Insurance Operations

Insurance Operations

Edited by

Ann E. Myhr, CPCU, MS, ARM, AU, AIM, ASLI

3rd Edition • 2nd Printing

The Institutes
720 Providence Road, Suite 100
Malvern, Pennsylvania 19355-3433

3rd Edition • 2nd Printing • March 2019

Library of Congress Control Number: 2018959465

ISBN 978-0-89462-274-8

Foreword

The Institutes are the knowledge partner that best provides educational activities related to risk management and property-casualty insurance, thereby empowering risk management and insurance professionals to help those in need. For more than 100 years, The Institutes have been meeting the public's changing insurance needs with customer-driven products and services.

In conjunction with outside experts and members of the academic community, our in-house professionals develop our course and program content, including Institutes study materials. Practical and technical knowledge gained from Institutes courses enhances qualifications, improves performance, and contributes to professional growth—all of which drive results.

The Institutes' proven knowledge helps individuals and organizations achieve powerful results with a variety of flexible, customer-focused options:

Recognized Credentials—The Institutes offer an unmatched range of widely recognized specialty credentials. Our flagship CPCU® designation provides learners with a broad understanding of the property-casualty insurance industry. Depending on their needs, CPCU students may select either a commercial insurance focus or a personal risk management and insurance focus and may choose from a variety of electives.

In addition, The Institutes offer certificate and designation programs in a variety of disciplines and on diverse topics, including these:

- Agent-broker
- Claims
- Commercial underwriting
- Cyber
- Fidelity and surety bonding
- General insurance
- Insurance accounting and finance
- Insurance information technology
- Insurance production and agency management
- Insurance regulation and compliance
- Management
- Marine insurance
- Personal insurance
- Premium auditing
- Quality insurance services
- Reinsurance
- Risk management
- Surplus lines

Ethics—Ethical behavior is crucial to preserving not only the trust on which insurance transactions are based but also the public's trust overall. All Institutes designations have an ethics requirement, which is delivered online and free of charge. Our ethics content relates to insurance issues and presents insurance-based case studies to outline an ethical framework.

Flexible Online Learning—The Institutes have an unmatched variety of technical insurance content covering topics from accounting to underwriting, which we now deliver through hundreds of online courses. These cost-effective self-study courses are a convenient way to fill gaps in technical knowledge in a matter of hours without ever leaving the office.

Continuing Education—A majority of The Institutes' courses are filed for CE credit in most states. We also deliver quality, affordable online CE courses quickly and conveniently through CEU. Visit CEU.com to learn more. CEU is powered by The Institutes.

College Credits—Most Institutes courses carry college credit recommendations from the American Council on Education. A variety of courses also qualify for credits toward certain associate, bachelor's, and master's degrees at several prestigious colleges and universities.

Custom Applications—The Institutes collaborate with corporate customers to use our trusted course content and flexible delivery options in developing customized solutions that help them achieve their unique organizational goals.

Insightful Analysis—Our Insurance Research Council (IRC) division conducts public policy research on important contemporary issues in property-casualty insurance and risk management. Visit www.Insurance-Research.org to learn more or purchase the IRC's most recent studies.

The Institutes look forward to serving the public through exemplary risk management and property-casualty insurance education solutions for another 100 years. In pursuit of this goal, we welcome your feedback, which helps us continually improve the quality of our study materials.

Peter L. Miller, CPCU
President and CEO
The Institutes

Preface

Insurance Operations is the assigned textbook for CPCU 520, one of the four foundation courses in The Institutes' Chartered Property Casualty Underwriter (CPCU) designation program.

The goal of CPCU 520 is to enable learners to improve their operational effectiveness by increasing their knowledge of how the various property-casualty insurance functions work together to create and deliver insurance products efficiently. The ten assignments in Insurance Operations support this goal.

Assignment 1 provides an overview of insurance operations, including classifications of insurers; insurers' major goals and the constraints on achieving them; and measurements used to evaluate insurers' success in meeting goals. Assignment 2 discusses insurance regulation and the regulatory activities that affect insurance operations.

Assignment 3 examines the characteristics of the competitive property-casualty insurance marketplace and the marketing and distribution systems and channels that insurers use. Assignment 4 provides an overview of the important role that the underwriting function plays in an insurer's operations and the steps in the underwriting process.

Assignment 5 examines the risk control and premium audit functions and how they support insurance operations. Assignment 6 provides an overview of the activities performed in the claims handling process.

Assignment 7 examines the two most prominent actuarial functions of insurers: ratemaking and estimation of loss reserves. Assignment 8 describes the principal functions and types of reinsurance and the factors that should be considered in the design of reinsurance programs.

Assignment 9 examines the importance of aligning information technology strategy with the goals of the insurance organization. Assignment 10 broadens the functional view of insurance and examines the strategic management process insurers can use to establish goals and to determine strategies for creating a competitive advantage.

The Institutes are grateful to the industry experts, insurance professionals, course leaders, and others who provided guidance and review during the planning of this text. Their thoughtful review and feedback contributed to making this content current, accurate, and relevant.

The Institutes continue to be equally thankful to the many insurance professionals who contributed to the development of earlier versions of this content. Although they are too numerous to name here, their valuable insights remain in the current content.

For more information about The Institutes' programs, please call our Customer Success Department at (800) 644-2101, email us at CustomerSuccess@TheInstitutes.org, or visit our website at TheInstitutes.org.

Ann E. Myhr

Contributors

The Institutes acknowledge with deep appreciation the contributions made to the content of this text by the following persons:

Doug Froggatt, CPCU, AINS

Beth Illian, CPCU, AINS, AIS

Kevin Kibelstis, CPCU, AINS, AIS

Lynn Knauf, CPCU, ARP

Eric C. Nordman, CPCU, CIE

Christian Schappel

Lawrence White, ACAS, MAAA, CPCU, ARM, AIAF, ARe

Contents

Assignment 6

The Claims Function	6.1
Overview of the Claims Function	6.3
Claims Department Structure, Personnel, and Performance	6.8
Measures Used to Ensure Regulatory Compliance	6.13
The Claims Handling Process	6.20
Framework for Coverage Analysis	6.27
Applying the Claims Handling Process and the Framework for Coverage Analysis	6.35
Summary	6.42

Assignment 7

Actuarial Operations	7.1
The Actuarial Function	7.3
Insurer Ratemaking Goals	7.5
Rate Components and Ratemaking Terms	7.7
Factors That Affect Ratemaking	7.9
Ratemaking Methods	7.14
Ratemaking Process Overview	7.18
Ratemaking Factor Variances by Type of Business	7.24
Loss Reserves and Analysis	7.28
Summary	7.35

Assignment 8

Reinsurance Principles and Concepts	8.1
Reinsurance and Its Functions	8.3
Reinsurance Sources	8.9
Reinsurance Transactions	8.12
Types of Pro Rata Reinsurance	8.15
Types of Excess of Loss Reinsurance	8.21
Alternatives to Traditional Reinsurance	8.24
Summary	8.27

Assignment 9

Business Needs and IT Alignment	9.1
Importance of Information Technology to an Insurer	9.3
The Importance of Data Quality in Meeting Insurer Information Needs	9.9
Types of Business Information Systems	9.14
Security and Control in Information Systems	9.20
Aligning Insurer and IT Strategy	9.25
Summary	9.30

Assignment 10

Insurer Strategic Management	10.1
Strategic Management Process	10.3
The Five Forces and SWOT Methods of Analyzing the Environment	10.8
Determining Strategy at Different Organizational Levels	10.13
Strategic Management Case Study	10.18
Summary	10.27
Index	1

Direct Your Learning ▶▶

Overview of Insurance Operations

Educational Objectives

After learning the content of this assignment, you should be able to:

▷ Categorize the internal and external constraints that impede insurers from achieving their major goals.

▷ Differentiate among the various classifications of insurers.

▷ Demonstrate how an insurer can measure its success at meeting established goals.

▷ Differentiate among the core and supporting functions performed by insurers.

▷ Explain how expanding data sources, the blockchain, and advanced analytics can transform insurance operations.

Overview of Insurance Operations

INSURER GOALS AND THE CONSTRAINTS ON ACHIEVING THEM

Like any other business, insurers operate with specific goals in mind—but they also often face constraints that many industries do not have.

These constraints can originate from an insurer's internal operation as well as its external environment. Navigating through these constraints is critical to securing an insurer's successful operation.

Insurer Goals

An insurer generally sets five major goals:

- Earn a profit
- Meet customer needs
- Comply with legal requirements
- Diversify risk
- Fulfill duty to society

Earn a Profit

The profit goal is most commonly associated with proprietary, or for-profit, insurers. **Cooperative insurers** also aim to earn a profit, but do not consider this goal to be the primary reason they are formed.

Insurers earn money by charging insureds a premium for the insurance contract, or policy. To meet the contract terms of payment of covered losses and to fulfill regulatory requirements, insurers take a portion of their surplus, or premiums not immediately needed to pay operating expenses, and invest it in stock, bonds, and real estate. These investments produce income in the form of interest, dividends, and, when sold, investment gains. This additional income can be further invested to pay future covered losses, expand the insurer's operations, or be returned to the insurer's investors.

A proprietary insurer must earn a profit to provide a return on the investment made by its stockholders. This is important because a proprietary insurer can attract capital only as long as its profits are comparable to or better than similar insurers. If investors do not believe that they will receive an acceptable

Cooperative insurers

Insurers owned by their policyholders and usually formed to provide insurance protection to their policyholders at minimum cost. Mutual insurance companies, reciprocal exchanges, and fraternal organizations are examples of cooperative insurers.

rate of return on their investment, they will seek investment opportunities elsewhere.

For cooperative insurers, one source of capital is funds from policyholders, usually in the form of premiums. Growth of surplus derived from underwriting operations is another. Profits are returned to policyholders in the form of dividends or are contributed to surplus to help ensure continued solvency and protect against unforeseen catastrophic losses. Under certain circumstances, a cooperative insurer can obtain additional capital by issuing surplus notes. These notes can usually be repaid only from profits, so gaining capital from them often depends on the insurer's anticipated profitability.

Whether cooperative or proprietary, an insurer can increase premium volume through policy sales, which in turn can be aided by marketing efforts. Additionally, when an insurer's underwriting operation evaluates risks effectively—avoiding risks that will require excessive loss payments—and prices insurance products appropriately, premium volume increases, resulting in greater profits for the insurer.

Meet Customer Needs

To attract customers, an insurer must provide the products and services those customers seek—and do so at a competitive price. This involves determining what customers need and what price is competitive and then finding the best way to satisfy those needs.

As in every retail or service organization, insurance customers expect prompt service and timely responses to inquiries. When insurance customers suffer a loss, they can be upset or under considerable stress. Consequently, the insurer must provide quick and professional assistance, which requires well-trained, customer-focused personnel and automated support systems.

Meeting customers' needs, however, may conflict with the profit goal. In some cases, offering high-quality insurance at a price that the customer can afford may not generate the profit that the insurer needs to attract and retain capital. Providing training, operating automated call centers, and maintaining current information technology can also be costly and conflict with achieving the profit goal in the near term. But the long-term benefits of these expenditures can reduce costs and help reduce premiums, and the improved customer service can create a competitive advantage by encouraging policy retention and new business.

Comply With Legal Requirements

Legal compliance is necessary for an insurer to be considered a responsible corporate citizen, and it promotes an insurer's good reputation in the business community. Therefore, it can enhance the insurer's ability to attract capital and customers; conversely, lack of compliance may lead to fines and penalties.

Compliance with state regulations is one of an insurer's greatest responsibilities. Unfortunately, compliance comes with expenses for filings, record keeping and accounting, and legal activities. Additional expenses are incurred for participation in assigned risk plans, Fair Access to Insurance Requirements (FAIR) plans, and government-required insolvency funds. To the extent that these expenses increase the cost of insurance, they create a conflict between the profit and customer needs goals.

Diversify Risk

Diversifying risk is a goal for property-casualty insurers because of the potential for catastrophic losses. For example, consider an insurer with a high concentration of policies along the coast of Florida. A single event, such as a hurricane, could result in staggering losses for the insurer to cover.

By spreading risk over a wider geographic area and multiple types of insurance business, insurers can help protect themselves from catastrophic losses. This goal complements the insurer's goals of earning a profit and fulfilling its duty to society.

Fulfill Duty to Society

At a minimum, the obligation for an insurer to fulfill its duty to society demands that the insurer avoid causing public harm. As responsible corporate citizens, many insurers go well beyond that minimum.

Many insurers contribute funds, and sometimes they volunteer employees' time, to public service organizations. Additionally, many insurers establish employee benefit plans that provide for the current and future well-being of their employees. Benefits such as medical insurance, disability insurance, retirement plans, employee assistance programs, and numerous other benefits help employees and retirees use personal resources to meet their needs and help minimize the use of public resources. Insurers' participation in philanthropic activities and employee benefits improves employees' job satisfaction and emotional well-being. In addition, these activities help with employee retention and attract qualified candidates to these organizations.

While fulfilling their duty to society through philanthropic activities and employee benefit programs, insurers strive to maintain a well-qualified, knowledgeable staff, which promotes the profit and customer needs goals. However, the required use of funds for these programs competes with these goals, so insurers must balance the use of funds to best meet their disparate goals.

Constraints on Achieving Insurer Goals

An insurer's path to achieving its goals is not always clear, as several internal and external constraints might prevent it from achieving its goals.

Internal Constraints

While some internal constraints are universal, others are imposed only in certain circumstances or on certain types of insurers:

- Efficiency—Inefficient insurers are at a disadvantage when competing with efficient ones. This competitive weakness might prevent them from meeting their profit and service goals, which can lead to an inability to meet humanitarian or societal goals. Inefficiency can also prevent an insurer from adequately meeting its customers' needs and, in extreme cases, can lead to insolvency and a consequent failure to meet legal and regulatory goals. An insurer's lack of efficiency may be caused by poor management, insufficient capital, outdated technology and inability to keep up with the growing influence of data analytics, inability to adapt to change, and other causes.

- Expertise—Considerable expertise is required to successfully operate an insurer. This is particularly true for insurers in niche or specialty markets. Lack of expertise may prevent an insurer from making a profit or meeting customers' needs and could eventually cause the insurer to fail to attain any of its goals. As with efficiency, in extreme cases, lack of expertise could ultimately lead to insolvency.

- Size—A small insurer may have more challenges than a large insurer in terms of available resources. Large insurers can take advantage of economies of scale and may find it easier to update technology or reach additional markets. They can also usually invest more in market research and product development than small insurers can. One advantage for a small insurer is that it can be more nimble, allowing it to respond quickly to emerging trends or changes in the external insurance environment.

- Financial resources—Insufficient financial resources can pose a serious threat to an insurer. When financial resources become strained, insurers are unable to effectively train staff, make new capital investments, or reach new markets. Management must make difficult decisions about allocating scarce resources among competing priorities.

- Other internal constraints—Examples of other internal constraints include lack of name or brand recognition, or a damaged reputation. A newly established insurer might lack the name recognition necessary to achieve its profit goals even if it has the expertise and financial resources to do so. If the insurer had past ethical or financial problems that have been corrected, overcoming its poor reputation will require work from all its employees. If the brand image has been damaged, the insurer may need to develop a concerted campaign to regain customer and public confidence as well as a plan to manage its image into the future. An insurer that fails to address all internal issues could develop problems retaining and hiring high-caliber managers and other staff because of its damaged image. These factors could prevent the insurer from meeting customers' needs and could jeopardize profitability.

External Constraints

In addition to internal constraints, insurers contend with several external constraints that may prevent them from meeting their goals:

- Regulation—Insurance operations are closely regulated, extending from incorporation to liquidation and encompassing most activities in between. Insurance regulators monitor insurers' solvency to protect the insurers' policyholders and members of the public who benefit from the existence of insurance. Insurance regulation is complex, extensive, and varies by state. Federal regulation adds another layer of complexity. Products that can be offered in one state may not be approved for use in another state. The variations in property-casualty laws in different states require a broader range of staff expertise. Consequently, regulation imposes a major constraint on insurers, requiring significant personnel and financial resources that can inhibit the insurer's ability to achieve its profit goals.

- Rating agencies—Financial rating agencies, such as A.M. Best, Standard & Poor's, and Moody's, rate insurers based on financial strength as an indication of an insurer's ability to meet policyholder obligations. To support their current ratings, well-managed and highly rated insurers typically must maintain capitalization levels in excess of the minimum amounts required. Because favorable financial ratings help to attract and retain customers, insurers try to conduct business to achieve the required capitalization levels to maintain or improve a favorable rating; however, this practice could also constrain insurers from meeting their profit goals.

- Public opinion—Public opinion about the insurance industry as a whole can inhibit individual insurers from meeting goals. While many customers are satisfied with their insurers, high-profile issues can lead to a negative perception of the insurance industry. Matters of ethics are major components in managing an insurer's reputation; therefore, efforts to manage reputation should include ethics initiatives, including ongoing training of all staff in ethical decision-making. Managing expenses to repair or protect an insurer's image or the image of the industry conflicts with the profit goal but helps attain the customer needs goal.

- Competition—Competition in the insurance industry is driven by the number of insurers in the marketplace, advances in technology, and customers seeking innovative products. Pricing and availability of insurance products fluctuate based on the amount of capital available to the industry, and, for many years, the industry experienced fluctuating underwriting cycles (or marketing cycles), referred to as hard or soft cycles. Although mergers and acquisitions have decreased the number of property-casualty insurers, so many insurers remain in the marketplace that competition remains high. Competition is further fueled in personal insurance by highly standardized products and technological advances, providing consumers with opportunities to easily explore multiple options. At the same time, technology allows insurers to compete for customers through personalized marketing, social media, and other digital interfaces.

- Economic conditions—Insurers' investment operations can be affected by economic downturns, potentially causing investment income to fall and thereby limiting insurers' policyholders' surplus for meeting the demands of customers' claims. Inflationary cycles can affect insurers, as well, affecting the costs of insurance losses through increased medical, construction, and other loss-related costs.

Apply Your Knowledge

Which one of the following is an external constraint faced by insurers?

a. Regulation

b. Expertise

c. Size

d. Lack of name or brand recognition

Feedback: a. Regulation is an external constraint faced by insurers.

CLASSIFICATIONS OF INSURERS

Insurance is a system under which participants (such as individuals, families, and businesses) make payments in exchange for the commitment to reimburse for specific types of losses under certain circumstances. Insurers, which are organizations within the financial services industry, may be classified in various manners.

The insurance organization or the entity that facilitates the pooling of funds and the payment of benefits is called an insurer. Participants in this mechanism, called insureds, benefit through reimbursement of covered losses that occur, reduction of uncertainty, additional services provided by the insurer to reduce the frequency or severity of losses, and financial protection against legal liability for damages to others. Additionally, insureds can benefit from the potential availability of credit from lenders, which may help enable them to purchase property. Because the risk of loss to property is transferred to the insurer, lenders are willing to loan money to insureds with greater confidence that the loan will be repaid.

The principal function of every insurer is the same: the acceptance of risks that others transfer to it through the insurance mechanism. This task is divided into core operations consisting of underwriting, claims, and marketing, which, in turn, are supported by several other functions. These operations are described in other sections.

Overview of Insurance Operations 1.9

Property-casualty insurers can be classified in these four ways:

- Legal form of ownership
- Place of incorporation
- Licensing status
- Insurance distribution systems and channels

The exhibit shows the general classifications of insurers. An insurer might be further classified by what types of insurance it writes or its specialty. See the exhibit "Classifications of Insurers."

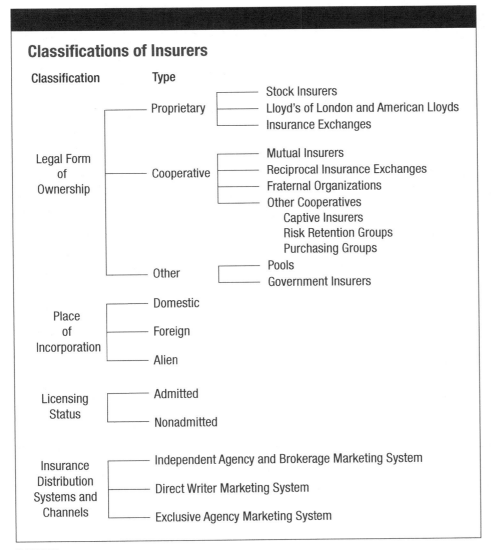

Classifications of Insurers

Classification	Type	
Legal Form of Ownership	Proprietary	Stock Insurers Lloyd's of London and American Lloyds Insurance Exchanges
	Cooperative	Mutual Insurers Reciprocal Insurance Exchanges Fraternal Organizations Other Cooperatives Captive Insurers Risk Retention Groups Purchasing Groups
	Other	Pools Government Insurers
Place of Incorporation	Domestic Foreign Alien	
Licensing Status	Admitted Nonadmitted	
Insurance Distribution Systems and Channels	Independent Agency and Brokerage Marketing System Direct Writer Marketing System Exclusive Agency Marketing System	

[DA06276]

Legal Form of Ownership

The first classification of insurers is by legal form of ownership. The two major types of insurers in this classification are proprietary and cooperative insurers.

Proprietary Insurers

Proprietary insurer
Insurer formed for the purpose of earning a profit for its owners.

Proprietary insurers include stock insurers, Lloyd's of London and American Lloyds, and insurance exchanges.

Stock insurers are the most prevalent type of proprietary insurer in the United States. These insurers are owned by their stockholders. By purchasing stock in a for-profit insurer, stockholders supply the capital needed to form the insurer or the additional capital the insurer needs to expand its operations. Stockholders expect to receive a return on their investment in the form of stock dividends, increased stock value, or both.

Stockholders have the right to elect the board of directors, which has the authority to control the insurer's activities. The board of directors creates and oversees corporate goals and objectives and appoints a chief executive officer (CEO) to carry out the insurer's operations and implement the programs necessary to operate the company.

Among the proprietary types of insurance ownership is a unique type known as Lloyds. Two types of Lloyds associations exist: Lloyd's of London and American Lloyds.

Lloyd's of London (Lloyd's) is technically not an insurer. However, it does provide the physical and procedural facilities for its members to write insurance. It is a marketplace, similar to a stock exchange. The members are investors who hope to earn a profit from the insurance operations.

American Lloyds associations are smaller than Lloyd's of London, and most are domiciled in Texas because of the favorable regulatory climate. Most of these associations were formed or have been acquired by insurers. Like most investors of Lloyd's of London today, members (called underwriters) of American Lloyds are not liable beyond their investment in the association.

An insurance exchange is a proprietary insurer similar to Lloyd's because it acts as an insurance marketplace. Exchange members underwrite any insurance or reinsurance purchased on the exchange. Members can be individuals, partnerships, or corporations, and they have limited liability. Members belong to syndicates and delegate day-to-day operations to the syndicate manager.

Cooperative Insurers

Cooperative insurers are the second type of insurer in the legal form of ownership classification. This type of insurer is owned by its policyholders and is usually formed to provide insurance protection to its policyholders at minimum cost. This classification includes mutual insurers, reciprocal insurance exchanges, fraternal organizations, and other cooperatives.

Mutual insurers constitute the largest number of cooperative insurers and provide low-cost insurance to their policyholders, who are the owners of the insurer. Because a traditional mutual insurer issues no common stock, it has no stockholders. Its policyholders have voting rights similar to those of a stock company's stockholders, and, like stockholders, they elect the insurer's board of directors that appoints officers to manage the company. Some profit is retained to increase surplus, and excess profit is usually returned to policyholders as dividends. Mutual insurers include some large national insurers and many regional insurers.

Mutual insurer

An insurer that is owned by its policyholders and formed as a corporation for the purpose of providing insurance to them.

Although initially formed to provide insurance for their owners, who otherwise could not obtain insurance, mutual insurers today generally seek to earn profits in their ongoing operations, just as stock companies do. A mutual insurer's retained profits ensure the future financial health of the organization.

A reciprocal insurance exchange, also simply called a reciprocal, consists of a series of private contracts in which subscribers, or members of the group, agree to insure each other. The term "reciprocal" comes from the reciprocity of responsibility of all subscribers to each other. Each member of the reciprocal is both an insured and an insurer. Because the subscribers are not experts in running an insurance operation, they contract with an individual or organization to operate the reciprocal. This manager is called an attorney-in-fact. The subscribers empower the attorney-in-fact to handle all the duties necessary to manage the reciprocal. An insurer may be formed as a reciprocal to receive favorable tax treatment.

Fraternal organizations resemble mutual companies, but they combine a lodge or social function with their insurance function. They write primarily life and health insurance.

Cooperative insurers include captive insurers, risk retention groups, and purchasing groups.

When a business organization or a group of affiliated organizations forms a subsidiary company to provide all or part of its insurance, the subsidiary is known as a captive insurer, or captive. This arrangement is sometimes referred to as "formalized self-insurance." For example, a large retail chain may decide it can insure itself at a more reasonable cost by using a captive rather than an unaffiliated insurer. The captive may also be formed to cover losses that other insurers will not cover at any price.

Captive insurers can take several forms, and their ultimate purpose is to fund the losses of their owners. Some states have enacted legislation to facilitate the formation and operation of captive insurers within their jurisdictions, while others do not permit the formation of captives.

Legislation has also allowed risk retention groups and purchasing groups to form. These cooperatives can be stock companies, mutuals, or reciprocal exchanges. They are usually organized so that a limited group or type of insured is eligible to purchase insurance from them. These types of insurers are becoming more significant in the evolving insurance marketplace.

Other Insurers

Other insurers are the third type of insurer in the legal form of ownership classification. Insurers that fall into this classification include pools and government insurers.

A pool consists of several insurers, not otherwise related, that join together to insure loss exposures that individual insurers are unwilling to insure. These loss exposures present the potential for losses that either occur too frequently or are too severe (catastrophic) for individual insurers to accept the risk. A major airplane crash is an example of such a catastrophic loss that might be insured under a pool arrangement.

Another catastrophic loss exposure that insurers may be unwilling to insure individually is a large nuclear power plant, for which losses could amount to billions of dollars for property and liability damage. Because no single insurer was willing to assume such tremendous liability, nuclear energy pools were formed. These pools allow many member insurers to spread any losses among members. Additionally, the pools buy reinsurance from nonmembers to increase their capacity.

Pools can be formed either voluntarily or to meet statutory requirements. They operate either as a syndicate or through reinsurance. A syndicate pool issues a joint (or syndicate) policy to the insured, listing all pool members and specifying the part of the insurance for which each member is responsible. Under such policies, the insured has a contractual relationship with each pool member and can sue any or all of them directly if a disagreement arises.

Under a reinsurance pool, one member of the pool issues the policy to the insured, and the other pool members reinsure an agreed proportion of the policy's insured loss exposures. The insured has a contractual relationship only with the member that issued the policy. The policyholder has no legal rights against the other members of the pool and might not even know that they exist.

Many pools are required by law. Virtually all states require some kind of pooling arrangement to provide auto liability insurance for drivers who cannot obtain such insurance in the standard market. Similar pools are required for workers compensation coverage in most states. **Fair Access to Insurance Requirements (FAIR) plans** are required by law in at least half of the states. These pools provide property insurance to qualified property owners who are unable to obtain coverage in the standard market.

Many states in the southeastern U.S., such as Florida, have pools that provide windstorm coverage for residents in storm-prone areas who cannot obtain coverage in the standard market. Similar statutory pools for other types of insurance are required by state law. The protection that these pools provide is

Fair Access to Insurance Requirements (FAIR) plans
An insurance pool through which private insurers collectively address an unmet need for property insurance on urban properties, especially those susceptible to loss by riot or civil commotion.

underwritten by private insurers and not by state governments, although state and federal governments do act as insurers in some situations.

Despite the size and diversity of private insurers in the U.S., private insurers do not provide some types of insurance. Some loss exposures, such as catastrophic flooding, do not possess the characteristics that make them commercially insurable, but a significant need for protection against the potential losses still exists. Both the federal government and state governments have developed insurance programs to meet specific insurance needs of the public. Some federal government insurance programs serve the public in a manner that only the government can. For example, only the government has the ability to tax in order to provide the financial resources needed to insure some of the larger loss exposures.

The federal government offers several forms of insurance. One of the largest property insurance programs it offers is the National Flood Insurance Program (NFIP), which is administered by the Federal Insurance Administration under the Federal Emergency Management Agency (FEMA). Most property insurance policies exclude flood coverage because the catastrophic loss potential of floods would significantly raise property insurance premiums for all customers. Customers located in an area prone to flooding can obtain the needed coverage through the NFIP program.

The federal government provides a government "backstop" insurance program through the original Terrorism Risk Insurance Act (TRIA) of 2002. In 2015, the Terrorism Risk Insurance Program Reauthorization Act (TRIPRA) extended the program for five years. TRIA ensures that commercial property owners can obtain reasonable and predictably priced terrorism coverage by specifying that the federal government will share the risk of loss from foreign terrorist acts. Without this backstop, financing for large commercial construction projects in high-population cities (terrorists' targets) would decline, stunting growth and hindering the economy. To qualify under TRIA, a terrorist act must be certified by the government. Federal assistance becomes available when such losses collectively exceed $5 million and when participating insurers pay a specified amount in related claims.

All states offer some form of government insurance. For example, some states provide workers compensation insurance for some or all employers in the state. Most state workers compensation programs compete with private insurers. However, in some states, workers compensation insurance is offered exclusively by the state.

Most states require motor vehicle owners to have auto liability insurance before registering their vehicles. However, drivers with poor driving records or with little driving experience may have difficulty obtaining insurance from private insurers. To make liability insurance available to almost all licensed drivers, all states have implemented automobile insurance plans through a **residual market**. The cost of operating such plans is spread among all private insurers selling auto insurance in the state.

Residual market

The term referring collectively to insurers and other organizations that make insurance available through a shared risk mechanism to those who cannot obtain coverage in the admitted market.

In most states, FAIR plans make property insurance more readily available to property owners who have exposures to loss over which they have no control, such as being in a neighborhood with a high property crime rate. These state-run plans spread the cost of operating the plan among all private insurers selling property insurance in the state. Without such a program, individuals and business owners located in such areas who have exposures to loss over which they have no control would be unable to obtain property insurance for their buildings or contents.

Beachfront and windstorm insurance pools are residual market plans similar to FAIR plans. These plans, available in states along the Atlantic and Gulf Coasts, provide insurance to property owners who are unable to obtain this coverage from private insurers. The plans provide coverage for wind damage from hurricanes and other windstorms. See the exhibit "The Rise of Insurtech Companies."

The Rise of Insurtech Companies

Emerging technologies have led to the growth of insurtech (that is, the coupling of insurance and technology) companies. These companies can assist traditional insurers with offering innovative new products and services. Categories of insurtech companies include these:

- Microinsurance—Firms offering insurance to economically disadvantaged and other traditionally underserved segments of the population that are united in risk pools whose members are connected to the insurer through web-enabled platforms on cell phones and other devices

- Firms that facilitate the use of sensors, Internet of Things (IoT)-enabled devices, and other data-capture technology to help insurers and brokers more accurately assess and price individual risks

- Peer-to-peer insurance—Firms that use web-enabled platforms to facilitate the formation of self-selected risk pools whose members (usually friends, relatives, or like-minded individuals) pool premiums and collectively pay for members' insured losses

- On-demand insurance (also known as need-based insurance)—Firms that use web-enabled customer interfaces and sensor technology to offer coverage that allows near-total customization for customers

---

[DA12776]

Place of Incorporation

The second classification of insurers is by place of incorporation and includes domestic insurers, foreign insurers, and alien insurers.

Insurance is regulated at the state level. Therefore, a domestic insurer is incorporated within a specific state or, if not incorporated, is formed under the laws of that state. An insurer is said to be operating in its own domiciled state when it is doing business in the state in which it is incorporated or was formed.

Reciprocal insurance exchanges are the only unincorporated insurers permitted in most states. Insurance exchanges and Lloyd's organizations are permitted under law in only a few states.

A foreign insurer is a domestic insurer that is licensed to do business in states other than its domiciled state. Alien insurers are incorporated or formed in another country.

Licensing Status

The third classification of insurers is by licensing status. An insurer's state license authorizes it to sell insurance in the state. A license indicates that the insurer has met the state's minimum standards for financial strength, competence, and integrity. If the insurer later fails to meet those standards or fails to comply with a state law, regulation, or rule, its license can be revoked.

A licensed insurer (admitted insurer) is an insurer that has been granted a license to operate in a particular state. An unlicensed insurer (nonadmitted insurer) has not been granted a license to operate in a given state.

Producers for primary insurance (except **surplus lines brokers**) are licensed to place business only with admitted insurers. Licensing status is also important for purposes of reinsurance.

Insurance Distribution Systems and Channels

The fourth classification of insurers is by their insurance distribution systems and distribution channels—that is, the method used to deliver insurance products to the marketplace. Insurers use many types of distribution systems and channels, designed to meet their particular marketing objectives. Most insurers use one or more of these insurance distribution systems:

- **Independent agency and brokerage marketing system**
- **Direct writer marketing system**
- **Exclusive agency marketing system**

Insurers also use these common **distribution channels** to promote products and services as well as to communicate with existing and prospective insureds: the internet, call centers, direct response, group marketing, and financial institutions.

Surplus lines broker

A person or firm that places business with insurers not licensed (nonadmitted) in the state in which the transaction occurs but that is permitted to write insurance because coverage is not available through standard market insurers.

Independent agency and brokerage marketing system

An insurance marketing system under which producers (agents or brokers), who are independent contractors, sell insurance, usually as representatives of several unrelated insurers.

Direct writer marketing system

An insurance marketing system that uses sales agents (or sales representatives) who are direct employees of the insurer.

Exclusive agency marketing system

An insurance marketing system under which agents contract to sell insurance exclusively for one insurer (or for an associated group of insurers).

Distribution channel

The channel used by the producer of a product or service to transfer that product or service to the ultimate customer.

MEASURING INSURER PERFORMANCE

Insurers use measurements that are specific to their industry to determine their success at meeting established goals.

Measuring the performance of an insurer involves determining how successful the insurer is at meeting established goals, including these:

- Meeting profitability goals
- Meeting customer needs
- Meeting legal requirements
- Meeting social responsibilities

As with any assessment, some measures are objective, while others may be subjective. Financial measurements are based on statistical evidence and are considered to be more objective. Measurements of legal requirements are also objective. Measurements of how well an insurer meets customer needs and social responsibilities are more subjective.

Meeting Profitability Goals

An understanding of how insurers make a profit is crucial to understanding how they meet their profitability goals. Like any business, an insurer generates income, or profits, when its revenue exceeds its expenses. The primary sources of revenue for insurers are insurance premiums (paid by insureds) and investment income. Insurers have investments because they receive premiums before they pay for losses and expenses. Insurers invest that money in the meantime and receive investment income as a result.

When determining expenses, insurers face a special challenge compared with other organizations. The largest portion of an insurer's expenses involves losses that will occur in the future and that are, by definition, more difficult to project than past or current expenses. Estimating these future expenses and setting aside the funds to pay for them is done through reserving.

Estimating insurer profitability is generally accomplished by examining premiums and either underwriting performance (underwriting gain or loss) or overall operating performance (gain or loss from operations). A review of these topics assists in understanding insurer profitability:

- Premiums and investment income
- Underwriting performance
- Overall operating performance
- Estimation of loss reserves

Premiums and Investment Income

An insurer's profits depend heavily on the premium revenue the insurer generates. Premiums are the amounts that insurers charge insureds for insurance coverages. Insurers use rates based on the insured's loss exposures to determine the premium to charge for insurance policies.

Insurers must charge premiums to have the funds necessary to make loss payments. In fact, an insurer's total revenue (premiums and investment income) must equal or exceed the amount needed to pay for losses and to cover its costs of doing business. For example, an insurer may use eighty cents of every premium dollar to pay for losses and twenty-five cents for other expenses. If the insurer can earn an amount equal to 5 percent of its premiums on its investments, it can break even. Consequently, an insurer's profitability must consider the volume of premium the insurer writes. Investment profit also depends, in part, on premium revenue that creates the funds used for investment.

Insurance operations generate substantial amounts of investable funds, primarily from loss reserves, loss adjustment expense reserves, and unearned premium reserves. Loss and loss expense reserves are especially significant for insurers that write liability insurance because the long delay inherent in the liability claim handling process generates very large loss reserves.

Measures of insurer profitability based on premiums consider premium growth issues and the rate of growth that is sustained over time. Premium growth is not always a positive indicator of an insurer's success. An insurer should achieve premium growth by writing new policies rather than depending solely on insurance rate increases or inflation. Premium growth, or the lack thereof, must be evaluated in light of current market conditions. During periods of intense competition, significant premium growth is difficult to achieve. However, rapid premium growth may be undesirable and could indicate lax underwriting standards or inadequate premium levels. Inappropriate premium growth can eventually lead to reduced profits as losses begin to exceed premiums collected for loss exposures. To determine profitability, an insurer should consider whether growth resulted from a competitive advantage, relaxed underwriting, inadequate insurance rates, or a combination of these factors.

Evaluating the rate of premium growth sustained over time helps determine insurer profitability. Establishing reasonable rules by which to measure the adequacy, inadequacy, or excessiveness of premium growth is difficult. Growth that is slower than the industry average usually indicates a problem. Likewise, a growth rate that is substantially higher than the industry average might indicate changes that could be unfavorable in the long term.

Underwriting Performance

An insurer's underwriting performance can be measured in terms of net underwriting gain or loss. This is determined as an insurer's earned premiums minus its incurred losses and underwriting expenses for a specific period. Incurred losses include loss adjustment expenses, and underwriting expenses include acquisition expenses, general expenses, taxes, and fees. Because net underwriting gain or loss ignores investment income (or investment losses)

and investment expenses, it represents the extent of the insurer's profit or loss derived strictly from the sale of insurance products.

The formula for calculating net underwriting gain or loss can be expressed as: net underwriting gain or loss = earned premiums – (incurred losses + underwriting expenses).

Three specific ratios are used to measure an insurer's underwriting performance: the loss ratio, the expense ratio, and the combined ratio (trade basis). See the exhibit "Measuring an Insurer's Underwriting Performance."

Measuring an Insurer's Underwriting Performance

The loss ratio compares an insurer's incurred losses with its earned premiums for a specific period. The figure for incurred losses includes loss adjustment expenses. The loss ratio is calculated in this manner:

$$\text{Loss ratio} = \text{Incurred losses} \div \text{Earned premiums}$$

The expense ratio compares an insurer's underwriting expenses with its written premiums for a specific period. The expense ratio is calculated in this manner:

$$\text{Expense ratio} = \text{Incurred underwriting expenses} \div \text{Written premiums}$$

The combined ratio (trade basis) combines the loss ratio and the expense ratio to compare inflows and outflows from insurance underwriting. The combined ratio (trade basis) is calculated in this manner:

$$\text{Combined ratio (trade basis)} = \frac{\text{Incurred losses (including LAE)}}{\text{Earned premiums}} + \frac{\text{Incurred underwriting expenses}}{\text{Written premiums}}$$

This can be simplified in this manner:

$$\text{Combined ratio (trade basis)} = \text{Loss ratio} + \text{Expense ratio}$$

[DA02738]

Overall Operating Performance

An alternative way to measure an insurer's profits is through overall results from operations. An insurer's overall gain or loss from operations is its net underwriting gain or loss plus its net investment gain or loss for a specific period. This overall figure gives a more complete picture of an insurer's profitability because investment income generally helps to offset any underwriting losses. The formula for overall gain or loss from operations is expressed as: overall gain or loss from operations = net underwriting gain or loss + investment gain or loss.

After an insurer pays losses, expenses, and taxes, and reserves money to pay additional incurred losses, the remainder is net operating income, which belongs to the company's owners. The owners (stockholders or policyholders) may receive a portion of this remainder as dividends. The amount that is left after dividends are paid is added to the policyholders' surplus. The increase in policyholders' surplus enables the insurer to expand its operations in the future and provides a cushion against catastrophic losses.

To obtain an accurate picture of an insurer's profitability, it is important to analyze the overall gain or loss from operations for several years because any insurer might have a single unprofitable year that is offset by a pattern of profitability over a longer period.

Insurers may lose money on their underwriting activities (that is, when the combined ratio is more than 100 percent) and yet still generate a profit on investments. Ideally, the investment profit is more than enough to offset the underwriting loss so that the insurer has an overall gain from operations, and the policyholders' surplus grows through time and generates a suitable return on equity for the insurer's owners. See the exhibit "Measuring an Insurer's Overall Performance."

Measuring an Insurer's Overall Performance

The investment income ratio compares the amount of net investment income (investment income minus investment expenses) with earned premiums over a specific period of time. The investment income ratio is calculated as shown:

Investment income ratio = Net investment income ÷ Earned premiums

The overall operating ratio, the trade basis combined ratio minus the investment income ratio, can be used to provide an overall measure of the insurer's financial performance for a specific period. Of all the commonly used ratios, the overall operating ratio is the most complete measure of an insurer's financial performance. The formula for overall operating ratio is as shown:

Overall operating ratio = Combined ratio (trade basis) − Investment income ratio

Return on equity, calculated by dividing the organization's net income by the average amount of owners' equity (policyholders' surplus) for a specific period, enables investors to compare the return that could have been obtained by investing in the insurer with the potential returns that could have been earned by investing their money elsewhere. In general, the owners' equity is invested in operations to generate income for the organization. For insurers, the policyholders' surplus is invested in underwriting activities. The formula for return on equity is as shown:

Return on equity = Net income ÷ Owners' equity

[DA02740]

The investment income ratio, overall operating ratio, and return on equity are more specific measures of an insurer's operational performance.

Estimation of Loss Reserves

One of the biggest problems in measuring insurer profitability arises from errors in estimating loss reserves. Loss reserves are generally the largest liability in the insurer's balance sheet and can have a significant effect on the insurer's overall profitability. Insurers establish loss reserves not just for reported claims, but also for losses that have occurred but that have not yet been reported (known as incurred but not reported [IBNR] losses), for losses that have been reported but for which established case reserves are inadequate (known as incurred but not enough recorded [IBNER] reserves), and for claims that have been settled and then reopened.

Errors in estimating outstanding loss amounts, by either underestimating or overestimating the final cost of claims, can distort the insurer's reported profits. This is true for both the year in which inaccurate estimates were originally made and the year in which corrections are made to the estimates. For example, if reserves are initially underestimated and subsequently increased, then net income and policyholders' surplus will decrease when the understatement is recognized. Also, because the insurer's pricing relies on historical loss data, inadequate reserves can result in reduced premium revenues. Therefore, in the long term, if an insurer does not have adequate reserves, it may not have the funds necessary to pay claims. Conversely, if the loss reserves are overestimated (higher than the ultimate loss payments), based on the artificially inflated reserve estimates, the statutory limits on premiums that could be written may be less, and the premiums may be inflated for new and existing risks. Although the reserve estimates may be decreased later, in the interim, these artificial results can cause the insurer to be less competitive in pricing, its financial strength ratings could be lowered, and the insurer's profitability may suffer. A pattern of underreserving or overreserving may ultimately lead to the insurer's insolvency.

Meeting Customer Needs

Determining how well insurers meet customers' needs is difficult because insurers are more likely to hear from customers who believe they have not been treated fairly.

Complaints and Praise

All insurers receive complaints, and each complaint should be evaluated. In some instances, a real problem exists that the insurer should address. In other instances, customers hold expectations that the insurer had not intended to fulfill.

Insurance producers can also be a source of information for evaluating an insurer's success in this area, as they are in frequent contact with customers and hear their complaints about and praise of insurers. Producers seldom keep formal records of such customer reactions, so their evaluations are likely to be subjective.

Customer Satisfaction Data

Many insurers emphasize a customer focus to maintain and raise levels of customer satisfaction with the insurer's products and services. Insurers often use response cards and phone surveys to determine whether customers feel properly treated after a transaction, particularly following a claim. Insurers can also conduct customer focus groups or interviews to determine how well a new or an existing product meets customers' needs. Additionally, insurers can survey customers to obtain an overall satisfaction rating associated with their products and services.

Insurer's Retention Ratio and Lapse Ratio

Two particularly telling measurements of customer satisfaction are the retention ratio and the lapse ratio (sometimes called the cancellation ratio). The data for developing these ratios are found in internal statistical reports. The retention ratio is the percentage of expiring insurance policies that an insurer renews, and it can be measured by policy count, premium volume, or both.

The lapse ratio is calculated by dividing the number of policies that lapse during a period by the total number of policies written at the beginning of that period. A lapse in insurance is defined as a point in time when a policy has been canceled or terminated for failure to pay the premium, or when the policy contract is void for other reasons.

These ratios can indicate the number of policies a company is losing, whether because of a service or price issue or some other issue (such as loss to competition).

Insurer-Producer Relationships

Insurers that market products through independent agents and brokers usually view this network of producers as their customers, in addition to the ultimate insurance customer. These insurers recognize that many other insurers are available to producers and that a competitive marketplace exists within their industry. Being responsive to producer requests and permitting access to insurer policy data and information systems are examples of how insurers maintain and strengthen the insurer-producer relationship. As is the case for customers, insurers can survey or meet with producers to measure their satisfaction with the insurer or to reveal unserved needs the insurer might be able to meet.

State Insurance Department Statistics

Several state insurance departments tabulate complaints they receive and publish lists showing the number of complaints received for each insurer. The number of complaints might indicate one insurer's customer relations success or failure relative to other insurers in the industry.

Consumer Reports

Consumers Union periodically surveys its membership to determine its level of satisfaction with the performance of auto and homeowners insurers. The results are published in that organization's magazine, *Consumer Reports*, including a list of the most satisfactory and least satisfactory insurers as indicated by the survey responses. Only a few of the largest insurers are included in the list because smaller insurers are not mentioned in the responses with sufficient frequency to evaluate their performance fairly.

Meeting Legal Requirements

An insurer's success or failure in meeting legal requirements is indicated by the number of criminal, civil, and regulatory actions taken against the insurer. These actions are automatically brought to the attention of management and should be evaluated carefully to see whether they result from a consistent disregard of legal requirements.

State insurance departments monitor the treatment of insureds, applicants for insurance, and claimants, and they oversee four insurer operational areas: sales and advertising, underwriting, ratemaking, and claim settlement. This regulatory oversight, called market conduct regulation, exists in addition to the role of state insurance regulation in solvency surveillance.

Most states publish a listing of regulatory actions against insurers. This information can be useful in showing how one insurer's performance in this area compares to that of its competitors.

Financial rating agencies provide summary information about insurer financial strength in the form of a financial rating. These rating agencies review all financial information presented in an insurer's balance sheet and financial statements, including any outstanding legal actions involving the organization. The prospective outcome of such actions affects the ratings that these organizations assign to insurers and are another indicator of how well an insurer meets its legal requirements.

Meeting Social Responsibilities

Meeting social responsibilities is the most difficult of the major insurer goals to evaluate. No standards exist for judging an insurer's performance in this area, and little information on an individual insurer's performance is publicly available. Of course, an insurer can get information from its own records to show its own performance, but comparisons with competing insurers are difficult to make because of the lack of available information. Many insurers use their websites to indicate their participation in home and workplace safety programs, support of community projects, and involvement in other social programs.

Another possible indicator of social responsibility is the benefits that an insurer provides for its employees. Some insurers have begun to promote family-friendly policies within their organization to assist employees with balancing work and family responsibilities.

Comparative information for employee benefits is available from the United States Chamber of Commerce and from various insurer trade associations. Additionally, some periodicals provide feature articles in which they rank employers according to their employee benefit programs.

Many insurers contribute to associations that do research and raise public concern for safety. Contributions to medical, welfare, and educational institutions and programs are another indication of humanitarian efforts and social responsibility.

Additionally, "green" initiatives are emerging for many insurers as they recognize their responsibility to preserve the environment. In addition to recycling and reusing materials used in the production of policies, handling claims, and reporting, insurers are increasingly interested in auto salvage programs. Salvage programs are better for the environment and more cost-effective for insureds.

FUNCTIONAL VIEW OF INSURANCE

The functional view of insurance examines the many and varied functions an insurer performs as it conducts its business operations.

To carry out the operations of an insurer, many people are needed, all of whom perform specific functions. A function generally describes a distinct type of work or an aspect of operations or management requiring special technical knowledge. An insurer's core functions are typically marketing and distribution, underwriting, and claims. These core functions represent the lifespan of the insurer's business operations, from getting the business (marketing and distribution), to pricing the business (underwriting), and then to administering the business (claims).

Insurers perform additional functions that are designed to support these three core functions. An insurer carries out these additional functions to facilitate risk transfer, to promote efficiency, and to meet its financial and nonfinancial goals.

This section provides an overview of these categories of insurer functions:

- Core functions
- Supporting functions
- Other common functional areas

All of the functions included in these categories interact to meet an insurer's goals. Some insurers may perform only some of these functions, some may combine or separate functions, and some may use different names for them.

Specific types of products might also drive an insurer's functional needs—for example, an insurer that offers surety bonds might have a surety bond function. Regardless of these differences, each function is closely linked to all the other functions, and none is performed in a vacuum. The interaction of these core and other functions is vital to an insurer's survival and success.

Core Functions

Although insurers may use varying organizational structures, three core functions exist within the structure of a typical insurer. These core functions—marketing and distribution, underwriting, and claims—form the basis of an insurer's business.

Marketing and Distribution

Marketing and distribution involves determining what products or services customers want and need, advertising the products (communicating their value to customers), and delivering them to customers. The marketing and distribution function contributes significantly to an insurer's goals of earning a profit and meeting customers' needs. The insurer cannot make a profit if it does not provide the products and services customers need.

The goals of the marketing and distribution function must be balanced with other insurer goals. For example, the objectives of the marketing and distribution function should support the insurer's overall growth and customer retention goals. If the insurer has targeted specific regions or lines of business as growth areas, the marketing and distribution function needs to align its efforts for overall growth and customer retention. An imbalance between the marketing and distribution function's goals and the goals of any other department within the organization may reduce the efficiency of the insurer.

Underwriting

Underwriting
The process of selecting insureds, pricing coverage, determining insurance policy terms and conditions, and then monitoring the underwriting decisions made.

Adverse selection
In general, the tendency for people with the greatest probability of loss to be the ones most likely to purchase insurance.

Once the marketing and distribution function has developed a relationship with potential customers, it is the job of the **underwriting** function to determine whether and under what conditions the insurer is willing to provide insurance products and services to the potential customers. The goal of underwriting is to write a profitable book of business for the insurer, which supports the insurer's profit goal. This is accomplished by developing appropriate underwriting guidelines, which underwriters use to evaluate risk. Underwriting serves both insurers and insurance buyers by helping the insurer avoid **adverse selection**. Avoiding adverse selection assists an insurer with remaining profitable and keeping premiums reasonable for insureds.

Claims

An insurance policy is a promise to make a payment to, or on behalf of, the insured if a covered event occurs. The purpose of the claims function is to fulfill the insurer's promise. To that end, the claims function is staffed by employees who are trained in the skills necessary to evaluate and settle claims and to negotiate or litigate the settlement of claims by or against insureds through the claim handling process.

The claim handling process is designed to achieve a fair settlement in accordance with the applicable insurance policy provisions. Claim settlements that exceed the amount payable under the policy increase the cost of insurance for all insureds. Settlements that are less than the coverage amount deprive the insured of benefits to which he or she is entitled under the insurance policy. Insurers have developed expertise in claim handling in all categories of loss exposures. Therefore, many insurance industry practitioners view claim handling as the primary service that insurers provide.

Supporting Functions

To support the core functions of marketing and distribution, underwriting, and claims, insurers provide a variety of supporting functions, including risk control, premium auditing, actuarial functions, reinsurance, and information technology. Although most insurers are able to provide these supporting functions in-house, many are available through third-party providers as well. These functions are not only necessary to the efficient operation of insurers, but are also used by a variety of other risk financing organizations, such as captives, pools, risk retention groups, and self-insurers:

- Risk control—An insurer's risk control function provides information to the underwriting function to assist in selecting and rating risks. The risk control function also works with commercial insureds to help prevent losses and to reduce the effects of losses that cannot be prevented. Insurers may also market their risk control services as a stand-alone product to third parties who have not purchased insurance policies from the insurer.

- Premium auditing—Although the premium for many types of insurance is known and guaranteed in advance, the premium is variable for some lines of insurance and cannot be precisely calculated until after the end of the policy period. For example, the premium for workers compensation insurance policies is calculated using wages paid during the policy period. Other commercial insurance policies may use rating variables such as sales or revenue to calculate the premium. Premium auditors ensure equitable treatment of insureds by reviewing the insureds' records to obtain accurate information on rating variables.

- Actuarial—Actuarial functions include calculating insurance rates, developing rating plans, estimating loss reserves, and providing predictive modeling services. The actuarial function also conducts sensitivity analysis to determine the financial security of the insurer. Furthermore, the actuarial function coordinates with the accounting and finance functions in developing reports for regulators to ensure that the insurer is adhering to all regulatory requirements.

- Reinsurance—When an insurer accepts a risk that is larger than it is willing or able to support, it can transfer all or part of that risk to other insurers through reinsurance transactions. Many insurers have a separate reinsurance department that arranges reinsurance and maintains reinsurance agreements.

- Information technology—The information technology function provides the infrastructure that supports all of an insurer's internal and external communications. Insurers use information technology to conduct their daily operations, manage marketing efforts, underwrite policies, track investments, and pay claims. Information systems are especially important to insurers because of the vast amounts of data associated with insurance operations.

Other Common Functional Areas

In addition to the core and supporting functions, insurers perform a host of other functions or outsource them to an external organization. Some common functions include investments, accounting and finance, customer service, legal and compliance, human resources, and special investigation units (SIUs).

- Investments—An insurer's investment operations enable it to earn investment income on the funds generated by its underwriting activities. This investment income enables the insurer to reduce the premium that it must charge in exchange for the risks it assumes. The nature of the insurance risks that an insurer assumes is a factor in determining the types of investments it acquires. For example, liability losses are paid out over a longer period than property losses. Therefore, liability policies can support more long-term investments, such as corporate bonds with long maturity periods, whereas property policies need to be supported by more liquid and short-term investments. An insurer that assumes only moderate underwriting risks might be able to assume greater investment risks with potentially higher investment yield, whereas an insurer that assumes high underwriting risks might need to be more conservative in its investment strategy.

- Accounting and finance—The primary responsibilities of the accounting and finance function are to ensure that the organization has funds to meet its obligations and to fairly and fully disclose the financial position of the insurer in conformance with generally accepted accounting principles (GAAP). Insurers, like all other types of businesses, use accounting to record, analyze, and summarize their financial activities and status. Once the information has been accumulated, an accountant must evaluate, interpret, and communicate the results to all stakeholders.

- Customer service—The customer service function can include an array of responsibilities that vary among insurers. Some insurers have customer service personnel assigned to specific work areas, such as customer billing, claims services, underwriting support, agency relations or billing, agency technology support, customer internet support, and information technology support services for internal users.

- Legal and compliance—The legal and compliance function provides legal counsel, support, and service to other functions within the insurer and ensures that statutory and administrative requirements are met. Large insurers may have legal counselors specifically assigned to their claim function. Activities of the legal and compliance function may include overseeing and managing litigation, managing corporate legal requirements, participating in legislative activities, and auditing all functions of the insurer for regulatory compliance and to ensure that organizational standards are met and procedures are followed.

- Human resources—The human resources function involves the selection, training, and dismissal of employees. The human resources area maintains employee records; supervises employee introduction to colleagues, performance reviews, and compensation management; conducts orientation and ongoing training; administers employee benefit programs; and performs related functions.

- SIUs—These units are established to combat insurance fraud, which includes any deliberate deception committed against an insurer or an insurance producer for the purpose of unwarranted financial gain. Fraud can occur during the process of buying, selling, or underwriting insurance, or making or paying a claim. Such fraud may be committed by applicants, insureds, claimants, medical and other service providers, and even by producers and the insurer's staff. SIU personnel investigate suspicious circumstances that affect claims such as underreporting payroll for a lower premium, overreporting square footage for the purpose of obtaining higher limits, or inflating the value on a proof of loss for a higher claim payment.

These other functional areas may be separated into additional functions. For example, in some insurers, the human resources function is divided into human resources and training and development. Other insurers may group several of these other functional areas into one such area. For example, the actuarial, investment, and internal audit functions may be combined to form the accounting and finance function.

THE DIGITIZATION OF INSURANCE

A single term resonates with increasing frequency throughout risk management and insurance: disruption. And it's not just an empty buzzword. Here's how Insurance Thought Leadership's chief innovation officer, Guy Fraker, distills the essence of the importance of innovation in the industry:

> The world is moving toward prevention—crash prevention, injury prevention, illness prevention. The entire history of the [risk management and insurance] industry is to clean up the unintended consequences from not preventing. And so the history of insurance has evolved over the past 100 years in the exact opposite direction of where the technologies are taking society. That gap is only going to continue to grow.[1]

Disruption entails equal parts threat and opportunity at every link in the insurance value chain. For every development that seemingly reduces the industry's reliance on human resources—a chatbot that potentially replaces a claims representative, for example—a breakthrough reveals potential revenue streams and the promise of new markets, like an app that connects impoverished populations with economical coverage options.

What's the best way to navigate this period of unprecedented uncertainty and opportunity? It starts with understanding how we got here—the rapid evolution of the three fundamental building blocks of the digitization of insurance: data capture, data storage, and data analytics. See the exhibit "How Big Data Has Transformed the Risk Management Environment."

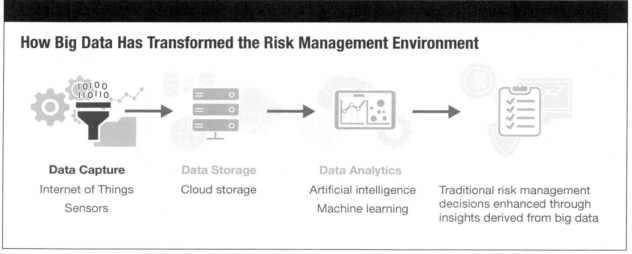

How Big Data Has Transformed the Risk Management Environment

Data Capture
Internet of Things
Sensors

Data Storage
Cloud storage

Data Analytics
Artificial intelligence
Machine learning

Traditional risk management decisions enhanced through insights derived from big data

[DA12739]

Data Capture: Expanding Data Sources

Data has always been everywhere. Any recorded piece of information that fortifies decision making is data. Today, however, there are more sources of data, more ways to record and transmit it, and more ways to use it than ever before. In fact, it's estimated that every second, nearly two megabytes of data are generated for every human on the planet. Much of that data is generated and ultimately leveraged on devices connected through the Internet of Things (IoT).

How is the IoT different from the internet? For most of its life, the internet's chief purpose has been to facilitate the use of centralized websites to connect people with information or with one another. That's still the case, but increasingly inexpensive bandwidth, cheap and widely available data transmission technology, and nearly universal connectivity also allow people to interact with devices and for those devices to meaningfully interact with each other without human intervention. The devices—whether a sensor that detects slow leaks in water heaters, a video doorbell system that repels intruders, or a jet engine that transmits diagnostic information to the cockpit—are the eponymous things that distinguish the IoT from the internet.

The ability of devices connected to the IoT to collect data about their surroundings and immediately transmit it to other devices or to people lies at the heart of the ongoing shift from risk transfer to risk prevention that is fundamentally changing the industry and the roles of those who work in it. Let's examine how.

Homes, cars, and businesses connected through the IoT can immunize themselves from loss in a myriad of ways, which may significantly change customers' expectations of the insurance product itself. That's because the demand for insurance stems from fundamental uncertainty—Will our warehouse burn down? What happens if I get sick?—and IoT environments that are increasingly adept at anticipating and controlling losses may considerably reduce or even eliminate that uncertainty and thereby radically alter the need to finance or transfer risk. Imagine, for example, a future in which autonomous vehicles have rendered their predecessors extinct, and the entire ground transportation grid hums with artificial-intelligence-governed efficiency that orchestrates each vehicle's speed and route to preclude collisions or other mishaps whose associated risks have consistently been covered under auto insurance.

But such a scenario—or similar ones in which, for instance, houses become smart enough to prevent most kinds of traditional losses that have always been covered under homeowners insurance—hardly spells doom for traditional insurers. Why? In addition to its risk control potential, the data that IoT-connected devices and sensors generate is already reshaping core insurer functions like underwriting, ratemaking, and claims.

The effectiveness of an insurer's underwriting function has always been largely reliant on the availability of quality data about the risk being evaluated. So it's easy to see how the volume of data the IoT produces could radically improve the process's efficiency and precision. Here's Chubb Limited Chairman and Chief Executive Officer Evan Greenberg on how the widening availability of data is changing underwriting data collection at one insurer:

> Right now, if you're a small business, to underwrite you, we ask you about thirty questions. For Chubb, in the next eighteen months, that'll come down to about seven questions, because we can just scrape the answers from data that is publicly available. . . . Eventually, we're going to have to ask you two questions: What's your name and what's your address? And we'll be able to figure out the rest to underwrite.[2]

In addition to leveraging IoT-generated data to streamline data collection, underwriters can use it to develop more accurate rates. For example, underwriters use a set of standard attributes (variables) to evaluate personal and commercial auto policyholders. However, when they can identify additional attributes that affect or reflect potential frequency and severity of loss, they can use that information to create more refined classification systems that produce more accurately priced accounts. The use of telematics presents such an opportunity: new attributes that correlate with auto losses are identified, and auto insurance classes and rates are refined.

For example, assume that an insurer categorizes as preferred its auto insurance applicants with good driving records and rating factors that suggest that they present minimal loss exposure. By offering lower rates to this category of insureds, the insurer hopes to attract and retain customers with a low risk of having an accident. Conversely, applicants with poor driving records or rating factors that suggest that they present greater loss exposure are categorized as nonstandard and are charged higher rates.

Using telematics could empower the insurer to better segment drivers into rating classifications. How? After a vehicle is monitored through telematics for a certain period, the insurer could present the insured with a new rate that takes actual driving experience into account. This does not mean that the primary factors for auto rates are ignored, but rather that the telematics data helps provide the insured with a more precise rate that accurately reflects the loss exposure.

Using the attributes provided by telematics, the insurer reclassifies the drivers based on a personalized driving score. Insurers use loss exposure data generated through telematics to supplement the data they have traditionally used for ratemaking. They analyze this data using sophisticated algorithms to determine the correlations and interactions among all the rating attributes being considered. This includes traditional rating attributes, such as vehicle use and type, and new attributes generated through telematics, such as braking, acceleration, and time of day. Increasingly, insurers are also using artificial intelligence (AI) to aid in the discovery of variable interactions that may not be evident when using a generalized linear model.

While ratemaking and underwriting rely on the IoT's data generation, an insurer's claims function can be transformed through its instantaneous communication. The IoT likewise can make claims handling more efficient through its ability to facilitate instantaneous communication between objects and people. A future in which an insured can just text a photo of a damaged car to trigger a claim's resolution is already here, but imagine a situation in which a home's sensors immediately detect a hailstorm intense enough to damage its roof and automatically dispatch a minidrone to capture dozens of high-resolution photographs of the damage, all without human intervention.

Data Storage: The Blockchain

The decision-making value of data produced by smart products, the IoT, and other data-capturing technology can be undermined by its volume, velocity, and veracity—more and faster is not necessarily better. Cloud computing enables the storage and sharing of vast amounts of data. But what if there was a way to ensure that the data used for risk management analysis was from a trusted source and independently verified? That is the premise underlying the data storage and sharing medium known as the blockchain.

Think of the blockchain as a virtual distributed ledger that maintains a dynamically updated list of data records (blocks). These records are not actually recorded in the ledger, however, until the veracity of data within them is confirmed and verified through a consensus process called mining. This verification process removes intermediary validation and establishes trust without the use of a centralized authority. After a block is confirmed and the data within it is verified through mining, the block is time stamped and added to the preexisting blocks in the chain—hence the term "blockchain." The blockchain is encrypted and protected against tampering and revision.

The myriad of risk management ramifications of the blockchain are a by-product of the medium's immutability, security, transparency, scalability, and ability to facilitate the sharing of verified, quality data. Here are some examples of its effects on the insurance value chain:

- Insurance products, pricing, and distribution—The supply chain for insurance is ripe for change through the implementation of blockchain. The use of smart contracts could alter the types of products insurers offer, such as parametric insurance or insurance that could be implanted in transactional purchases. Blockchain can also help make smaller insurance policies, covering specific days or actions, more efficient to offer, thereby increasing availability while decreasing costs.

- Underwriting, risk management, and reinsurance—Risk registries and data-sharing capabilities could increase through blockchain-enabled peer-to-peer insurance models and the like. Shared industry ledgers could also come into play, allowing interinsurer claims to be settled quickly.

- Policyholder acquisition and servicing—Onboarding new customers and clientele could be much easier for insurers that adopt blockchain. With third-party requests for information removed from the process, new customer data would be verified almost immediately. The insurance life-cycle documents could be easily updated, and any repetition of data entry and verification would become avoidable.

- Claims management—The use of smart contracts, reliant on triggering events rather than indemnification, could simplify the traditional claims management process. If the industry establishes a communal ledger via the blockchain process, that could also help quicken the handling of multilayer settlements and fraud investigations.

- Finance, payments, and accounting—Integrating blockchain into how an insurer works could make international payments easier to process, creating greater efficiency when dealing with matters of subrogation.

- Insurance regulation and compliance—By giving regulators the ability to keep an eye on insurance variables throughout their jurisdictions, blockchain would help free resources for individual departments of insurance. It could also help create an industry-wide proof-of-insurance ledger, rather than putting the onus on individual insureds to prove that they have insurance.

Data Analytics: Advanced Analytics

Insurers are already using data analytics across various functions, including underwriting and claims. While applications such as chatbots (which mimic human speech) are taking over some basic claims and customer service functions, insurance professionals who embrace changes and enhancements are positioned to help the industry and traditional roles evolve.

In particular, auto insurance has been influenced by data analytics. In the auto insurance field, telematics devices track driving habits; dashboard cameras detect distracted driving; and front-facing computer-vision technology identifies, analyzes, and then prevents risks. For example, a truck's brakes may automatically be applied because a front-facing camera determines that a vehicle has stopped directly in front of the truck. The data gained by telematics programs can help insurers more accurately price their products and classify insureds. For instance, awareness that drivers the insurer had previously classified as preferred are actually standard can help the insurer more accurately classify insureds.

Data analytics has allowed underwriters to segment policies and rates based on attributes that might have once been considered obscure, such as geospatial data. More precise underwriting of property exposures can be critical to insurers' success as climate and environmental changes become more common.

Workers compensation has been influenced by data analytics that enable the identification of which workers are likely to be injured, which injuries are likely to be expensive, and which claims are fraudulent. For example, an employee's delay in reporting a claim may go unnoticed by a manager but trigger a response in data analysis. As claims managers are often involved in developing treatment plans, the ability to flag a claim because of complications related to an individual's health and recovery can reduce cost and the risk of reinjury.

Also in personal and commercial lines claims, techniques such as network analysis and clustering (essentially, finding similar claims and claimants) identify and prevent fraud. These methods allow claims departments to keep up with the ever-changing techniques of fraudsters rather than relying on traditional fraud indicators. And the ability to scan claims without manual human involvement saves time and resources. Automatic detection stops the fraud process before the insurer's money is lost.

While the claims process benefits from the automation of analytics, claims professionals with skills are still necessary to properly use this data. Emphasizing the need for competent risk management and insurance professionals, Michael Skiba, vice president of counter fraud strategies for Inform, remarked:

> I think many carriers are aware that the future of fighting fraud is all about data: data management, inclusion and integration, and at the core of this data is the technology that surrounds it. But we can't forget the "people" aspect of what is to come in fraud fighting. Many companies are failing to recognize that they need people who have the ability to leverage the power of this data and, furthermore, have some degree of comfort using technology to assist with fraud-fighting efforts.[3]

SUMMARY

Although an insurer usually maintains overall goals that are similar to any other organization's, it often also faces numerous constraints within its internal operation and external environment. Navigating through these constraints to ensure operational profit while maintaining a strong reputation is critical to an insurer's success.

Insurers can be classified in several ways, including legal form of ownership, place of incorporation, licensing status, and the insurance distribution systems and channels the insurer uses to deliver its products and services to the marketplace.

Measuring the performance of an insurer involves determining how successful the insurer is at meeting established goals. Measuring how well an insurer meets its profitability goals and legal requirements is more objective, while measuring how well an insurer meets customer needs and social responsibilities is more subjective.

An insurer's core functions are marketing and distribution, underwriting, and claims. Other supporting functions include risk control, premium auditing, actuarial functions, reinsurance, and information technology. Additional common functional areas in an insurer may include investments, accounting and finance, customer service, legal and compliance, human resources, and SIUs. While insurers vary regarding their structure and the exact role of each functional area, the interaction of the core functions and the other functions is vital to insurers' survival and success.

The best way to navigate this period of unprecedented uncertainty and opportunity in risk management and insurance starts with understanding how we got here—the rapid evolution of the three fundamental building blocks of the industry: data capture, data storage, and data analytics.

ASSIGNMENT NOTES

1. Swiss Re Institute, "The insurance industry has to promote innovation," December 8, 2017, www.youtube.com/watch?v=C-IVCPmxd6M (accessed September 10, 2018.)

2. "Insurance is moving toward 'predict and prevent' using big data," CNBC, July 30, 2018, www.cnbc.com/video/2018/07/30/chubb-ceo-insurance-moving-toward-predict-and-prevent-with-big-data.html?__source=sharebar | email&par=sharebar (accessed August 29, 2018).

3. Michael Skiba, Jeffrey Rapattoni, and Chris McKibbin, "Secrets to combating insurance fraud with data analytics," February 5, 2018, www.propertycasualty360.com/2018/02/05/secrets-to-combating-insurance-fraud-with-data-ana/?slreturn=20180721134130 (accessed August 31, 2018).

Direct Your Learning ▶▶

2

Insurance Regulation

Educational Objectives

After learning the content of this assignment, you should be able to:

▷ Explain how insurance regulation protects consumers, contributes to maintaining insurer solvency, and assists in preventing destructive competition.

▷ Summarize the regulatory activities of state insurance departments, including state insurance commissioners' duties.

▷ Describe the licensing requirements for insurers and insurance personnel.

▷ Describe the methods that regulators use to maintain the solvency of insurers.

▷ Examine the goals of insurance rate regulation, the major types of state rating laws, and the reasons supporting and opposing rate regulation.

▷ Explain how the contract language contained in insurance policies is regulated.

▷ Summarize the regulation of insurance market conduct and consumer protection.

Insurance Regulation

REASONS FOR INSURANCE REGULATION

Because a well-functioning insurance market is essential to society, regulation is necessary to correct market imperfections, whether those imperfections result from externalities, incomplete information, costs, or other causes. However, the reasons for regulation can differ; each market participant, each regulator, and each observer may offer different reasons for regulating a particular market.

The insurance industry is regulated primarily for three reasons:

- To protect consumers
- To maintain insurer solvency
- To prevent destructive competition

Although these purposes clearly overlap, each is examined separately.

Consumers may not have complete information about the product of insurance, yet they need the product and often are required to purchase it. Because of consumers' incomplete information, insurance regulators must ensure that the products are beneficial to consumers and available at an equitable price. In addition, inadequate information, destructive competition, and mismanagement (among other things) can threaten the solvency of insurers. Implementation and enforcement of insurance regulation is necessary to correct each of these market imperfections. If regulation can correct or reduce the effect of the market imperfections, it can encourage insurer solvency.

Protect Consumers

The primary reason insurance is regulated is to protect consumers. When consumers buy electronics, clothing, or furniture, they can usually inspect the products before purchasing them to ensure that the products meet their needs. Even if consumers inspect the insurance policies they purchase, they might not be able to analyze and understand complex legal documents.

Regulators help to protect consumers by reviewing insurance policy forms to determine whether they benefit consumers and comply with state consumer protection laws. State legislatures can set coverage standards and specify policy language for certain insurance coverages. State insurance regulators can review policy language and disapprove policy forms and endorsements that are inconsistent with state consumer protection laws.

Insurance regulators also protect consumers against fraud and unethical market behavior. Departments of insurance receive complaints about these behaviors:

- Producers have intentionally sold unnecessary insurance.
- Producers have misrepresented the nature of coverage to make a sale.
- Producers have stolen or misused insured or insurer funds.
- Claim representatives have engaged in unfair claim practices, refusing to pay legitimate claims or unfairly reducing claim payments.
- Insurance managers have contributed to the insolvency of insurers through their dishonesty.

In addition to protecting consumers against such abuses, regulators also try to ensure that insurance is readily available, especially the insurance that is viewed as a necessity. For example, all states now try to ensure that continuous personal auto insurance coverage is available by restricting the rights of insurers to cancel or nonrenew personal auto insurance policies. At the same time, regulators recognize that insurers sometimes must break long-term relationships with insureds whose loss exposures no longer match those the insurer wants to cover. Cancellation restrictions aimed at promoting availability can therefore lead insurers to reject more new-business applications, which reduces insurance availability.

Insurance regulators also provide information about insurance matters so that consumers can make more informed decisions.

Maintain Insurer Solvency

Another reason insurance is regulated is to maintain insurer solvency. Solvency regulation protects insureds against the risk that insurers will be unable to meet their financial obligations. Consumers and even some sophisticated businesspeople may find it difficult to evaluate insurers' financial ability to keep their promises. Insurance regulators try to maintain a sound financial condition of private insurers for several reasons:

- Insurance provides future protection—Premiums are paid in advance, but the period of protection extends into the future. If insurers become insolvent, future claims may not be paid, and the insurance protection already paid for may become worthless.
- Regulation is needed to protect the public interest—Large numbers of individuals and the community at large are adversely affected when insurers become insolvent.
- Insurers have a responsibility to insureds—Insurers hold substantial funds for the ultimate benefit of insureds. Government regulation is necessary to safeguard such funds.
- Insurers have become insolvent despite regulatory reviews. The goal of regulation is not to eliminate all insolvencies but rather to minimize

the number of insolvencies. To eliminate insolvencies would mean that regulations must be set to allow the most inefficient insurer to continue to operate, which is not a desirable regulatory goal.

Prevent Destructive Competition

Insurance regulation also seeks to prevent destructive competition. Regulators are responsible for determining whether insurance rates are high enough to prevent destructive competition. At times, some insurers underprice their products to increase market share by attracting customers away from higher-priced competitors. This practice drives down price levels in the whole market. When insurance rate levels are inadequate, some insurers can become insolvent, and others might withdraw from the market or stop writing new business. An insurance shortage can then develop, and individuals and firms might be unable to obtain the coverage they need. Certain types of insurance can become unavailable at any price, such as when both products liability and directors and officers coverage became unavailable in the 1980s.

INSURANCE REGULATORS

Insurance is a highly regulated industry, with regulations guiding the licensure and operations of insurers and their employees. To be successful, insurance professionals should have a basic understanding of the sources of those regulations.

The primary source of insurance regulation is state insurance departments, led by state insurance commissioners. **The National Association of Insurance Commissioners** coordinates state-level insurance regulation, though it has no direct regulatory authority of its own. Because insurers are businesses, however, they are also subject to certain federal regulations.

National Association of Insurance Commissioners (NAIC)
An association of insurance commissioners from the fifty U.S. states, the District of Columbia, and the five U.S. territories and possessions, whose purpose is to coordinate insurance regulation activities among the various state insurance departments.

State Insurance Departments

Every state has three separate and equal branches of government: the legislative branch makes the laws, the judicial branch (the court system) interprets the laws, and the executive branch implements the laws. Day-to-day regulation of insurance business is performed by state insurance departments, which fall under the executive branch of each state government. The laws that state insurance departments enforce are enacted by the legislature.

A state Insurance Department engages in a wide variety of regulatory activities, which typically include these:

- Licensing insurers
- Licensing producers, claims representatives, and other insurance personnel
- Approving policy forms

- Holding rate hearings and reviewing rate filings
- Evaluating solvency information
- Performing market conduct examinations
- Investigating policyholder complaints
- Rehabilitating or liquidating insolvent insurers
- Issuing cease-and-desist orders
- Fining insurers that violate state law
- Publishing shoppers' guides and other consumer information (in some states)
- Preventing fraud

The Insurance Commissioner

Every state Insurance Department is headed by an insurance commissioner, superintendent, or director appointed by the governor or elected by the voting public. This commissioner delegates the duties he or she is charged with to the personnel in the state Insurance Department.

The duties of a typical state insurance commissioner include these:

- Overseeing the state Insurance Department's operation
- Declaring orders, rules, and regulations necessary to administer insurance laws
- Determining whether to issue business licenses to new insurers, producers, and other insurance entities
- Reviewing insurance pricing and coverage
- Conducting financial and market examinations of insurers
- Holding hearings on insurance issues
- Taking action when insurance laws are violated
- Issuing an annual report on the status of the state's insurance market and Insurance Department
- Maintaining records of Insurance Department activities

Although most commissioners are appointed, some states elect their commissioners. Which selection method better serves the public interest is a matter of debate. See the exhibit "State Insurance Commissioners: Election Versus Appointment."

Many commissioners were employed in the insurance business before they entered public office, and many are employed by insurers or insurance-related organizations after leaving office. The expertise and understanding of insurance operations needed to regulate effectively will most likely be found in a person who has worked in the insurance business. However, some allege that such insurance commissioners have a less-than-objective relationship with the insurers they regulate.

State Insurance Commissioners: Election Versus Appointment

Elective systems offer these benefits:

- An elected commissioner is generally in office for a full term, while an appointed insurance commissioner is subject to dismissal.
- An elected commissioner is more likely to change the Insurance Department's stance, rather than regulating in the same manner as his or her predecessor.
- An elected commissioner is more aware of the issues important to the public.
- An elected commissioner is not obligated to any particular group or special interest.

Appointment systems offer these benefits:

- An appointed commissioner has no need to campaign and is less likely to be unduly influenced by political contributors.
- An appointed commissioner is less likely to be swayed by ill-informed public opinion than an elected one.
- An appointed commissioner is more likely to be perceived as a career government employee interested in regulation than as a politician interested in political advancement.

[DA12799]

State insurance commissioners usually deny that they are overly responsive to insurers. Commissioners frequently issue cease-and-desist orders, fine or penalize insurers for infractions of the law, forbid insurers to engage in mass cancellations, limit insurance rate increases, and take numerous other actions that benefit policyholders at insurers' expense.

State Regulation Funding

State insurance departments are partly funded by state premium taxes, audit fees, filing fees, and licensing fees, but premium taxes are the major source of funding. Although state premium taxes are substantial, only a relatively small proportion is spent on insurance regulation. Premium taxes are designed primarily to raise state revenues.

The National Association of Insurance Commissioners (NAIC)

The NAIC coordinates insurance-regulation activities among the state insurance departments but has no direct regulatory authority. However, by providing a forum to develop uniform policy when appropriate, the NAIC has a profound effect on state regulation.

The NAIC meets three times a year to discuss important issues in insurance regulation. It developed uniform financial statements that all states require insurers to file. It collects and compiles financial information from insurers for use by insurance regulators. It also assists state insurance departments by sharing financial information about insurers that are potentially insolvent and by developing model laws and regulations. The NAIC's Financial Analysis Working Group serves as both a coordinator and a failsafe mechanism for state insurance regulators as they oversee nationally significant insurers.

Model Laws and Regulations

Model law

A document drafted by the NAIC, in a style similar to a state statute, that reflects the NAIC's proposed solution to a given problem or issue and provides a common basis to the states for drafting laws that affect the insurance industry. Any state may choose to adopt the model bill or adopt it with modifications.

Model regulation

A draft regulation that may be implemented by a state insurance department if the model law is passed.

Many states' insurance laws and regulations incorporate at least the primary concepts of the NAIC's **model laws**, which results in some degree of uniformity among the states. If the model law is passed, the state may draft a **model regulation**. Examples of model laws include model legislation on the regulation of risk retention groups and a model property and liability insurance rating law.

Accreditation Program

In addition to developing model laws, the NAIC's accreditation program increases the uniformity of insurer solvency regulation across the states. To become accredited, a state Insurance Department must prove that it has satisfied the program's minimum solvency regulation standards.

The NAIC's Financial Regulation Standards and Accreditation Program has certain criteria:

- The state's insurance laws and regulations must meet the basic standards of the NAIC models.
- The state's regulatory methods must be acceptable to the NAIC.
- The state's Insurance Department practices must be adequate as defined by the NAIC.

Federal Regulation

While state governments, rather than the federal government, hold the regulatory power over insurers, some federal regulations still apply. For example, insurers are subject to federal employment laws just like any other business, and stock insurers are subject to the same regulations as other businesses that sell stock to the public.

The federal Insurance Fraud Prevention Act protects consumers and insurers against insolvencies resulting from insurance fraud. It prohibits anyone with a felony conviction involving trustworthiness from working in the business of insurance unless he or she secures the written consent of an insurance regulator. Moreover, it establishes that it is illegal for an insurer, reinsurer, producer, or other similar entities to employ a felon with a conviction involving breach of trust or dishonesty. The act also identifies crimes related to the business of insurance, such as making false statements or reports about insurers to influence regulations.

Apply Your Knowledge

Carla, a claims manager, is training new claims representatives and talking to them about regulations that apply to their jobs. Carla wants them to understand the primary source of insurance regulation. Which one of the following should Carla therefore focus on?

- State insurance departments
- The NAIC
- Federal regulation
- Model laws and acts

Feedback: a. When discussing regulation with the new claims representatives, Carla should focus on state insurance departments so that the claims representatives understand the primary source of insurance regulation.

INSURANCE REGULATORY ACTIVITIES: LICENSING INSURERS AND INSURANCE PERSONNEL

Insurers can reap strategic advantages by anticipating regulatory requirements and processes at the start of a business development plan. Noncompliance with these requirements could lead to regulatory intervention, the loss of an insurer's license, or damage to an insurer's reputation.

Although the review processes for insurer licensing vary from state to state, all states require property-casualty insurers to receive approval before operating within the state. In addition to the authority to regulate insurers and related entities, departments of insurance (DOIs) also have authority to regulate insurance producers, claims representatives, and other insurance personnel through state laws.

Licensing Insurers

When a state issues a license to an insurer, it indicates that the insurer meets minimum standards of financial strength, competence, and integrity. As such, the insurer is authorized to write certain types of insurance in the state but is subject to all applicable state laws, rules, and regulations. If the state's standards for licensure change at a later time and the insurer fails to meet those news standards, its license can be revoked.

In response to complaints about the length of time regulators took to license a new insurer, regulators developed the Uniform Certificate of Authority Application (UCAA) to streamline the process. With the participation of all states and the District of Columbia, the UCAA process is designed to allow insurers to file copies of the same application for admission in numerous states. While each state still performs its own independent review of each application, insurers no longer need to file different applications in different formats.

Licensing standards vary among admitted domestic, foreign, alien, and nonadmitted insurers, and risk retention groups face a set of standards of their own.

Domestic Insurers

Domestic insurer

An insurer doing business in the jurisdiction in which it is incorporated.

Foreign insurer

An insurer licensed to operate in a state but incorporated in another state.

Alien insurer

An insurer domiciled in a country other than the United States.

Paid-in surplus

The amount stockholders paid in excess of the par value of the stock.

Reciprocal insurer

An insurer owned by its policyholders, formed as an unincorporated association for the purpose of providing insurance coverage to its members (called subscribers), and managed by an attorney-in-fact. Members agree to mutually insure each other, and they share profits and losses in the same proportion as the amount of insurance purchased from the exchange by that member.

If a **domestic insurer** obtains a license in a state other than that of its domicile, that state would consider it a **foreign insurer**. While a domestic insurer's license usually has no expiration date, licenses of foreign insurers and **alien insurers** generally require annual renewal.

An applicant for a domestic insurer license usually must apply for a charter and provide the names and addresses of the incorporators, the name of the proposed corporation, the territories and types of insurance it plans to market, the total authorized capital stock (if any), and its surplus. The application will be reviewed by the state insurance commissioner to determine whether the applicant meets the state's licensing requirements.

Part of the requirements for licensure is that the insurer must be financially sound. State laws require that domestic stock insurers satisfy certain minimum capital, surplus, and **paid-in surplus** requirements before a license is granted. Minimum initial capital and paid-in surplus requirements vary widely by state, by amounts, and by type of insurance written. Minimum initial capital requirements range from as little as $100,000 to as much as $15 million.

For mutual or **reciprocal insurers**, the minimum financial requirement applies only to surplus. (A mutual insurer does not have capital derived from the sale of stock.) A mutual insurer's initial surplus can be derived from premium deposits paid by prospective policyholders, or a portion could be borrowed. Most states require mutuals to have an initial surplus equal to the minimum capital and paid-in surplus requirement for stock insurers writing the same type of insurance, but some have set a lower minimum surplus requirement. In most states, reciprocal insurers face the same minimum surplus requirements as mutuals.

For mutual insurers, many states require the organizers to have a minimum number of applications with deposit premiums for a minimum number of separate loss exposures and aggregate premium exceeding a specific amount. These requirements help guarantee that the insurer has a sufficient book of business before it officially begins operations.

In addition to financial requirements, states impose other requirements on new insurers. For example, the proposed name for a new mutual insurer must include the word "mutual," and the proposed name of a new insurer must not be so similar to that of any existing insurer that it would be misleading. The commissioner might have the authority to refuse a license if he or she believes the insurer's incorporators or directors are not trustworthy. Some states even permit the commissioner to deny a license to an otherwise worthy applicant if the commissioner believes that no additional insurers are needed in the state.

Foreign Insurers

To be licensed in an additional state as a foreign insurer, an insurer must show that it has satisfied the requirements imposed by its home state (its state of domicile) and generally must satisfy the minimum capital, surplus, and other requirements imposed on the domestic insurers of the state in which it is applying.

Alien Insurers

Alien insurers (insurers domiciled outside the United States) must satisfy the requirements imposed on domestic insurers by the state in which they want to be licensed. Additionally, they usually must establish a branch office in any state and have funds on deposit in the U.S. equal to the minimum capital and surplus required.

Nonadmitted Insurers

From an insured's point of view, an admitted insurer is licensed by a state insurance department to do business in the insured's home state. A nonadmitted insurer is not licensed in the insured's home state (though it could be an admitted insurer in other states, and may even be an alien insurer).

A nonadmitted insurer is typically a surplus lines insurer, which is a mechanism that allows U.S. consumers to buy property-casualty insurance from nonadmitted insurers when the insurance they need is not available from admitted insurers. Surplus lines insurers provide a positive, legal supplement to the admitted insurance market because the business that surplus lines insurers generally accept includes distressed risks (those with underwriting problems), unique risks (those that are difficult to evaluate), high-capacity risks (those that require very high coverage limits), and new or emerging risks. Additionally, a nonadmitted insurer writing business in the surplus lines market will not face regulatory constraints on insurance rates and forms. Surplus lines coverages commonly include products liability, professional liability, employment practices liability, special events, and excess and umbrella policies.

Under surplus lines laws, a nonadmitted insurer might be permitted to transact business through a specially licensed surplus lines producer if the insurance is not readily available from admitted insurers, the nonadmitted insurer is considered acceptable, and the producer has a special license authorizing him or her to place such insurance.

An acceptable nonadmitted insurer generally must file a financial statement that the insurance commissioner finds satisfactory; supply documentation of transactions to state regulators; obtain a certificate of compliance from its home state or country; and, if an alien insurer, maintain a trust fund in the U.S. Some states leave the determination of acceptability to the producer. A few states permit producers to use other nonadmitted insurers if the desired insurance cannot be obtained from either admitted or acceptable nonadmitted insurers.

The National Association of Insurance Commissioners (NAIC) maintains an International Insurers Department (IID) to examine nonadmitted alien insurers' financial condition, trust funds, and trust deposits. The IID maintains a list of alien insurers that meet its standards, known as the NAIC Quarterly Listing of Alien Insurers. The IID standards cover four primary areas:

- Capital and surplus requirements
- Trust fund requirements
- Biographical affidavits from the directors and officers of insurers
- Annual filing of insurers' audited financial statements

The IID list is recognized as a credible list of financially sound insurers, and a number of states used the list as a de facto eligibility list for alien nonadmitted insurers. Under provisions of the federal Nonadmitted and Reinsurance Reform Act (NRRA), no state may prohibit a licensed surplus lines broker from "placing or procuring" insurance with an insurer on the list.

In addition to recognizing the IID list, the NRRA initiated several state-level reforms that made the surplus lines market more efficient and established a modern, consistent, and more effective framework for surplus lines regulation.

Modernized surplus lines regulation, along with requirements for capital and trust accounts, help ensure that nonadmitted insurers will be able to pay their claims, counteracting the fact that surplus lines insurance is not usually protected by a state's guaranty fund.

Risk Retention Groups

A risk retention group is a special type of assessable mutual insurer enabled by the 1986 Liability Risk Retention Act. Risk retention groups are often formed under state captive laws, which generally establish lower capital and surplus requirements for captives than for traditional property-casualty insurers. Once licensed as a commercial liability insurer under the laws of at least one state, a risk retention group can write insurance in other states without a license by filing the appropriate notice and registration forms with the nonchartering state. A risk retention group can write only commercial liability insurance for its members and may not write other lines of business. However, in a nonchartering state, a risk retention group might be subject to some state laws, such as unfair claim settlement practice laws, and to premium taxes. The risk retention group might also be required to become a member of a joint underwriting association or a similar association through which insurers share losses in such areas as assigned-risk auto insurance.

Some state regulators have expressed concerns about the financial security of risk retention groups, particularly when the group providing the insurance is licensed in another state. Congress helped address these concerns by allowing the licensing state to request and, if necessary, mandate an examination of a group's financial condition—even when the commissioner has no reason to believe that the group is financially impaired.

Licensing Insurance Personnel

In addition to insurers, state regulators also license some categories of insurance personnel. States license many of the people who sell insurance, give insurance advice, or represent insurers, including producers, claims representatives, and insurance consultants.

Producers

Producers must be licensed as a resident producer in each state where they do business. To obtain a license to sell a particular type of insurance, a producer must pass a written examination. Insurance producers operating without a license are subject to civil, and sometimes criminal, penalties. When doing business in a state other than their home state, producers must meet the nonresident licensing requirements in that state. This process can sometimes be cumbersome because each state has its own specific licensing requirements.

Traditionally, the differences between states' licensing requirements have been a source of frustration and expense for producers licensed in more than one state. Provisions in the Gramm-Leach-Bliley (GLB) Act have led to greater licensing reciprocity among states, although the ultimate goal of regulators is to move beyond reciprocity and to resolve issues related to uniformity in producer licensing.

The development of the National Insurance Producer Registry (NIPR) has eliminated many of the inconveniences that arise from a multistate regulatory system. The NIPR is a unique public-private partnership that supports the work of the states, Puerto Rico, the District of Columbia, the U.S. Virgin Islands, and the NAIC in making the producer-licensing process more cost effective, streamlined, and uniform for the benefit of regulators, insurance producers, insurers, and consumers. The NIPR vision is to provide a single electronic communication network producers can use to meet all aspects of the licensing and appointment processes. To this end, the NIPR developed and implemented the Producer Database (PDB) and the NIPR Gateway:

- The PDB is an electronic database that provides participating state regulatory licensing systems with one common repository of producer information. The PDB also includes data from the NAIC Regulatory Information Retrieval System to provide a more comprehensive producer profile. Some of the key benefits of the PDB are increased productivity, lower cost, reduced use of paper, access to real-time information, and the ability to conduct national verification of the license and status of a producer.

- The NIPR Gateway is a communication network that links state insurance regulators and the entities they regulate to facilitate the electronic exchange of producer information. Data standards have been developed for the exchange of license application, license renewal, appointment, and termination information.

The National Association of Registered Agents and Brokers Reform Act of 2015 (NARAB II) was a second attempt by the federal government to establish a centralized organization that, with the compliance of jurisdictions throughout the U.S., would work with individual states to streamline the nonresident-producer-licensing process. This law is designed to create a central clearinghouse for nonresident producers, without affecting any individual state's laws or rights to regulate insurance within its borders. Under NARAB, which will be run as a private, not-for-profit corporation, member producers would need to be licensed only as a resident producer by their state to qualify as a nonresident producer in other participating states. Producer participation in NARAB is completely voluntary.

Claims Representatives

Some states require claims representatives to be licensed so that they are aware of prohibited claims practices, have a minimum level of technical knowledge and skill, and understand how to handle insureds' claims fairly. This licensing typically includes an examination, which is important because of the complex and technical nature of insurance policies and the claims process. The licensing process also typically involves a background check, as well as ethics requirements, to help protect consumers from unfair, unethical, and dishonest claims practices.

Public adjusters, who represent insureds for a fee, are generally required to be licensed to ensure technical competence and protect the public.

Insurance Consultants

Insurance consultants give advice, counsel, or opinions about insurance policies. Some states require insurance consultants to be licensed, the requirements of which vary by state. Separate examinations are usually required to be an insurance consultant in both life-health and property-casualty insurance.

Apply Your Knowledge

To be licensed in an additional state, which one of these types of insurers must show that it has satisfied the requirements imposed by its home state (its state of domicile) and generally must satisfy the minimum capital, surplus, and other requirements imposed on the domestic insurers of the state in which it is applying?

- Alien insurer
- Foreign insurer
- Admitted insurer
- Nonadmitted insurer

Feedback: b. To be licensed in an additional state, a foreign insurer must show that it has satisfied the requirements imposed by its home state (its state of domicile) and generally must satisfy the minimum capital, surplus, and other requirements imposed on the domestic insurers of the state in which it is applying.

INSURANCE REGULATORY ACTIVITIES: MONITORING INSURER SOLVENCY

Insurers must remain solvent to pay their customers' covered claims. To ensure this, the United States' regulatory framework has made provisions to monitor insurers' financial strength.

Because insurers hold large sums of customers' money for long periods of time, their financial strength and claim-paying ability must be closely monitored. Monitoring insurer solvency protects insureds and the public by reducing the insolvency risk and protecting the public against loss when insurers fail. Whether directly or indirectly, insurers and consumers both pay for the cost of regulation; however, the long-term result is keeping insolvencies infrequent and manageable.

Methods to Maintain Solvency

The U.S. regulatory framework is a national system of state-based regulation. State insurance regulators are assisted by the National Association of Insurance Commissioners (NAIC), an organization of the chief insurance regulatory official from each state, the District of Columbia, and five U.S. territories. The NAIC provides financial, actuarial, legal, technological, research, and economic expertise to state regulators to assist them in meeting regulatory goals.

The mission, or purpose, of U.S. insurance regulation is to protect the interests of the insured and those who rely on the insurance coverage provided to the insured, while also facilitating an effective and efficient marketplace for insurance products. To accomplish this, insurance regulators must have appropriate regulatory authority and be able to operate without too much influence from insurers or other groups.

The U.S. regulatory framework relies on an extensive system of peer review, featuring frequent communication and collaboration to provide the necessary checks and balances needed to make the system work. Much of this collaboration occurs through the NAIC, where the diverse perspectives of its members are reflected in solutions embodied in model laws and regulations. These solutions have resulted in a risk-focused approach that is constantly evolving to meet changing local, national, and international developments.

Uniformity of approach to financial regulation has been facilitated by the NAIC accreditation program. As part of the peer review process, the accreditation program subjects state insurance regulators to a thorough and comprehensive review to determine whether the state has met minimum, baseline standards of solvency regulation.

To become accredited, the state must pass a full on-site accreditation review. To remain accredited, an accreditation review must be performed at least once every five years with interim annual reviews. These reviews look at the state's ability to protect consumers, meet standards, and cooperate with officials. See the exhibit "Financial Solvency Core Principles."

The U.S. regulatory framework has evolved over time into the risk-focused approach used by regulators today. A wide variety of insurers, ranging from small to large, serve a variety of state-based, regional, and national markets. This wide range of regulated entities calls for a flexible approach to regulation that focuses on the risks undertaken by each regulated entity. Here are some examples of solvency requirements insurers must comply with:[1]

- Insurers must submit annual and quarterly financial statements to the domestic regulator and the NAIC using a prescribed format called the annual statement or the blank. The NAIC maintains a data warehouse for use by state financial regulators.

- Insurers are required to use the NAIC's manual and instructions for consistency of accounting treatment and financial reporting.

- Most insurers (except the very small) must submit their financial statement to a certified public accountant for audit and have an actuary attest to the accuracy of reserve estimates.

- Insurers must perform a risk-based capital (RBC) calculation and report the results to regulators. The RBC calculation uses a standardized formula to benchmark a specified level of regulatory actions for weakly capitalized insurers. The RBC amount, based on industry experience, explicitly considers the size and risk profile of the insurer.

- Insurers are required to adhere to state minimum capital and surplus requirements.

Financial Solvency Core Principles

Core Principle 1	Regulatory reporting, disclosure, and transparency	• Insurers are required to file standardized reports annually and quarterly to assess the insurer's risk and financial condition. • These reports contain both qualitative and quantitative information, and are updated as necessary to incorporate significant common insurer risks.
Core Principle 2	Off-site monitoring and analysis	• Assess on an ongoing basis the financial condition of the insurer as of the valuation date and to identify and assess current and prospective risks through risk-focused surveillance. • The results of the off-site analysis are included in an insurer profile for continual solvency monitoring. • Many off-site monitoring tools are maintained by the NAIC (such as the NAIC Financial Analysis Solvency Tools—FAST).
Core Principle 3	On-site, risk-focused examinations	• U.S. regulators carry out risk-focused, on-site examinations in which an insurer's corporate governance, management oversight, and financial strength are evaluated, including the system of risk identification and mitigation both on a current and prospective basis. • The reported financial results are assessed through the financial examination process and a determination is made of the insurer's compliance with legal requirements.
Core Principle 4	Reserves, capital adequacy, and solvency	• Insurers are required to maintain reserves and capital at all times and in such forms so as to provide an adequate margin of safety. • The most visible measure of capital adequacy requirements is associated with the risk-based capital (RBC) system. The RBC calculation uses a standardized formula to benchmark specified level of regulatory actions for weakly capitalized insurers.
Core Principle 5	Regulatory control of significant, broad-based, risk-related transactions/ activities	The transactions/activities encompass these: • Licensing requirements • Change of control • The amount of dividends paid • Transactions with affiliates • Reinsurance
Core Principle 6	Preventive and corrective measures, including enforcement	• The regulatory authority takes preventive and corrective measures that are timely, suitable, and necessary to reduce the impact of risks identified during on-site and off-site regulatory monitoring. • These regulatory actions are enforced as necessary.
Core Principle 7	Exiting the market and receivership	• The legal and regulatory framework defines a range of options for the orderly exit of insurers from the marketplace. • Solvency is defined and a receivership scheme established to ensure the payment of insured obligations of insolvent insurers subject to appropriate restrictions and limitations.

"The United States Insurance Financial Solvency Framework and Core Principles," National Association of Insurance Commissioners, April 14, 2013, pp.4-5, www.naic.org/documents/committees_e_us_solvency_framework.pdf (accessed August 10, 2018). [DA06398]

- State investment laws limit the types and quantity of investments an insurer may make, encouraging insurers to maintain a conservative and diversified investment portfolio.
- State laws specify limitations on the amount on any single insured risk a property-casualty insurer may underwrite.
- Treatment of reinsurance is governed by the NAIC Credit for Reinsurance Model Law, which imposes standards on credits allowed to the reporting insurer.

Liquidation of Insolvent Insurers

Insolvency

A situation in which an entity's current liabilities (as opposed to its total liabilities) exceed its current assets.

If an insurer falls into **insolvency**, the insurance commissioner places it in receivership—at which time, another party, typically the insurance commissioner, manages the insurer. With proper management, successful rehabilitation might be possible.

If the insurer cannot be rehabilitated, it is liquidated according to the state's insurance code. Many states now rehabilitate and liquidate insolvent insurers according to the Uniform Insurers Liquidation Act, the Insurers Rehabilitation and Liquidation Model Act, and the Insurer Receivership Model Act.

State Guaranty Funds

Guaranty fund

A state-established fund that provides a system for the payment of some of the unpaid claims of insolvent insurers licensed in that state, generally funded by assessments collected from all insurers licensed in the state.

Guaranty funds do not prevent insurer insolvency, but they mitigate its effects. All states have property-casualty insurance guaranty funds that pay some of the unpaid claims of insolvent insurers licensed in the particular state.

Typically, insurers doing business in the state are assessed their share of the unpaid covered claims of the insolvent insurer. Although the amounts involved are not trivial, they still represent a very small percentage of total premiums.

State guaranty funds vary by state. However, these characteristics are common:

- Assessments are made only when an insurer fails (except in New York)—The definition of "failure" varies by state. Some states regard an insolvency order from a state court as evidence of failure. Others require a liquidation order from the state. All states limit the amounts that insurers can be assessed in one year.
- Policies usually terminate within thirty days after the failure date— Unpaid claims before termination, however, are still valid and paid from the guaranty fund of the insured's state of residence if the insolvent insurer is licensed in the state. Under the NAIC's model act, if the failed insurer is not licensed in the state, an insured or claimant cannot file a claim with the guaranty fund but must seek payment by filing a claim against the failed insurer's assets that are handled by the liquidator.

- Claims coverage varies by state—No state guaranty fund covers reinsurance or surplus lines insurance (except New Jersey).

- Claims are subject to maximum limits—The maximum limit is usually the lesser of $300,000 or the policy limit. Some states have limits under $300,000, and a small number of states have higher limits, such as $500,000 or $1 million.

- Most states provide for a refund of unearned premiums—A few states have no unearned premiums claim provision. In these states, an insured with a failed insurer is not entitled to a refund of the unearned premiums from the guaranty fund.

- Most states apply a $100 deductible to unpaid claims—Many states exempt workers compensation claims from a deductible.

- Most states divide their guaranty funds into separate accounts, usually auto, workers compensation, and other types of insurance—Auto or workers compensation assessments can be limited to insurers that write only that line of insurance.

- Assessment recovery varies by state—Some states permit insurers to recover assessments by an insurance rate increase. The remaining states generally reduce annual state premium taxes, usually over a period of five years. Consequently, taxpayers and the general public, as well as insureds, subsidize the unpaid claims of insolvent insurers.

Homeowners and auto insurance claims are covered by all state funds, but some types of insurance, such as annuities, life, disability, accident and health, surety, ocean marine, mortgage guaranty, and title insurance, often are not covered. Self-insured groups are not protected by guaranty funds. Risk retention groups are prohibited by federal law from participating in the state guaranty fund system.

Reasons for Insolvency

It is difficult to state the exact reasons for an insurer's failure. Usually, there isn't a single event or mistake that causes an insurer to become insolvent; rather, poor management and adverse events combine to cause insolvencies. Increased competition among insurers, leading to lower premium prices during soft phases of the underwriting cycle, often contributes to an increase in insurer insolvencies. Some insolvencies occur when an insurer is overexposed to losses resulting from a major insured catastrophe, especially during periods when intense competition causes lower insurance prices.

Experts have identified these factors that frequently contribute to an insurer's insolvency:

- Rapid premium growth
- Inadequate insurance rates
- Inadequate reserves

- Excessive expenses
- Lax controls over managing general agents
- Uncollectible reinsurance
- Fraud

Poor management is at the root of most of these factors. A combination of inadequate insurance rates and lax underwriting standards can start deterioration in a book of business. If these problems are not detected and corrected promptly, the decay in the quality of the business accelerates.

Rapid premium growth precedes nearly all major insolvencies. Rapid growth by itself is not harmful, but it reduces the margin for error in insurers' operations—and it usually indicates larger issues. If insurance rates are inadequate and losses understated, net losses and capital deterioration rise more quickly than management can effectively respond to.

Apply Your Knowledge

Greatview Insurance is experiencing rapid premium growth because of its recently lowered personal lines rates. Which one of the following is reduced for Greatview because of this growth?

a. Fraud
b. Reinsurance
c. Margin for error
d. Chance of insolvency

Feedback: *c*. An insurer's rapid premium growth reduces its margin for error in insurer operations.

INSURANCE REGULATORY ACTIVITIES: REGULATING INSURANCE RATES

Although rate regulation laws are intended to protect consumers, adherence to these laws also supports insurers' financial stability—which, in turn, protects insurers.

States use a variety of approaches to regulate insurance rates, but they all have the same broad fairness goals: to ensure the financial health of insurers and to protect consumers who could be hurt by an organization's financial collapse. Each approach, however, has its own benefits and drawbacks.

Insurance Rate Regulation Goals

Rate regulation ensures that rates are adequate, not excessive, and not unfairly discriminatory.

Adequate

When an insurer offers a specific type of insurance, the rates it charges should be high enough to pay for all the claims and expenses the insurer will encounter for that type of insurance. This requirement helps maintain insurer solvency. If an insurer fails because its rates are inadequate, it cannot pay for any losses accrued by its insureds and third-party claimants, who would consequently be financially harmed.

Several factors complicate the regulatory goal of rate adequacy:

- An insurer usually does not know what its expenses will be when a policy is sold. The rate could become inadequate if there is an unexpected increase in claims frequency or severity.
- Insurers might charge inadequate rates in response to strong price competition.
- State rate-approval systems may not approve a request for rates an insurer believes are adequate for public policy reasons or because of disagreement over the level of requested rates.
- Natural and other unanticipated catastrophic events could lead to higher losses than those projected when rates were set.
- Regulatory actuaries and insurer actuaries may disagree about the assumptions used to determine trends or account for socioeconomic components of a proposed rate change.

Unfortunately, no method of rate regulation guarantees that rates will be adequate.

Not Excessive

Although rates should be adequate, they should not be excessive just so insurers can earn disproportionate or unreasonable profits. Regulators have considerable latitude and discretion in determining whether rates are excessive for a given type of insurance, and they consider several factors, including these:

- Number of insurers selling a specific coverage in the rating territory
- Relative market share of competing insurers
- Degree of rate variation among the competing insurers
- Past and prospective loss experience for a given type of insurance
- Possibility of catastrophe losses
- Margin for underwriting profit and contingencies

- Marketing expenses for a given type of insurance
- Special judgment factors that might apply to a given type of insurance

Regulators sometimes use the fair rate of return approach in determining whether an insurer's rates are adequate or excessive. This approach is based on the premise that an insurer should expect at least some minimum rate of return on the equity invested in its insurance operations and that a fair rate of return should be similar to the rate of return of other types of businesses—especially if insurers are to attract investment capital. However, regulators, insurers, and investors often disagree as to what constitutes a fair rate of return for insurers.

Not Unfairly Discriminatory

Rates also have to avoid being unfairly discriminatory. The word "discrimination" carries negative connotations and is generally associated with prejudicial behavior, but it also has a secondary, neutral meaning, focused on the ability to differentiate among like items.

Discrimination in this neutral sense is essential to insurance rating. However, insurers' discrimination must be fair and consistent, resulting in substantially similar rates for insureds with loss exposures that are roughly similar. As an example, two drivers, each age twenty-five, operating similar vehicles in the same rating territory who buy the same type and amount of auto insurance from the same insurer should be charged the same rates.

Regulation seeks to prohibit only unfair discrimination, not fair discrimination.

If loss exposures are substantially different in terms of expected losses and expenses, then different rates can be charged. For example, if a woman age twenty-five and another age sixty-five are in good health and purchase the same type and amount of life insurance from the same insurer, it is not unfair rate discrimination to charge the older woman a higher rate. The higher probability of death for a woman at age sixty-five clearly and fairly justifies a higher rate.

The number of factors involved in determining rates has been illuminated through use of sophisticated computer simulation modeling for catastrophes and of innovative risk classification systems, such as credit-based insurance scores. This influx of data has greatly complicated regulatory evaluation of whether rates are unfairly discriminatory.

Types of Rating Laws

A state's rating laws influence how it achieves its three major rate regulation goals and the rates property-casualty insurers can charge. Rating laws apply not only to rates for a new type of insurance but also to changes in rates for existing types. The major types of state rating laws are these:

- Prior-approval laws require rates and supporting rules to be approved by the state Insurance Department before they can be used. In some cases, a prior-approval law contains a deemer provision, which means that a filing is deemed approved if the insurer has not heard from the regulator within a given time (usually thirty to ninety days).

- File-and-use laws allow the insurer to use the new rates immediately after filing with the state Insurance Department. The department has the authority to disapprove the rates if they cannot be justified or if they violate state law.

- Use-and-file laws, a variation of file-and-use laws, allow insurers to use the new rates and later submit filing information that is subject to regulatory review.

- No filing laws (information filing, or open competition) do not require insurers to file rates with the state Insurance Department. Market prices driven by the economic laws of supply and demand, rather than the discretionary acts of regulators, determine the rates and availability. However, insurers might be required to furnish rate schedules and supporting statistical data to regulatory officials, and the state Insurance Department has the authority to monitor competition and to disapprove rates if necessary. The goals of adequate, nonexcessive, and equitable rates still apply.

- Flex rating laws require prior approval only if the new rates exceed a certain percentage above (and sometimes below) the rates filed previously. Insurers can increase or decrease their rates within the established range without prior approval. Typically, a range of 5 percent to 10 percent is permitted. Flex rating permits insurers to make rate adjustments quickly in response to changing market conditions and loss experience, but it prohibits wide swings within a short period of time. Flex rating also can restrict insurers from drastically reducing rates to increase market share. The result should be smoother insurance pricing cycles.

Variations of these filing approaches exist. For example, open competition might apply as long as insurers meet certain tests, such as providing evidence of competitive markets or keeping rate increases to less than 25 percent per year. Insurers that fail to meet these criteria would be subject to prior approval or another type of regulatory review.

Apply Your Knowledge

Which one of the following types of rate regulation laws allows an insurer to use a new rate immediately after filing it with the state, although it may be disapproved if found to violate state law or be unjustifiable?

- Prior-approval laws
- No filing laws
- Flex rating laws
- File-and-use laws

Feedback: d. File-and-use laws allow an insurer to use a new rate immediately after filing it with the state, although it may be disapproved if found to violate state law or be unjustifiable.

INSURANCE REGULATORY ACTIVITIES: REGULATING INSURANCE POLICIES

Regulation of insurance policies helps to protect insurance consumers, who often may not understand complex policy language. Regulation can protect insureds from policies that are narrow, restrictive, deceptive, or that fail to comply with state laws and regulations.

Contract language contained in insurance policies is regulated through legislation and insurance departments' rules, regulations, and guidelines. Regulation may require certain forms, provisions, or standards, or it may prohibit certain provisions.

Legislation

Insurance policy regulation starts with a state legislature passing laws that control the structure and content of insurance policies sold in the state. Legislative policy regulation affects these five areas: standard forms, mandatory provisions, prohibited provisions, forms approval, or readability standards.

Legislation might require insurers to use a standard policy to insure property or liability loss exposures. A standard policy is one policy all insurers must use if a coverage is sold in the state.

Legislation might also require that certain standard mandatory policy provisions appear in certain types of insurance policies. The required and optional provisions might be based on a model bill developed by the National Association of Insurance Commissioners (NAIC). For example, states usually require that workers compensation insurance, no-fault auto coverage, and often uninsured motorists coverage contain mandated policy provisions. State laws and regulations might require that the mandated policy provisions meet certain minimum standards, providing at least a basic level of protection.

Legislation might mandate that policies be filed and/or approved by the state to protect policyholders against ambiguous, misleading, or deceptive policies. Many states require that a policy be submitted for approval before it is used. However, if a specified period elapses and the policy has not been disapproved, the policy is considered approved. (Some states permit the state insurance department to extend the review period.) The purpose of such approval is to encourage a prompt review of the policy. However, it can cause a perfunctory review.

Finally, legislation might require that insurance policies meet a readability test. Legislation may specify policy style and form as well as the size of print. Readability legislation has influenced the drafting of both personal and commercial insurance policies, but readability tests do not necessarily measure how well the policies can be understood.

Policy Rules, Regulations, and Guidelines

State insurance departments implement specific directives from the legislature or exercise the general authority they have to regulate insurance policies. Administrative rules, regulations, and guidelines can be stated in (1) regulations communicated by the state insurance department to insurers, (2) informal circulars or bulletins from the same source, and (3) precedents set during the approval process. For example, the state insurance department might require specific wording in certain policy provisions or might notify insurers that certain types of policy provisions will be disapproved.

Courts

Although the courts do not directly regulate insurers, they do influence them by determining whether insurance laws are constitutional and whether administrative rulings and regulations are consistent with state law. The courts also interpret ambiguous and confusing policy provisions, determine whether certain losses are covered by the policy, and resolve other disputes between insurers and insureds over policy coverages and provisions.

Court decisions often lead insurers to redraft their policy language and to modify provisions. For example, based on the legal doctrine of concurrent causation, certain courts ruled that if a loss under a risk of direct physical loss (formerly "all-risks") policy is caused by two causes of loss, one of which is excluded, the entire loss is covered. As a result of this doctrine, insurers were required to pay certain flood and earthquake claims they had believed were excluded by their property insurance policies. Subsequent revision of the language in many such property policies explicitly excluded coverage for flood and earthquake losses in cases in which a nonexcluded cause of loss contributed to the loss.

INSURANCE REGULATORY ACTIVITIES: MARKET CONDUCT AND CONSUMER PROTECTION

Consumer protection lies at the heart of insurance regulation. Regulators help protect insurance consumers from unfair practices and promote competition within the insurance marketplace.

In practice, regulators have monitored three key areas of market conduct:

- Producer practices
- Underwriting practices
- Claims practices

However, these traditional market conduct examinations have begun to play less of a role in regulation as regulators have moved toward market analysis to maintain the industry's health. Additionally, state insurance departments provide information and assistance directly to insurance consumers to protect them from possible unfair practices.

Monitoring Market Conduct

Laws regarding unfair trade practices prohibit abusive practices. Currently, all United States jurisdictions except American Samoa and Guam have laws against unfair trade practices. Unfair trade practices acts at the state level regulate the trade practices of the business of insurance as required under the McCarran Act.

If an insurer is accused of engaging in unfair trade practices, the case can be decided by the insurance commissioner of the state in which the practice occurred. An insurer that violates the unfair trade practices act is subject to at least one, if not both, of two penalties:

- Fine per violation—Fines are often increased significantly if the activity is considered flagrant, with conscious disregard for the law.
- Suspension or revocation of license—This may occur if the practice occurred frequently and if the insurer's management knew or should have known of it.

If an insurer disagrees with the commissioner's findings, it can usually file for judicial review. If the court agrees with the commissioner, the insurer must obey the commissioner's orders.

The National Association of Insurance Commissioners (NAIC) Model Unfair Trade Practices Act prohibits insurers from any activity that would restrain trade or competition in the business of insurance. The act also prohibits an insurer from misrepresenting its own or another insurer's financial status.

Additionally, there are numerous provisions in the Model Act to protect insurance consumers.

The key insurer market conduct areas that are regulated by the Model Act and state-level unfair trade practices acts include producer practices, underwriting practices, and claims practices.

Producer Practices

A producer might be penalized (through fines, license revocation, and so forth) for engaging in practices that violate the state's unfair trade practices act, such as these:

- Dishonesty or fraud—A producer might embezzle premiums paid by insureds or misappropriate some claims funds.

- Misrepresentation—A producer might misrepresent the losses that are covered by an insurance policy to induce a client to purchase that policy under false pretenses.

- Twisting—A producer might induce an insured to replace one policy with another, to the insured's detriment. This is a special form of misrepresentation called twisting.

- Unfair discrimination—A producer might engage in any number of acts that unfairly favor one insured over another.

- Rebating—A producer might engage in rebating, the practice of giving a portion of the producer's commission or some other financial benefit to an individual as an inducement to purchase a policy. Rebating is illegal in almost all states.

Underwriting Practices

Insurance regulators attempt to prevent improper underwriting that could result in insurer insolvency or unfair discrimination against an insurance consumer. See the exhibit "Examples of Unfair Trade Practices With Respect to Underwriting."

Examples of Unfair Trade Practices With Respect to Underwriting

- Discriminating unfairly when selecting loss exposures
- Misclassifying loss exposures
- Canceling or nonrenewing policies contrary to statutes, rules, and policy provisions
- Using underwriting rules or rates that are not on file with or approved by the insurance departments in the states in which the insurer does business
- Failing to apply newly implemented underwriting and rating factors to renewals
- Failing to use correct policy forms and insurance rates
- Failing to use rules that are state specific

[DA02905]

To protect consumers, insurance regulators take actions such as these:

- Constrain insurers' ability to accept, modify, or decline applications for insurance—To increase insurance availability, states often require insurers to provide coverage for some loss exposures they might prefer to not cover.

- Establish allowable classifications—Regulators limit the ways in which insurers can divide consumers into rating classifications. For example, unisex rating is required in some states for personal auto insurance. This promotes social equity rather than actuarial equity.

- Restrict the timing of cancellations and nonrenewals—All states require insurers to provide insureds with adequate advance notice of policy cancellation or nonrenewal so that insureds can obtain replacement coverage. Insurers are typically allowed to cancel or nonrenew only for specific reasons.

Apply Your Knowledge

Greta is a new producer working at a small agency. Feeling pressure to increase her sales numbers, she considers offering a portion of her commissions back to new clients who purchase a policy from her as an incentive for them to close the deal with her. What unfair trade practice would Greta be engaging in if she went through with this action?

a. Twisting
b. Fraud
c. Misrepresentation
d. Rebating

Feedback: d. If Greta gives a portion of her commission or some other financial advantage to new clients as an inducement to purchase a policy, she would be engaging in the unfair trade practice of rebating.

Claims Practices

All states prohibit certain claims practices by law. Claims practices are regulated to protect insureds and maintain public confidence in the insurance promise: to pay valid claims promptly and fairly. Apart from regulatory penalties, failure to practice **good-faith claims handling** can lead to claims for damages that allege **bad faith** on the insurer's part. Unfair claims practices laws prohibit unethical and illegal claims practices. The laws are generally patterned after the NAIC Model Unfair Claims Settlement Practices Act. See the exhibit "Examples of Unfair Claims Settlement Practices."

Good-faith claims handling

The manner of handling claims that requires an insurer to give consideration to the insured's interests that is at least equal to the consideration it gives its own interests.

Bad faith (outrage)

A breach of the duty of good faith and fair dealing.

Examples of Unfair Claims Settlement Practices

- Knowingly misrepresenting important facts or policy provisions
- Failing to properly investigate and settle claims
- Failing to make a good-faith effort to pay claims when liability is reasonably clear
- Attempting to settle a claim for an amount less than the amount that a reasonable person believes he or she is entitled to receive based on advertising material that accompanies or is part of the application
- Failing to approve or deny coverage of a claim within a reasonable period after a proof-of-loss statement has been completed

[DA02906]

In some cases, courts have ruled that an insurer's improper claims handling constitutes not only a breach of contract or violation of regulations, but also an independent tort—bad faith. Legal remedies for bad-faith actions can lead both to first-party actions (involving the insured) and to third-party actions (involving a claimant). An insurer that violates good-faith standards can be required to honor the policy's intent (paying the claim) and pay extracontractual damages (damages above the amount payable under the terms of the insurance policy), such as emotional distress and attorney fees.

Market Analysis

Insurance regulators are moving away from traditional market conduct examinations in favor of market analysis. Market analysis enables regulators to identify general market disruptions, promotes uniform analysis by applying consistent measurements between insurers, and facilitates communication and collaboration among regulators from different states. One of the fundamental components of market analysis is the collection of regulatory information from insurers using the Market Conduct Annual Statement (MCAS).

The MCAS allows regulators to monitor, benchmark, and analyze the insurance market in almost every jurisdiction in the U.S. on a state or national level. It began as a source of information on life insurance and annuities alone, but has since been used to track homeowners, auto, and long-term care data as well.

Ensuring Consumer Protection

While all insurance regulatory activities protect insurance consumers at least indirectly, certain activities are designed specifically to support consumers. For example, state insurance departments respond to consumer complaints and also inform and educate consumers.

State insurance departments often assist with complaints about rates or policy cancellations or with consumers' difficulty finding insurance. Although state insurance departments usually have no direct authority to order insurers to pay claims when facts are disputed (such disputes are typically resolved through the courts), most state insurance departments can investigate and follow up on a consumer complaint, at least to the extent of getting a response from the insurer involved.

Many states compute complaint ratios, and some make them readily available to consumers through the internet. To help make consumers more knowledgeable about the cost of insurance, some states publish shoppers' guides and other forms of consumer information, much of which can be found online.

SUMMARY

Insurance regulation is considered necessary to protect consumers, to maintain insurer solvency, and to avoid destructive competition.

Every state has an Insurance Department, headed by a commissioner responsible for regulating insurance in that state. State insurance regulators belong to the NAIC, which has no regulatory authority of its own but has substantial influence in coordinating the activities of state regulations. Some federal regulation also affects insurers.

Insurance regulators govern the formation and licensing of insurers, as well as the licensing of insurance personnel. By issuing a license to an insurer, a state indicates that the insurer meets minimum standards of financial strength, competence, and integrity. States also license many of the people who sell insurance, give insurance advice, or represent insurers, including producers, claims representatives, and insurance consultants.

Regulators in the U.S. have a framework to prevent insurer insolvencies and to manage those that do occur despite preventive efforts. The NAIC provides tools for uniformity and a risk-based approach in solvency regulation. State guaranty funds, financed through assessments of insurers operating in the insolvent insurer's state, provide payments for insurers' valid claims after the insolvency. Most insurer insolvencies occur because of poor management practices.

States regulate insurance rates to help maintain insurer solvency and protect consumers. The three major goals of rate regulation are to ensure that rates remain adequate, not excessive, and not unfairly discriminatory. These goals are generally achieved through rating laws at the state level. The major types of state rating laws are prior-approval laws, file-and-use laws, use-and-file laws, no filing laws, and flex rating laws.

Regulating contract language contained in insurance policies is necessary because insurance policies are complex documents. Insurance policy regulation starts with a state legislature passing laws regarding insurance policy form and content. State insurance departments implement specific directives from the legislature or exercise their general authority to regulate insurance policies through administrative rules, regulations, and guidelines.

The primary focus of insurance regulation is to prevent unfair trade practices and to protect consumers. Regulators are moving away from traditional market conduct examinations and toward market analysis, an approach that enables them to review the practices of an entire market, consisting of multiple insurers. In addition to their monitoring insurers' conduct, regulators also protect those who purchase insurance by providing information and assistance directly to consumers.

ASSIGNMENT NOTE

1. "The United States Insurance Financial Solvency Framework and Core Principles," National Association of Insurance Commissioners, April 14, 2013, p.6,www.naic.org/documents/committees_e_us_solvency_framework.pdf (accessed August 13, 2018).

3

Insurance Marketing and Distribution

Educational Objectives

After learning the content of this assignment, you should be able to:

▷ Explain how insurers differentiate marketing for different types of customers.

▷ Explain how unique economic factors shape the insurance marketplace.

▷ Explain how typical insurer marketing activities are performed and why they are performed.

▷ Distinguish among the main types of insurance distribution systems and channels.

▷ Describe the functions performed by insurance producers.

▷ Describe the key factors an insurer should evaluate during the distribution-system and distribution-channel selection process.

Insurance Marketing and Distribution

3

PROPERTY-CASUALTY INSURER MARKETPLACE

The property-casualty insurance marketplace is the intersection of customers' needs and insurers' ability to meet them. But how does an insurer distinguish itself when it has to contend with regulation, unanticipated catastrophic losses, and a competitive landscape in which data-driven personalized service has given consumers and businesses more choices than ever before? One way is through marketing strategies tailored for specific types of customers.

Five distinguishing characteristics drive consumer demand for insurance products and services:

- Insurance needs
- Knowledge of the insurance market
- Methods of accessing the insurance market
- Negotiating ability
- Access to alternative risk financing measures

These characteristics underlie an insurer's marketing strategy for each customer group. To understand how, though, it's useful to first examine each of the four types of customers and how the five characteristics define them. See the exhibit "The Property-Casualty Insurance Marketplace."

Characteristics of Property-Casualty Insurance Customers

Property-casualty insurance customers can be divided into individuals, small businesses, middle markets, and national (or larger) accounts.

Individuals

Generally, individuals share the same needs for property coverage to protect real and personal property and liability coverage for losses arising out of their personal actions and their ownership and use of property. Because so many individuals have the same insurance needs, insurers can pool individual insureds' loss exposures based on relevant underwriting factors to determine the appropriate premiums for their policies.

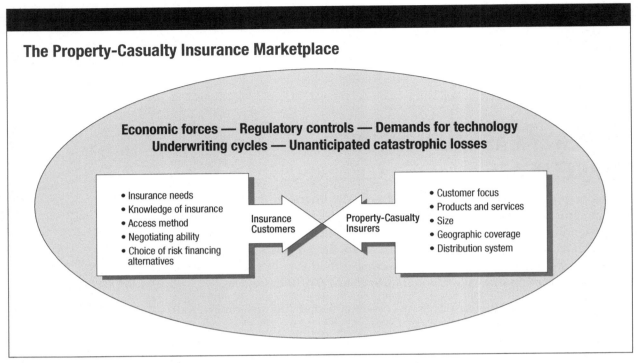

The Property-Casualty Insurance Marketplace

Economic forces — Regulatory controls — Demands for technology
Underwriting cycles — Unanticipated catastrophic losses

Insurance Customers
- Insurance needs
- Knowledge of insurance
- Access method
- Negotiating ability
- Choice of risk financing alternatives

Property-Casualty Insurers
- Customer focus
- Products and services
- Size
- Geographic coverage
- Distribution system

[DA06182]

Individuals are typically the least knowledgeable about insurance markets and the insurance mechanism. Therefore, they often need to rely on the expertise of a producer to help them decide which coverages, policy limits, and deductible levels are most appropriate for their particular circumstances. Individuals may also use direct access to insurers through apps, websites, or call centers to purchase insurance products.

Aside from retention and insurance, few risk financing alternatives are available to individuals.. In addition, they are often required to purchase insurance by mortgagors and lenders. Individuals must also purchase auto liability coverage to meet state requirements because retention alternatives are financially unfeasible.

Individuals have little negotiating power in insurance transactions. Most personal lines insurance contracts are offered on an as-written basis by the insurer; therefore, very little negotiation occurs. If an individual customer is not satisfied with the policy's terms or price, typically his or her only option is to look to other insurers for coverage.

Small Businesses

Small businesses do not usually have any employees with full-time risk management responsibilities. Often, the owner, or a designated partner or manager with a limited knowledge of insurance markets, is responsible for making risk management decisions—including the risk financing decision to purchase insurance. This decision is often made with the help of a local agent or a small local broker. Small businesses are not the typical target market for regional or national brokers because such businesses often do not generate sufficient commissions.

The insurance needs of small businesses can usually be covered by a limited number of commercial insurance policies, such as a businessowners policy, a workers compensation policy, and commercial auto policies.

Small businesses have little negotiation power with insurers and a limited number of choices when it comes to risk financing alternatives. Some small businesses have been able to join with similar organizations to form small risk retention groups or purchasing groups as alternatives to the standard commercial insurance market.

Middle Markets

Organizations that can be classified as middle markets are larger organizations with insurance needs that vary considerably according to the products or services they provide. For example, a company that manufactures airplane components has significantly higher products liability insurance needs than a company that manufactures greeting cards.

Middle-market organizations are often large enough that their loss histories provide credible statistics for use in projecting future losses. These organizations may have a risk manager (or a small risk management department) to assist with coverage decisions. The risk managers typically use brokers to access the insurance markets and may be targeted by small (local), regional, or national brokers. They typically have some negotiating power with insurers because they have a more credible loss history, generate more premium income for the insurer, and have broker representation that can assist in their presentations to insurers. Finally, middle-market organizations have increasing access to risk financing alternatives such as large-deductible plans.

National Accounts

The national accounts/large accounts segment includes the largest organizations seeking insurance coverage, such as Fortune 500 companies, chemical and other manufacturing organizations, and large municipalities. By virtue of their size and scope, these organizations have the most complex insurance needs, the most comprehensive knowledge of the insurance market (with a large risk management department and regional or national broker representation), and the widest variety of risk financing alternatives relative to other customer types.

These accounts often generate millions of dollars in premiums annually, giving national account brokers the most negotiating power with insurers. This power can be used to negotiate broader coverages, lower deductibles, higher limits, or premium reductions.

Organizations in this category are likely to have complex insurance programs that combine commercial insurance coverages with sophisticated retention plans and captive insurers. The use of captives by large organizations provides them with additional flexibility to bypass the standard commercial insurance market and access reinsurance markets directly. Furthermore, unique loss exposures that require extremely high limits or highly specialized underwriting consideration are often insured by a consortium of insurers that work together to provide the necessary insurance program. See the exhibit "Comparison of Insurance Consumers."

Comparison of Insurance Consumers

	Individuals	Small Business	Middle Markets	National Accounts
Insurance Needs	Least complex	Somewhat complex	Complex	Highly complex
Knowledge of the Insurance Market	Least knowledgeable	Some knowledge	Risk manager on staff—more knowledgeable	Full-time risk management department—most knowledgeable
Access Method	Direct access/ agents	Agents/small brokers	Brokers—small/ regional/national	Brokers— regional/national
Negotiating Ability	Little, if any, negotiating ability	Little, if any, negotiating ability	Some negotiating ability	Most negotiating ability
Choice of Risk Financing Alternatives	Retention only alternative	Retention/ few other alternatives	Some alternatives— rent-a-captives, risk retention groups	Wide variety of alternatives

[DA02712]

Property-Casualty Insurer Marketing Differentiations

An insurer's marketing differentiations uniquely match the characteristics of the customer groups or segments of those groups that it targets for sales.

Customer Focus

To be customer focused, an insurer must understand the characteristics of specific customer groups and provide products and services that respond to those characteristics. Customer focus is improved through market intelligence, which provides information relevant to understanding customers' current and future needs, preferences, attitudes, and behaviors. This depth of understanding leads to better customer interaction through an intensified customer-market view. Through market intelligence, often augmented by increasingly sophisticated analysis of the massive amount of data available about individual consumers, the insurer understands where its insurance offer fits and discovers untapped or underserved potential markets.

Products and Services

Property-casualty insurers can be further differentiated by line (for example, personal or commercial). Personal or commercial lines insurers may focus on property or liability insurance, package policies, or specialty lines, but they often sell a range of insurance products that meet the needs of their customers. Services are also tailored to respond to customers' needs identified through market intelligence.

Size

An important driver of competition is the size of the organizations in an industry. For a given number of organizations, the level of competition is usually greater if all organizations are approximately the same size than if there are two or three large organizations and many small ones. The larger companies may dominate the market, reducing competition.

An insurer's size influences its decision regarding the customer groups to whom it chooses to market. If a market is dominated by a large organization, a smaller insurer might select a subsection of the market or a niche market to target and tailor its product to better meet the precisely defined needs of that group.

Similarly, a small insurer might avoid the national accounts market, where large written premiums must be reinsured or offset by significant reserve levels, reducing an insurer's ability to write a substantial number of other accounts. For a small insurer that relies on a single large account, the risk of losing that account can be disproportionate to the benefits of serving a single account.

Geographic Area

Property-casualty insurers are differentiated by the geographic areas they serve. An insurer's decision regarding geographic area is based on its size, its level of expertise in writing coverage in broader geographic areas, the level of competition in those areas, and its customer focus. An insurer that chooses a regional area for operation can more narrowly focus its marketing intelligence to address customers' insurance needs in the smaller area. In contrast, writing insurance nationally or internationally requires substantially more marketing intelligence to understand customers and successfully meet a wider range of insurance needs.

Distribution System

An insurer's choice of marketing system(s) is influenced by its customers' knowledge of insurance products and the risk financing alternatives available. For example, individuals generally have limited knowledge of insurance products and limited risk financing alternatives that are usually in the form of deductible selections. Insurers focused on mature customers with homes, autos, and valuable personal property may choose a distribution system based on exclusive agents or independent agents, who can assist them with coverage, limits, and deductible selections. Alternatively, an insurer targeting sales of personal auto insurance to young drivers who have a high probability of selecting the lowest-priced coverage might choose an internet-based or app-based distribution system.

Similar decisions regarding the selection of marketing systems are made for small-business, middle-market, and national accounts. Small businesses lack sufficient personnel to dedicate to risk management and insurance placement tasks; therefore, an independent-agent distribution system is appropriate to provide that assistance. As accounts grow larger and have risk management staff to make selection decisions or work with brokers for coverage selection, broker-based distribution systems might be the selected option.

UNIQUE FACTORS IN THE PROPERTY-CASUALTY INSURER MARKETPLACE

All marketplaces are influenced by changes in the economy. Business cycles, interest rates, rates of unemployment, and changing consumer demographics and social pressures gradually require shifts in operations, products, and distribution systems.

The property-casualty insurance marketplace is also shaped by unique economic forces, regulatory controls, and technology demands that set the parameters within which insurers must operate. Underwriting cycles, as well as the financial shock of unanticipated catastrophic losses, further affect it. Within this changing environment, insurers adjust to maintain the competitive dynamic required for the functioning of the marketplace.

Economic Forces

Property-casualty insurers manage a narrow margin of underwriting profitability to remain competitive. Inflation is a factor in increasing the costs of losses and the costs of an insurer's operations. Similarly, the availability of reinsurance influences the price and the cost of insurer operations. Investment earnings frequently offset high losses and rising costs. When investment earnings are diminished or the prospect of catastrophe losses increases, insurers must raise premiums to sustain risk-appropriate rates of return.

Many companies invest reserve funds to gain investment earnings. The importance of investment earnings to a property-casualty insurer's profitability is a key feature of the industry. Insurers' operations are frequently dependent on investment earnings because premiums are held competitively low to attract customers.

Regulatory Controls

State-based insurance regulations stipulate the financial requirements that insurers must sustain to operate within a state and the marketing conduct to which insurers must adhere. In this way, insurance regulation is a stabilizing control that ensures the sustainability of insurance companies and their ability to reliably provide compensation for insureds' losses and fair treatment to insureds in business practices.

Insurance regulatory controls are a marketplace feature unique to the insurance industry, creating an environment in which a minimum standard of practice is required for all competitors.

Demands for Technology

The demand for technology is a powerful factor in the insurance marketplace because of the computer networks that connect insurers and producers and the technological connections between insurers and customers through the internet. Producers complete applications and access insureds' information through computer networks to facilitate service. Customers obtain coverage information and compare premium quotations through insurers' websites or sites that provide quotes from multiple insurers.

The primary demand for technology in these marketing applications is ease of use. Both producers and customers are drawn to user interfaces that are easy to understand and navigate. This requires significant engineering to provide point-of-use instruction and easy user operation.

Underwriting Cycles

Underwriting cycles, a key feature of the insurance marketplace, create additional competitive shifts to which insurers continuously adapt. Because underwriting cycles have numerous causes, they have varying duration and depth. As a result, insurers must also adapt as the cycle patterns reveal themselves to remain competitive.

Pricing and availability of insurance products fluctuate based on the amount of capital available to the industry. A hard market is characterized by periods of decreased competition, with rising prices and increased insurers' profitability. A soft market occurs as competition increases and insurers lower premiums to compete, which eventually leads to diminished profitability and the need to increase pricing. During periods of abundant marketplace capital, protracted soft market conditions can prevail.

Unanticipated Catastrophic Losses

Insurers maintain reserves and reinsurance to pay catastrophe losses. However, catastrophes of unanticipated severity can cause losses that exceed maximum anticipated losses. These exceptional losses can result from disasters such as record-breaking hurricane losses, terrorist attacks, and oil spills, or extraordinary tort awards and class action lawsuits. Unplanned losses can result in insurer insolvencies, withdrawal of insurers from geographic markets, and reinsurance shortages.

Every year, insurers are challenged to price products for which loss costs can only be estimated. In years of extraordinary catastrophes, the market must respond with improved catastrophe ratemaking and forecasting that anticipate even greater unforeseen events.

INSURER MARKETING ACTIVITIES

Marketing is an insurer's information portal to insurance customers. Through this portal, insurers gather information about customers, make decisions about segments of customers whose needs they can address, and disseminate information to existing and prospective customers.

An insurer's marketing activities are focused on information gathering, synthesis, and dissemination. The goal is the development of products for groups of customers with results that meet the insurer's strategies and objectives.

Activities performed by marketing can be divided into these categories:

- Marketing research
- Market development
- Marketing information
- Marketing planning
- Product development
- Advertising and promotion
- Customer and public relations
- Sales fulfillment

Marketing Research

Marketing research is the systematic gathering and analyzing of data to assist in making decisions. Marketing research cannot guarantee success, but it can improve an insurer's chances of making correct decisions.

Marketing research is typically done on a project basis with a stated objective, research design, data collection, analysis, and formal report. Effective marketing research results include conclusions and implications or recommendations. Ideally, cost-benefit measures are used to track the value of information developed from the various studies. Decisions based on the research are then implemented and evaluated on a cost-benefit basis. See the exhibit "Market Research Project Examples."

Market Research Project Examples

- Test prospecting sources through wholesale clubs to determine whether the concept is worthy of prototype development and pilot testing on a larger scale

- Determine why policies lapse or are terminated by policyholders and the cost-benefit of implementing a conservation program to retain those policyholders

- Examine the insurance purchase behaviors of first-time car owners to determine what actions are needed to attract those customers

- Identify the relationship between a policyholder's claim experience and retention of the policyholder through subsequent renewals

- Use secondary data from the U.S. Government's Standard Industrial Classification (SIC) coding system combined with Metropolitan Statistical Areas (MSAs) to identify businesses within the insurer's preferred business types and geographic areas for targeted advertising

[DA06195]

Insurers use increasingly sophisticated marketing research methods to gather meaningful information, such as customer profiles, product preferences, and refinements to improve distribution channels. One important result of this research is the development of market segments in which the insurer will compete for customers.

Market Research Methods

The best marketing research is conducted as scientifically as possible. A researcher should strive for objectivity, eliminating preconceptions and bias to the extent possible. The research may consist of qualitative studies, such as **focus groups** and observer impressions, and quantitative studies that use survey research techniques and statistical analysis of the data included in corporate databases.

The two broad categories of market data are secondary data and primary data. Research typically begins with secondary data, which is data collected by other parties, because it is immediately available at little or no cost. Many research questions can be answered at minimal expense from secondary data

Focus group

A small group of customers or potential customers brought together to provide opinions about a specific product, service, need, or other issue.

before the more costly primary data research is conducted, requiring the collection of data first-hand by the insurer. Primary data collection is more expensive, but it addresses issues specific to the marketing research project.

Increasingly, insurers are applying **predictive analytics** to improve the outcome of market research. The forms of predictive models applied in analytics vary depending on the behavior or event they are predicting.

Predictive analytics
Statistical and analytical techniques used to develop models that predict future events or behaviors.

Most predictive models generate a score, with the higher score indicating a higher likelihood that the given behavior or event will occur. Predictive scores are typically used to measure the risk or opportunity associated with a specific customer or transaction. These evaluations assess the relationships between many variables to estimate risk or response.

Predictive analytics models are used in many aspects of marketing. For example, insurers can use models to examine the purchasing patterns of insurance customers and can use the resulting information to increase the marketing function's hit ratio and retention ratio. An insurer could also use models to answer specific questions, such as, "What characteristics of small businesses result in the most profitable commercial insurance accounts?" Variables such as premium size, geography, business type, years in business, and form of ownership could affect the profitability of an account. A predictive model would weigh the importance of each relevant variable to provide an estimate of the likely profitability of each characteristic.

Insurers can take advantage of additional applications for predictive analytics in marketing:

- Cross-selling—identifying existing policyholder groups to whom efforts to sell additional policies will be most successful
- Target marketing—defining and refining marketing efforts on a specific group of customers
- Individualized customer support—tailoring customer support to specific customers' needs
- New agent contracting—determining which characteristics of exclusive and independent agents result in the most successful market penetration
- Designing and evaluating marketing campaigns—defining aspects of advertising efforts that result in the highest response rates from prospective customers

Market segmentation
The process of identifying and dividing the groups within a market that share needs and characteristics and that will respond similarly to a marketing action.

Target marketing
Focusing marketing efforts on a specific group of consumers.

Niche marketing
A type of marketing that focuses on specific types of buyers who are a subset of a larger market.

Market Segmentation

Insurers use **market segmentation** to differentiate themselves from other insurance providers to meet the needs of customer groups. **Target marketing** is a practice of more closely defining a group of customers within a market segment. **Niche marketing** is a well-defined, often small marketing segment of the population that has specific needs. For example, a market segmentation of small businesses can include a target market of retailers with a niche market of jewelry stores.

By identifying the characteristics of the various market segments, target market groups, and niches, insurers build a competitive advantage through designing specific marketing strategies to address their needs and characteristics. The more closely a group of customers is defined, the more closely an insurer can develop expertise regarding the customers' needs and tailor products and services to meet those needs. As groups are more closely defined, insurers are less likely to encounter competition for that group than in the open market.

- Behavioristic segmentation—the division of a total consumer market by purchase behavior
- Geographic segmentation—the division of markets by geographic units
- Demographic segmentation—the division of markets based on demographic variables, such as age, gender, education, occupation, ethnicity, income, family size, and family life cycle
- Psychographic segmentation—the division of markets by individuals' values, personalities, attitudes, and lifestyles

Marketing management defines logical market segments that provide an opportunity for success. Criteria regarding the segments, as well as the external environment and the insurer's internal environment, are considered in the market segment selection. See the exhibit "Market Segment Selection Considerations."

Market Development

Market development activities provide leadership when an insurer enters a new market. The new market may be a new territory, a new customer type, or a new product. Other examples of major projects managed might include new approaches to selling the insurer's products or delivering web-based applications for insurance policies.

Market development involves actions required to ensure the success of the venture, including development and implementation of a broad range of activities:

- Training programs
- Problem resolution
- Process documentation
- Funding assistance
- Technical assistance
- Public relations campaigns

The market development staff includes project managers who generate and screen ideas. Project managers are also skilled in developing project scope documents, decision grids, task outlines, progress reports, and project reports. The project manager usually handles only one or two projects at a time because of the high level of effort and responsibility involved in each project.

Market Segment Selection Considerations

Each marketing segment should be:

- Accessible—Segments should be able to be effectively reached and served.

- Substantial—Size and purchasing power should suggest potential profitability.

- Responsive—Actions taken by the insurer should produce satisfactory results.

Internal marketing environment:

- Technical resources—What technical resources are needed to support the customers and products sold?

- Type of products sold—Do the products available meet the specific segment's needs, or do they address homogeneous needs of a larger group? What is the product fit to the market segment?

- Age of product—Do the products available meet current customer needs?

- Product mix—Do the products we will sell to this market segment help us achieve our optimum product mix?

- Distribution channels—Are our distribution channels appropriate to the characteristics of this market segment?

- Corporate ownership—Does our ownership affect our ability to obtain the sources of funds needed for growth, expansion, or financial stability to market successfully to this market segment?

- Company size and resources—Are we limited by our company size and resources to compete for customers in this market segment?

External marketing environment:

- Market segment competition—How significant is the competition within this market segment? What are the characteristics of competing insurers in this market segment (such as customer focus, size, distribution systems, and technological capabilities)?

- Economic environment—Are there issues in the current economic environment (such as inflation, investment earnings, customers' spending habits, availability and cost of employees) that affect our chances of success in this market segment?

- Social environment—What behaviors or beliefs in the population of this market segment will increase or decrease our chances of success in offering our products and services?

- Regulatory environment—Are the products and services we are proposing for this marketing segment permitted under applicable laws and regulations?

[DA06196]

Marketing Information

Marketing information activities develop and maintain information needed in market planning to support management at all levels in answering specific questions concerning markets, customers, producers, and competitors. The marketing information function serves the company best when it can deliver timely and cost-effective information essential to decision making.

Marketing information is divided into two major systems: internal accounting and market monitoring.

- The internal accounting system provides report and analysis capability based on transactions associated with sales activity. Much of the essential information on production, retention, and policies in force is available as a byproduct of the systems that keep track of commissions and billings.

- The market monitoring system provides intelligence about the external environment to inform senior management about important developments and changing conditions. The market monitor should provide current, unfiltered, and unbiased information about customers, producers, and competitors. Customers and producers are monitored to determine their satisfaction levels with the service they receive from the insurer, and the resulting information helps the insurer shape decisions related to growth and profitability strategies. The market monitor also maintains up-to-date competitive intelligence about the strategies and actions of key competitors. Competitor monitoring also includes benchmark studies of competitors that excel in success factors crucial to a property-casualty insurer. Benchmark information helps management develop strategies for closing the gap between company performance and key competition.

Marketing Planning

Marketing planning provides the tools and facilitation skills to assist management in developing fact-based marketing plans. This activity also assists in the development and updating of the company's strategic plans.

Before introducing a new insurance product or service, the insurer completes a comprehensive marketing plan. The plan identifies the product or service to be promoted and the customers to be targeted, and it details the resources and strategies that will be used to create, price, promote, and sell the product or service. Because marketing plans affect many other insurer functions, representatives from other departments often participate in the creation or review of marketing plans.

Marketing plans are as varied as the products and services they promote. However, all plans serve the same fundamental purpose: they provide the "roadmaps" necessary to profitably and effectively acquaint sellers with potential buyers.

A marketing plan for a typical insurance product or service might include, but is not limited to, these items:

- Product proposal and sales goals—A summary of the new product's operation, a description of the unmet need the product is designed to fulfill, and summarized sales projections.
- Situational analysis—A SWOT (strengths, weaknesses, opportunities, threats) analysis of the current marketplace, including analyses of the competition; critical factors required for success; resource, technology, and training requirements; and an assessment of the existing legal and regulatory environment.
- Marketing goals—An outline of the proposed target market, including detailed sales projections and specifics as to how success will be measured.
- Marketing strategies—Plans and proposals for how the product will be developed, priced, promoted, and sold. These strategies include determining the appropriate distribution channels for products and services.
- Projected outcome—The pure loss ratio and ultimate loss ratio over a five-year period.

Product Development

An insurer's management team must decide which insurance products and services will be sold to which markets. There are many product decisions to be made, ranging from what product lines to offer to what coverages, limits, and deductibles will be included in the policy.

Insurers usually follow a series of steps in product development. See the exhibit "Product Development Steps."

Advertising and Promotion

The advertising function is responsible for managing the company's communications through mass media with its chosen target markets. The advertising program is developed to be consistent with strategic direction and marketing plans and supportive of distribution system efforts. Advertising is intended to build and reinforce the company's image as an acceptable choice in the minds of target customers.

Advertising is expensive. Insurers face a dilemma when trying to decide how much advertising is enough to communicate effectively with customers while staying within a reasonable budget. The effectiveness of marketing communications can be measured in several ways. For example, an insurer might pilot test advertising to determine its effectiveness or might also show proposed advertising to a focus group to obtain feedback.

Sales promotion reinforces the image and positioning created by the insurer's advertising efforts when carried down to the agency level. Sales promotion includes brochures used in the sales process, giveaway items promoting the

Product Development Steps

1. Opportunity assessment

- Monitor market
- Identify opportunity
- Relate opportunities to business strategy
- Develop specifications
- Secure senior management approval to proceed

In the first step, market monitoring results in the identification of an opportunity for a new product. Marketing personnel evaluate the opportunity against the insurer's business strategies and continue the process if there is a successful match by developing specifications for the product and obtaining approval.

2. Development of contract, underwriting, and pricing

- Develop coverage and policy forms
- Develop guidelines for underwriting and claims
- Develop classifications
- Develop pricing structure
- Secure approval from functional managers to proceed

The second step is to develop the policy forms, guidelines, classifications, and prices in a cooperative effort across the insurer functions of underwriting, actuarial, claims, reinsurance, premium audit, and risk control. This step concludes with a tangible product plan.

3. Business forecast

- Review the product plan with profit center management
- Identify requirements for statistics
- Develop business forecast
- Secure senior management approval to proceed

In the third step, the product is submitted to an assessment of sales potential. The business forecast establishes benchmarks for evaluating the success of the product including expected premium volume, producers' participation, loss ratio, and methods of gathering data that can be used to analyze the product success or failure.

4. Regulatory requirements

- File with regulators
- Develop statistical information systems
- Communicate regulatory approval

The fourth step moves the development process to the regulatory arena. At a minimum, state regulators require notification of new policy forms, rating plans, and policy writing rules. Some states require regulatory approval of new products and changes in existing products to protect policyholder interests.

5. Distribution requirements

- Develop advertising and sales promotional information
- Develop sales training
- Plan roll-out strategy

In the fifth step, the insurer determines distribution requirements, which include the overall plan for effectively advertising and distributing the new product to targeted customers.

6. Introduction

- Implement sales training and promotion
- Measure and compare results to plan

The sixth step is the introduction of the product in one or more states with advertising and sales promotions. The results are monitored, and marketing management takes actions to improve the product performance or eliminates weak products in this step if the actual results do not achieve profitability objectives.

[DA06197]

insurer and the producer, and awards merchandise. Regular communications with producers and sales management, such as newsletters, may be part of the sales promotion function.

Customer and Public Relations

The customer relations function manages communications with individual customers from the home office. This functional area ensures that all written communications seen by customers are understandable and consistent in quality and tone.

The customer relations function also provides a forum for communications to the insurer initiated by customers, including complaints, suggestions, and questions. Insurers are often asked to respond to state insurance departments, which themselves are responding to consumer complaints about the insurer. Typically, a complaint is addressed to an insurer's CEO and must be addressed within a specified period, often ten working days.

The customer relations function also provides management with low-cost, high-value information about the evolving wants and needs of policyholders.

Public relations activities include communications with the public on behalf of the insurer to ensure a strong public image. Individuals performing these activities may also be called communications or media specialists. They design and implement a consistent description of the organization and its actions.

The public relations staff provides periodic information to the insurer's community about the organization's activities. They may communicate with employees to request their participation in media or educational events, such as conferences or public speaking engagements, to ensure that the insurer's messages are included and a positive image provided. In times of crisis, the public relations staff coordinates a consolidated message to the media to provide consistent communication as well as to respond to negative publicity, if necessary.

Sales Fulfillment

Sales fulfillment is the satisfactory delivery of the products and services that result from the product development activity. Fulfillment of a product plan affects many of an insurer's functional areas. For example, the introduction of policies and services to target high-net-worth individuals as a market segment must include participation by customer service, underwriting, claims, and other functional areas. The senior management team must communicate the goals, strategies, and action plans to all areas of the organization. Each functional area must determine the impact of the plan on operations, budget, and performance standards.

Milestones should be established for the functional areas with metrics to periodically check the results of the marketing plan and take action in any area where goals are not met. If sales results do not meet projections, marketing analysis can help determine why and recommend improvements.

INSURANCE DISTRIBUTION SYSTEMS AND CHANNELS

Insurers are driven by competition to address customer preferences. In this environment, insurers examine the efficiency of their distribution systems and channels.

No single approach to distribution meets the needs of all insurers and all insurance customers. Insurers select one or a combination based on overall business plans, customer needs, and their core products and services.

Insurers use many types of **distribution systems** based on their organizational structure, business and marketing plans, growth goals, technological capabilities, staffing, and other resources necessary to support the selected system(s). The principal characteristics that distinguish one distribution system from another include the relationship to the insurer and customers, ownership of expirations, compensation methods, and functions performed. These are the main insurance distribution systems:

Distribution system

The necessary people and physical facilities to support the sale of insurance products and services.

- Independent agency and brokerage marketing systems
- Exclusive agency marketing system
- Direct writer marketing system

Mixed marketing systems include more than one distribution system, such as using independent agents for commercial lines and exclusive agents for personal lines. Insurers use these common distribution channels to promote products and services as well as to communicate with existing and prospective insureds:

- Internet
- Call centers
- Direct response
- Group marketing
- Financial institutions

Independent Agency and Brokerage Marketing Systems

The independent agency and brokerage marketing system uses agents and brokers who are independent contractors rather than employees of insurers. These independent agents and brokers are usually free to represent as many or as few insurers as they want.

Independent Agents and Brokers

An independent agency is a business, operated for the benefit of its owner (or owners), that sells insurance, usually as a representative of several unrelated insurers. An insurance broker is an independent business owner or firm that sells insurance by representing customers rather than insurers. Brokers shop among insurers to find the best coverage and value for their clients. Because they are not legal representatives of the insurer, brokers are not likely to have authority to commit an insurer to write a policy by binding coverage, unlike agents, who generally have binding authority. See the exhibit "Similarities and Differences Between Brokers and Agents."

Similarities and Differences Between Brokers and Agents

In practice, despite the technical distinctions between brokers and independent agents, the differences are minimal. Both brokers and independent agents are intermediaries between insurers and insurance buyers, and both collect premiums from insureds and remit them to insurers. Both are in the business of finding people with insurance needs and selling insurance appropriate to those needs. In fact, the same person can act as an agent in one transaction and as a broker in another. A person acts as an agent when placing insurance with an insurer for which he or she is licensed as an agent but may act as a broker when placing insurance with other agents or insurers.

[DA06205]

The independent agency or brokerage can be organized as a sole proprietorship, a partnership, or a corporation.

Agency expiration list

The record of an insurance agency's present policyholders and the dates their policies expire.

One of the main distinguishing features between independent agents and brokers and other distribution systems is the ownership of the **agency expiration list**. If an insurer ceases to do business with an agency, the agency has the right to continue doing business with its existing customers by selling them insurance with another insurer. The ownership of expiration lists is an agency's most valuable asset. An independent agency has the right to sell its expiration lists to another independent agent.

Compensation for independent agents and brokers is typically in two forms:

- A flat percent commission on all new and renewal business submitted
- A contingent or profit-sharing commission based on volume or loss ratio goals

Disclosure of the commission paid to agents or brokers enhances the transparency of the transaction for prospective insureds.

National and Regional Brokers

National and regional brokers generally represent commercial insurance accounts that often require sophisticated knowledge and service. In addition to insurance sales, large brokerage firms may provide extensive risk control, appraisal, actuarial, risk management, claim administration, and other insurance-related services that large businesses need. These brokers are often equipped to provide services that are supported by offices in multiple states.

Large insurance brokerage firms operate regionally and nationally, and some even operate internationally. They can tailor insurance programs for customers or groups of customers who require a particular type of coverage for multiple locations. Examples of such programs are insurance marketed to attorneys, which might include professional liability coverage, and an insurance program for daycare centers that includes coverages for exposures related to child care.

The brokers receive negotiated fees for the services they provide, or they receive fees in addition to commissions, subject to state regulation.

Independent Agent Networks

Independent agent networks, also known as agent groups, agent clusters, or agent alliances, consist of independent agencies and brokerages that join together to gain advantages normally available only to large national and regional brokers. Agent networks operate nationally, regionally, or locally and, in the majority of cases, allow their agent-members to retain individual agency ownership and independence.

By combining individual agency forces into a single selling, negotiating, and servicing unit, an agent network can offer many benefits to its agent members, including these:

- Obtaining access to an increased number of insurers
- Meeting **countersignature law** requirements for businesses in multiple states
- Combining premium volume to meet insurer requirements for profit-sharing
- Generating additional sales income
- Facilitating agency succession planning
- Providing expertise in risk management services
- Enabling resource sharing and expense reduction
- Increasing market share

Countersignature laws

Laws that require all policies covering subjects of insurance within a state to be signed by a resident producer licensed in that state.

Managing General Agents

Managing general agents (MGAs), also referred to as management general underwriters (MGUs), serve as intermediaries between insurers and the agents and brokers who sell insurance directly to the customer, similar to wholesalers in the marketing system for tangible goods.

The exact duties and responsibilities of an MGA depend on its contracts with the insurers it represents. MGAs can represent a single insurer, although

Managing general agent (MGA)

An authorized agent of the primary insurer that manages all or part of the primary insurer's insurance activities, usually in a specific geographic area.

they more commonly represent several insurers. Some MGAs can be strictly sales operations, appointing and supervising subagents or dealing with brokers within their contractual jurisdiction. That jurisdiction can be specified in terms of geographic boundaries, types of insurance, or both. A few MGAs cover large multistate territories, although frequently only for specialty insurance.

An insurer operating through an MGA reaps several advantages:

• A low fixed cost—An insurer who writes business through an MGA does not have to staff and support a branch office. The MGA is usually compensated by a commission override on business its subagents sell. The MGA, by writing relatively small amounts of business for each of several insurers, generates enough commissions to cover its expenses and earn a profit. The MGA might also receive a contingent commission based on the profitability or the volume of business it writes.

• Specialty expertise—MGAs develop expertise in particular markets and design insurance programs in collaboration with the insurers they represent. Specialty insurance programs offered by MGAs include those for such diverse risks as petroleum distributors, fire departments, horse farms, employment practices liability, and directors and officers liability.

• Assumption of insurer activities—Full-service MGAs can provide an array of benefits to their subagents and brokers, including claim administration, information management, risk management services, underwriting and marketing services, policy issuance, and premium collection. Insurers must supervise the MGAs that represent them, and most states regulate the MGAs' activities and contracts.

Surplus Lines Brokers

Most agents and brokers are limited to placing business with licensed (or admitted) insurers. The circumstances under which business can be placed with an unlicensed (or nonadmitted) insurer through a surplus lines broker vary by state. Normally, a reasonable effort to place the coverage with a licensed insurer is required.

The agents and brokers, who must be licensed to place surplus lines business in that state, might be required to certify that a specified number (often two or three) of licensed insurers have refused to provide the coverage. In some states, agents and brokers must provide letters from the insurers rejecting the coverage. Some state insurance departments maintain lists of coverages that are eligible for surplus lines treatment without first being rejected by licensed insurers. Some states also maintain lists of eligible surplus lines insurers, requiring producers to place business only with financially sound insurers.

Surplus lines brokers have access to insurers that have the capacity to provide the needed insurance, which might not be available from insurers licensed to do business in the state. This provides a system for insuring specific customers or exposures:

- A customer that requires high limits of insurance
- A customer that requires unusually broad or specialized coverage
- An unusual or a unique loss exposure
- Loss exposures requiring a tailored insurance program
- An unfavorable loss exposure, such as a poor claim history or difficult-to-treat exposures

Surplus lines brokers work to ensure that coverage is placed only with eligible nonadmitted insurers, the customer's unique or unusual requirements can be met by the prospective surplus lines insurer, and the financial security of the surplus lines insurer is properly evaluated.

Exclusive Agency Marketing System

The exclusive agency marketing system uses independent contractors called exclusive agents (or captive agents), who are not employees of insurers. Exclusive agents are usually restricted by contract to representing a single insurer. Consequently, insurer management can exercise more control over exclusive agents than over independent agents. However, some exclusive agency companies allow their agents to place business with other insurers if the exclusive agency insurer does not offer the product or service needed.

Exclusive agents are usually compensated by commissions. During initial training, some of them might receive a salary, a guaranteed minimum income, or income from a drawing account. In terms of overall compensation, insurers in the exclusive agency system commonly pay one commission rate for new business and another, lower rate for renewal business. For exclusive agents, the focus is on new-business production, and a reduced renewal commission rate encourages sales and supports growth.

Exclusive agents typically do not own expirations as independent producers do. However, some insurers that market through the exclusive agency system do grant agents limited ownership of expirations. Usually, such ownership of expirations applies only while the agency contract is in force. When the agency contract is terminated, the ownership of expirations reverts to the insurer. The insurer might be obligated to compensate the agent for the expirations upon termination of the agency contract; however, the agent does not have the option of selling the expirations to anyone other than the insurer.

The exclusive agency insurer handles many administrative functions for the exclusive agent, including policy issuance, premium collection, and claim processing. Exclusive agents might offer loss adjustment services similar to those offered by independent agents and brokers; however, these agents might be restricted in their ability to offer some risk management services to their customers.

Direct Writer Marketing System

The direct writer marketing system uses sales agents (also known as sales representatives) who are employees of the insurers they represent. The sales agents sell insurance for the insurer at office locations provided by the direct writer insurer. Sales agents in the direct writer system may be compensated by salary, by commission, or by both salary and a portion of the commission generated.

Because sales agents are employees of the insurers they represent, they usually do not have any ownership of expirations and, like exclusive agents, are usually restricted to representing a single insurer or a group of insurers under common ownership and management. Also, insurer management exercises greater control over its employee sales agents compared to exclusive agents, who are independent contractors.

Sometimes a customer needs a type of policy not available from the direct writer insurer that the sales agent represents. When this happens, the sales agent may act as a broker by contacting an agent who represents another insurer and applying for insurance through that agent, who usually shares the commission with the direct writer sales agent. Insurance sold in this manner is referred to as brokered business. Sales agents are largely relieved of administrative functions by their employers. These insurer-assumed functions include policy issuance, premium collections, and claim functions.

Distribution Channels

The distribution channels used by insurers and their representatives are conduits for contacting and establishing communication with their customers and prospective customers. Insurers' increasing use of omnichannel marketing has been driven by technology and customer preference. Customers who are familiar with the prompt, efficient delivery and service they obtain from other product providers expect the same type of response from their insurers.

Insurers and their representatives are constantly searching for ways to quote and issue policies more quickly, while keeping costs reasonable. At the same time, customers desire competitive pricing, customized insurance products, high-quality service, and increased interaction with insurers.

Internet

As a distribution channel, the Internet can be used to provide online access to all parties to the insurance transaction: the insurer, its representatives, and the customer. Interactions range from exchanges of email to multiple-policy quoting, billing, and policy issuance.

The customers' ability to access information has increased dramatically, as has the speed of the insurance transaction itself. Customers also interact with insurers on the Internet via web-based insurance distributors, also called insurance portals or aggregators. These portals deliver leads to the insurers whose products they offer through their websites. Portals benefit customers by offering the products and services of many insurance providers on one Internet site, in a form of cyberspace one-stop shopping. Although the leads that portals generate must subsequently be screened and fully underwritten by the insurers accepting the coverage, those leads can increase market share and brand awareness.

Call Centers

Call centers sell insurance products and services through telemarketing. Call centers operate with customer service representatives, touch-tone service, or speech-enabled (voice response) service.

The best-equipped call centers can replicate many of the activities of producers. In addition to making product sales, call center staff can respond to general inquiries, handle claim reporting, answer billing inquiries, and process policy endorsements. In some cases, a customer can begin an inquiry or a transaction on the Internet, then have a customer service representative at the insurer's call center access the Internet activity and answer the inquiry or conclude the transaction.

Direct Response

The direct response distribution channel markets directly to customers. No agent is involved; rather, direct response relies primarily on phone and/or Internet sales. Although this distribution channel is also called direct mail, customers can also contact insurers via telephone and the Internet. Direct response relies heavily on advertising and targeting specific groups of affiliated customers.

With direct response, commission costs, if any, are greatly reduced. However, a disadvantage is that advertising costs are typically higher. The customer can sometimes "opt out" and speak with a call-center customer service representative or be assigned to a local servicing office.

Group Marketing

Group marketing sells insurance products and services through call centers, the Internet, direct mail response, or a producer to individuals or businesses that are all members of the same organization. Distributing insurance to specifically targeted groups is known by a number of terms, including these:

Affinity marketing

A type of group marketing that targets various groups based on profession, association, interests, hobbies, and attitudes.

- **Affinity marketing**—Insurers target various customer groups based on profession, interests, hobbies, or attitudes. For example, the insurer, agent, or broker might decide to market personal insurance products to university alumni groups, chambers of commerce, bar associations, or users of a particular credit card. Coverage is sometimes offered at a discounted premium.

- Mass marketing or mass merchandising—Insurers design an offer for their policies to large numbers of targeted individuals or groups. Coverage is frequently offered at a discounted premium, and the insurer retains the right to underwrite each applicant, with guaranteed policy issuance available as an option.

- Worksite marketing or payroll deduction—Employers can contract directly with an insurer or through a producer to offer voluntary insurance coverage as a benefit to their employees. Worksite marketing (or "franchise marketing") of insurance is used frequently to offer personal insurance coverages or optional life, health, and disability coverage to employees. Premiums for employees are usually discounted and are deducted (after tax) from employees' paychecks, with an option available for employees to pay for the coverage in another way.

- Sponsorship marketing—A trade group sponsors an insurer in approaching a customer group. The sponsor participates in the profitability of the program. For example, a wholesale club sponsors an insurer to market to club members for a fee based on the success of the program.

The success of any marketing group program depends on the support of the sponsoring organization or employer, offering discounted premiums, treating the employees as a preferred group for underwriting purposes, and facilitating program operation, particularly from the employer's administrative perspective.

Financial Institutions

Insurers and producers can elect to market their products and services through a bank or another financial services institution, either exclusively or through using additional distribution channels. Marketing arrangements can range from simple to complex. For example, a small insurance agency may place an agent at a desk in a local bank, or a large insurer may form a strategic alliance with a regional or national financial holding company to solicit customers.

The prospect of diversifying into new markets appeals to many financial institutions. In fact, some financial institutions have expanded into insurance by participating in renewal rights arrangements by which they purchase only a book of business and not the liabilities of an agency or insurer.

Insurers view financial institutions as beneficial strategic partners because of these qualities:

- Strong customer base
- Predisposition to product cross-selling
- Strength at processing transactions
- Efficient use of technology for database mining geared to specific products and services

To sustain distribution relationships with financial institutions, insurers must focus on providing saleable products and efficient administration and support while also protecting their professional presence in financial institutions from competitors.

Omnichannel Marketing System

Omnichannel marketing allows insurers to market to customers in multiple channels and meet the needs of customers seeking alternative methods to purchase insurance. By using an omnichannel approach, insurers can target various market segments using methods such as online, mobile applications, call centers, or other approaches based on the customers' preferred method of interaction. This approach is supported by developments in data analytics, which assists insurers in using customer data to make better and more consistent marketing decisions.

Insurers are using an omnichannel approach to more effectively communicate with customers. Combining marketing channels requires consideration of several issues:

- Maintaining consistent customer communications—An insurer must send customers the same clear, consistent message about its products and services. In addition, the insurer's internal communications must be consistent across marketing systems and distribution channels, and workflows, data management, and underwriting standards must be communicated.

- Providing a consistent customer experience—The experience a customer has when interacting with an insurer must be consistent across all marketing channels. Customers' access to the Internet and its wealth of information has created knowledgeable, demanding insurance customers with distinct preferences and expectations.

- Matching the type of insurance with an appropriate channel—Some marketing systems are more suitable than others based on the product being sold. Personal insurance and commercial insurance vary in terms of the products' levels of complexity and in terms of the expertise insurers, agents, and brokers need in order to properly sell the products to consumers and service them after the sale. The combination of systems and channels selected depends on the particular type of insurance to be sold.

FUNCTIONS OF INSURANCE PRODUCERS

The functions insurance producers perform vary widely from one marketing system to another and from one producer to another within a given marketing system. Although technology has changed the process, producers are often the initial contact with insurance customers and provide expertise and ongoing services. This is particularly true for commercial insurance customers.

Insurance producers represent one or more insurance companies. As a source of insurance knowledge for their customers, producers provide risk management advice, solicit or sell insurance, and provide follow-up services as customers' loss exposures or concerns change.

Insurance producers typically perform these functions:

- Prospecting
- Risk management review
- Sales
- Policy issuance
- Premium collection
- Customer service
- Claim handling
- Consulting

Prospecting

Virtually all producers prospect. Prospecting involves locating persons, businesses, and other entities that may be interested in purchasing the insurance products and services offered by the producer's principals. Prospects can be located using several methods:

- Referrals from present clients
- Referrals from strategic partners, such as financial institutions and real estate brokers
- Advertising in multimedia and direct mail
- Interactive websites, social media, and mobile marketing
- Telephone solicitations
- **Cold canvass**

Cold canvass

Contacting a prospect without an appointment.

Large agencies and brokerages may have employees who specialize in locating prospective clients. However, a producer is typically responsible for his or her own prospecting. Insurers might also participate in prospecting, especially in the exclusive agent and direct writer marketing systems.

Risk Management Review

Risk management review is the principal method of determining a prospect's insurance needs. The extent of the review varies based on customers and their characteristics.

Individual or Family

For an individual or a family, the risk management review process might be relatively simple, requiring an interview or completion of an online questionnaire that assists in identifying the prospect's loss exposures, which are often associated with property ownership and activities. Using the results of the questionnaire, the producer suggests methods of risk control, retention of loss exposures, and insurance.

Businesses

The risk management review process for businesses is likely to be more complex because they have property ownership, products, services, employees, and liabilities that are unique to the size and type of organization. Substantial time is required to develop and analyze loss exposure information for a large firm with diversified operations.

A review of previous losses, or a "loss run," can guide the producer in helping the business owner develop risk management plans, track the results of current risk management efforts, identify problem areas, and project costs. Loss runs include, at a minimum, lists of losses and their total cost. For large commercial customers, the producer may work with the customer's Risk Management Department in identifying loss exposures and risk analysis. Based on this analysis, risk treatment decisions, including insurance coverage, can be made. The producer can then coordinate further coverage discussions between the customer and the insurer.

Sales

Selling insurance products and services is one of the most important activities of an insurance producer because it is essential to sustaining the livelihood of the agency or brokerage. Commission on business sold is the principal source of income for producers, and the ownership of policy expirations applicable to the business sold is the principal asset of an insurance agency.

Policy Issuance

At the producer's request, insurers issue policies and their associated forms, sending them either directly to policyholders or to the producer for delivery. In paperless environments, the policies and forms may be produced digitally, along with endorsements, bills, and loss history information.

Premium Collection

Producers who issue policies may also prepare policy invoices and collect premiums. After deducting their commissions, they send the net premiums to the insurers, a procedure known as the agency bill process.

To give the producer some protection against policyholders' late payments, premiums are usually not due to the insurer until thirty or forty-five days after the policy's effective date. This delay also permits the producer to invest the premiums collected until they are due to the insurer. The resulting investment income can be a significant part of the producer's remuneration.

Agency billing may be used for personal insurance policies, but it is more commonly used with large commercial accounts. For small commercial accounts and the vast majority of personal insurance, the customer is usually directed to send premium payments to the insurer, bypassing the producer in a procedure known as the direct bill process.

Customer Service

Most producers are involved to some degree in customer service. For independent agents and brokers, value-added services and the personalization of insurance packages are what differentiate them in the marketplace. For the producer of a direct writer, service might consist of providing advice, handling an endorsement request, providing coverage quotes, or referring a policyholder who has had a loss to the Claims Department.

Producers are expected to facilitate contacts between policyholders and the insurer, including these:

- Responding to billing inquiries
- Performing customer account reviews
- Answering questions regarding existing coverage and additional coverage requirements
- Corresponding with premium auditors and risk control representatives

Claim Handling

All producers are likely to be involved to some extent in handling claims filed by their policyholders. Because the producer is the policyholder's principal contact with the insurer, the policyholder usually contacts the producer first when a claim occurs.

In some cases, the producer might provide information on contacting the insurer. Alternatively, the producer might obtain some basic information about the claim from the policyholder, relay it to the insurer, and arrange for a claim representative to contact the policyholder. Frequently, insurers issue their policies with a "claim kit" that informs their policyholders about the proper procedures and contacts in the event of a loss.

Some producers are authorized by their insurers to adjust some types of claims. Most often, the authorization is limited to small first-party property claims. However, a few large agencies or brokerages that employ skilled claim personnel might be authorized to settle large, more complex claims. The limitations on the producer's claim-handling authority should be specified in the agency contract.

Claim handling by qualified producers offers two major advantages: quicker service to policyholders and lower loss adjustment expenses to the insurer. Conversely, if the producer is not properly trained in how to handle claims, overpayment of claims can offset the savings.

Consulting

Many producers offer consulting services, for which they are paid on a fee basis. Such services are usually performed for insureds, but they may also be performed for noninsureds or for prospects. Services might be provided for a fee only, or the producer might set a maximum fee to be reduced by any commissions received on insurance written because of the consulting contract.

Laws in some states prohibit agents from receiving both commission and a fee from the same client. Fees are billed separately from any insurance premiums due, whereas commissions are included in the premium totals billed.

SELECTING INSURANCE MARKETING DISTRIBUTION SYSTEMS AND CHANNELS

Any firm that sells a product has a distribution system to carry out some of its marketing functions. Distribution systems for intangible products, such as insurance, are more flexible and adaptable than those for tangible products because they are not constrained by large investments in physical facilities. This intangibility gives insurers options to meet a wide array of customers' needs as well as their own operational needs. Distribution channels provide even more options for communicating with existing and potential customers.

Insurance distribution systems and channels provide the necessary people, physical facilities, and conduits for communication between insurers and customers.

An insurer usually selects a distribution system before it begins writing business. Changing distribution systems for existing business can be difficult and expensive because of existing agency contracts and possible ownership of expirations. However, an insurer might decide to use a different distribution system when entering a new territory or launching a new insurance product. In contrast, distribution channels selected by insurers and their representatives are more readily changeable.

The key factors in selecting distribution systems and channels are based on customers' needs and characteristics as well as the insurer's profile. See the exhibit "Distribution Systems and Conduits for Insurance Marketing."

Distribution Systems and Conduits for Insurance Marketing

Distribution systems consist of the necessary people and physical facilities to support the sale of the insurance product and services.	Independent agency and brokerage marketing system • Independent agents and brokers • National and regional brokers • Independent agent networks • Managing general agents (MGAs) • Surplus lines brokers Exclusive agency marketing system Direct writer marketing system
Distribution channels are communication conduits for promoting and servicing products as well as communicating with existing and prospective insureds.	• Internet • Call centers • Direct response • Group marketing • Financial institutions

[DA06250]

Customers' Needs and Characteristics

The needs and characteristics of customers—both existing and those in target markets—are key factors in an insurer's selection of distribution systems and channels because their satisfaction drives their purchase decisions. These are examples of customer needs and characteristics:

- Products and services—What are customers' expectations regarding coverage, accessibility, price, and service? Customers with low service expectations, such as those who purchase minimum-coverage personal auto insurance, may be satisfied with the ease of shopping online for direct writers' policies. Conversely, a large commercial account's risk manager will seek the expertise of an agent or broker to provide advice, assist in coverage placement, and respond to changing needs as the organization's internal and external environments change.

- Price—To what degree is the price of products and services a factor for customers? Some consumers' paramount concern is the price of insurance. Others are concerned with price to a degree but are unlikely to make changes if they are satisfied with a product. Still others seek risk management alternatives that will minimize the adverse effects of losses for the organization over the long term.

- Response time—How quickly can inquiries and transactions be processed? Customers can quickly conduct many financial services transactions, and they often expect the same response from their insurance providers.

Insurer's Profile

An insurer's profile—including its strategies and goals, strengths, existing and target markets, geographic location, and the degree of control over producers it needs or desires—frames the business and marketing environments within which it operates. The insurer must evaluate these key factors when selecting distribution systems and channels.

Insurer Strategies and Goals

An insurer's strategies, defined by high-level organizational goals, provide purposeful direction for the organization. These strategies and goals often address issues regarding market share, sales, service, and the markets in which the insurer competes. They may also relate to acquisitions, strategic alliances, or mergers.

Changes in market strategies or aggressive goals can be a catalyst for an insurer to reexamine its distribution systems and channels if current approaches are inadequate to achieve required results. For example, a regional personal lines insurer that contracts independent agents as a distribution system may adopt a strategy to expand to the national market. Rather than contracting additional independent agents in the expanded geographic territory, the insurer assumes the role of a direct writer and uses an online distribution channel to reach customers through web-based insurance distributors. This approach can reduce long-term costs and accelerate the insurer's market-share growth.

Insurer Strengths

Organizations evaluate their internal and external environments to assess their strengths and weaknesses compared with external opportunities and threats. Once an insurer determines where its strengths lie, it selects those distribution systems and channels that maximize its opportunities to capture market share and minimize its weaknesses. In doing so, the insurer may analyze these factors:

- Financial resources—The initial fixed cost of entering a market through the exclusive agency system or direct writer system is greater than doing so through the independent agency system. The insurer must hire, train, and financially support the direct writer and exclusive agency producers at substantial cost before they become productive. Similarly, online distribution channels have high start-up costs for supporting information systems. In comparison, the cost of conducting a direct response campaign can be much lower. Consequently, insurers with the financial resources to initiate distribution systems and channels with high start-up costs have the option of competing in markets that are best served by those marketing methods.

Insurers without those financial resources may be limited in the target markets they can enter.

- Core capabilities—Core capabilities include the abilities of an organization's staff, processes, and technology. An insurer whose strength is successfully servicing large, complex commercial accounts can capitalize on the firm's core capabilities. Complex commercial accounts require personalized service and are well served by agents and brokers, who can provide advice and ongoing service to expand the types of businesses to which the insurer markets or its geographic market.

- Expertise and reputation of producers—Because agents and brokers are the point of contact with customers, their expertise and reputation can be a crucial strength or weakness for the insurer. The level of expertise required of a producer depends on the lines of insurance written. Specialty target markets, such as international manufacturing, high-net-worth individuals, and large public entities, require knowledgeable and prominent producers to advise them. Having producers with those attributes in a direct writer distribution system allows the insurer to expand into similar or secondary markets. An insurer attempting to enter specialty markets without the skill base on staff must compete for agents and brokers who can provide the needed expertise and reputation.

Existing and Target Markets

The characteristics of an insurer's existing book of business should be considered before any change in distribution system or channel. If agents or brokers own the expirations for current accounts, the insurer must either give up that business and start over or purchase the expirations from producers. Either option might be expensive, depending on the quality of the existing business.

Disruptions in communication channels can also result in policyholder dissatisfaction and lost accounts. As a result, insurers change market systems and channels for existing customers with great caution. However, some catalysts are sufficiently threatening to cause an insurer to change marketing approaches. For example, an insurer that is losing market share to an aggressive new competitor has ample incentive to change its approach to better address customers' needs and characteristics.

Customers' needs and characteristics are driving factors for an insurer that is considering changing its marketing approach or adopting an omnichannel approach for a new target market. If an insurer's existing distribution systems and channels do not adequately address the customers' profiles as determined through marketing research, the insurer is less likely to gain market share. To make an optimum choice, the insurer carefully balances the cost of changing its distribution systems and channels with expected benefits resulting from the new accounts it will write.

Insurers can apply data analytics approaches to more clearly define customer needs based on existing information regarding purchasing preferences, demographics, coverage needs, and other factors. This analysis can assist in determining appropriate distribution systems or channels for existing business and to target new markets.

Geographic Location

The geographic location of existing policyholders or target markets is a key concern in selecting a distribution system and channels because the insurer's fixed costs of establishing an exclusive or direct writer agent in a territory are substantial. Exclusive agent or direct writer marketing systems can be successful only when a sufficient number of prospects exist within a relatively small geographic area.

Because the cost of appointing an independent agent is generally lower than that of appointing an exclusive or direct writer agent, those systems can be used in sparsely populated areas or when customers in the target market are widely dispersed. Emerging digital technologies are also providing opportunities for insurers to reach these customers. This is especially true for personal lines or small commercial lines customers who may be better served through omnichannel marketing approaches, such as online or through call centers.

Degree of Control Required

The extent of control the insurer wants to exercise over its marketing operations may influence its choice of a distribution system:

- An insurer can exercise the greatest control over producers in the direct writer system. Under that system, the producer is an employee of the company, and the company can exercise control over both the results achieved and the methods used to achieve them. For example, an insurer can specify the number and type of new applications the producer must submit each month (results) as well as the marketing approaches the producer can use (methods).

- Under both the agency and brokerage system and the exclusive agency system, the producers are independent contractors; therefore, the insurer can control only the results they produce, not the methods they use to produce them. For example, an insurer can specify the number and type of new applications the producer must submit each month (results). To achieve those results, however, the agent or broker can engage in any advertising or marketing campaign that does not violate insurance regulations or contractual agreements with the insurer.

- Producers are not involved in the direct response system. Consequently, the insurer has complete control of its distribution system.

Degree of control becomes important in meeting the needs of some customers. For example, pharmaceutical manufacturers require specialized risk management advice that includes a risk control recovery plan in case a tainted drug or defective medical device is released to the public. The insurer may wish to control the nature of the risk management alternatives recommended to those insureds, preferring those that foster transparency and immediate response following products liability losses.

Other insurers value discretion in the producers who represent them. For example, an insurer that specializes in church insurance or distributes insurance through religious affinity groups will expect to have some control over the producers' use of social media. A producer's indiscretions posted in public forums can cause an insurer to lose accounts. Therefore, the insurer might choose a direct writer distribution system under which producers are employees and subject to the insurer's guidelines for media use.

SUMMARY

The property-casualty insurance marketplace is the unique environment where insurance customers' needs and characteristics are addressed by insurers. Key features of the insurance marketplace include these:

- Insurance customers who come to the market with varying insurance needs, knowledge of insurance, access methods, negotiating ability, and choice of risk financing alternatives
- Insurers that compete in the market for customers based on differentiations in customer focus, products and services, size, geographic area, and distribution system

The property-casualty insurance marketplace is the unique environment in which insurance customers' needs and characteristics are addressed by insurers. Marketplace features that are unique to the industry include economic forces, regulatory controls, demands for technology, underwriting cycles, and unanticipated catastrophic losses.

An insurer's marketing activities collectively gather and analyze information so that the organization can make optimal and informed choices in market segmentation, efficient product development, and effective communication to customers to promote product sales. Marketing activities include these examples:

- Marketing research
- Market development
- Marketing information
- Marketing planning
- Product development
- Advertising and promotion
- Customer and public relations
- Sales fulfillment

Insurance distribution systems consist of the necessary people and physical facilities to support the sale of insurance products and services. The main insurance distribution systems are these:

- Independent agency and brokerage marketing system
- Exclusive agency marketing system
- Direct writer marketing system

Insurers use distribution channels to promote products and services as well as to communicate with existing and prospective insureds. These are common insurance distribution channels:

- Internet
- Call centers
- Direct response
- Group marketing
- Financial institutions

No one distribution system or channel is best; insurers may select multiple distribution systems and/or channels based on their marketing and business needs, and on customer needs and preferences.

Insurance producers represent one or more insurance companies and perform these typical functions:

- Prospecting
- Risk management review
- Sales
- Policy issuance
- Premium collection
- Customer service
- Claim handling
- Consulting

Insurers should evaluate various factors when selecting distribution systems and channels. These factors include customers' needs and characteristics, such as the products and services they require, the price they are willing to pay, and the response time they require.

Insurers' profiles serve as guidelines that affect their choice of distribution systems and channels. Insurers' profiles include their strategies and goals, strengths, existing and target markets, geographic location, and the degree of control required.

The Underwriting Function

Educational Objectives

After learning the content of this assignment, you should be able to:

▷ Distinguish among the underwriting activities typically performed by line and staff underwriters.

▷ Explain why it is important to comply with underwriting authority in individual account selection.

▷ Describe the constraining factors considered in the establishment of underwriting policy.

▷ Explain why insurers implement underwriting guidelines and conduct underwriting audits.

▷ Summarize the steps in the underwriting process and the purpose of each.

▷ Explain how an insurer's underwriting results are measured and how financial measures can be distorted.

The Underwriting Function

UNDERWRITING ACTIVITIES

Insurers assume billions of dollars in financial risk through coverage decisions based on underwriters' analysis of data drawn from both traditional sources and the increasingly significant universe of technology-driven big data. An insurer's underwriting activities—the coordinated efforts of **line underwriters** and **staff underwriters**—can therefore influence its profitability more than any other single factor.

Line underwriters evaluate new submissions and perform renewal underwriting, usually by working directly with insurance producers and applicants. Staff underwriters, meanwhile, manage risk selection by working with line underwriters and coordinating decisions about products, pricing, and guidelines. Collectively, these activities enable the insurer to avoid adverse selection, maintain adequate policyholders' surplus, and enforce underwriting guidelines, all of which contribute to the primary underwriting goal of sustaining profitable growth.

Let's examine the line underwriting and staff underwriting roles more closely.

Line Underwriting Activities

Line underwriters evaluate accounts for acceptability and make their decisions according to the **underwriting guidelines** outlined by staff underwriters. The individual activities these tasks entail include these:

- Selecting insureds—Line underwriters select new and renewal accounts (and evaluate existing ones) by identifying suitable applicants and charging appropriate premiums that accurately reflect the loss exposures covered. Techniques driven by customer-generated data, such as predictive analysis, generalized linear models, and credit-scoring models, often help line underwriters make these decisions. Line underwriters also look for unusual patterns of policy growth or loss and monitor real-time data, such as information from vehicle-based telematic devices, wearable sensors, and devices connected to the Internet of Things. Optimized insured selection helps line underwriters fulfill one of underwriting's chief purposes—to avoid adverse selection, which can significantly undermine profitability.

- Classifying and pricing accounts—Account classification entails grouping similar accounts so that they can be priced competitively while still allowing the insurer to make a profit and maintain an adequate **policyholders'**

Line underwriter
Underwriter who is primarily responsible for implementing the steps in the underwriting process.

Staff underwriter
Underwriter who assists underwriting management with making and implementing underwriting policy.

Underwriting guidelines (underwriting guide)
A written manual that communicates an insurer's underwriting policy and that specifies the attributes of an account that an insurer is willing to insure.

Policyholders' surplus
An insurer's assets minus its liabilities, which represents its net worth.

surplus. Like account selection, this activity is often reinforced with data-driven decision making.

- Recommending or providing coverage—Line underwriters may make sure that existing accounts are adequately protected through non-insurance risk management techniques, such as retention or risk control, so that any coverage gaps are addressed. They might also collaborate with producers to ensure that applicants obtain the coverage they request. Finally, producers and applicants often want to know how coverage will respond to a specific type of loss; line underwriters respond (usually through the producer) by explaining the types of losses covered and the endorsements that can be added to provide coverage not included in standard policies.

- Managing a book of business—Some insurers' line underwriters are responsible for the profitability of a book of business accepted from a producer or written in a territory or line of business. In such cases, the line underwriter works to ensure that each book of business achieves established goals, such as product mix, loss ratio, and written premium.

- Supporting producers and customers—Because customer service activities and underwriting are often interwoven, line underwriters have a vested interest in ensuring that producers' and insureds' needs are met. Line underwriters usually work directly with producers to prepare policy quotations.

- Coordinating with marketing efforts—An insurer's marketing efforts and underwriting policy should be compatible.

Staff Underwriting Activities

Staff underwriters work closely with underwriting management to perform activities essential to profitable risk selection, such as these:

- Performing market research—Market research may entail evaluating the effect of adding or deleting entire lines of business, of expanding into additional states, or of retiring from states an insurer operates in; determining optimal product mix for a book of business; and examining premium-volume goals. Market research can also be refined using data-fueled predictive analysis methods.

Underwriting policy (underwriting philosophy)

A guide to individual and aggregate policy selection that supports an insurer's mission statement.

- Formulating underwriting policy— **Underwriting policy (underwriting philosophy)** translates an insurer's mission and goals into specific strategies that, in turn, determine the composition of the insurer's book of business. Insurers often develop their underwriting policy within the context of the market(s) they serve—the standard market, the nonstandard market, or the specialty market. Beyond these broad market selections, the goals for an insurer's book of business and resulting underwriting policy may be established according to types of insurance and classes of business to be written; territories to be developed; or forms, insurance rates (such as filed rates and surplus lines pricing), and rating plans to be used.

- Revising underwriting guidelines to reflect changes in underwriting policy—Some insurers' underwriting guidelines include systematic instructions for handling particular classes of commercial accounts, including pricing instructions. Such guidelines may identify specific hazards to evaluate, alternatives to consider, criteria to use when making the final decision, ways to implement the decision, and methods to monitor the decision. Other insurers use less comprehensive guidelines.

- Evaluating loss experience—Insurance products with greater-than-anticipated losses are usually targeted for analysis. Staff underwriters research loss data to determine the specific source of the excess losses. Part of this research includes analyzing—often augmented with big data—the insurance industry's loss experience, which may reveal trends affecting the insurer's products. Based on their evaluation, staff underwriters, usually with the agreement of other key departments, adjust the insurer's underwriting guidelines.

- Researching and developing coverage forms—When an insurer develops its own forms, staff underwriters collaborate with the insurer's actuarial and legal departments to meet changing consumer needs and competitive pressures. Additionally, insurers modify existing coverage forms so that the coverage provided will respond as anticipated.

- Reviewing and revising pricing plans—Staff underwriters review and update rates and rating plans continually, subject to regulatory constraints, to respond to changes in loss experience, competition, and inflation. Insurers and advisory organizations gather historical loss data to develop **prospective loss costs**. Each insurer then examines its own operational profit and expense requirements. Staff underwriters combine prospective loss costs with an insurer-developed profit and expense loading to create a final rate used in policy pricing. Insurers must develop their own rates for any coverage for which advisory organizations do not develop loss costs. In such situations, reviewing and revising rating plans become even more crucial to ensuring that the loss costs adequately reflect **loss development** and **trending**.

- Assisting others with complex accounts—Staff underwriters often serve as consultants to other underwriters. Generally, staff underwriters have significant first-hand experience in line underwriting. They regularly see complex and atypical accounts, unlike most line underwriters. Staff underwriters also function as referral underwriters, reviewing and approving the risk when an application exceeds a line underwriter's authority.

- Conducting underwriting audits—Staff underwriters are often responsible for monitoring line underwriters' activities and their adherence to **underwriting authority**, which can be evaluated by conducting **underwriting audits**. These audits focus on proper documentation; adherence to procedure, classification, and rating practices; and conformity of selection decisions to the underwriting guidelines. Staff underwriters also monitor underwriting activity by analyzing statistical results by type of insurance, class of business, size of loss exposure, and territory. Statistical data shows

Prospective loss costs

Loss data that are modified by loss development, trending, and credibility processes, but without considerations for profit and expenses.

Loss development

The increase or decrease of incurred losses over time.

Trending

A statistical technique for analyzing environmental changes and projecting such changes into the future.

Underwriting authority

The scope of decisions that an underwriter can make without receiving approval from someone at a higher level.

Underwriting audit

A review of underwriting files to ensure that individual underwriters are adhering to underwriting guidelines.

the extent to which underwriting goals are met, but it does not conclusively demonstrate whether the results are a product of the insurer's underwriting guidelines.

UNDERWRITING AUTHORITY

The levels of underwriting authority granted to underwriters reflect their experience and knowledge in risk selection decisions. Authority may also be granted to producers and managing general agencies. Compliance with levels of authority is crucial to maintaining the appropriate controls over risk selection.

Underwriters have different levels of authority. As their levels of underwriting authority increase, the responsibility for accurately applying experience and judgment also increases. Compliance with levels of authority ensures that the insurer accepts applicants within its underwriting policy.

Before accepting an applicant, a line underwriter must determine whether he or she has the necessary underwriting authority to make the decision. The underwriting authority granted typically varies by position, grade level, and experience.

Underwriting authority requirements are usually communicated to an underwriter through the insurer's underwriting guidelines. A notation next to a specific classification in the underwriting guide, for example, might indicate that a senior underwriter must review and approve an application from that classification before it is processed further. Depending on the concerns that underwriting management places on a classification, underwriting approval might be required from the line underwriter's branch manager or a staff underwriter at the home office. Another approach to controlling underwriting authority is to specify in the underwriting guidelines the policy limits at which the accounts must be submitted to a higher authority.

In addition, some rating plans, such as composite rating, might require higher underwriting authority to review the merits of the account. Similarly, certain endorsements or coverage forms named in the underwriting guidelines might require specific levels of authority for approval.

Compliance with levels of underwriting authority ensures that the individuals making application-selection decisions have the experience necessary to evaluate which risks are acceptable and the unique knowledge required to judge risk for specialized lines of insurance.

To place controls on levels of underwriting authority, insurers generally grant authority in these ways:

- Underwriters gain underwriting authority with experience and positive results.
- Producers may gain underwriting authority based on experience, profitability, and contractual arrangements. Authority, if granted, may be only for certain types of insurance within specific limits of coverage.
- Managing general agents (MGA), when appointed, assume decentralized underwriting authority, which capitalizes on an MGA's familiarity with local conditions.

Insurers with conservative internal underwriting philosophies may not grant underwriting authority to any entities beyond their own internal underwriters. Specialty insurers, such as those offering surety bonds, aviation insurance, and livestock mortality insurance, also usually centralize underwriting authority.

CONSTRAINTS IN ESTABLISHING UNDERWRITING POLICY

An insurer's underwriting policy promotes the type of insurance anticipated to produce a growing and profitable book of business. However, various factors constrain what an underwriting policy can accomplish.

An insurer's senior management formulates an underwriting policy that guides individual and aggregate underwriting decisions. Underwriting policy determines the composition of the insurer's book of business, including the lines and classes of business that the insurer will offer, the amount of business the insurer is willing to write, the rating philosophy and forms the insurer will apply, and the territories to be developed. See the exhibit "Lines of Business."

Lines of Business

The National Association of Insurance Commissioners (NAIC) Annual Statement, which is prescribed for financial reporting in all states, divides property and liability coverages into thirty-three separate lines of business. Examples of these statutory prescribed lines of business are fire, allied lines, workers compensation, commercial multiperil, and ocean marine. A complete listing appears in the NAIC Annual Statement. Insurers must report premiums, losses, and expenses by the lines of business, but related lines of business are combined to create insurance products. For example, an insurer who markets commercial auto insurance will have to offer the following NAIC Annual Statement lines of business: commercial auto no-fault (personal injury protection), other commercial auto liability, and commercial auto physical damage. When they use the term "line of business," underwriters are mentally combining several related NAIC Annual Statement lines into a single reference, such as "commercial auto."

[DA06262]

All insurers would like to obtain profitable results, and most insurers would like to expand premium writings or increase market share. However, when these changes involve the insurer's underwriting policy, major constraining factors must be considered. See the exhibit "Constraints of Underwriting Policy."

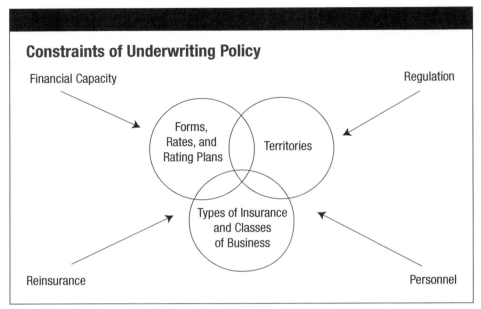

[DA06270]

Financial Capacity

Premium-to-surplus ratio, or capacity ratio

A capacity ratio that indicates an insurer's financial strength by relating net written premiums to policyholders' surplus.

Statutory accounting principles (SAP)

The accounting principles and practices that are prescribed or permitted by an insurer's domiciliary state and that insurers must follow.

An insurer's financial capacity refers to the relationship between premiums written and the size of the policyholders' surplus, which is an insurer's net worth. That relationship is crucial in evaluating insurer solvency. The National Association of Insurance Commissioners (NAIC) has developed a series of financial ratios that it uses in conjunction with analytical evaluations to identify insurers that should receive additional solvency surveillance from regulators. The **premium-to-surplus ratio** is one of those key ratios, and it is considered too high when it exceeds 300 percent, or 3-to-1.

Insurers may exceed the premiums-to-surplus ratio through the rapid growth of premiums written. Because of conservative **statutory accounting principles** used in insurance, rapid growth results in a reduction in policyholders' surplus to pay for expenses generated by that growth. This constraint often precludes premium expansion unless the insurer purchases reinsurance or obtains more capital. See the exhibit "Statutory Accounting Rules."

Statutory Accounting Rules

Since the beginning of state oversight of insurance, insurance regulators have been primarily concerned with insurer solvency. The National Association of Insurance Commissioners (NAIC) was formed in 1871 to reduce the inconsistencies and confusion caused by multiple state financial reporting requirements. The accounting system that evolved to satisfy insurance regulations is called statutory accounting principles (SAP). SAP are conservative accounting rules designed to determine whether an insurer can meet its obligations to policyholders. Most other businesses use generally accepted accounting principles (GAAP), which focus on the organization as an ongoing enterprise, for financial reporting.

[DA06271]

Insurers recognize the limitations of their capacity and seek to write those lines of business or accounts that maximize **return on equity**. These activities help realize maximization:

- Setting return thresholds—Insurers typically establish a return-on-equity threshold against which capacity allocation proposals are evaluated. If, for example, the insurer wants a 10 percent return on equity and the sale of workers compensation insurance in a specific state is expected to generate a 12 percent return on equity, then the insurer should expand into this territory and line of business if no better opportunity is present.

- Redirecting focus on target business classes—An insurer may decide to stop pursuing one class of business and, instead, use capacity elsewhere. For example, an insurer may stop pursuing a class of general liability accounts whose losses exceed expectations and develop a marketing campaign for accounts that offer more promising returns.

- Adjusting underwriting policy based on jurisdiction—Jurisdiction can be relevant in this process. For example, inadequate rate levels and rising benefit levels for claimants in many states led some insurers to develop restrictive acceptance criteria for workers compensation submissions.

Effective account selection allows insurers to be commercially viable by rationing their available capacity to obtain an optimum spread of loss exposures by territory, business class, size of risk, and line of business. See the exhibit "Return on Equity."

Return on equity (ROE)

A profitability ratio expressed as a percentage by dividing a company's net income by its net worth (book value). Depending on the context, net worth is sometimes called shareholders' equity, owners' equity, or policyholders' surplus.

Regulation

States promulgate insurance regulations that take the form of statutes enacted by state legislatures and regulations adopted by the state insurance department. Insurance is a highly regulated industry, and regulations directly and indirectly affect most insurer activities.

Return on Equity

Return on equity is not only a benchmark for employing capacity but also a fundamental measure of insurer profitability. This financial ratio relates net operating gain (after taxes) as a percentage of prior-year capital and surplus.

The SAP and GAAP approaches to calculating return on equity differ, as shown below:

$$\text{Return on equity (SAP basis)} = \frac{\text{Net income}}{\text{Average policyholders' surplus}}$$

$$\text{Return on equity (GAAP basis)} = \frac{\text{Net income}}{\text{Average owners' equity}}$$

Stock insurers calculate both ratios since they report their financial performance using both SAP and GAAP bases. Mutual insurers calculate return on equity using only the SAP basis.

Return on equity is also a key financial ratio used by insurance regulators for solvency surveillance. An acceptable value for return on equity falls between 5 and 15 percent.

[DA06272]

Regulation affects underwriting policy in several ways:

- Insurers must be licensed to write insurance in each state in which they write insurance.
- Rates, rules, and forms must be filed with state regulators.
- Some states specifically require underwriting guidelines to be filed.
- If consumer groups believe that the insurance industry has not adequately served certain geographic areas, regulatory focus on insurance availability can lead to requirements to extend coverage to loss exposures that an insurer might otherwise not write.

Market conduct examination

An analysis of an insurer's practices in four operational areas: sales and advertising, underwriting, ratemaking, and claim handling.

State regulators perform **market conduct examinations** to ensure that insurers adhere to the classification and rating plans they have filed. When a market conduct examination discloses deviations from filed forms and rates or improper conduct, the insurer is subject to penalties.

Insurance regulation is not applied uniformly across states. In some jurisdictions, insurers may be unable to get rate filings approved, or approval may be granted so slowly that rate levels are inadequate relative to rising claim costs. Some insurers have chosen to withdraw from states that impose regulations they consider too restrictive.

Personnel

Insurers require the talent of specialists to market their products effectively, underwrite specific lines of business, service their accounts, and pay claims for losses that occur. An insurer must have a sufficient number of properly trained underwriters to implement its underwriting policy. No prudent insurer, for example, would pursue the highly technical lines of aviation, surety, or ocean marine insurance without a sufficient number of experienced underwriting specialists in those lines of business.

In addition to having personnel with the necessary skills, the insurer must have the personnel where they are needed. As a general practice, an insurer should obtain premiums from a broad range of insureds to create the widest possible distribution of loss exposures. However, regulatory expenses and policyholder service requirements make it difficult for small insurers to efficiently handle a small volume of business in many widespread territories. Insurers must have a sufficient volume of premium to operate efficiently in an area. Information systems are especially important; many growth plans have been abandoned because computer support was not available.

Reinsurance

The availability and cost of adequate reinsurance can influence underwriting policy. Reinsurance treaties may exclude certain types of insurance or classes of business, or the cost of reinsurance may be prohibitive.

Reinsurers are also concerned about the underlying policy forms offered by the insurer. A reinsurer may not have any reservations about an insurer's use of forms developed by advisory organizations. However, it may expressly exclude reinsurance coverage for loss exposures covered by manuscript forms developed for a particular insured or covered by forms developed independently of an advisory organization.

IMPLEMENTING UNDERWRITING POLICY

Staff underwriters develop underwriting guidelines, which distill underwriting policies into directions for line underwriters' policy selection. Underwriting audits ensure that established underwriting standards are reasonably consistent.

Insurers convey underwriting policy through their underwriting guidelines. The guidelines describe the parameters of acceptable applicants for insurance for which the insurer has priced its insurance products.

Underwriting audits are the insurer's quality control check for uniform application of the underwriting guidelines and for continuous improvement.

Purposes of Underwriting Guidelines

An insurer's underwriting policy is communicated to underwriters through underwriting guidelines, which are continually updated to reflect changes in policy. Underwriting guidelines identify the major elements that underwriters should evaluate for each type of insurance, as well as boundaries, such as maximum coverage limits, for application selection.

Some underwriting guides include step-by-step instructions for handling particular classes of insureds. Such guides might identify specific hazards to evaluate, alternatives to consider, criteria to use when making the final decision, ways to implement the decision, and methods to monitor the decision. Some guidelines also provide pricing instructions and reinsurance-related information. Other insurers use underwriting guides that are less comprehensive. For example, they may list all classes of business and indicate their acceptability by type of insurance. Codes are then assigned to indicate the desirability of the loss exposure and the level of authority required to write the class of business.

Because underwriting guidelines usually specify the attributes of accounts that insurers are willing to insure, insurers consider them trade secrets. Disclosure of this proprietary information might cause an insurer to lose its competitive advantage over others. See the exhibit "Sample Commercial Underwriting Guidelines."

Underwriting guidelines serve these purposes:

- Provide for structured decisions
- Ensure uniformity and consistency
- Synthesize insights and experience
- Distinguish between routine and nonroutine decisions
- Avoid duplication of effort
- Ensure adherence to reinsurance treaties and planned rate levels
- Support policy preparation and compliance
- Provide a basis for predictive models

Provide for Structured Decisions

Underwriting guidelines provide a structure for underwriting decisions by identifying the major considerations underwriters should evaluate for each type of insurance the insurer writes. For example, the section of an insurer's underwriting guidelines addressing contractors' equipment might indicate that equipment use is of paramount importance in determining acceptability and pricing. Contractors' equipment used in mountainous areas is more likely to be subject to upset and overturn and therefore requires more scrutiny and premium than contractors' equipment used on flat terrain.

Sample Commercial Underwriting Guidelines

I. GENERAL:

The Risk Selection Guide is a comprehensive alphabetical listing by class of business showing what the Midley Insurance Companies believe to be the desirability of insuring an average risk in the class. The Guide grades each class for Property, Commercial Automobile, Workers Compensation, Burglary and Robbery, Fidelity, Premises/Operations Liability, and Products/Completed Operations Liability. In addition, the final column titled "Form" indicates whether the General Liability coverage must be written on a Claims-Made Form (indicated by a "CM"), or whether the Occurrence Form is available (indicated by an "O"). Please remember the risk selection guide is only a guide. The company retains final authority regarding the acceptance or rejection of any specific risk.

II. CLASSIFICATION ACCEPTABILITY RATINGS:

The Risk Selection Guide is being published as a section of this agent's manual to answer this question: "Are risks within a particular class likely to be accepted by the Midley Insurance Companies?" In light of this question, the risk grades as found in the Risk Selection Guide are defined as follows:

E—Excellent

This class of business is considered to have excellent profit potential. Unless a specific risk in this class has unusual hazards or exposures, it will rarely present any underwriting problems. Risks graded as "E" may be bound by the agent without prior underwriting consent.

G—Good

This class of business is considered to have good profit potential. Normally this risk may be written before obtaining an inspection or developing additional underwriting information other than that present on the application. The agent may bind risks graded as "G" without prior underwriting consent.

A—Average

Potential for profit is marginal because of high variability of risks within the class. It is understood that the underwriter might think it is necessary to inspect the risk before authorizing binding. In all instances, it is recommended that the agent call the underwriter and discuss the risk before binding.

S—Submit

The account presents little potential for profit. These risks will require a complete written submission before binding. The underwriter must obtain a complete inspection and evaluate any other underwriting information deemed necessary before authorizing the binding of this risk.

D—Decline

Due to the lack of potential for profit, this class of risk is prohibited and will not be considered. Under no circumstances may a risk classified as "D" be bound without the prior written approval of the Vice President of Commercial Underwriting.

III. FOOTNOTES:

Footnotes sometimes are indicated as applying to an individual classification for a specific line of insurance. These footnotes are displayed at the bottom of each page and are designed to make you aware of certain hazards or exposures that are unacceptable or need to be addressed in an acceptable manner.

We hope the Risk Selection Guide will be valuable in understanding the types of business our companies want to be writing. However, please do not hesitate to call your underwriter if you are unsure as to how to classify a particular risk, or if you feel the factors associated with a specific risk make it considerably better or worse than the grading assigned by this guide.

Description	Property	Auto	Workers Compensation	Burglary and Robbery	Fidelity	Premises and Operations	Products and Completed Operations	Form
Painting—exterior—buildings or structures—three stories or less in height	A[1]	G	A	A	A	G[2]	G	O
Painting—interior—buildings or structures	A[1]	G	G	A	A	G[2]	G	O
Painting—oil or gasoline tanks	A[1]	G	D	A	A	D	D	O
Painting—ship hulls	A[1]	G	D	A	A	D	D	O
Painting—shop only	S[1,3]	G	S	A	A	G	G	O
Painting, picture, or frame stores	G	G	G	G	G	E	G	O
Paper coating or finishing	D	A	D	A	A	G	A	O
Paper corrugating or laminating—workers compensation only			D					
Paper crepeing—workers compensation only			D					
Paper goods manufacturing	D	A	D	A	A	G[4]	G[4]	O
Paper manufacturing	D	A	D	A	A	G[4]	G[4]	O
Paper products distributors	S	A	A	A	A	G[4]	G[4]	O
Paper, rag, or rubber stock dealers and distributors—secondhand	D	D	D	D	D	D	D	O
Paperhanging	G	G	G	G	G	G	G	O
Parachute manufacturing	D	A	D	D	D	D	D	O
Parades	D	D	D	D	D	D	D	O
Parking—private	A	A	S	S	S	A	A	O
Parking—public—open air	A	A	S	S	S	A	A	O
Parking—public—operated in conjunction with other enterprises	A	A	S	S	S	A	A	O
Parking—public—not open air	A	A	S	S	S	S	A	O
Parking—public shopping centers—(lessor's risk only)	G	G	S	G	G	G	G	O
Parks or playgrounds	A[5]	A	A	A	A	S[5]	S[5]	O
Paste, ink, or mucilage manufacturing—workers compensation only			S					

[1] Flammable liquid storage must be minimal and controlled.

[2] A minimum property damage deductible of $250 on premises and operations coverage is mandatory.

[3] The risk is unacceptable if any painting or finishing is done inside without an approved spray booth.

[4] Acceptability will depend on the specific nature of the operation and specific types and uses of the products.

[5] This risk is unacceptable unless this classification constitutes only a small part of other properties or operations.

[DA06292]

By identifying the principal hazards associated with a particular class of business, underwriting guidelines ensure that underwriters consider the primary hazard traits of the exposures they evaluate.

Ensure Uniformity and Consistency

Underwriting guidelines help ensure that selection decisions are made uniformly and consistently by all of the insurer's underwriters. Ideally, submissions that are identical in every respect should elicit the same response from different underwriters. Guidelines facilitate uniformity because they include acceptable approaches to evaluating applicants and the overall desirability of a particular type of risk or class of business.

Synthesize Insights and Experience

Underwriting guidelines synthesize the insights and experience of seasoned underwriters. Staff underwriters, who assist with the insurer's unique or challenging accounts on a referral basis, often are able to include the approaches they have taken in underwriting particular classifications and lines of business. For many insurers, underwriting guidelines serve as a repository for an insurer's cumulative expertise.

Distinguish Between Routine and Nonroutine Decisions

Underwriting guidelines help line underwriters distinguish between routine and nonroutine decisions:

- Routine decisions are those for which the line underwriter clearly has decision-making authority according to the underwriting guidelines.
- Nonroutine decisions involve submissions that fall outside the underwriter's authority.

Underwriting guides usually indicate that the classifications and lines of business must be either declined or submitted to a higher level of authority for approval.

Avoid Duplication of Effort

Many underwriting situations recur. If the problems inherent in a particular situation have been identified and solved, the solution should apply to all similar situations that might arise in the future. Underwriting guidelines contain the information necessary to avoid costly duplication of effort.

Ensure Adherence to Reinsurance Treaties and Planned Rate Levels

Compliance with underwriting guidelines ensures that coverage limits and accepted loss exposures will not exceed the insurer's treaty reinsurance, because staff underwriters reflect those treaty limitations in the guidelines.

Compliance with underwriting guidelines also ensures selection of loss exposures in an overall book of business commensurate with the planned rate levels for those policies. The importance of compliance with underwriting guidelines as it affects the profitability of a book of business is illustrated by an example of the outcome when compliance with guidelines fails. Many home-owners policy underwriting guidelines require property to be insured to within a percentage (such as 100 percent) of the replacement cost of the dwelling. Because most property losses are partial losses, rates are developed with the expectation that total losses will be rare. If property insured in a portfolio is significantly undervalued, average losses will equal a larger percentage of the average dwelling-coverage limits. The portfolio might also experience a greater number of losses equal to the total dwelling-coverage limit. Overall, the profitability of the book of business will decline as losses exceed expectations.

In resolving this profitability problem, one alternative is to increase the rates charged. However, that does not resolve the underlying problem of undervaluing the property insured, and the increased rates might not be competitive in the market. A better alternative is to enforce compliance with underwriting guidelines, ensure adequate coverage to replacement cost at the time of the initial application, and implement a program to increase dwelling coverage to keep pace with inflation and building cost increases.

Support Policy Preparation and Compliance

Underwriting guides provide information to assist underwriters and support staff in policy preparation. Rules and eligibility requirements for various rating plans are also included. Specialized information, such as eligibility for experience and retrospective rating together with appropriate rating formulas, often appears in the underwriting guide. Underwriting guidelines also support compliance with state regulatory requirements, as staff underwriters incorporate applicable regulations in the guidelines.

Provide a Basis for Predictive Models

Predictive modeling

A process in which historical data based on behaviors and events is blended with multiple variables and used to construct models of anticipated future outcomes.

Underwriters use **predictive modeling** to identify applications that present lower underwriting risk. Predictive modeling incorporates underwriting thought processes with underwriting guidelines by assigning a rank or score to all of the variables presented by an account and its loss exposures. Predictive models function in this way:

- Multiple data variables of individual risks are developed to rank the relative likelihood of insurance loss.
- Data variables are based on underwriting guidelines along with the insurer's loss experience, loss data collected from external sources, and underwriting expertise.
- The ranking or score developed from the data variables is a predictive measure of future profit potential based upon the account's characteristics.

Predictive modeling can provide a consistent way to review individual applications that improves the overall profitability of a book of business. It can also help in managing a large book of business for which conducting an in-depth underwriting review on every account would be too costly.

Purposes of Underwriting Audits

Staff underwriters conduct periodic audits to monitor line underwriters' adherence to the practices and procedures outlined in the underwriting guidelines. Audits are a management tool used to achieve uniformity and consistency in the application of underwriting standards.

Underwriting audits are typically conducted on-site at the branch or regional office being audited. A typical underwriting audit may involve selecting accounts at random or reviewing files that had experienced notable claims. These accounts are then scrutinized to determine whether prescribed procedures were followed and whether the underwriter acted in accord with the insurer's underwriting policy. Feedback from the audit of individual files provides individual line underwriters with strategies to improve future underwriting decisions.

Underwriting audits can also be used to monitor statistics for books of business. This can provide indications of applications written in excess of underwriting guidelines. For example, an excessive number of workers compensation applications accepted with hazardous classification codes in one territory could indicate an imbalance of product mix. It can also indicate inconsistent adherence to underwriting guidelines.

An underwriting audit provides staff underwriters with information on the effectiveness of the underwriting guidelines. Underwriting guidelines that are not being followed may be either outdated or considered unrealistic. This could indicate that a critical review for updates is required. Line underwriters, for example, might ignore the underwriting guidelines when changes in the insurance marketplace have occurred without corresponding changes having been made to the underwriting guidelines. As a result, staff underwriters might learn that producers are not receptive to complying with the insurer's underwriting guidelines. If compliance with underwriting guidelines is not leading to the desired results, such information is valuable in the ongoing effort of developing or revising effective underwriting guidelines.

STEPS IN THE UNDERWRITING PROCESS

Whether relying on independent judgment or the guidance of automated underwriting systems, underwriters engage in a series of steps and tasks designed to ensure that insurers are ultimately able to reach their business goals.

Application

A legal document that provides information obtained directly from an applicant requesting insurance and that an insurer can use for underwriting and claims handling purposes.

Underwriter

An insurer employee who evaluates applicants for insurance, selects those that are acceptable to the insurer, prices coverage, and determines policy terms and conditions.

Underwriting submission

Underwriting information for an initial application, or a substantive policy midterm or renewal change.

After a producer submits an **application** for insurance to an insurer, the application must be qualified for acceptance. **Underwriters** qualify an application by following the steps in the underwriting process. The underwriting process is also applied to renewal policies and certain policy changes, such as requests to add new locations to a property policy. For ease of discussion, applications, renewals, and policy changes to which the underwriting process is applied are referred to as **underwriting submissions**.

The underwriting process is a series of steps to determine which submissions will be accepted, for what amount of insurance, at what price, and under what conditions. In addition to considering the merits of an individual submission, underwriters consider how a submission fits into the insurer's business portfolio mix and whether it provides opportunity for profitability.

These general steps in the underwriting process provide a sound framework within which underwriters can make decisions:

- Evaluate the submission
- Develop underwriting alternatives
- Select an underwriting alternative
- Determine an appropriate premium
- Implement the underwriting decision
- Monitor underwriting decisions

Evaluate the Submission

Loss exposure

Any condition or situation that presents a possibility of loss, whether or not an actual loss occurs.

Hazard

A condition that increases the frequency or severity of a loss.

The first step in the underwriting process is evaluating a submission's **loss exposures** and associated **hazards.**

Underwriters must understand the activities, operations, and character of each applicant. To do so, they determine the information needed to make decisions regarding acceptance, coverage amounts, conditions, and price. However, trade-offs are necessary to control underwriting expenses and to handle a reasonable number of submissions.

Information efficiency

The balance that underwriters must maintain between the hazards presented by the account and the information needed to underwrite it.

Before gathering the information necessary to evaluate a submission, underwriters must determine what information is essential and what information may be desirable or available, but not essential. Underwriters seek to achieve **information efficiency** by weighing the need for information against the cost to obtain it. For example, an underwriter is likely to investigate a chemical manufacturer extensively but may require much less information to underwrite a gift shop. Sometimes a submission's premium size drives the decision regarding the amount of information gathered or the resources used to gather it. A submission with a small premium volume may not justify expensive research.

Underwriters can use various sources to obtain the information needed to evaluate a submission. These are the principal sources of underwriting information:

- Producers—The producer usually prequalifies applicants and often has firsthand knowledge of the applicant's business operations and reputation.

- Applications—Insurance applications provide general information required to process, rate, and underwrite loss exposures of the applicant and specific information necessary to evaluate the acceptability of an applicant's loss exposures for a particular type of insurance. In addition, insurers often use supplemental applications or questionnaires for certain coverages or classes of business to obtain more pertinent information when evaluating the submissions.

- Inspection reports—Inspections or risk control reports provide useful information about the property's physical condition, the business operations' safety record, and the applicant's management.

- Government records—Motor vehicle reports; criminal court records; civil court records, including records of suits, mortgages and liens; business licenses; property tax records; Securities and Exchange Commission filings; and bankruptcy filings may all provide relevant underwriting information.

- Financial rating services—An applicant's financial status provides important underwriting information. Dun & Bradstreet, Standard & Poor's, and Experian are examples of services that can provide an overall picture of the applicant's financial status.

- Loss data—The applicant's loss history may provide information on loss frequency and severity, types of losses, and trends in loss experience and reporting. Loss data analysis is a significant tool for predicting future losses and is also important for policy pricing.

- Premium audit reports—A **premium audit** report can provide useful information about the insured's operations that may have underwriting implications.

- Claims files—Underwriters can obtain insights into renewal policies by reviewing insureds' claims files. Claims representatives typically accumulate and document a significant amount of underwriting information during their investigations.

Choosing the right tools requires a holistic understanding of the information available and of the usefulness of that information in predicting which submissions are likely to provide an **underwriting profit**. See the exhibit "Underwriting Evaluation Tools."

Develop Underwriting Alternatives

The second step in the underwriting process is developing underwriting alternatives. Such alternatives include accepting a submission as is, rejecting

Premium audit

Methodical examination of a policyholder's operations, records, and books of account to determine the actual exposure units and premium for insurance coverages already provided.

Underwriting profit

Income an insurer earns from premiums paid by policyholders minus incurred losses and underwriting expenses.

Counteroffer

A proposal an offeree makes to an offeror that varies in some material way from the original offer, resulting in rejection of the original offer and constituting a new offer.

Rating plan

A set of directions that specify criteria of the exposure base, the exposure unit, and rate per exposure unit to determine premiums for a particular line of insurance.

Experience rating

A rating plan that adjusts the premium for the current policy period to recognize the loss experience of the insured organization during past policy periods.

Schedule rating

A rating plan that awards debits and credits based on specific categories, such as the care and condition of the premises or the training and selection of employees, to modify the final premium to reflect factors that the class rate does not include.

Retrospective rating

A ratemaking technique that adjusts the insured's premium for the current policy period based on the insured's loss experience during the current period; paid losses or incurred losses may be used to determine loss experience.

Facultative reinsurance

Reinsurance of individual loss exposures in which the primary insurer chooses which loss exposures to submit to the reinsurer, and the reinsurer can accept or reject any loss exposures submitted.

Underwriting Evaluation Tools

- Telematics—the use of Global Positioning System (GPS) tracking to collect and analyze data regarding driver behavior and vehicle use

- Predictive analytics—statistical and analytical techniques used to develop models that predict future events or behaviors

- Predictive modeling—a process in which historical data based on behaviors and events are blended with multiple variables and used to construct models of anticipated future outcomes

- Catastrophe (CAT) modeling—a type of computer program that estimates losses from future potential catastrophic events

- Internet of Things (IoT) and connected devices—wearables and other smart products provide additional information on customer behavior and assist in more efficient risk selection and pricing

[DA06331]

the submission, or making a **counteroffer** to accept the submission subject to certain modifications.

The underwriter typically makes a counteroffer to accept a submission from among these major types of modifications:

- Require risk control measures—A counteroffer may require the applicant to implement additional risk control measures. Measures such as installing an automatic fire-extinguishing sprinkler system, adding guard service, and improving housekeeping and maintenance can reduce physical hazards. Installing machinery guards can reduce the frequency of employee bodily injuries. If the applicant accepts the counteroffer, the insurer generally establishes controls to verify that the required risk control measures have been implemented.

- Change insurance rates, **rating plans**, or policy limits—A rate modification could either increase or decrease the premium. Using a different rating plan can provide pricing flexibility; the underwriter can properly price a submission based on its loss exposures. Examples of rating plans for commercial applicants include **experience rating**, **schedule rating**, and **retrospective rating**. An underwriter may also counteroffer with different policy limits. The insurer's underwriting guidelines usually specify the maximum limits of insurance that an underwriter can approve; these limits generally reflect reinsurance limitations or reinsurance availability and possible catastrophic loss from a single loss exposure. If high policy limits are requested, the underwriter may suggest lower limits or use **facultative reinsurance**.

- Amend policy terms and conditions—When the requested coverage cannot be provided, the underwriter might counteroffer to amend policy terms and conditions by modifying the policy to exclude certain causes of loss, add or increase a deductible, or make another coverage change. For example, an insurer may be unwilling to provide replacement cost coverage on a poorly maintained building but may be willing to provide a more limited coverage form. Increasing a deductible might make coverage more viable for a small commercial account with a high number of small losses that have caused unsatisfactory loss experience in the past. The underwriter's flexibility varies by type of insurance. Coverage modification is not always permitted on policies that have been approved by state regulators.

- Use facultative reinsurance—If an applicant is in a class of business or has atypical loss exposures that are excluded from the insurer's **treaty reinsurance** agreement, or if the amount of insurance needed exceeds the limits of the treaty reinsurance agreement, the underwriter may be able to transfer a portion of the liability for the applicant's loss exposures to a facultative reinsurer. An alternative to purchasing facultative reinsurance is for the producer to divide the insurance among several insurers—an approach sometimes called agency reinsurance.

Treaty reinsurance

A reinsurance agreement that covers an entire class or portfolio of loss exposures and provides that the primary insurer's individual loss exposures that fall within the treaty are automatically reinsured.

Select an Underwriting Alternative

The underwriter must evaluate each underwriting alternative carefully and select the optimal one under the circumstances. In some cases, the underwriter has no choice but to reject a submission; however, rejections produce neither premium nor commission, only expense. Therefore, underwriters try to make submissions acceptable whenever possible.

Selecting an alternative involves weighing a submission's positive and negative features, including the loss exposures contemplated in the insurance rate, risk control measures, and management's commitment to loss prevention. These factors also should be considered before selecting an underwriting alternative:

- Underwriting authority—Before accepting a submission, an underwriter must determine whether he or she has the necessary underwriting authority. If not, the submission must be referred to an individual with higher underwriting authority.
- Supporting business—A submission that is marginal by itself might be acceptable if the applicant has desirable supporting business. The **account underwriting** approach evaluates all lines together.
- **Mix of business**—The underwriter must consider whether accepting the submission supports the insurer's goals for mix of business.
- Producer relationships—The relationship between underwriters and producers should be based on mutual trust and respect. Underwriters should consider the opinions and recommendations of the producer before determining an underwriting alternative. While differences of opinion are

Account underwriting

A method of underwriting in which all of the business from a particular applicant is evaluated as a whole.

Mix of business

The distribution of individual policies that compose the book of business of a producer, territory, state, or region among the various lines and classifications.

common, collaboration and a willingness to see the other's viewpoint are essential to building a satisfactory working relationship.

- Regulatory restrictions—State regulations restrict underwriters' ability to accept or renew business. Many states also establish timeframes within which a submission must be declined or a policy nonrenewed, with notice of refusal to renew provided. Underwriters must know these restrictions and make timely decisions to avoid mandatory acceptance or renewal of an otherwise unacceptable submission.

Determine an Appropriate Premium

Loss costs

The portion of the rate that covers projected claim payments and loss adjusting expenses.

Underwriters must ensure that each loss exposure is accurately classified so that it is properly rated, with the appropriate premium charged. Insurance **loss costs** are typically based on a classification system that combines similar loss exposures into the same rating classification. Rating classifications enable the insurer to match potential loss costs with an applicant's particular loss exposures. Consequently, the insurer can develop an adequate premium to pay losses and operating expenses and to produce a profit.

Accurate classification ensures a pool of loss exposures with similar expected loss frequencies and loss severity. Misclassification can produce adverse results, including insufficient premium to cover losses and expenses and the inability to sell policies because prices are higher than competitors' prices. For most types of personal insurance and some commercial insurance, proper classification automatically determines the premium. For major types of commercial insurance, such as general liability, the underwriter might have the option of adjusting the premium based on the characteristics of the submission's loss exposures.

Implement the Underwriting Decision

Once an underwriter has evaluated a submission, selected and applied any appropriate modifications, and determined the premium, the next step is to implement the underwriting decision. Implementing underwriting decisions generally involves three tasks.

First, the underwriting decision is communicated to the producer. If the decision is to accept the submission with modifications, the reasons must be clearly communicated to the producer and applicant, and the applicant must agree to accept or implement any modifications made as a counteroffer. If the submission is rejected, the underwriter must provide a clear explanation of why that applicant does not meet the insurer's underwriting requirements. Effective communication of both positive and negative decisions clarifies the insurer's standards and helps the producer understand what kinds of business the insurer wants to write.

The second task is issuing any required documents. For example, when accepting a submission, the underwriter may need to issue a **binder** or prepare **certificates of insurance**.

The third task is to record data about the applicant and the policy for policy issuance, accounting, statistical, and monitoring purposes. Data may include location, limits, coverages, price modifications, and class of business. This data is coded so that the insurer and the industry can accumulate and aggregate information on all accounts for ratemaking, statutory reporting, financial accounting, and book-of-business evaluations. Such information is also used to monitor the account, trigger renewals, and flag situations requiring special attention.

Monitor Underwriting Decisions

The final step, an ongoing one, in the underwriting process is monitoring underwriting decisions. After an underwriting decision has been made on a new-business submission or a renewal, the underwriter is tasked with monitoring both individual policies and books of business to ensure that satisfactory results are achieved.

When monitoring individual policies, underwriters must be alert to changes in insureds' loss exposures. Changes in the nature of an insured's business operation, for example, could significantly raise or lower the insured's loss potential. Underwriters do not have the resources necessary to constantly monitor all individual policies, so existing policies are usually monitored in response to one or more of these triggering events that may indicate a change in the account:

- Substantive policy change requests
- Significant and unique loss occurrences
- Risk control and safety inspection reports
- Premium audit results

Policy monitoring also frequently occurs on renewal. As a policy's expiration date approaches, the underwriter may need to repeat the underwriting process before agreeing to renew the policy for another term. Renewal underwriting, however, can generally be accomplished more quickly than new-business underwriting because the insured is already known to the insurer and more information might be available if claims reports or risk control reports have been added to the file.

In addition to monitoring individual policies, underwriters must monitor books of business. Monitoring a book of business means evaluating the quality and profitability of all the business written for any group of policies. The evaluation should identify specific problems for each type of insurance, which can be subdivided into class of business, territory, producer, and other policy subgroups. Monitoring a book of business is also necessary to ensure that

Binder

A temporary written or oral agreement to provide insurance coverage until a formal written policy is issued.

Certificate of insurance

A brief description of insurance coverage prepared by an insurer or its agent and commonly used by policyholders to provide evidence of insurance.

premium volume covers the fixed costs and overhead expenses of each book of business.

Underwriters use premium and loss statistics to identify aggregate problems in a deteriorating book of business. Reviewing the book of business can also help determine compliance with underwriting policy and may detect changes in the type, volume, and quality of policies that may require corrective action.

MEASURING UNDERWRITING RESULTS

An insurer's underwriting results are a key indicator of its profitability. Without a clear understanding of their underwriting performance, insurers may not be able to respond to conditions that adversely affect them or recognize opportunities to improve their performance.

Insurers typically track their underwriting results through the use of financial and nonfinancial measures. The most common financial measure of underwriting results over a specific time period—typically one year—is the insurer's combined ratio. Proper underwriting should produce an underwriting profit or perhaps a small underwriting loss that is more than offset by investment profits. However, financial measures are not always reliable indicators of underwriting success in the short term.

Nonfinancial measures can be used to evaluate the actions of individual underwriters and underwriting departments, rather than their results.

Financial Measures

Combined ratio

A profitability ratio that indicates whether an insurer has made an underwriting loss or gain.

Many insurers use the **combined ratio** (or combined loss and expense ratio) to measure the success of underwriting activities. See the exhibit "Combined Ratio."

From an insurer's perspective, the lower the combined ratio, the better. For example, a combined ratio of 95 percent means that an insurer has an outflow of $0.95 for every premium dollar, while a combined ratio of 115 percent means that the insurer has an outflow of $1.15 for every premium dollar. Therefore, a lower combined ratio reflects higher profitability for an insurer.

Although the combined ratio is the most commonly cited measure of underwriting success, the results it produces are generally subject to an additional analysis of its components. For example, individual categories of insurer expenses may be compared with those of other insurers or industry norms, or the specific lines of business that exceeded anticipated losses may be examined. An in-depth analysis enables an insurer to make changes to its underwriting guidelines that yield desired results in the future.

Changes in premium volume, major catastrophic losses, and delays in loss reporting can distort the combined ratio, making it difficult to evaluate the effectiveness of underwriting. Additionally, any discussion of insurer

Combined Ratio

$$\text{Combined ratio (or trade-basis combined ratio)} = \frac{\text{Loss and loss adjustment expenses incurred}}{\text{Premiums earned}} + \frac{\text{Underwriting expenses incurred}}{\text{Premiums written}}$$

When the combined ratio is:

Exactly 100 percent	Every premium dollar is being used to pay claims and cover operating costs, with nothing remaining for insurer profit.
Greater than 100 percent	An underwriting loss occurs: more dollars are being paid out than are being taken in as premiums.
Less than 100 percent	An underwriting profit occurs because not all premium dollars taken in are being used for claims and expenses.

Most insurers consider any combined ratio under 100 percent to be acceptable because it indicates a profit from underwriting results, even before income from an insurer's investment activity is considered in its overall financial performance.

[DA06399]

underwriting profitability needs to be considered within the context of the underwriting cycle.

Distortions Created by Changes in Premium Volume

An insurer's combined ratio must be evaluated, taking into consideration fluctuations in premium volume and the distortions they can create. Premium volume and underwriting policy are related: restrictive underwriting policy usually reduces premium volume, while a less restrictive underwriting policy generally increases premium volume.

Changes in underwriting policy, however, often do not have the immediate effect desired. For example, an insurer that becomes more restrictive in its underwriting criteria will usually see a reduction in premiums written. Because incurred losses remain outstanding from the prior period that had a less restrictive underwriting policy, the loss ratio component of the combined ratio will likely deteriorate. With this reduction in premiums written, the expense ratio will increase, even though the insurer's underwriting expenses might have remained relatively unchanged. Similarly, a significant relaxation of underwriting standards, at least in the short term, can make an insurer appear profitable and even cost conscious when its book of business is underpriced.

Distortions Created by Major Catastrophic Losses

Underwriting results are usually evaluated annually. However, major hurricanes, major earthquakes, and other natural catastrophes occur too irregularly to be predicted annually. Floods, for example, are typically predicted over a hundred-year period. Certain flood plains are predicted to average one flood every one hundred years or, in lower-elevation areas, every ten or twenty years.

Catastrophes such as industrial explosions, airplane crashes, nuclear reactor breakdowns, or terrorist activities likewise occur with too little regularity to create a predictable pattern. Ideally, insurance rates allow for unpredicted losses. Still, a major catastrophe is likely to cause an underwriting loss for that year for most, if not all, affected insurers. However, failure to predict the unpredictable does not necessarily indicate inadequate underwriting.

Distortions Created by Delays in Loss Reporting and Loss Development

Delays in loss reporting reduce the value of the information provided by the combined ratio. If premiums and losses could be readily matched, an insurer could determine whether its book of business was underpriced and then make corrections in its pricing structure. This information is valuable to insurance regulators as well, because an inadequately priced book of business is a significant threat to an insurer's solvency.

Insurers establish a loss reserve when a claim is reported. Reserved losses are included in incurred losses and reflected in the combined ratio. The type of loss usually determines how quickly the insurer is notified of a claim and how quickly the reserve is replaced with the amount of final payment. With certain types of insurance, particularly liability insurance, a considerable amount of time can elapse between when a loss is reported and when a claim is settled. Reserves are established as soon as the loss is reported, but significant inaccuracy exists in estimating ultimate loss costs that will be paid at some future date. The longer the time between the estimate and the ultimate claim settlement, the greater the inaccuracy is likely to be.

These delays in loss reporting and loss settlement can result in an understatement of losses in one year and an overstatement in another year that appear in the combined ratio. However, these misstatements do not reflect changes in actual underwriting results.

Distortions Created by Underwriting Cycle

Historically, insurance industry underwriting cycles have consisted of a period of underwriting profits followed by a period of underwriting losses, as measured by the combined ratio. When insurers earn underwriting profits, they may use those profits to reduce their premium rates and offer broader coverage to increase their market share.

At times of underwriting losses, insurers may need to increase premium rates and restrict the availability of coverage to increase underwriting profits. These tactics may be necessary for the insurer to maintain the **policyholders' surplus** it needs to support its level of business.

Policyholders' surplus
Under statutory accounting principles (SAP), an insurer's total admitted assets minus its total liabilities.

Because premium levels, capital-allocation strategies, investment strategies, and insurer profitability are affected by this market phenomenon, insurers have tried to better understand what factors cause the underwriting cycle to shift to a different phase. Insurers essentially want to be able to maintain their competitive advantage and market share regardless of the cycle phase.

In addition, insurance regulators are concerned about the effects of the underwriting cycle on insurance availability and affordability. Although most of the factors affecting the underwriting cycle have been identified through examination of past cycles, changes in the insurance marketplace have reduced the predictive value of these factors. This increases the difficulty of determining when the next cycle phase will begin.

Individual insurers cannot change the underwriting cycle. However, effective underwriting and financial management can enable an insurer to periodically reposition itself through changes in its underwriting guidelines and allocation of capital to underwriting. This allows the insurer to maximize profits and market share growth during the cycle phases. See the exhibit "Phases of the Underwriting Cycle."

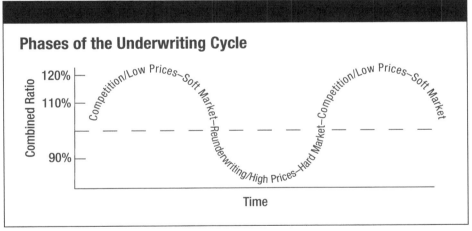

[DA02639]

Nonfinancial Measures

The success of an insurer depends on the ability of every underwriter to attain and maintain profitable results over the long term. This profitability goal is accomplished in part by using nonfinancial measures to assess performance.

Nonfinancial measures link an organization's business strategy and its outputs to its performance. These measures evaluate individual underwriters and underwriting departments based on their actions rather than on their results. If underwriters adhere strictly to underwriting guidelines, underwriting should produce favorable financial results over the long term, barring uncontrollable variables. Underwriting performance standards include these areas of underwriting:

- Selection
- Product or line-of-business mix
- Pricing
- Accommodated accounts
- Retention ratio
- Hit ratio
- Service to producers
- Premium to underwriter

Some of these nonfinancial measures apply only to commercial lines underwriting departments. Others apply to both personal and commercial lines. Portions of both types may be automated , while some measures can be evaluated during an underwriting audit. Insurer management and underwriting staff typically work together to agree on the nonfinancial measures or standards that constitute underwriting goals.

Selection

Insurers often establish selection goals for underwriters in order to ensure that the quality of the underwriter's book of business does not deteriorate. For example, an underwriter might be required to have specific percentages of its book of business be considered "highly desirable," "average," and "below average." For this type of performance standard to be effective, the insurer's underwriting guidelines need to clearly delineate among account categories. Selection standards for individual underwriters usually support overall underwriting goals and are evaluated during an underwriting audit.

Product or Line of Business Mix

Measuring product or line of business mix is one way to evaluate an underwriter's contribution to a profitable book of business. Building a proper mix in a book of business requires that underwriters have a thorough knowledge of the insurer's business goals, including the types of products it prefers to write and the insurer's appetite for certain types of risks. For example, if product liability losses are causing an adverse effect on the insurer's entire book of business, the product-mix standard might require a reduction in manufacturing classes and a concerted effort to increase the writing in the contractor, service, and mercantile classes.

This performance measure requires a statement in the insurer's underwriting guidelines of the desired product or line of business mix for new and renewal business. Underwriters are often held accountable for supporting product or line-of-business mix goals, provided that the goals are clearly stated in the insurer's underwriting guidelines.

Pricing

Insurers generally establish pricing standards as a nonfinancial measure. Pricing standards enable insurers to determine levels of premium adequacy by comparing premiums charged with the established pricing standards. In commercial insurance, for example, underwriters typically modify rates for each account being underwritten to reflect specific features of that account. Pricing standards indicate the extent to which these modifications depart from the insurer's regular, or standard, pricing. If one or more underwriters continually apply excessive premium credits to accounts to obtain new business or to retain it on renewal, an underwriting audit might reveal that profitability is being sacrificed in return for short-term growth.

Insurers use information systems to track the extent to which their underwriters deviate from the insurer's established pricing for specific classifications. This information might be useful in determining the extent to which the underwriter's book of business is underpriced or overpriced and where pricing adjustments might be made, should market conditions change.

Accommodated Accounts

Making an underwriting accommodation usually means accepting substandard exposures in return for other, more profitable accounts. Some insurers require that underwriters note the accommodation in the file for the account. Other insurers require underwriters to keep a log in which all accommodated risks are entered, along with the reasons for the accommodations. Evaluating the accommodation notes in the files or the log as part of underwriting audits and reviews can reveal whether the underwriter is making excessive accommodations and can ensure that the producer has increased volume or has fulfilled some other promise in exchange for the accommodations.

Retention Ratio

The retention ratio is the percentage of expiring policies an insurer renews. Retention can be measured by policy count, premium volume, or both. Because most, if not all, of the underwriting investigation work has been completed for existing policies, retaining those policies offers more profit potential than acquiring new business, which involves acquisition costs.

A low retention rate might indicate serious deficiencies in the way insurers do business, including poor service to producers, noncompetitive pricing, or unfavorable claims service. This standard of performance requires careful monitoring of the renewal rate and evaluation of any trends detected.

Hit Ratio

Increasingly, underwriters have dual responsibilities: they are responsible not only for underwriting a profitable book of business, but also for meeting any new business sales goals the insurer makes applicable to their book of business, which is often referred to as **production underwriting**. The **hit ratio**, sometimes called the success ratio, is a nonfinancial measure used to determine how well underwriters (or the insurer as a whole) are meeting their sales goals.

Underwriting management usually monitors this performance measure more closely than the other standards of performance because the hit ratio provides information about the insurer's competitiveness in the current insurance market. Ratios that are inordinately high or low might require further investigation. A high hit ratio might indicate any of these conditions:

- Competition is easing.
- Rates are inadequate or lower than other insurers' rates.
- Coverage is broader than other insurers'.
- The underwriter has the skill set for production underwriting.
- Underwriting-selection criteria are deteriorating.
- An extremely good relationship exists between the insurer and the producer.

A low hit ratio might indicate one of more of these conditions:

- Competition is increasing.
- Rates are higher than other insurer's rates.
- Coverages or forms are too restrictive.
- The underwriter does not have the skill set for production underwriting.
- Selection criteria are too stringent.
- Service is poor.
- A poor relationship exists between the insurer and the producer.

Service to Producers

Producers work most frequently with insurers who work most cooperatively with them. Because producers usually rank insurers on the basis of service received, an insurer must be able to evaluate its own performance.

This standard requires establishing a set of minimum acceptable standards for certain types of service to producers. The actual performance of each underwriter, branch, or region being evaluated is then compared with the targeted level of performance.

Production underwriting

Performing underwriting functions in an insurer's office as well as traveling to visit and maintain rapport with agents and sometimes clients.

Hit ratio

The ratio of insurance policies written to those that have been quoted to applicants for insurance.

Premium to Underwriter

The volume of premium an underwriter is able to handle is an often-used measure of performance. Underwriting management uses this measure to determine whether individual underwriters are assuming their share of work compared with other underwriters in the same company handling similar accounts.

SUMMARY

Line underwriters evaluate new submissions and perform renewal underwriting, usually by working directly with insurance producers and applicants. Staff underwriters, meanwhile, manage risk selection by working with line underwriters and coordinating decisions about products, pricing, and guidelines.

Underwriting authority reflects an insurer's underwriting policy. Compliance with levels of underwriting authority is important because it ensures that people with the proper experience and knowledge are making risk selection decisions.

An insurer's senior management formulates an underwriting policy to guide underwriting and the composition of the insurer's book of business. These major constraining factors are considered in establishing an underwriting policy:

- Financial capacity
- Regulation
- Personnel
- Reinsurance

Underwriting guidelines describe the parameters of acceptable applicants for insurance for which the insurer has priced its insurance products. Underwriting guidelines can provide for structured decisions and ensure consistency in overall underwriting decision making. Underwriting audits are a quality control check for uniform application of underwriting guidelines. Continuous improvement results from audits in the form of feedback to underwriters and from enhancements to the underwriting guidelines.

The underwriting process is a series of steps with related tasks applied to determine which submissions will be insured and for what amount of insurance, at what price, and under what conditions.

An insurer's underwriting results are a key indicator of its profitability. However, the combined ratio, a widely used measurement, can be distorted by changes in premium volume, major catastrophic losses, delays in loss reporting and loss development, and underwriting cycles.

Nonfinancial measures are useful in evaluating individual underwriters' and underwriting departments' performance. Such measurements include selection, accommodated accounts, service to providers, and others.

Direct Your Learning ▶▶

Risk Control and Premium Auditing

Educational Objectives

After learning the content of this assignment, you should be able to:

▷ Describe the goals of insurer risk control activities.

▷ Describe the risk control services provided by insurers.

▷ Explain how risk control cooperates with other insurer functions.

▷ Explain why premium audits are conducted and why they must be accurate.

▷ Describe the premium auditing process.

▷ Explain how premium auditing contributes to other insurer functions.

Outline

Insurer Risk Control Goals

Risk Control Services Provided by Insurers

Cooperation Between Risk Control and Other Insurer Functions

Reasons for Premium Auditing

Premium Auditing Process

Premium Auditing Contributions

Summary

5

▶▶

5.1

Risk Control and Premium Auditing

5

INSURER RISK CONTROL GOALS

The primary purpose of an insurer's risk control function is to evaluate loss exposures to assist with underwriting decisions. Another important risk control function is to recommend strategies to customers to prevent or mitigate losses.

Insurers conduct risk control activities to achieve several goals:

- Earn a profit
- Meet customer needs
- Comply with legal requirements
- Fulfill duty to society

Earn a Profit

Risk control activities can help insurers reach their profit goals in several ways:

- Improving underwriting decisions—By inspecting the premises and operations of insurance applicants, risk control representatives can improve the information on which the underwriting department bases its decisions about which applicants to accept and how to price coverage. Better underwriting information enables the insurer to do a better job of selecting insureds and pricing its coverage at a competitive level to produce an underwriting profit.

- Improving premium volume—Risk control personnel often recommend risk control measures that can change a marginal account to an acceptable account, thereby increasing the insurer's premium volume while meeting underwriting guidelines. In addition, risk control personnel and the services they offer can be instrumental in winning new business by helping producers demonstrate added value to their prospective clients.

- Encouraging insureds to improve risk control—Risk control representatives can influence insureds to implement more effective risk control initiatives by working with them to identify risk control opportunities and safety improvements.

- Reducing insureds' losses—Risk control representatives can continue to monitor insureds and suggest appropriate risk control measures as the nature or extent of the insureds' loss exposures change. Consequently, risk control representatives can reduce losses that the insurer must pay, thereby helping to keep the insurer's book of business profitable.

- Providing an additional revenue source—Traditionally, insurers provided risk control services only to their insureds and did not charge a fee in addition to the policy premium. Now, many insurers also sell unbundled risk control services to firms that have chosen to retain, or self-insure, their losses. Some insurers also provide their insureds with supplemental risk control services for a fee in addition to the policy premium. Several major insurers offer access to a variety of experts, such as nurses, ergonomic specialists, industrial hygiene specialists, engineers, attorneys, and chemists.

- Reducing errors and omissions claims against the insurer—Competent risk control service reduces the possibility of errors and omissions claims by insureds or others alleging injury because of the insurer's negligence. In addition, the errors and omissions liability loss exposure can influence an insurer's decision about what types or levels of risk control services to provide.

Meet Customer Needs

Some insurers offer risk control activities in response to the needs of insurance customers—usually their commercial and industrial customers.

These needs have resulted partly from the pressures of legislation such as the Occupational Safety and Health Act, the Consumer Products Safety Act, the Comprehensive Environmental Response Compensation and Liability Act, and the Americans with Disabilities Act. The threat of large liability judgments in certain areas has also contributed to the demand for risk control services.

By exercising sound risk control, organizations make their accounts more attractive to underwriters (especially during a hard market); help control their insurance premiums and possibly even lower them; reduce disruption to operations following accidents; remain socially responsible; comply with occupational safety and health standards; comply with local, state, and federal laws; and improve their financial performance.

Insurers who rely on the independent agency system to market their products often provide risk control services to help agents develop their relationships with insureds and potential accounts. By providing risk control services, the insurer can also experience these additional benefits:

- Enhance its relationship with the producers, staff, and customers of the independent agency
- Increase its own market share as well as that of the agency
- Attract and retain higher-quality accounts
- Help the agency and its customers accomplish their goals

By satisfying customer needs for risk control services, insurers can attract new customers, retain satisfied customers, and gain a competitive advantage over insurers that do not provide these services.

Comply With Legal Requirements

Some states require insurers to provide a minimum level of risk control service to commercial insureds. This requirement applies most often to workers compensation insurance but may also exist for other lines of coverage. Some insurers charge an additional fee for providing risk control services that exceed what the law requires. Charges for services often depend on the premium volume associated with the account. Insurers comply with these laws to not only meet the state's legal requirements and avoid financial penalties, but also to minimize the possibility of errors and omissions claims by insureds.

Fulfill Duty to Society

Insurers benefit society by providing financial resources to help individuals and businesses recover from accidental losses. However, preventing accidental losses is clearly preferable. An occupational injury can cause pain, suffering, and loss of income for an individual and his or her family. A fire at a large factory can cause loss of business income, employee layoffs, and contingent business income losses for the firm's suppliers. Accidental losses collectively have a profound adverse effect on society.

Insurers have an ethical obligation to use their expertise wisely. By assisting insureds in preventing or reducing accidental losses, insurers pursue humanitarian goals and benefit society. This is true even when the insurer derives no direct financial benefit from its risk control services.

RISK CONTROL SERVICES PROVIDED BY INSURERS

Many insurers employ individuals who specialize in risk control. Insurance personnel who perform risk control activities have varying titles, such as safety specialist, risk control specialist, loss control representative, or loss control engineer. The term "risk control representative" refers to all risk control personnel, regardless of job title. Risk control representatives are often members of an insurer's Risk Control Department.

Insurers provide three types of risk control services: conducting physical surveys, performing risk analysis and improvement, and developing safety management programs.

An insurer with the necessary resources might provide all three services for some of its insureds. Insurers' decisions regarding the risk control services they provide to their insureds are influenced by several factors, including the line of insurance provided, the size of a commercial insured, the types of loss exposures insured, and the potential legal liability.

Some insurers employ a limited number of risk control staff, or none at all. These insurers often choose to contract with private firms to provide risk control services on an as-needed basis. An insurer that has its own Risk Control Department might also contract with private firms to provide services in geographically remote areas, for highly specialized risks, or to augment its in-house staff during busy times or major underwriting initiatives.

Conducting Physical Surveys

Conducting physical surveys consists mainly of collecting underwriting information on a customer's loss exposures by looking at things like building construction type(s), worker occupations, site diagrams, and fire protection systems. During a typical survey, a risk control representative inspects a customer's premises on a walking tour and interviews the customer's management to discover details that might not be apparent from the tour. The risk control representative evaluates loss exposures and associated hazards relating to these factors:

- Fire, windstorm, water damage, burglary, and other causes of property loss
- Legal liability arising out of the premises, operations, products, completed operations, automobile use, mobile equipment, environmental impairment, and other sources of liability
- Employee injuries relative to working conditions, machinery hazards, and employee safety practices

Technology is playing an ever-increasing role in the risk control survey process. See the exhibit "Technology's Growing Impact on the Survey Process."

In addition to evaluating loss exposures and physical hazards, risk control representatives determine management's ability to control exposures effectively. Specifically, they look at the level of the management team's experience, and for consistent use of rules and procedures, use of engineering controls and protective clothing, and safety systems such as safety committees and job safety analysis.

Two key components of successful risk control measures are management's commitment to risk control and employee attitudes about safety. By carefully evaluating management's approach to accident prevention, the risk control representative can obtain important insight into the possibility and extent of **moral hazards** and **morale hazards**.

After completing the walking tour, the risk control representative meets with management to ask questions, discuss loss exposures and hazards, and provide recommendations for controlling hazards. Then, he or she organizes the information in a formal report and sends the report to the insured, along with any resource information to help implement the recommendations.

Moral hazard

A condition that increases the likelihood that a person will intentionally cause or exaggerate a loss.

Morale hazard (attitudinal hazard)

A condition of carelessness or indifference that increases the frequency or severity of loss.

Technology's Growing Impact on the Survey Process

Mobile inspection and survey software allows risk control representatives to input survey data, property measurements, and photos in real time from smartphones, laptops, and tablets into an insurer's central database. This software can facilitate the automatic creation of letters, assignments, and reports, as well as increase data accuracy by eliminating the need to forward paper survey forms to other individuals in the Risk Control Department who would then have to enter the data manually into the insurer's database.

The biggest example of the growing influence of technology on the risk control survey process is the use of drones in property inspections and monitoring. The recent loosening of Federal Aviation Administration regulations on drone usage has paved the way for wide adoption of commercial applications.

Because of the ease with which drones can reach areas that are difficult or dangerous for humans to access—like rooftops, towers, smokestacks, construction sites, mines, pipelines, and catastrophe sites—insurers are increasingly deploying drones in the survey and inspection process. Drones can take high-quality photos, videos, and measurements of areas difficult and often expensive for people to access. New software also allows drones to automatically flag problematic conditions like damage, corrosion, and flooding.

[DA12786]

Resource information might include training materials, an example of a written safety program, a self-inspection checklist template, or regulatory compliance information. Risk control correspondence is typically shared with the Underwriting Department and producer, and it may also be shared with the Claims Department and other areas.

The risk control representative's written recommendations can help a customer eliminate or control loss exposures. And they help the Underwriting Department and the producer follow up on the customer's progress in addressing the identified hazards.

Typically, recommendations are generated when a risk control representative identifies a loss exposure that falls below a satisfactory level. With merchant loss exposures, for example, a common recommendation is to control slip-and-fall hazards by improving the maintenance program for aisles, steps, and stairwells.

Recommendations should be as practical as possible, conform to industry and regulatory standards, and be explained in enough detail to allow successful implementation by the insured. While the cost of addressing a particular hazard should be considered, it should not stop the implementation of a recommendation. When the cost of addressing a hazard in the traditional manner is prohibitive, more cost-effective alternatives should be offered to control risk. A simple cost-benefit analysis can be done to help ensure that recommendations are not unnecessarily burdensome. Too often, recommendations are limited to fixing what is broken or upgrading an item to meet regulatory standards. It is in the best interest of the insured and the insurer to offer recommendations that are not merely minimum requirements but, in fact, best practices.

A survey report might also include information about a property valuation (appraisal) that has been conducted by others. This can be important if the actual value differs from the coverage limits requested by the customer. For example, if a customer has requested $500,000 insurance coverage (actual cash basis) on an older building, and a professional appraisal values that building at $750,000 (functional replacement cost basis), a coverage gap can be avoided. The underwriter, and even the producer, might use a software program to determine the current estimated value of a property. However, most insurers choose to avoid making an official determination of property values for policy-limit purposes, as doing so can subject them to errors and omissions claims.

Physical surveys provide benefits to both the underwriter and the insured in these ways:

- The survey report helps the underwriter gain a better understanding of the loss exposures being insured. Underwriters often provide an insurance quote with the condition that various risk control recommendations in the survey report be implemented.

- The insured can gain a better understanding of its loss exposures and the steps that could be taken to reduce losses, comply with laws and regulations, and provide a better working environment for employees, all of which can increase employee morale and productivity.

- If a property valuation is part of the survey, the insured can be more confident of an adequate recovery in the event of a total loss and less likely to incur a coinsurance penalty in the event of a partial loss.

Performing Risk Analysis and Improvement

In addition to completing a physical survey and loss exposure and hazard evaluation, the risk control representative might analyze the customer's loss history (risk analysis) and submit recommendations (improvements) to the business owner or manager about how to reduce hazards that have led to previous losses. A risk control representative or the producer usually contacts the insured to follow up on the insured's progress in complying with the recommendations. Some insurers' risk control departments follow up on recommendations on a scheduled basis—for example, sixty to ninety days from when the recommendations were made. Depending on the procedures of the particular insurer, follow-up might also occur as part of the renewal process.

Some insurers require the producer to conduct the follow-up. However, the process can also be handled using risk control management software that can be accessed by the insurer and the insured simultaneously. Using this software, the insurer (or one of its risk control representatives) can input recommendations into a program, which then notifies the insured that a recommendation was made. Often, the insurer can use this software to track recommendations until resolution, assigning and monitoring individual tasks remotely. This can eliminate the need for phone calls and frequent check-ins. Ultimately, the goal is for the Underwriting Department to obtain confirmation from the insured that the recommendations were implemented.

To support the risk analysis and improvement effort, the insurer's risk control representatives can provide training, information, or counseling services, such as these:

- Coordinated safety programs
- Technical risk-control information resources
- Workers compensation risk management strategies
- Fire protection systems testing and evaluation
- Preconstruction counseling

A safety training program includes a series of presentations on safety-related subjects to raise workers' awareness of loss exposures and appropriate safety behaviors. Typically, the subjects covered are fire safety, driver safety, and machine operation safety. Subjects are selected based on an analysis of the insured's loss exposures or trends in loss experience. Priority is given to subjects that could significantly improve the insured's loss experience. Videos and slide shows can be shown in conjunction with training programs or sent to insureds upon request.

Safety programs can help develop positive safety attitudes among all workers, improve workers' understanding of safety-related matters, and help workers accept responsibility for their role in the organization's safety program. To prepare the insured's managers for assuming a leadership role in risk control, the insurer might also conduct supervisory safety training sessions.

A written safety program is a collection of policies and procedures the insured uses in its operations to facilitate risk control. Written safety programs generally include information on awareness and training, life safety, accident reporting and investigation, reporting of safety concerns, employee responsibilities, supervisory responsibilities, and regulatory compliance.

Many insurers also serve as a source of technical risk control information. Information sought by the insured might relate to specific hazards and controls, the interpretation of standards, or particular safety management products or suppliers. By providing this information, the insurer helps the insured save time and effort when making risk control decisions. Doing so also helps the insurer build a relationship with the insured, which can help retain the insured's business.

When business owners expand existing facilities or build new structures, they often overlook the connection between construction features and insurance rates. Generally, rating credits can be given for noncombustible or fire-resistive construction, sprinkler systems, smoke detectors, burglar alarms, security hardware, and other features. A preconstruction review by the insurer of the drawings and specifications allows the insured to see how insurance rates and underwriting acceptability will be affected by the new construction. Any plan alterations can be made more cost-effectively before construction begins.

Apply Your Knowledge

Following a tour of an insured's retail facility, Thomas, a risk control representative from Sota Insurance, provides a recommendation to the retailer for controlling a hazard he identified during his survey of the building. However, the retailer says the cost of addressing the hazard in the traditional manner is prohibitive. What should Thomas do next in regard to the hazard?

a.   Require the retailer to address the hazard exactly as recommended

b.   Offer more cost-effective solutions to control risk

c.   Waive the need for the retailer to address the hazard

d.   Hire a contractor to address the hazard

Feedback: b. When the cost of addressing a hazard in the traditional manner is prohibitive, more cost-effective alternatives should be offered to control risk. A simple cost-benefit analysis can be done to help ensure that recommendations are not unnecessarily burdensome.

Developing Safety Management Programs

The development of safety management programs is often coordinated by senior risk control staff, as they generally have the advanced technical and communication skills needed for more in-depth consultation work.

Developing safety management programs begins with a complete evaluation of the insured's operations, just as in risk analysis and improvement risk control services. After reviewing the evaluation, the more experienced risk control representative or risk control consultant assists the insured in establishing risk control goals, selecting appropriate risk control measures, organizing the resources necessary to implement the chosen risk control measures, and establishing procedures to monitor the program.

Because of several concerns, the insured is ordinarily responsible for implementing the program on a daily basis without direct assistance from the risk control consultant. These concerns include errors and omissions liability, lack of authority to exercise a management role in the insured's business, and the need for management to have program ownership.

After being implemented, the program must be monitored to determine whether adjustments are needed. The risk control consultant can provide a great deal of technical assistance in the monitoring phase of the program.

The consultation process normally requires several visits to the insured's premises to gather initial information, plan the review with management, and follow up to monitor the program. Depending on the needs, abilities, and preferences of the insured, ongoing risk control visits may occur on a semiannual, quarterly, or monthly basis.

Factors Affecting Service Levels

Every insurer must decide what levels of risk control service to provide and which insureds to accept as clients for such service. Several factors influence insurers' decisions.

Line of Insurance

One of the factors that will influence an insurer's decision about the level and type of risk control service to provide is the line of insurance. An insurer that writes only personal insurance is unlikely to provide extensive risk control services. The relatively small premium for a typical personal auto or homeowners account does not justify the cost of on-site safety inspections.

During personal insurance underwriting, insurers sometimes request that their agents or salespeople photograph a house or an auto (the latter to verify a car's vehicle identification number). Insurers might provide producers with checklists to ensure that certain items are either requested specifically of the applicant or identified during the producer's drive-by inspection. Producers can effectively implement risk control programs when insurers provide explicit instructions. When insuring exceptionally high-value property, such as a mansion or yacht, the insurer might use specially trained risk control representatives to develop underwriting information or recommendations for reducing physical hazards.

In addition to conducting on-site inspections, an insurer can promote risk control among its personal lines insureds by publishing educational bulletins or offering rate discounts for home security systems, deadbolt locks, automobile plug-in monitoring equipment (telematics), anti-theft devices, driver education, or other risk control measures.

Commercial Insured Size

The large premiums generated by commercial insureds and the increased values at risk often make it economically feasible to provide these insureds with risk control services. The level of service rendered to a commercial insured can depend on the size of the account. Typically, an insurer devotes more resources to accounts that generate a substantial premium. Still, some insurers make risk control services available to smaller accounts that request them.

Insurers may provide options for insureds to purchase supplemental risk control services. By not including the cost for such supplemental services in the premium, insurers allow insureds who do not want or need these additional services to avoid subsidizing the costs associated with them.

Types of Loss Exposures Insured

The risk control services an insurer provides depend to some degree on the types of loss exposures the insurer is willing to cover. An insurer that covers large and complex industrial firms needs skilled personnel and sophisticated equipment to meet those firms' risk control requirements, including these:

- Testing and evaluating the effects of noise levels on employees
- Assessing the hazards to employees from solvents, toxic metals, radioactive isotopes, and other substances
- Assisting in the design of explosion suppression systems or fire-extinguishing systems for dangerous substances or easily damaged equipment
- Evaluating products liability loss exposures and preparing programs to minimize such loss exposures
- Consulting on complex and specialized risk control problems

An insurer that deals primarily with habitational, mercantile, and small manufacturing loss exposures might be able to maintain a less-sophisticated Risk Control Department.

Potential Legal Liability

Making recommendations to existing insureds is an important risk management tool for insurers. However, the threat of being named in a lawsuit for negligence in providing risk control services may lead some insurers to choose not to offer risk control services or limit what they offer.

Some states have enacted statutes that protect insurers by preventing insureds, their employees, and third parties (including applicants) from bringing suit against an insurer for injuries or damages sustained as a result of providing, or failing to provide, risk control services. Although relatively infrequent, negligent inspection claims do occur. If an insurer's Underwriting Department chooses to require certain controls as a prerequisite to providing coverage, such controls should be expressed as conditions of the insurance quote and the subsequent insurance agreement, rather than risk control recommendations to avoid exposure to potential legal liability.

COOPERATION BETWEEN RISK CONTROL AND OTHER INSURER FUNCTIONS

An insurer's risk control efforts are most effective when they complement the activities of its other departments and various external organizations.

Cooperation between risk control representatives and the representatives of other insurer functions can improve the quality of information available to an insurer and the services it offers. Insurers and insureds can also benefit from cooperative relationships between the risk control function and various external organizations, particularly producers.

These are the principal opportunities for risk control cooperation:

- Underwriting
- Marketing and sales
- Premium auditing
- Claims
- Producers

Underwriting

The risk control function provides information to underwriters that enables them to make better underwriting decisions. This information consists primarily of field inspection reports on the premises and operations of new applicants and existing insureds renewing their policies. Inspection reports should provide a clear profile of the applicant's loss exposures and related hazards. Additionally, an insurer's Risk Control Department can provide technical support to its Underwriting Department in many areas, such as fire hazards of new building materials, health hazards of materials or production processes, and new techniques or equipment for materials handling.

The risk control function can also help underwriters modify a new applicant's loss exposures to meet eligibility requirements. After an applicant has been accepted, risk control can help the insured to remain within underwriting guidelines and qualify for policy renewal. Risk control can even help "rehabilitate" a marginal account that underwriting has accepted because of competitive considerations.

Marketing and Sales

The risk control function also can be instrumental in helping the insurer's marketing and sales staff meet its goals. By evaluating an applicant's premises and operations, interviewing management staff, and evaluating the nature of historical losses, risk control representatives can help determine if an applicant's current risk controls are acceptable or if there are ways to improve an accepted applicant's risk controls. The risk control representative's evaluation can make the difference between an applicant's acceptance or rejection.

By making marginal accounts acceptable, risk control helps marketing reach its sales goals. Risk control can also help marketing by proving to applicants and insureds that the insurer understands their business operations and associated hazards, and is prepared to help them protect their interests. The risk control representative can offer crucial advice on improving safety.

After applicants become insureds, risk control can play a key role in retaining them as customers. In fact, a commercial insured might have more regular contact with the insurer's risk control representatives than with any other employee of the insurer. By providing professional and courteous service, risk control personnel can create customer goodwill.

Premium Auditing

In one respect, the roles of risk control representatives and premium auditors are similar, because both visit the insured's premises and have direct insured contact. However, risk control representatives typically visit the insured at the beginning of the policy period and as needed throughout the policy period, while premium auditors visit at the end of the policy period. Premium auditors often visit the insured after the point at which recordkeeping deficiencies resulting from the insured's lack of knowledge or misunderstanding can be corrected. Risk control personnel can use the opportunity provided by their own inspections, as well as information from recent premium audits, to help improve insured documentation and the accuracy of premium audits. During the premium auditing process, a new exposure or an increase in exposure that is discovered by an auditor can prompt risk control involvement.

To take advantage of this opportunity, however, premium auditors must communicate their needs to risk control representatives so that they can, for example, note the location of the accounting records and the name of the person to contact at audit time. They can also record the names, titles, and duties of executive officers.

The risk control representative's description of operations could be a starting point for the auditor's classification of loss exposures. They might help estimate the payroll by classification or at least the number of employees per department. They can report the existence of any new operations. If properly informed, they can also advise the insured about recordkeeping requirements and the need for good risk transfer practices, including certificates of insurance with additional insured-specific language and written contracts that include hold-harmless language.

Claims

A partnership between risk control and claims can be just as valuable to an insurer as the partnership between risk control and underwriting, marketing, or premium auditing. The Risk Control Department needs claims experience information to direct risk control resources and efforts to crucial areas. The Claims Department relies on risk control for loss exposure data and background information that can support the loss adjusting process. Claims and risk control personnel should discuss common concerns and review loss cases regularly. The claims experience information that can be useful to the risk control function includes frequency and severity of losses by type of insurance, by cause of loss, by the kind of business the insured engages in, and by worker occupation.

Regarding individual accidents, particularly in the workers compensation area, risk control can also benefit from information about the type of accident, the body part injured, how the accident occurred, and perhaps other details from the adjuster's report. Risk control staff can use this information for these purposes:

• Identifying areas for research

• Targeting loss exposures for additional attention

• Identifying characteristics associated with particular types of losses

• Developing alternatives to control losses

Risk control representatives are usually well informed in engineering, mechanical, and technological areas with which claims personnel might be unfamiliar. Therefore, the Risk Control Department can provide codes, standards, technical advice, laboratory analyses, valuable insight based on experience, and other assistance to the Claims Department when investigating and settling claims. A risk control specialist can design product recall procedures to assist claims personnel and insureds in controlling specific product losses. Risk control representatives can also support the claims function by reviewing and emphasizing the importance of thorough loss documentation and proper claims reporting procedures.

Producers

Traditionally, producers encouraged the insured's risk control activities and coordinated the efforts of the insurer's risk control representatives with the insured. Producers still perform this role. However, many large agencies and brokerages maintain their own Risk Control departments, and some can furnish services equivalent to those offered by insurers. If an insured is receiving risk control services from both the insurer and its producer, the risk control entities of both organizations should strive to coordinate their efforts for the mutual benefit of all parties involved, particularly the insured.

REASONS FOR PREMIUM AUDITING

Premium auditing plays a vital role in insurance. With knowledge of insurance principles, accounting procedures, and particular state regulations, premium auditors can obtain the information needed to calculate premiums accurately and collect the data used to establish future insurance rates. By ensuring the accuracy of the information on which insurance premiums are based, premium auditing helps make the insurance mechanism work as intended and supports the insurer's profit goal by making sure appropriate premiums are charged for policies provided. Accurate premium auditing also contributes to insureds' confidence that they are being treated fairly.

Insurers conduct premium audits for these reasons:

- To determine correct premiums
- To collect ratemaking data
- To meet regulatory requirements
- To deter and detect fraud
- To reinforce insureds' confidence
- To obtain additional information

The need for a premium audit arises because some insurance policies have adjustable premiums. For these kinds of policies, loss exposure varies substantially by individual insured. A standard premium rate might be far from reflecting an insured's actual exposure to loss. When entering an adjustable premium contract, the insured pays a standard premium, which is adjusted the following year based on the actual loss exposure. Adjustable premium policies include a clause that allows the insurer to perform premium audits to determine the actual amount of **exposure units** on which the premium will be based.

Exposure unit

A fundamental measure of the loss exposure assumed by an insurer.

For many commercial insurance policies, the premium paid at the beginning of the policy period is a provisional premium based on an estimate of the extent of operations to be insured. At the end of the policy period, typically one year, the insured's records are examined, or audited, by a premium auditor to determine the exposure units. After the auditor reports the data, the audit processors apply the rates and various factors, such as **experience modification** and premium discounts, to determine the final earned premium. If the insured's operations were more extensive than estimated, an additional premium is charged. If less extensive, the insured receives a partial refund.

Experience modification

A rate multiplier derived from the experience rating computation.

Accuracy in premium audits is critical. If audit errors go undetected, some insureds may pay more than their proportional share for covered loss exposures, while others may pay less than their share. Auditing errors also result in incorrect experience modifications, which leads to incorrect premiums. Plus, if an error is detected, the rating bureau cannot calculate the correct experience modification until it receives the correct data. In addition, errors in premiums can reduce insureds' confidence in auditors, the insurer, and insurance in general.

Premium auditing is performed for many coverages, including workers compensation, general liability, and commercial auto policies for large fleets. Although premium auditing most often involves liability insurance, some property insurance policies, such as those covering fluctuating inventory values, are also subject to premium audit.

Determine Correct Premiums

The primary reason for premium auditing is to determine the correct premium for the policy period. The insurer bears this responsibility.

Unless premiums are sufficient for the loss exposures covered, the insurer cannot operate profitably. If, however, the insurer overcharges the insured, it will certainly encounter negative reactions when the error is discovered and will probably lose the insured's business. As a result, the premium determination process requires certainty and precision. A premium audit provides that accuracy.

When a policy is written subject to audit, the actual premium can be calculated only after the end of the policy period, when the exact exposure units or premium bases during the period are known. In most cases, the applicable manual for the type of insurance involved has rules that strictly define the procedure to be followed, specifying inclusions and exclusions in the premium base and defining distinct rating classifications.

For example, for workers compensation coverage, manual rules specifically indicate how to assign payroll for clerical or construction employees. Mastering these rules requires considerable effort and practice.

Insureds have the accounting information or other data that is used to determine the premium base, but they rarely understand insurance manual rules well enough to present the information in the form in which insurers need it. As a result, a skilled premium auditor, employed by the insurer, usually assembles the information and determines the actual earned premium. Even if the insured can provide the premium data requested, having a premium auditor inspect the original books of account (in which business transactions are initially recorded) makes the insurer more confident that the data is accurate. However, because of staff shortages, heavy workloads, expenses, or company policies, some insurers do not have their own premium auditors and may rely on voluntary audit reports or external premium auditing consultants.

A premium audit is also important to provide the insurer with current and accurate information to determine whether the renewal premium estimate is in line with the audited exposures. This allows the insurer to collect sufficient premium in advance in the event that the insured experiences financial problems during the policy period, which could make collection of a retrospective premium adjustment difficult.

Incorrect or incomplete audits can cause extra work for several insurer departments. For example, redoing the audit drains resources from the Premium Audit Department, other departments may have to explain the error and perform damage control with insureds, the Underwriting Department may have to correct records, the Accounting Department may have to issue corrected bills, the Marketing Department may have to regain insureds' confidence, and the Premium Collection Department may have to spend time resolving payment or billing issues. See the exhibit "The Importance of Premium Auditing for the Insurer."

The Importance of Premium Auditing for the Insurer

A prompt and accurate premium audit can benefit the insurer's financial position in three ways:

- Accurate classification of loss exposures helps ensure equitable and accurate insurance rates. For example, misclassifying hazardous business into a lower-rated classification results in loss of premium volume, which might make an otherwise-profitable policy unprofitable.

- Delay in audits and the resulting billing delay can hurt the insurer's cash flow. Even more important is the effect of increasing the deposit premium for a renewal policy based on the premium audit. Keeping the deposit premiums at a realistic level provides additional cash at policy inception and prevents collection problems later.

- Premium that has been developed by audit is fully earned and, consequently, has an immediate effect on profit and policyholders' surplus (an insurer's assets minus total liabilities), which represents an insurer's net worth and ability to write new business.

[DA12785]

Collect Ratemaking Data

Insurance advisory organizations collect ratemaking data and, in most cases, project the costs of future losses, or loss costs. To these loss costs, insurers add their own expense component to determine a final insurance rate.

Calculating actuarially credible rates begins with data about claim payments, earned premiums, and insured exposure units for each rating classification. Claims reports provide the necessary information on claims for a given period. The premium volume and total insured loss exposures by class are determined by compiling data from premium audits.

A detailed classification breakdown of exposure units obtained by a premium audit is necessary for the insurer's statistical report to the advisory rating organizations (rating bureaus), as well as for billing purposes. When an advisory organization has credible statistics showing premium volume, loss experience, and total insured exposure units for each rating class, its actuaries can calculate appropriate loss costs that are used to establish rates. This data usually must be filed with state regulators to support rate increases or other rate filings. Lack of consistency in audit classification of loss exposure causes inequity not only in the level of current premium paid but also in the resulting distortion of the classification of loss results, which can negatively affect future rates.

Premium audits affect the equity and accuracy of rates in two ways:

- Classification determinations—If premium auditors in one area of a state consider a particular industrial class to be in classification X, while the premium auditors in another part of the state consider it to be in class Y, then the inconsistency distorts the resulting loss data from both classes and leads to inequitable rates for all insureds in the state for those two classes. Equally important is accurately classifying claims. By notifying the Claims Department when additional classifications are assigned and by reviewing the classification of past claims at the time of an audit, premium auditors can assist the Claims Department in accurately classifying losses as well as loss exposures.
- Measurement of the exposure unit base—An audit error, not in classification but in determining the exposure units, also distorts the rate structure. Either underreporting or overreporting the exposure units affects the rate for that class.

Meet Regulatory Requirements

Although requirements vary by state, premium audits are often required to meet workers compensation insurance regulations. Compared with other types of insurance, workers compensation regulation tends to be more restrictive because of the compulsory nature of the coverage.

Uniform workers compensation rules and rates are usually prescribed even in states allowing open competition for other types of insurance. The rules in some states stipulate that the insurer must audit the records of insureds that meet certain criteria, usually related to premium size or type of business, within specific time frames, such as every three years.

Deter and Detect Fraud

Premium auditing tends to deter fraud. Insureds are less likely to submit false or misleading information to an insurer when they know the information might be verified by a premium auditor.

Although uncovering fraud is not the primary purpose of premium auditing, premium auditors have often uncovered deceptive business practices during routine audits. Such discoveries can lead to a maze of falsified or missing records. The insurer's usual recourse is not to renew the policy, and those decisions depend on accurate and precise information from the auditor. Therefore, even when performed randomly, premium audits are an effective control on the integrity of the premium computation and collection process.

Reinforce Insureds' Confidence

Accurate premium audits can contribute to insureds' confidence that they are receiving fair treatment. Seeing that premiums are computed from a meticulous audit, in which the auditor exercised due care collecting and verifying data, counters the notion that premium adjustments are arbitrary and conveys to insureds they are, and in fact must be, treated according to uniform and equitable standards. A good premium auditor also explains the audit procedure to the insured so that a premium adjustment will not be a surprise.

In addition, an insured with a favorable impression of the insurer is less likely to look for another insurer at renewal time or when the need for additional coverage arises. Having gained from the audit procedure a greater understanding of how the premium is determined, an insured might also improve record keeping, especially when having organized records reduces the premium. The insured might even be more receptive to risk control advice after a well-conducted premium audit. Conversely, insureds who experience an inaccurate premium audit might be less cooperative when it comes to claims investigations, paying premium bills, or implementing risk control advice, and they may be more inclined to consider switching to another insurer.

Obtain Additional Information

A premium audit might generate additional underwriting information about the insured, such as an incorrect classification or a new loss exposure the underwriter had not previously identified. A premium audit can also identify all named insureds on the policy to make sure all exposures from additional entities are included in the premium. Such information can be extremely useful to the underwriter in determining whether to renew a policy.

Premium audit information can also identify marketing opportunities and assist the Claims Department in adjusting certain types of losses. Finally, a premium audit is a source of feedback on the insurer's image and effectiveness.

Apply Your Knowledge

The premium auditors for Danforth Insurance Co., an insurer operating in the western part of a state, consider a commercial industry exposure to be Classification X. The premium auditors for Forthley Insurance Co., an insurer operating in the eastern part of the state, consider the same commercial industry exposure to be Classification Y. How will these different classifications likely affect insurance rates in the state?

a. They will drop rates equally for all insureds in those two classes.

b. They will raise rates equally for all insureds in those two classes.

c. They will lead to inequitable rates for all insureds in those two classes.

d. They will lead to similar rates for all insureds in those two classes.

Feedback: c. The inconsistency between the companies' premium auditors distorts the resulting loss data from both classes and leads to inequitable rates for all insureds in the state in those two classes.

PREMIUM AUDITING PROCESS

Premium auditors must follow a systematic process for each audit. This helps ensure that their information is accurate and complete and that their work is reliable.

At each stage of the auditing process, premium auditors make judgments and decide how to proceed. To proceed, they sometimes need more information about the insured's operations, additional records, or an explanation of a discrepancy. These judgments are necessary because premium auditors must be satisfied that the information they receive is reasonable and reliable.

These are the typical stages of the premium auditing process:

- Planning
- Reviewing operations
- Determining employment relationships
- Finding and evaluating books and records
- Auditing the books or records
- Analyzing and verifying premium-related data
- Reporting the findings

Each stage is not necessarily a clearly defined step; many of them blend into each other.

Planning

Planning greatly improves a premium audit's efficiency and quality. Insurers cannot afford to audit every policy every year, so they must decide which ones warrant the expense. In some cases, an insurer might determine that an audit is not worth the cost and elect to waive it, if permitted by regulators. Factors that weigh into this decision include the policy and its endorsements, prior audit reports, and the reliability of the insured's voluntary report.

A voluntary report (also called a policyholder's report) is a form the insured completes and returns to the insurer. The insurer includes instructions to help the insured compile the **exposure unit (unit of exposure)** information required to adjust the premium for the expired policy period. Once the insurer receives the voluntary report, it might choose to accept it (to perform a two-year audit at the end of the next policy period) or to initiate an immediate field audit to confirm the voluntary report.

Exposure unit (unit of exposure)
The unit of measure (for example, area, gross receipts, payroll) used to determine an insurance policy premium.

To conduct a field audit (also called a physical audit), an auditor examines the insured's books and records at the insured's premises. For each audit, the auditor must anticipate the classification and loss exposure concerns and determine the premium base and any necessary allocations. The next step is to plan how to approach the audit, what records to use, how to locate the records, how much time to dedicate to the audit, whom to contact, and which questions to ask.

The decision of whether to conduct a field audit is influenced by legal requirements, premium size, the insured's operations, prior audit experience, the nature of the policy, the cost of auditing, geographical factors, and staffing requirements. For example, a workers compensation audit might be legally required, and advisory organizations' rules usually require audits of all policies with a premium above a certain amount and might restrict audit waivers to no more than two in a row. Advisory organizations' rules might also restrict classification changes.

When planning both mandatory and discretionary audits, some audit teams use predictive modeling. This can help with mandatory audits by scheduling the order of audits (according to contract terms) with the goal of affecting the insurer's earned premium in the most optimal way. For discretionary audits, auditors may use modeling to determine not only which insureds to audit but also how to audit them.

Reviewing Operations

Before they look at the books, skilled premium auditors determine the nature of the operation being insured; compare it with similar businesses; look for classifications that might not be on the policy; assess management's quality and cooperation to determine how to proceed with the audit; and report significant information to the Underwriting Department. Additionally, auditors note organizational changes and stay alert for clues about changes in the nature and direction of the insured's business.

The process the premium auditor uses is also known as auditing the risk, rather than auditing the policy. By reviewing the operations, organization, and business processes, the premium auditor notes existing exposures and reports changes or additional exposures, both new and previously unidentified, to the underwriter. The underwriter may request additional information from the insured or have a risk control representative inspect the operation and make recommendations. If an auditor identifies new exposures, the underwriter may decide to cancel the policy, not renew it, or propose coverage changes.

Some audit and underwriting teams also use predictive modeling during this stage. Advanced software can take raw data obtained from the insured and turn it into indicators that can help predict future outcomes—most notably, the potential for future losses. Predictive modeling can help modify or develop rating plans and improve premium accuracy.

Insureds may fail to communicate changes in operations. Even if such information is reported, it might be faulty or otherwise insufficient for underwriting purposes. A premium auditor should supply the Underwriting Department with details sufficient for rating purposes.

In addition, the auditor should indicate the proper classifications for any new loss exposures. The Underwriting Department will also want information on the experience of a new operation's management, its financing, its marketing, the basis of its income, and any unusual hazards.

The Insurance Services Office, Inc. (ISO) Premium Audit Advisory Service (PAAS) offers numerous guides and publications to assist premium auditors as they review insureds' operations. Classification guides (available electronically) provide detailed descriptions of all ISO general liability classifications and National Council on Compensation Insurance (NCCI) workers compensation classifications, as well as state exceptions to these classifications. PAAS also publishes a series of e-bulletins to provide updates relevant to premium auditors.

Determining Employment Relationships

After analyzing the insured's operations, premium auditors must determine which employees are covered by insurance with payroll-based premium—but this not always simple. For example, payroll might constitute the premium base for both workers compensation and general liability policies, but each coverage might define "employee" differently.

The premium basis of workers compensation policies includes the payroll of every person considered an employee under workers compensation laws. Therefore, the premium auditor must distinguish between employees and independent contractors (who are not covered under workers compensation). Moreover, applicable workers compensation laws vary by state. Many insureds do not realize that they must obtain certificates of insurance from their subcontractors; otherwise, premium auditors must include the subcontractors' payroll in the premium base.

Each state has also imposed regulations regarding workers compensation for corporate officers, sole proprietors, and partners. Most states exclude sole proprietors and partners from workers compensation coverage, although coverage may be extended to them under the voluntary compensation endorsement. Some states allow corporate officers to be excluded, and all states regulate the payroll amount to be used to set the premium for corporate officers.

Many states' workers compensation **Test Audit** programs also review the claims filed under workers compensation policies to verify that injured employees were valid employees or under the insured's direction and control, that they were subject to coverage, and that their class assignment is correct. This process was developed to validate the ratemaking process and the experience-modification calculation. As a result, many insurers require their

Test Audit

An audit conducted by an insurance advisory organization or bureau to check the accuracy of insurers' premium audits.

premium auditors to review and verify the claims for each workers compensation audit.

Finding and Evaluating Books or Records

Premium auditors can examine all of the insured's books or records related to insurance premiums. Auditors must decide, however, which records provide the necessary information most efficiently and reliably. They must evaluate the accounting system to determine record accuracy and identify any alternative sources that can confirm the data. The quality of the insured's accounting system and records can reflect the quality of its management. Low-quality accounting records will reduce the auditor's confidence in their reliability and accuracy, so the auditor should take special care to verify the information obtained from those records.

Sophisticated technology, like blockchain, can increase efficiency and decrease the resources needed in this stage of the premium audit process. See the exhibit "Blockchain's Impact on Premium Auditing."

Blockchain's Impact on Premium Auditing

Blockchain technology is a giant leap forward in digital recordkeeping. It is a decentralized, real-time ledger and data-storage technology that contains a history of transactions that cannot be altered or hacked.

For both insurers and insureds, blockchain's advantage is that it enables transactions among authorized participants to be approved and recorded immediately, without the need for an official recordkeeper or third party to act as an intermediary. It creates an instantaneous and permanent transaction record that can be viewed (in read-only format) by authorized entities, like an insurer and its audit team.

Blockchains can eliminate the need to verify the accuracy of insureds' data. As a result, rather than having to spend time trying to double-check past data, audit teams can now spend more time on forward-looking functions, like predictive analysis or forecasting. This could not only lower expense ratios, but also improve the accuracy of the ratemaking process.

[DA12793]

In addition to meeting accounting standards, insureds should set up their records to take full advantage of insurance rules and requirements. Producers can assist with this. For example, insureds should separate their payroll records by classification and arrange their records so that auditors can easily identify previously unreported classifications. Payroll records should identify the overtime **premium pay (shift differential)**, which is not typically included in the premium basis. Severance and per diem pay can be excluded. However, other forms of compensation are included, such as vacation pay, tool allowances, bonuses, commissions, sick pay, the value of board and lodging, and certain types of nonmonetary compensation.

Premium pay (shift differential)

A payroll system that increases the regular hourly wage rate for the night shift or other special conditions.

The premium auditor's role includes determining what benefits and compensation are included in both the workers compensation premium base and the general liability premium base. The PAAS Chart of State Exceptions can help the premium auditor make these determinations. See the exhibit "Example of Premium Auditor's Determination of Excludable Benefits."

Example of Premium Auditor's Determination of Excludable Benefits

For nonunion construction companies that are required to pay prevailing wage rates, fringe benefits (additional benefits paid by employers in addition to wages), that are usually paid to the union at union companies, may be deducted for workers compensation premium calculation. These fringe benefits, however, would not be deducted for general liability premium calculations.

[DA06137]

For large accounts, auditors frequently visit the business either before or shortly after the insurer accepts the account. During this pre-audit survey, the premium auditor confirms the information on the application and may help establish bookkeeping procedures.

Auditing the Books and Records

The auditor's job involves not only counting the loss exposures but also classifying them correctly, which can be complex. Rating manuals contain numerous rules and exceptions, and insureds' operations change over time. A premium audit can uncover any classification changes necessary to revise coverage, particularly when a policy does not generate a large enough premium to justify an on-site inspection or risk control report.

The premium auditor's expertise with classification questions can help underwriters maintain the proper classifications of the insured's operations and align the **deposit premium** with the loss exposures covered by the policy. Proper classifications are important—if a classification is wrong and the rate on the policy is too high, the insured is overcharged; if the classification is wrong and the rate on the policy is too low, the account is less likely to be profitable for the insurer.

When premium auditors examine the insured's accounting records, they must decide how much evidence is sufficient to determine the loss exposures and classifications. If evidence is not readily available, auditors must decide whether its potential effect on the audit is worth the resources required to obtain it.

When the insured uses an automated accounting system, the premium auditor must evaluate the system's capabilities and the accounting process's reliability, decide what data to accept, and decide what additional data to request. If the

Deposit premium

The amount the primary insurer pays the reinsurer pending the determination of the actual reinsurance premium owed.

data does not include all the necessary information, the premium auditor must determine the steps to take to obtain the information; making the effort at the beginning of the audit to arrange for the computer to produce the necessary data can save time.

Analyzing and Verifying Premium-Related Data

Once premium auditors have obtained the data needed to calculate the premium, they must decide whether the data is reasonable. The premium auditor might ask these questions:

- Is the data logical?
- Does the data seem complete?
- Does the data reflect enough detail for the insured's operations?
- Is the data consistent with industry averages? (For example, are the ratios of payroll-to-sales or labor-to-materials reasonable, considering the nature of the operation?)
- Can deviations from expected amounts be explained?

Premium auditors should verify premium-related data against the general accounting records and reconcile any discrepancies. If a risk is misclassified as a lower-rated class, the auditor should attempt to correct the error and notify the underwriter as soon as possible. The NCCI Basic Manual requires insurers to add or change a classification during either the audit or the policy period if the addition or change results in a premium decrease. If the appropriate class is rated higher, the correction may not be applied until the next renewal. There are exceptions in some states, such as Delaware and Pennsylvania, which are independent from the NCCI and use only authorized classes, regardless of the effect on rate.

Usually, the rates for workers compensation policies are based on an exposure unit of $100 of payroll. However, other premium bases may be used, such as per capita for domestic workers, upset payroll (factors based on wood production) for loggers, and per shift for taxi drivers. General liability policies may use a number of different premium bases, such as units, area, frontage, payroll, sales, costs, or gallons. Sales and payroll are usually based on exposure units of $1,000 or 10,000 gallons. Because they are not regulated by any bureaus, general liability policies may also be written on a composite-rated basis, based on what was agreed to when the policy was written. Most importantly, all parties should understand the premium basis being used for all policies and how records should be maintained to develop the final premium.

Verification and analysis ensure that the audit is appropriate in relation to the insured's actual loss exposures and should confirm expectations developed in the audit planning and operations review.

Apply Your Knowledge

Kristian, a premium auditor for Valentin Insurance, is conducting a field audit of an insured's operation. The insured uses a lot of subcontractors. Kristian should make sure that the insured has

a. A Test Audit program.
b. Certificates of insurance from its subcontractors.
c. Blockchain.
d. A risk audit of the subcontractors' facility.

Feedback: b. Many insureds do not realize that they must obtain certificates of insurance from their subcontractors; otherwise, premium auditors must include the subcontractors' payroll in the premium base.

Reporting the Findings

No premium audit is complete until the results are submitted. The premium-related data should be recorded and the billing information clearly summarized so that the audit can be processed and billed immediately. In addition, premium auditors must show in their reports how they obtained the data so that others can retrace their steps.

The premium auditor should succinctly describe the insured's operations and explain any deviations from the usual operations for that type of business. Premium auditors must also identify other significant information obtained during the audit and communicate it effectively to the appropriate people, such as underwriters.

PREMIUM AUDITING CONTRIBUTIONS

Effective insurer management capitalizes on the opportunities for premium auditing to contribute to other insurer functions.

Premium auditors may be one of the few insurer representatives to meet insureds, see their operations, and review their financial records. This direct contact not only significantly influences the insured's impression of the insurer, but also provides a channel to communicate relevant information to other insurer functions, including these:

- Underwriting
- Marketing and sales
- Claims
- Risk control

Underwriting

Premium auditing contributes most directly to underwriting. Premium audit reports constitute a valuable source of information for underwriters, and effective cooperation between underwriters and premium auditors is essential to ensuring that existing accounts remain profitable. Premium auditing can contribute significant information to many areas of underwriting. These examples are some of the more important and common ones. The premium auditor should develop an underwriter's perspective of an account and use the premium auditor's report, or an acceptable substitute, to communicate the desired information.

A crucial responsibility of the premium auditing function is to classify insured exposures correctly. The audit is often the only source of information for proper classifications. Although underwriting must establish the classifications when the policy is issued, the information submitted is occasionally incomplete or inaccurate. Properly classifying an account can be complex, and the operations of insureds can change. The premium audit, conducted at the end of the policy period, can reveal any classification changes necessary to update the policy.

Another important contribution of the premium auditing function to underwriting is the identification of inadequate exposure estimates. When the insured exposure has been underestimated or incorrectly classified, an inadequate deposit premium for a renewal will result. Although the premium audit will help develop the proper exposure, it is possible that additional premium charged after the end of the policy period will never be collected.

A premium audit report can also provide a comparison of anticipated loss exposures to actual loss exposures. In a well-managed insurance operation, anticipated loss exposures should not differ significantly from actual loss exposures. Unless the insured has changed its business operations, the premium audit assessment at the end of the policy period should correspond with the underwriting assessment at the beginning of the policy period.

For large accounts, advance audits—or pre-audit surveys—can be used to support underwriting decisions by ensuring that insurers issue policies based on correct business classifications and exposure bases. During these advance audits, the premium auditor can classify the operation, verify the estimated premium base, and observe the operation.

New exposures are another important area in which underwriting information might be deficient. New exposures can result from a change in operations or a new venture. The insured often does not communicate such changes to the producer or insurer, and even if it is reported, the information might not be sufficient for underwriting purposes. Premium auditing can assist underwriting by identifying new exposures during a review of the insured's operations. The premium auditor can also indicate the proper classifications for the new exposures.

Premium auditors are also in a position to provide underwriting with information on the desirability of an account. Premium auditors visit the insured's premises, meet with management, review business records, and observe the employees and operations. These activities provide valuable insight that can help the underwriter determine an account's desirability and guide underwriting decisions about the most appropriate coverage options and amounts.

While on the insured's premises, a premium auditor may become aware of physical, moral, and morale hazards. Examples of physical hazards include construction, hazardous materials, and poor safety or hygiene practices. Moral hazards can be indicated by questionable business practices or a failing business. Indicators of morale hazards include indifference to proper maintenance or poor financial records. Any of these hazards should be promptly communicated to underwriting.

Marketing and Sales

Premium auditing can also play a significant role in marketing and sales. It is important that premium audits be conducted in a timely manner. A delay of a return premium due to an insured could adversely affect the insurer's future marketing efforts. The auditor's professional conduct and skill are also important factors in retaining an account. Auditors must often be able to convince an insured of the accuracy of an audit that results in additional premium owed by the insured. This additional premium might significantly affect the profit margin and thus the insurer's decision about retaining the account.

During a premium audit, insureds may mention plans to expand operations or erect new buildings. They may be considering an employee benefits plan or business interruption insurance, or they may have gaps in present coverage observed during the audit. All of these situations may present new marketing opportunities for the insurer, and the auditor can benefit both the insured and insurer by referring the insured to marketing or sales.

Claims

During a premium audit, claims information can help verify employment classifications. However, premium auditing provides an even more valuable contribution to the claims function by verifying or correcting the classification codes assigned to an insured's claims. Various insurance regulators have emphasized the importance of improving claims-coding accuracy. This review also ensures that claims and premiums are matched in the same classifications, thus improving the credibility of rates.

Premium auditors can also verify that injured employees in workers compensation claims were employees of the insured when their injuries occurred. The premium audit can help verify injured employees' earnings. If there are any discrepancies in employment dates or wages, the premium auditor can notify claims.

Additionally, premium auditors can provide values of inventories, contractors' equipment lists and values, automotive equipment values, and other facts that are important to the claims function. For example, the claims department might request that the auditor review crime and fidelity losses during the premium audit. Although this line does not usually have auditable exposures, the premium audit can help determine that the amount claimed was accurately calculated from the insured's books and records.

Risk Control

Risk control also has an interest in the premium auditor's observations. Since risk control representatives cannot visit every insured, the premium auditor can serve as a source of information for risk control. The premium auditing process can contribute information about unsafe procedures or working conditions, observations of insureds' vehicles, and any hazards that provide opportunities for further risk control investigation and recommendations.

SUMMARY

The primary purpose of an insurer's risk control function is to evaluate loss exposures to assist with underwriting decisions and to help the insured prevent losses or reduce their effect. Insurers conduct risk control activities to achieve several goals: earn a profit, meet customer needs, comply with legal requirements, and fulfill their duty to society.

Insurers provide three types of risk control services: conducting physical surveys, performing risk analysis and improvement, and developing safety management programs. Every insurer must decide what levels of risk control services to provide to which insureds, as well as whether to contract with private firms to provide some or all of these services. Several factors that influence insurers' decisions regarding the type and extent of risk control services they provide to insureds include the line of insurance provided, the size of a commercial insured, the types of loss exposures insured, and the potential legal liability.

An insurer's risk control function is most effective when performed in cooperation with other insurer functions, such as underwriting, marketing and sales, premium auditing, and claims. Additionally, both insurers and insureds can benefit from risk control cooperation with external organizations, such as producers.

Premium auditing plays an important role in the insurance mechanism because of the number and size of policies now written with a variable premium base. Premium audits are used to determine correct policy premiums; to collect ratemaking data; to meet regulatory requirements; to deter and detect fraud; to reinforce insureds' confidence; and to obtain additional information about the insured that may be useful to other insurer functional areas, such as underwriting, marketing, and claims. Accuracy in premium audits is critical.

Audit errors that go undetected can lead to improper experience modifications, in turn resulting in incorrect and inequitable premiums.

A systematic process for conducting premium audits is necessary to provide complete, accurate reports and to effectively use premium audit resources. The stages in the premium auditing process include planning, reviewing operations, determining employment relationships, finding and evaluating books or records, auditing the books and records, analyzing and verifying premium-related data, and reporting the findings.

Because premium auditors are often the only insurer representatives that have direct contact with insureds, premium auditing can provide important contributions to other insurer functions, such as underwriting, marketing and sales, claims, and risk control.

Direct Your Learning ▶▶

6

The Claims Function

Educational Objectives

After learning the content of this assignment, you should be able to:

▷ Explain how an insurer's claims function achieves its primary goals, provides valuable information to other departments, and interacts effectively with its outside contacts.

▷ Examine how Claims Department results can be optimized by:

- Department structure

- The types and functions of claims personnel

- Claims performance measurements

▷ Examine how the following measures are used to ensure regulatory compliance:

- Claims guidelines, policies, and procedures

- Controls

- Supervisor and manager reviews

- Claims audits

▷ Describe the activities in the claims handling process.

▷ Describe the framework for coverage analysis and the information obtained by following it.

▷ Given a claims resolution scenario, demonstrate how a claims representative handles the claim and analyzes coverage.

The Claims Function

OVERVIEW OF THE CLAIMS FUNCTION

An insurer's claims function must fulfill its responsibility to the insured and pay covered claims, while also supporting an insurer's financial goals.

An insurer's success is greatly influenced by the proper and efficient performance of its claims function. The claims function generates a vast amount of information that is essential to an insurer's marketing, underwriting, and actuarial departments. Because claims personnel are among the most visible of insurer's employees, they must be able to effectively interact with individuals inside and outside of the insurance organization.

Claims Function Goals

When establishing goals for the claims function, senior management should recognize the effect the claims function has on both the insurance customer and the insurer itself. The claims function has these two primary goals:

- Complying with the contractual promise
- Supporting the insurer's financial goals

Complying With the Contractual Promise

The first goal of the claims function is to satisfy the insurer's obligations to the insured as set forth in the insurance policy. Following a loss, the promise of the insuring agreement to pay, defend, or indemnify in the event of a covered loss is fulfilled.

The insurer fulfills this promise by providing fair, prompt, and equitable service to the insured, either (1) directly, when the loss involves a first-party claim made by the insured against the insurer, or (2) indirectly, by handling a third-party claim made by someone against the insured to whom the insured might be liable.

From the insurer's perspective, claims are expected, and claims representatives must deal with them routinely. For the individuals involved, the loss occurrence and its consequences are not routine and can be overwhelming. Claims representatives, therefore, routinely deal with insureds and claimants in stressful situations. A claims representative should handle a claim in a way that treats all parties involved fairly and equitably, and do so in a timely manner.

Were it not for insurance, administered through the claims handling process, recovery would be slow, inefficient, and difficult.

Supporting the Insurer's Financial Goals

The second goal of the claims function is supporting the insurer's financial goal. Achieving this goal is generally the responsibility of the marketing and underwriting departments. However, it would be shortsighted not to recognize the role of the claims function in helping insurers achieve an underwriting profit by controlling expenses and paying only legitimate claims.

By managing all claims function expenses, setting appropriate spending policies, and using appropriately priced providers and services, claims managers can help maintain an insurer's underwriting profit. Similarly, claims staff can avoid overspending on costs of handling claims, claims operations, or other expenses. Finally, by ensuring fair claim settlement, claims representatives prevent any unnecessary increase in the cost of insurance and subsequent reduction in the insurer's underwriting profit.

Insureds and other claimants are entitled to a fair claim settlement. By overcompensating an insured or a claimant, the insurer unnecessarily raises the cost of insurance for all of its insureds. Overpaid claims can lower insurer profits and result in higher policy premiums.

Conversely, underpaid claims can result in dissatisfied insureds, litigation, or regulatory oversight. Insureds and claimants who believe they are being treated fairly are likely to accept the claims representative's settlement offer, but if insureds and claimants are treated unfairly, they might sue the insurer or file a complaint with their state Insurance Department.

An insurer's success in achieving its financial goal is reflected in its reputation for providing the service promised. A reputation for resisting legitimate claims can undermine the effectiveness of insurer advertisements or its goodwill earned over the years. Consequently, the two goals of the claims function work together to help bring about a profitable insurance operation.

Claims Information Users

The claims function provides valuable information to other insurer departments. The three primary recipients of claims information are the marketing, underwriting, and actuarial departments.

Marketing

The Marketing Department needs information about customer satisfaction, timeliness of settlements, and other variables that assist in marketing the insurance product. The Marketing Department recognizes that the other services the insurer performs for the insured are forgotten quickly if the insurer fails to perform well after a loss occurrence.

Producers must be prepared to explain any premium changes and changes to policy provisions to their insureds. Producers must have insured loss information to prepare renewal policies properly because many commercial policies are subject to rating plans that affect the policy premium, based partly on the insured's loss experience. In personal insurance, personal auto policies might be surcharged when property damage claims are paid during the policy year. Additionally, claims personnel often inform producers of court rulings that affect the insurer's loss exposures or pricing, such as interpretations of policy exclusions or application of limits.

Underwriting

The insurance business operates effectively if underwriters accept loss exposures that are likely to experience only the types and amounts of losses anticipated in the insurance rates. If underwriters accept loss exposures that experience more losses than anticipated, the rates charged by the insurer will be inadequate, and the insurer could become financially insolvent. Claims personnel help underwriters in this regard by ensuring that claims are paid fairly and according to the policy. Proper, consistent, and efficient claims handling enables underwriters to evaluate, select, and appropriately price loss exposures based on consistent claims costs.

When claims representatives inspect accident scenes in homes or at work sites as part of the claims investigation, they sometimes notice loss exposure characteristics, either negative or positive, that were not readily apparent in the insurance application. When claims representatives report such findings to the underwriter, the underwriter may adjust the premium or take other actions to accommodate the difference in the exposure. For example, based on information from the claims representative, the underwriter may cancel coverage or renew it only if the insured implements corrective measures. Alternatively, the underwriter may grant a premium credit based on a claims representative's report of an above-average loss exposure.

A number of similar claims may also alert underwriting management to a problem for a particular type or class of insured. These claims might be the result of new processes or technologies being used by the class of insureds as a whole. For example, some roofing contractors might have tried to speed the process of replacing composite roofs by moving the tar smelter to the roof of the structure being repaired. This practice might have caused a number of fire losses. An adverse court ruling could also cause the loss experience of a class of business to deteriorate or could increase the number of claims presented.

Actuarial

Actuaries need accurate information not only on losses that have been paid but also on losses that have occurred and are reserved for payment, collectively called incurred losses. Loss reserves can be increased or decreased as the claim develops, and reserve change reports help actuaries more accurately predict loss development. Incurred loss information helps actuaries establish reserves for incurred but not reported (IBNR) losses and project the development of open claims for which the reserves might change substantially before the claim is finally settled.

In addition to incurred loss information, actuaries need accurate information on loss adjusting expenses and recoverable amounts associated with claims, such as salvage and subrogation, any ceded reinsurance recoverable, and deductibles (when the insurer pays an entire claim and then asks the insured to reimburse the deductible amount).

All of the claims information that actuaries collect from claims personnel must be accurately represented through appropriate reserving methods in the insurer's financial statements. Actuaries must update these statements for reporting at various times during the year. When claim payments are recorded accurately and realistic reserves are set in the insurer's claims processing system, then the raw data that actuaries use to develop rates will be accurate and the rates will reflect the insurer's loss experience.

Claims Department Contacts

Other than the producer, Claims Department personnel are the contacts within the insurer who are most visible to the public. Therefore, the Claims Department must interact effectively with outside contacts, such as the public, lawyers, and state regulators.

The Public

Although many insurers have a Public Relations Department that handles advertising, the insurer's public image is determined largely by the Claims Department's behavior.

Because the claims representative is an insured's and a claimant's primary contact with the insurer, claims service significantly affects an insured's or a claimant's (referred to as "claimant" through the remainder of this section) satisfaction with an insurer. The claims representative's skill at communicating directly with claimants influences their satisfaction with the insurer.

Claims representatives' first contact with a claimant occurs after the claimant has sustained a loss. Most claimants suffer some type of emotional reaction to a loss, which may include anger, depression, frustration, or hopelessness. Claims representatives must empathize with claimants to interact effectively with them.

Most claimants' knowledge of insurance is less sophisticated than that of an insurance professional. Claims representatives must be prepared to explain the policy's claims provisions to the claimant as those provisions apply to the claimant's property damage or injury. A well-prepared, professional claims representative who empathizes with the claimant will gain the claimant's confidence and increase the likelihood of reaching a mutually agreeable settlement.

Technological improvements have allowed many insurers to improve the quality and speed of their claims service. Starting with the growth of cell phones and the internet and progressing to improvements in wireless technologies, claims departments have found new ways to streamline the claims process and improve customer satisfaction.

Technology facilitates communications among field personnel, regional or local claims offices, claimants, vendors, and service providers. In catastrophe losses, floods, tornadoes, hurricanes, and earthquakes can cause significant damage to the infrastructure used for traditional communication systems. Satellite transmissions and other modern communication devices used in wireless technology may overcome these problems to enable continued electronic communications for claims personnel and, ultimately, faster and better customer service for claimants when they need it most.

Lawyers

For some types of claims and in certain areas of the United States, claimants are more likely to hire lawyers, often leading to costly litigation. Although legal representation can result in a higher payment by the insurer, representation does not necessarily result in higher settlements for claimants, because claimants must pay expenses and legal fees from settlements. Legal representation also does not guarantee a faster settlement. Even if litigation ensues, claims representatives should continue to interact in a cordial, professional manner with claimants' lawyers.

When an insurer needs a lawyer either to defend the insured or to defend itself, it will typically hire a lawyer from the jurisdiction in which the claim is submitted. The lawyer will provide advice regarding specific losses and legal issues. Claims representatives will assist the insurer's lawyers as needed by sharing claims details and assembling information that supports the insurer's legal position.

State Regulators

State insurance regulators monitor insurers' activities in the claims handling process. Regulators exercise controls by licensing claims representatives, investigating consumer complaints, and performing market conduct investigations. Enforcement is usually handled through the Unfair Claims Settlement Practices Act or similar legislation.

Not all states currently license claims representatives, and no standard procedure or uniform regulation exists for those that do. Some states require licensure only for independent adjusters, who work for many insurers, or for public adjusters, who represent insureds in first-party claims against insurers. Other states require staff claims representatives to be licensed.

State insurance regulators also handle customer complaints made against an insurer. Most states have a specific time limit within which the insurer must answer or act on inquiries from the Insurance Department. Failure to respond can result in expensive fines and even in the loss of the claims representative's—or his or her employer's—license.

Insurance regulators periodically perform market conduct investigations either as part of their normal audit of insurer activities or in response to specific complaints. The typical market conduct audit includes more than just claims practices; it audits all departments that interact directly with insureds and claimants.

CLAIMS DEPARTMENT STRUCTURE, PERSONNEL, AND PERFORMANCE

Information generated by a Claims Department, including about loss payments and expenses, is essential to marketing, underwriting, and pricing insurance products. In this way, the claims function is crucial to fulfilling an insurer's promise to pay covered losses, creating an accompanying need for an insurer's Claims Department to operate efficiently.

The results of a Claims Department can be optimized by its structure, personnel, and performance measures. Let's look at all three.

Claims Department Structure

An insurer's Claims Department can be organized in several ways. Usually, a senior claims officer heads the Claims Department and reports to the chief executive officer (CEO), the chief financial officer, or the chief underwriting officer. The senior claims officer may have staff located in the same office. This staff often makes up the home office Claims Department. Within this area, any number of technical and management specialists can provide advice and assistance to remote claims offices and claims representatives.

The senior claims officer may have several claims offices or branches countrywide or even worldwide. Staff from remote claims offices can all report directly to the home office Claims Department, or regional/divisional claims officers may oversee the territory.

Third-party administrator (TPA)
An organization that provides administrative services associated with risk financing and insurance.

Regional claims officers may have one or more branch offices reporting to them—for example, in both Boston and New York City. And a branch office in New York City may have smaller offices in Albany, New York, and Erie, New York, reporting into it. Each branch office could have a claims manager, one or more claims supervisors, and a staff of claims representatives. Similar department structures are adopted by **third-party administrators (TPAs)**.

Claims Personnel

Claims personnel are among the most visible employees of an insurer and must therefore be able to interact well with a variety of people.

A **claims representative** fulfills the promise to either pay the insured or on behalf of the insured by handling claims when losses occur. People who handle claims may be staff claims representatives, independent adjusters, employees of TPAs, or **producers** who sell policies to insureds. Public adjusters also handle claims by representing the interests of insureds to the insurer.

Claims representative
A person responsible for investigating, evaluating, and settling claims.

Producer
Any of several kinds of insurance personnel who place insurance and surety business with insurers and who represent either insurers or insureds, or both.

Staff Claims Representatives

Staff claims representatives are employees of an insurer and handle most claims, usually while working from branch or regional offices rather than at the insurer's home office. They may include inside claims representatives, who handle claims exclusively from the insurer's office, and field claims representatives (also called outside claims representatives), who handle claims both inside and outside the office. Field claims representatives handle claims that require such tasks as investigating the scene of the loss; meeting with insureds, claimants, lawyers, and others involved in the loss; and inspecting damage. If the branch or region covers a large territory, the insurer may set up claims offices in areas away from the branch office to enable the claims representative to serve insureds more efficiently.

Independent Adjusters

Some insurers may find it economically impractical to establish claims offices in every state in which insureds reside. In such instances, insurers may contract with **independent adjusters** to handle claims in strategic locations.

Some insurers employ claims personnel in their home or branch offices to monitor claims progress and settle claims but use independent adjusters to handle all field work. Other insurers hire independent adjusters when their staff claims representatives are too busy to handle all claims themselves.

Independent adjuster
An independent claims representative who handles claims for insurers for a fee.

For example, if a disaster strikes, staff claims representatives may need assistance to handle the large number of claims quickly enough to satisfy the insurer and its insureds. Insurers may also use independent adjusters to meet desired service levels or when specialized skills are needed, such as to investigate aircraft accidents.

Some independent adjusters are self-employed, but many work for adjusting firms that range in size from one small office with a few adjusters to national firms with many offices employing hundreds of adjusters.

Third-Party Administrators

Businesses that choose to self-insure do not use agents, underwriters, or other typical insurer personnel. However, they do need personnel to handle losses that arise. Self-insured businesses can employ their own claims representatives or contract with TPAs, which handle claims, keep claims records, and perform statistical analyses. TPAs are often associated with large independent adjusting firms or with subsidiaries of insurers. Many property-casualty insurers have established subsidiary companies that serve as TPAs.

Producers

Producers can also function as claims representatives for certain claims. The term "producer" includes agents, brokers, sales representatives, and intermediaries who place insurance with insurers.

Insurers may allow producers to pay claims up to a certain amount, such as $2,500. Those producers can issue claim payments, called drafts, directly to insureds for covered claims, thus reducing an insured's wait time. In this capacity, producers function like inside claims representatives.

Public Adjusters

Public adjuster

An outside organization or person hired by an insured to represent the insured in a claim in exchange for a fee.

If a claim is complex, or if settlement negotiations are not progressing satisfactorily with the insurer, the insured may hire a **public adjuster** to protect his or her interests.

Some states have statutes that govern the services public adjusters can provide. But in general, the public adjuster prepares an insured's claim and negotiates the settlement with the staff claims representative or independent adjuster. The insured, in turn, pays the public adjuster's fee, which is usually a percentage of the settlement.

Apply Your Knowledge

A natural disaster just struck a large number of homes and businesses insured by Watkins Insurance Company. The company is receiving more claims than its staff claims representatives can handle in a timely manner. Which kind of professional would Watkins Insurance Company look to hire to make sure that it can satisfy its insureds?

a.   Independent adjuster

b.   Third-party administrator

c.   Producer

d.   Public adjuster

Feedback: *a.* Watkins Insurance Company would hire independent adjusters, which are independent claims representatives who handle claims for insurers for a fee. Some insurers hire independent adjusters when their staff claims representatives are too busy to handle all claims themselves.

Claims Performance Measures

Because Claims Department members have diverse roles and are spread over a wide geographic area, insurers face special issues when it comes to evaluating and measuring the performance of their Claims Department staff.

Insurers are businesses, so they must make a profit to survive. Claims departments play a crucial role in insurer profitability by paying fair amounts for legitimate claims and providing accurate, reliable, and consistent ratemaking data. Because paying claims fairly does not conflict with insurer profit goals, an insurer measures its claims and underwriting departments' performance using a **loss ratio**, which is a profitability measure.

In addition to reaching profit goals, an insurer strives to ensure that its Claims Department meets quality performance goals. Internally identified best practices, claims audits, and customer-satisfaction data are tools that provide measures of quality.

Loss ratio

A ratio that measures losses and loss adjustment expenses against earned premiums and that reflects the percentage of premiums being consumed by losses.

Profitability Measures

A loss ratio is one of the most commonly used measures for evaluating an insurer's financial well-being. It compares an insurer's losses and **loss adjustment expenses (LAE)** with its collected premiums and reveals the percentage of premiums being consumed by losses. An increasing loss ratio could indicate that the insurer is improperly performing the claims function. Increasing losses could also mean that the Underwriting Department elected to cover loss exposures that were more costly or occurred more frequently than it estimated or that the Actuarial Department failed to price the insurer's products correctly.

Loss adjustment expense (LAE)

The expense that an insurer incurs to investigate, defend, and settle claims according to the terms specified in the insurance policy.

When an insurer's loss ratio increases, the Claims Department, along with other insurer functions, is pressured to reduce expenses. Claims representatives could quickly reduce LAE in the short term by offering the settlement payments insureds and claimants demand rather than spending resources on investigating claims and calculating and negotiating fair payments.

However, to reduce LAE in the long term, inflated settlement demands should be resisted; researched; negotiated; and, if necessary, litigated. LAE can also be reduced by making sure that claims procedures are always properly performed by claims representatives.

Apply Your Knowledge

An insurer's CEO is analyzing the organization's profitability. He sees that three years ago, the insurer's loss ratio was 0.67, while two years ago, the insurer's loss ratio was 0.70. Last year, the loss ratio was 0.75. Further analysis indicates that the Actuarial Department is pricing the insurer's products correctly and that the Underwriting Department was selecting appropriate loss exposures. This leads the CEO to focus on the Claims Department as potentially undermining the organization's profitability. Which of the following are measures the Claims Department could employ in an attempt to reduce LAE long term?

a. Immediately offering the settlement payment insureds and claimants demand.

b. Resisting; researching; negotiating; and, if necessary, litigating inflated settlement demands.

c. Skipping claims procedures.

d. None of these measures will reduce LAE long term.

Feedback: *b.* Resisting; researching; negotiating; and, if necessary, litigating inflated settlement demands reduces LAE long term.

Quality Measures

Three frequently used tools provide quality measures for evaluating a Claims Department's performance: best practices, claims audits, and customer-satisfaction data.

In a Claims Department, the term "best practices" generally refers to a system of identified internal practices that produce superior performance. Best practices are usually shared with every claims representative. An insurer can identify best practices by studying its own performance or the performance of similar successful insurers.

Claims Department best practices are often based on legal requirements specified by regulators, legislators, and courts. For example, a Claims Department may have a best practice stating that claims will be acknowledged within twenty-four hours of receipt. This time frame may have been selected because of a regulation, law, or court decision.

Insurers use claims audits to ensure compliance with best practices and to gather statistical information on claims. A claims audit is performed by evaluating information in a number of open and closed claims files. Claims audits can be performed by the claims staff who work on the files (called a self-audit), or they can be performed by claims representatives from other offices or by a team from the home office. Claims audits usually evaluate both quantitative and qualitative factors. See the exhibit "Quantitative and Qualitative Audit Factors."

The quality of a Claims Department's performance is also measured by customer satisfaction. Claims supervisors and managers monitor correspondence they receive about the performance of individual claims representatives. While compliments are usually acknowledged, supervisors or managers must respond to complaints. Claims Departments have procedures for responding to complaints, which can come directly from insureds, claimants, or vendors or be submitted on their behalf by a state insurance department.

Quantitative and Qualitative Audit Factors

Quantitative	Qualitative
Timeliness of reports	Realistic reserving
Timeliness of reserving	Accurate evaluation of insured's liability
Timeliness of payments	Follow-up on subrogation opportunity
Number of files opened each month	Litigation cost management
Number of files closed each month	Proper releases taken
Number of files reopened each month	Correct coverage evaluation
Percentage of recovery from subrogation	Good negotiation skills
Average claim settlement value by claims type	Thorough investigations
Percentage of claims entering litigation	
Percentage of cases going to trial	
Accuracy of data entry	

[DA02267]

No matter the source, complaints must be investigated by management and responded to in a timely manner. Complaints, such as not receiving a return phone call, may indicate legitimate service issues. Other complaints may simply indicate dissatisfaction with an otherwise valid claim settlement. Review of complaints received in a claims office can show whether problems exist with a particular claims representative, supervisor, or manager.

MEASURES USED TO ENSURE REGULATORY COMPLIANCE

Insurers institute compliance measures, which are various guidelines that insurers ask personnel to use or other actions that they take to ensure that legal and regulatory requirements are met and to promote good-faith claims handling practices.

Compliance measures include these:

- Claims guidelines, policies, and procedures
- Controls, such as reports, access security, authority levels, and tracking
- Supervisor and manager reviews
- Claims audits

A combination of compliance measures helps insurers enforce good-faith claims handling; encourages claims personnel to provide complete and accurate information to management, producers, reinsurers, lawyers, insureds, claimants, and others; and makes the insurer's operation run efficiently and with sound expense management.

Claims Guidelines, Policies, and Procedures

Claims guidelines

A set of guidelines and instructions that specify how certain claims handling tasks should be performed by setting policies and procedures for claim handling.

Some insurers have claims guidelines, which are policies and procedures that serve as a compliance measure. **Claims guidelines** specify how certain claims handling tasks should be performed by setting policies and procedures for claims handling. For example, claims guidelines might specify when an independent adjuster should be assigned to a claim. Such a guideline helps ensure that the insurer pays an independent adjuster only when necessary and helps claims managers control Claims Department expenses so that they can help meet corporate goals. A sample page from a hypothetical insurer's claims guidelines can be instructive. See the exhibit "Claims Guidelines Sample Page."

Claims Guidelines Sample Page

WORTHY INSURANCE COMPANY CLAIMS GUIDELINES

Subject:	Activity Log
Category:	File Documentation
Purpose:	The activity log is a chronological record of file development that describes the activities and analysis on the claim file.
Procedure:	The activity log form should be completed as events occur and include the day, month, year, time, and person making notes. The activity log should be a brief notation of file activities and analysis. Detailed explanations may appear in other documents and file reports.
Responsibility:	Anyone who conducts activity on the file must comply with this procedure.

[DA03173]

Steps for performing some tasks can be clearly specified in claims guidelines so that claims personnel ensure that information is accurate and that claims are handled properly and in good faith. Claims departments can use guidelines in training new claims personnel because they provide instruction for performing tasks properly. They are also useful as a reference for performing infrequent tasks or when one employee must perform another employee's duties because of vacation, illness, or another absence.

Claims guidelines, policies, and procedures can also be useful when an insurer must defend a bad-faith lawsuit. Evidence that good-faith claims handling procedures were prescribed and followed demonstrates that the insurer takes measures to help guarantee good-faith claims handling. When claims personnel consistently follow company policies and procedures, insureds and claimants are less likely to find fault with the claims handling.

Supervisors and managers often use diaries as reminders to review claim files or perform another activity. Claims representatives usually have many claims to handle at the same time; therefore, a reminder system is essential to helping them handle all of them properly. A **diary, or suspense**, is a system to remind claims personnel to perform a particular task on a claim. An automated diary system might send a computer message at set intervals to remind the claims representative to review the file or reserves; to make a payment; to contact the insured, the claimant, or witnesses; or to request additional information from service providers. See the exhibit "Sample Automated Diary."

Diary, or suspense

A system to remind claims personnel to perform a particular task on a claim.

Sample Automated Diary

Claim # 12345678

Pol # 78-02-3359   **Ins** Brown, Jackie   **DOL** 12/12/X0   **TOL** Collision

Diary 12/14/X1   **Claims rep** Stone   **Date set** 12/12/X1

Notes: Insured is to call today. Follow up if no response. Need vehicle location for inspection.

[DA03174]

An **activity log** is a record of all the activities and analyses that occur regarding a particular claim. See the exhibit "Sample Activity Log."

Activity log

A record of all the activities and analyses that occur while handling a claim.

Because claims representatives handle a large volume of claims, the activity log is a crucial record of activity that has occurred on each claim. Claims representatives who rely on their memories to recall all the activity on a claim are likely to forget important information. A claim file should speak for itself so that anyone reading the activity log and other documents knows exactly what has occurred. Claims representatives should carefully document every activity on a claim.

Many insurers use a team approach to claims handling and offer extended hours to provide better service to insureds and claimants. As a result, one claims representative might take an insured's statement during the day shift, and another claims representative might answer a question from the same insured during the evening shift. Without an accurate, complete activity log, the two claims representatives might give contradictory or confusing information to the insured. Especially when more than one claims representative might work on a claim, the activity log is crucial.

Sample Activity Log

Activity Log

Claim # 12345678

Date	Activity	Diary
12/12/X1	Rec'd claim from home office. Called insured— no answer. Left msg on answering machine.	12/14/X1
12/14/X1	No response from Mrs. Darlington. Called again. Spoke with 16-yr.-old daughter. She will have her mother (the insured) call me tomorrow.	12/15/X1
12/15/X1	Spoke with insured. Took recorded statement. Mrs. Darlington backed out of her driveway and hit the neighbor's mailbox across the street, which belongs to Mr. Bounds, of 1220 NW 84th Street, Anytown, PA 19344. His evening phone number is 111-123-4567. The mailbox was mounted on a concrete post that suffered no damage, and Mr. Bounds told Mrs. Darlington that he would not file an insurance claim for damages. Mrs. Darlington's car is at Sam's Auto Repair. Arranged for inspection. Explained claims process to Mrs. Darlington. Phoned Mr. Bounds to verify that his mailbox was not damaged and that he will not file a claim.	12/20/X1
12/20/X1	Estimates rec'd and differences analyzed to ensure fair comparison. Called Mrs. Darlington and reviewed repair estimate with her. Agreed on settlement amount. Processed payment today. Closed file.	

[DA03175]

Activity logs are also useful in claims audits. Producers are sometimes interested in the details of how a claim was handled, and claims personnel can review activity logs to provide those details.

Controls

Claims departments can use various electronic controls as compliance measures, such as claims reports, access security, authority levels, and claims information tracking systems.

Most insurers' claims information systems can be used to generate periodic claims reports. Claims representatives, supervisors, and managers review those reports to ensure that claims have been entered correctly. Reports might include information such as this:

- Claims with reserves above a specified amount
- Claims assigned to independent adjusters
- Claims in litigation
- Claims closed by agents
- Claims with reserve changes larger than a specified amount
- Claims closed without payment by a claims representative

Reports can help insurer personnel monitor claims practices by indicating possible errors. For example, managers might review a daily report listing all claims with reserves above $100,000. If claims personnel mistakenly entered a $10,000 reserve as a $100,000 reserve, the daily report would alert managers to the error. The error could then be corrected before it affected reports produced for parties outside the insurer and agents' commission calculations.

Reports of claims assigned to independent adjusters can help an insurer meet corporate goals for expense management. If the reports indicate that many claims are assigned to independent adjusters, the insurer can examine the reasons for those assignments and determine whether a staff claims representative should be assigned to a different territory to reduce independent adjusting expenses. Similarly, claims in litigation can be reviewed to ensure that legal expenses are managed properly.

Access security refers to an individual's ability to review, enter, and change information in a claims information system. These systems limit access to claims information using these three methods:

- The first method of access security requires a person attempting to access claims information to enter a password maintained by the Information Systems Department.
- The second method of access security restricts access to certain data in the claims information system to managers only.
- The third method of access security prevents unauthorized individuals from changing crucial information in the claims information system, such as reserve amounts or claims codes.

Authority levels restrict claims personnel from making changes to claims information that exceed their authority and are described next. **Authority levels** refer to the reserve amounts and payment amounts that claims personnel are allowed to set and make. Claims information systems might be designed to allow different authority levels for different types of employees. For example, experienced personnel might be allowed to set reserves and request payments for larger amounts than inexperienced personnel. Supervisors might have an authority level that is higher than that for experienced claims personnel.

Access security

A security setting that controls an individual computer user's ability to review, enter, and change information in a claims information system.

Authority level

A designated dollar amount assigned to claims personnel to limit the reserve amounts they can set and the payment amounts they can make.

Authority levels help control claims in several ways. First, if a claim requires high reserves or payments, authority levels ensure that experienced, qualified personnel handle those reserves or payments. Second, if inexperienced claims personnel enter a reserve amount or payment inaccurately and the inaccurate amount exceeds their authority level, the claims system prevents the error.

Claims information tracking systems can be designed to automatically capture information such as the date a reserve was changed, the name of the individual who made the change, the date a payment was requested, and the name of the individual who made the request. Such information is stored in the claims information system and cannot be altered. Tracking systems discourage fraud and are useful for identifying training needs.

Supervisor and Manager Reviews

In addition to the various claims guidelines and controls, supervisor and manager reviews are another type of compliance measure that insurers can use. Supervisors and managers use diary systems as reminders to review claims. During a review, they might check the claims codes, reserves, and payments entered for the claim. They might review the claims representative's reports to the file; the activity log; and other file documentation, such as police reports, physician reports, and damage estimates. During the review, supervisors and managers might detect errors that can be corrected.

The review also allows supervisors and managers to coach claims representatives on how to handle claims, on additional investigation that might be needed, and on negotiation or settlement approaches. Supervisor and manager reviews are essential to helping claims personnel learn how to improve job performance.

Claims Audits

Claims audit

A review of claim files to examine the technical details of claim settlements; ensure that claims procedures are followed; and verify that appropriate, thorough documentation is included.

Internal claims audit

A review of claim files conducted by an insurer's staff to examine the technical details of claim settlements; ensure that claims procedures are followed; and verify that appropriate, thorough documentation is included.

Most insurers use claims audits as a type of compliance measure. **Claims audits** are a review of claim files, both paper and electronic, to ensure that claims are being handled properly. Claims audits can be conducted by an insurer's internal personnel or by others.

An **internal claims audit** is a review of claim files conducted by an insurer's staff to examine the technical details of claim settlements; ensure that claims procedures are followed; and verify that appropriate, thorough documentation is included. Generally, internal claims audits are conducted by claims personnel, but they might also be conducted by personnel from other departments, such as accounting, underwriting, or human resources and training.

Internal claims audits can be conducted by managers, supervisors, technical support staff, or other claims representatives. The reason for the audit determines which claim files are audited. For example, to ensure that claims representatives comply with procedures and policies, a random sample of claim files might be appropriate as a routine, regularly scheduled audit. If a specific catastrophe generated many claims complaints, managers might audit claims only from that catastrophe. A supervisor might audit a specific claims representative's claims to prepare for a performance review. Technical support staff might audit a sample of files involving only subrogated or only litigated claims.

An actuary might review claim files to examine how reserves are set, how frequently they are changed, and how accurate the initial reserves were compared to the final settlement amount. If reserves are habitually lower than the amount of the final claim settlement, the actuary might increase total reserves beyond the amounts set by the Claims Department. Such a change would help ensure that total reserves for all claims are adequate to maintain the insurer's financial condition.

The Underwriting Department might audit claim files to see the kinds of claims that are being reported; how much is being paid for those claims; and what, if any, coverage or underwriting standards should be changed to address those claims. For example, if an underwriter notices many claims for damage from sewer backup, the underwriter might decide that underwriting standards should be made more strict for properties likely to experience sewer backup.

Human resources and training might audit claim files to identify training needs for the Claims Department. For example, a trainer might discover that a claims code for a particular kind of loss is often entered incorrectly. Based on that finding, the trainer might develop a short class to teach support staff about that type of loss and how to code it correctly.

Internal claims audits might also be conducted to ensure that employee fraud is not occurring. In addition, if employees know that claims will be audited, it might deter them from committing fraud.

External claims audits are claim file reviews conducted by someone other than an insurer's own employees. External claims audits are conducted to review overall claims handling practices; to review reserves and other technical details of claim settlements; to investigate consumer complaints; to ensure that claims procedures were followed; and to verify that appropriate, thorough documentation was included.

State insurance regulators might conduct a claims audit to review an insurer's claims handling practices. The purpose of the review is to determine whether an insurer is violating any unfair claim settlement practices acts or laws and whether the insurer routinely engages in any illegal claims handling practices.

Many state insurance regulators are interested in insurers' reserving practices because adequate reserves are crucial to insurers' financial condition. Regulators can evaluate reserves based on an insurer's annual financial statement. However, if regulators need additional information, they might conduct a claims audit to review reserves and reserving practices. Regulators might find that an insurer routinely sets claims reserves lower than necessary and then increases the reserves in steps.

External claims audit

A review of claim files conducted by organizations other than the insurer that involves reviewing overall claims handling practices; reviewing reserves and other technical details of claim settlements; investigating consumer complaints; ensuring that claims procedures were followed; and verifying that appropriate, thorough documentation was included.

Insurance advisory organizations such as Insurance Services Office, Inc. (ISO) and the American Association of Insurance Services (AAIS) are also interested in insurers' reserves but rarely conduct a claim audit to study reserves or reserving practices. Instead, such organizations rely on the information provided in insurers' Annual Statements.

THE CLAIMS HANDLING PROCESS

To ensure that every claim is handled properly, the claims representative must follow a systematic claims handling process.

The claims handling process begins when the insured reports the loss to the producer or directly to the insurer's claim center. Losses can be reported using a loss notice form, which varies by type of loss, through a letter, or as part of a lawsuit. Once a loss notice has been received and the associated information has been entered into the insurer's claims information system, the insurer begins the claims handling process.

The claims handling process consists of a series of standard activities. The activities are not always sequential. Depending on the severity and complexity of the claim, the process may be completed quickly, or may take months or even years. These activities provide a framework for handling all types of property, liability, and workers compensation claims:

- Acknowledging and assigning the claim
- Identifying the policy
- Contacting the insured or the insured's representative
- Investigating and documenting the claim
- Determining the cause of loss, liability, and the loss amount
- Concluding the claim

Acknowledging and Assigning the Claim

Generally, the first activity of the insurer in the claims handling process involves two functions—acknowledging receipt of the claim and assigning the claim to a claim representative. The purpose of the acknowledgment is to advise the insured that the claim has been received. The acknowledgment also provides the name and contact information of the assigned claims representative and the claim number. Insurers acknowledge claims in a timely manner to comply with insurance regulations.

Insurers use different methods of assigning claims to claims representatives. Some assign claims based on territory, type of claim, extent of damage, workload, or other criteria contained in the insurer's claims information system. The goal is to assign the claim to a claims representative who possesses the appropriate skills to handle it. Some states require claims representatives who handle claims in the state to have an adjuster license. These licensing requirements must also be considered when assigning a claim to a claims representative.

After receiving the claim assignment, the claims representative contacts the insured, and possibly the claimant (if it is a third-party claim), to acknowledge the claim assignment and explain the claim process. For insurers that do not make contact immediately after receiving the loss notice, this contact serves as the claim acknowledgment. For some types of losses, the claims representative may give the insured instructions to prevent further loss, such as to cover roof damage with a tarp. If the claim involves property damage, the claim representative may arrange a time with the insured to inspect the damage or the damage scene. As an alternative, the claims representative may advise the insured or claimant that an appraiser or an independent adjuster will be in contact to inspect the property damage. If the claim involves bodily injury, the claims representative should get information about the nature and extent of the injury. See the exhibit "How Blockchain Can Assist in Processing Claims."

How Blockchain Can Assist in Processing Claims

Blockchain can make the claims handling process quicker and more cost efficient through the use of smart contracts. As an example, consider flight insurance that provides coverage for late or canceled flights. The insurance contract, which insures the on-time performance of a flight, is recorded on the blockchain. If the flight is late or canceled, data can be verified digitally by a trusted third party, which automatically triggers a claim payment.

Even when the entire insurance contract isn't recorded on the blockchain, smart contracts can help. For example, a smart contract tied to sensors or telematics in a car involved in an accident can provide the first report of loss to the insurer while simultaneously notifying recommended repair shops and alerting the insured of next steps. As with any new technology or process, care must be given that this process is used in compliance with applicable laws.

[DA12778]

Identifying the Policy

Usually, the claims representative first identifies the policy under which the claim has been made upon receiving the assignment in order to determine what types of coverage apply to the loss. If it is apparent from the loss notice that coverage may not be available for the loss, the claims representative must notify the insured of this concern through a **nonwaiver agreement** or a **reservation of rights letter**.

Claims representatives may also establish claim or case (loss) reserves, often in conjunction with identifying the policy. This can occur at almost any point in the claim handling process. While the exact timing may differ among insurers,

Nonwaiver agreement
A signed agreement indicating that during the course of investigation, neither the insurer nor the insured waives rights under the policy.

Reservation of rights letter
An insurer's letter that specifies coverage issues and informs the insured that the insurer is handling a claim with the understanding that the insurer may later deny coverage should the facts warrant it.

the setting of an initial reserve(s) usually occurs early in the claim handling process.

Setting accurate reserves is an important part of the claims representative's job. Establishing and maintaining adequate reserves is important for the insurer's financial stability because reserves affect the insurer's ability to maintain and increase business. See the exhibit "Setting Accurate Reserves Can Be Difficult."

Setting Accurate Reserves Can Be Difficult

After the claims representative receives notice of a loss, obtains initial information, and verifies coverage, a loss reserve (or case reserve) for that claim is established. Assume, for example, that an insured had a minor auto accident in which the insured's car hit a guardrail on a foggy night and that no injuries or other cars were involved. After obtaining initial information concerning the accident, verifying coverage, and receiving written estimates of the cost to repair the insured's car, the claims representative establishes a case reserve of $5,000. This figure is probably a very accurate estimate because a single-car collision loss is relatively easy to evaluate. Two weeks later, the repairs are made to the insured's car, and the insurer issues a check for $5,000. Once the loss is paid, the reserve is reduced to zero because no future loss payment is expected. Therefore, the $5,000 claim paid by the insurer equals the initial case reserve.

Conversely, complex claims are often difficult to estimate, especially liability claims. Assume, for example, that an insured was involved in a serious auto accident and that two persons in the other car were hospitalized with severe injuries. The cause of the accident is not immediately clear because of conflicting testimony of witnesses, and it is difficult to determine whether the insured is responsible for the accident. What case reserve should be established? The amount eventually paid because of this accident could range from almost nothing (if the insured is not found to be legally responsible) to hundreds of thousands of dollars (if the insured is responsible and the injured victims die or are permanently disabled). The eventual payment on this particular claim, which may not be made for several years, can vary significantly from the original reserve.

[DA07639]

Contacting the Insured or the Insured's Representative

Another activity in the claims handling process, which occurs soon after the loss is assigned to a claims representative and initial reserves are established, is contacting the insured or the insured's representative. For some insurers (or in certain claims as specified in the insurer's guidelines), this contact occurs at the same time as the claim acknowledgment. Generally, the claims representative reviews the initial loss report and policy and then contacts the insured and schedules a time to speak with the insured or a party representing the insured about the facts of the loss. This can be a face-to-face meeting at the insured's location or the loss location, or it can be a telephone discussion. If the loss involves a third-party claimant, then the claims representative also contacts the claimant and schedules a meeting with the claimant or a party representing the claimant (such as a public adjuster or an attorney) to discuss the facts of the loss. Once contact is made, the claims representative should take these actions:

- Inform the insured of what is required to protect damaged property and to document the claim.
- Describe the claims inspection, appraisal, and investigation process.
- Tell the insured what additional investigation is needed to resolve potential coverage issues.
- Explain potential coverage questions or policy limitations or exclusions, and obtain a nonwaiver agreement when necessary.
- If medical and wage loss information is part of the claim, obtain the necessary authorizations.
- Explain the amount of time it will take to process and conclude the claim.
- Supply the insured with a blank proof of loss form for property damage and any necessary written instructions so that the insured can document the claim.

Investigating the Claim

Claims representatives begin investigating a claim as soon as it is assigned. They can develop an outline or notes to logically organize the investigation and to ensure that information that may be available only for a short time is investigated first (such as accident scenes or damaged property that may be destroyed or discarded). Claims representatives should contact any third-party claimant early in the investigation. Doing so establishes rapport with claimants, facilitates the investigation, and contributes to a timely settlement.

Claims representatives must also know when they have sufficient information on which to base a decision. Investigations should be geared to obtain information that will help determine the cause of loss, the amount of loss, and liability. The insurer's claim handling guidelines help claims representatives determine the types and extent of investigation needed for a satisfactory claim settlement. Once sufficient information is obtained to make a reasoned determination, the claims representative does not need to continue the investigation, unless the determination is disputed.

During the course of an investigation, the claims representative may discover that the insured was not at fault and that a third party caused the accident. When an insurer pays a claim to an insured for a loss caused by a negligent third party, the insurer can recover that payment amount from the negligent third party through the right of **subrogation**. Subrogation rights are established by insurance policies and by law. Claims representatives investigate subrogation possibilities concurrently with other investigations.

Subrogation
The process by which an insurer can, after it has paid a loss under the policy, recover the amount paid from any party (other than the insured) who caused the loss or is otherwise legally liable for the loss.

Documenting the Claim

Along with the investigation, documentation of the claim must continue throughout the life of the claim. All aspects of a claim must be documented to create a complete claim file. Three crucial parts of the claims documentation are diary systems, file status notes, and file reports.

Because claims representatives simultaneously handle many claims, they must have a system for working on and reviewing each claim. Whether this system is called a diary system, a suspense system, or a pending system, the purpose is the same. The system allows the claims representative to work on a claim one day and then diary it or calendar it for review. For example, the claims representative may ask an insured to provide a repair estimate and then diary that file for review on a date two weeks in the future. During that time, the claims representative would expect to receive the requested estimate. If the estimate has not been received by then, the review would prompt the claims representative to follow up.

File status notes (or an activity log) must accurately reflect and document investigations, evaluations of claims, decisions to decline coverage, or decisions to settle the claims. Because lawyers and state regulators can obtain copies of claim files, the file status notes and other file documentation must reflect these elements:

- Clear, concise, and accurate information
- Timely claim handling
- A fair investigation considering the insured's and the insurer's interests
- Objective comments about the insurer, insured, or other parties associated with the claim
- A thorough good-faith investigation

File reports to various parties are developed by claims representatives to document claim activity. The reports include various types of internal and external reports:

- Internal reports—for parties within the insurance organization who have an interest in large losses or loss of a specific nature, such as death, disfigurement, or dismemberment
- Preliminary reports—acknowledge that the claims representative received the assignment, inform the insurer about initial activity on the claim, suggest reserves, note coverage issues, and request assistance, if needed
- Status reports—periodically report the progress of the claim, recommend reserve changes, and request assistance and settlement authority when necessary

- Summarized reports—detailed narratives that follow an established format with captioned headings that give them structure, usually filed within thirty days of the assignment date
- External reports containing information collected by claims representatives—inform producers, some states' advisory organizations, and others who have an interest in the claim about details of the losses, such as the amount paid and the amount in outstanding reserve

Determining the Cause of Loss, Liability, and the Loss Amount

Claims representatives use the information gained about a claim during their investigation to determine the cause of loss, liability, and the loss amount. The facts of the loss determine the cause of the loss. For example, in a fire loss, the claims representative may find that a toaster caused the fire. The claims representative also determines the liability for the loss based on the facts of the case. For example, in an auto accident, the claims representative applies statutory and case law on negligence to determine liability of the parties involved.

Concurrent to the determination of the cause of the loss and the liability for the loss, the claims representative may determine the amount of the loss. For a property claim, the claims representative investigates the amount of damage to the property and the cost to repair or replace it and may also investigate the amount of business income lost. To determine a loss amount in a bodily injury claim, the claims representative investigates the extent of the injury, the residual and lasting effects of the injury, and the amount of pain and suffering the individual has endured.

Concluding the Claim

When the investigation has been completed and all documentation has been received, the claims representative must decide whether to pay the claim or deny it.

Payments

When a covered claim is concluded through negotiation or other means, the claims representative or claims personnel must issue a claim payment. When issuing claim payments, claims personnel must ensure that the proper parties are paid. Other parties, such as mortgagees on homes and loss payees on autos and personal property, can have a financial interest in the property. Parties named in the policy have rights, described in the policy, to be included as a payee under certain circumstances, such as for property that has been destroyed. For third-party liability claim payments, the claims representative must determine whether an attorney or a lienholder, such as a medical service provider, should be named as an additional payee on the payment. The claims representative is responsible for including all required payees when issuing a claim payment.

Claim Denial

When claims investigations reveal that a policy does not provide coverage for a loss or when an insured fails to meet a policy condition, the claims representative must make a timely claim denial. Insurers often have strict guidelines that claims representatives must follow when denying claims, and some insurers require a claims manager's approval to issue a claims denial. Before denying a claim, the claims representative must analyze the coverage carefully, investigate the loss thoroughly, and evaluate the claim fairly and objectively. Courts often favor insureds when a claims denial fails to meet these requirements, and the insurer can be assessed penalties in addition to the loss amount.

Once claims management gives authority to deny a claim, the claims representative must prepare a denial letter as soon as possible. Insurers usually send denial letters by certified mail with a return receipt requested to be signed by the addressee. Some insurers also send a copy of the letter by regular mail, marked "personal and confidential," in case the certified mail is not claimed. These procedures help ensure that the denial letter reaches the correct party, and they provide documentation that it was received.

Alternative Dispute Resolution and Litigation

If an insurer and an insured or a claimant cannot agree on the claim value or claims coverage, they may resolve the disagreement in court. However, court costs and delays in the court system have encouraged insurers, insureds, and claimants to seek alternative dispute resolution (ADR) techniques for settling disputes outside the traditional court system, including these:

- **Mediation**
- **Arbitration**
- **Appraisals**
- **Mini-trials**
- **Summary jury trials**

Despite the variety of ADR methods available, many cases are concluded through litigation. Litigation can occur at almost any point during the life of a claim. However, it occurs most often when the parties to the claim are unable to reach an agreement by negotiation or ADR, or when a claim is denied. ADR reduces, but does not eliminate, the possibility that a claimant will sue and take a case to trial. Accordingly, insurers must be prepared to litigate some claims. Many insurance policies require insurers to defend their insureds at trial. The duty to defend usually ends when the amount the insurer has paid in settlements or judgments on the claim reaches the insurer's limit of liability.

Mediation

An alternative dispute resolution (ADR) method by which disputing parties use a neutral outside party to examine the issues and develop a mutually agreeable settlement.

Arbitration

An alternative dispute resolution (ADR) method by which disputing parties use a neutral outside party to examine the issues and develop a settlement, which can be final and binding.

Appraisal

A method of resolving disputes between insurers and insureds over the amount owed on a covered loss.

Mini-trial

An alternative dispute resolution method by which a case undergoes an abbreviated version of a trial before a panel or an adviser who poses questions and offers opinions on the outcome of a trial, based on the evidence presented.

Summary jury trial

An alternative dispute resolution method by which disputing parties participate in an abbreviated trial, presenting the evidence of a few witnesses to a panel of mock jurors who decide the case.

When litigation cannot be avoided, claims representatives participate in developing a litigation strategy for the insured's defense and for litigation expense control. Claims representatives must carefully select and direct defense lawyers. The lawyer's role is to be the insured's advocate. To mitigate the claim against the insured and to encourage the claimant to settle out of court, the lawyer must address every aspect of the claimant's case, from liability to damages.

Closing Reports

When a claim is resolved, the claims representative may complete a closing or final report, which can include the claims representative's recommendations on subrogation, advice to underwriters, and other suggestions. In some instances, subrogation claims representatives use these reports to evaluate the likelihood of a successful subrogation action.

Claims supervisors and managers may use the reports to audit the claims representative's performance. These reports can also be submitted to reinsurers for reimbursement of loss payment. Claims representatives should be aware of claims that should be referred to reinsurers and must complete reports on those claims based on the insurer's internal guidelines and reinsurance agreements.

FRAMEWORK FOR COVERAGE ANALYSIS

Coverage analysis is the process of examining a policy by reviewing all its component parts and applying them to the facts of a claim.

A claims representative begins the process of coverage analysis by carefully reading the policy form and all endorsements. With experience, claims representatives learn to recognize the types of losses covered under the policy forms.

A systematic framework for coverage analysis can guide the claims representative to the parts of the policy that may provide or exclude coverage. It also ensures that all of the component parts are reviewed and reduces the incidence of erroneous coverage determinations. These questions outline a systematic framework for coverage analysis and the information it will yield:

- Is the person involved covered?
- Did the loss occur during the policy period?
- Is the cause of loss covered?
- Is the damaged property covered?
- Is the type of loss covered?
- Are the amounts of loss or damages covered?
- Is the location of the loss covered?
- Do any exclusions apply?
- Does other insurance apply?

Is the Person Involved Covered?

Some policies cover only insureds named or listed in the policy. Most policies define "insured" broadly, so the claims representative must determine whether the persons who suffered the loss are covered. For example, the homeowners (HO) policy covers the financial loss that the insured suffers as the result of a fire. For coverage to apply, the policy must cover the person who has suffered the financial loss. For example, the Personal Auto Policy (PAP) Part A—Liability Coverage defines "insured" as:[1]

> B. "Insured" as used in this Part means:
>
> 1. You or any "family member" for the ownership, maintenance or use of any auto or "trailer".
>
> 2. Any person using "your covered auto".
>
> 3. For "your covered auto", any person or organization but only with respect to legal responsibility for acts or omissions of a person for whom coverage is afforded under this Part.
>
> 4. For any auto or "trailer", other than "your covered auto", any other person or organization but only with respect to legal responsibility for acts or omissions of you or any "family member" for whom coverage is afforded under this Part. This provision (B.4.) applies only if the person or organization does not own or hire the auto or "trailer".

According to the PAP definition, a friend who borrows your car and drives it is an insured. A friend who uses your car and pays you for that use is not an insured because of the last sentence in Item 4.

In contrast, the HO-3 defines "insured" in part as:[2]

> 3. "Insured" means:
>
> a. You and residents of your household who are:
>
> (1) Your relatives; or
>
> (2) Other persons under the age of 21 and in the care of any person named above;…

According to the HO-3 definition, a sixteen-year-old international exchange student who lives in the household is an insured. An independent twenty-four-year-old friend who visits over the weekend is not an insured. "Insured" may be defined differently in other sections of the policy. For example, the definition of "insured" is expanded for Part B—Medical Payments Coverage of the PAP to include:[3]

> 1. You or any "family member":
>
> a. While "occupying"; or
>
> b. As a pedestrian when struck by;
>
> a motor vehicle designed for use mainly on public roads or a trailer of any type.
>
> 2. Any other person while "occupying" "your covered auto".

Most property insurance policies limit recovery to the amount of a person's insurable interest in the damaged or destroyed property. However, insurable interest alone does not guarantee coverage. An individual may have an insurable interest in a building but not be considered an insured under the policy because the person's name is not listed in the declarations or on an endorsement.

For example, Kathy owns a house jointly with her parents, who live in another state. All three have an insurable interest in the house, but Kathy is the only named insured on the policy. If a tornado damages the house, Kathy would be paid for the loss because she has an insurable interest in the house and is a named insured. Kathy's parents are not residents of the house or named insureds, so even though they have an insurable interest, they are not insureds under the policy. See the exhibit "Adjusting Tip."

Adjusting Tip

Claim representatives must determine whether others have an insurable interest in the property on which a claim is based. In Kathy's case, the claim representative, on discovering that Kathy's parents have an insurable interest in the house, should check with a supervisor or manager to determine how to handle the claim payment. Lienholders or mortgagees often have an insurable interest in property, and the claim representative must determine when they should be included as payees on any claim payments.

[DA03105]

Did the Loss Occur During the Policy Period?

Many policies are written to cover only losses that occur during the policy period. The HO-3 states:[4]

> P. **Policy Period**. The policy applies only to loss which occurs during the policy period.

The policy period typically begins and ends at one minute after midnight. The Loss of Use section contains an exception to the policy period provision. For example, if a fire leaves a home unfit to live in, the insured can claim expenses for living elsewhere, even if the policy expires the next day. However, the fire must have begun during the policy period.

The date and time of loss occurrence is used to determine whether a loss occurred during the policy period. However, court decisions have offered different interpretations of date of occurrence. For example, a court may determine that the date of occurrence for an occupational disease is the first date of exposure to the harmful condition that caused the disease, the last date of exposure to the harmful condition that caused the disease, or the date the disease was diagnosed.

Is the Cause of Loss Covered?

Covered causes of loss, or perils, vary by type of policy and may include fire, theft, hail, windstorm, collision, or a legal obligation to pay damages.

Specified causes of loss coverage, also called named-perils coverage, covers a loss only if it is a direct result of a specifically listed or named cause of loss in the policy. For example, in the HO-3 policy, personal property is covered for specified perils.

Causes of loss are not often defined in the policy because the definitions are subject to court interpretation and therefore vary by state. For example, fire may seem easy to define, but does fire include smoke or excessive heat with no actual flame? Does it include damage the firefighters cause while extinguishing the fire? See the exhibit "Adjusting Tip."

Specified causes of loss coverage

Coverage for direct and accidental loss caused by fire, lightning, explosion, theft, windstorm, hail, earthquake, flood, mischief, vandalism, or loss resulting from the sinking, burning, collision, or derailment of a conveyance transporting the covered auto.

Adjusting Tip

When the policy does not define a cause of loss or another term, claim representatives can use other resources to determine the meaning. For example, statutory provisions and court decisions have defined many terms that are not defined in policies. Standard dictionaries are also resources for defining terms.

[DA03107]

Special form coverage

Property insurance coverage covering all causes of loss not specifically excluded.

Special form coverage, also called all-risks or open-perils coverage, covers every cause of direct physical loss that is not excluded. The HO-3 provides special form coverage on the dwelling and other structures. Section I—Perils Insured Against in the HO-3 states, in part, "We insure against *risk of direct loss to property* described in Coverages A and B" [emphasis added].[5] Following that statement is a list of causes of loss that the policy does not cover, such as smog, rust, birds, and rodents. Any cause of loss that is not listed among the excluded causes of loss is covered. See the exhibit "An HO-3 Claim Example."

An HO-3 Claim Example

An insured accidentally spills a caustic chemical in the kitchen. The chemical splashes on the linoleum floor, table, chairs, and area rug. Because spills are not excluded under special form coverage on the dwelling, the damage to the linoleum floor is covered. Because spills are not a named peril under specified perils coverage on the contents, the damage to the table, chairs, and area rug is not covered.

[DA03108]

In answering the question "Is the cause of loss covered?," claims representatives should thoroughly investigate all the facts concerning the loss and apply them to the language in all the provisions of the policy.

Is the Damaged Property Covered?

In following the framework for coverage analysis, the claims representative must determine whether the damaged property is covered. Insurance policies may not cover all of the insured's property. Certain property must be specified in order for coverage to apply. For example, the PAP defines "your covered auto" as:[6]

1. Any vehicle shown in the Declarations.
2. A "newly acquired auto".
3. Any "trailer" you own.
4. Any auto or "trailer" you do not own while used as a temporary substitute for any other vehicle described in this definition which is out of normal use because of its:
   a. Breakdown;
   b. Repair;
   c. Servicing;
   d. Loss; or
   e. Destruction

If a claim investigation reveals that an auto involved in an accident does not appear in the declarations or fall within the definition of "your covered auto," a coverage question may exist. However, the question may be easily resolved if the insured can prove that the car was recently purchased but has not yet been added to the policy or is a temporary substitute vehicle.

Is the Type of Loss Covered?

Losses can be classified as **direct losses** or **indirect losses**. A crumpled car fender is a direct loss. Indirect losses reduce future income, increase future expenses, or both. For example, if fire destroys an insured's home, the cost of rebuilding the home is a direct loss. The rental cost for temporary living quarters for the insured while the home is being rebuilt is an indirect loss. The loss of earnings and the extra expenses incurred over a period of time after a fire damages a business are also indirect losses.

Many property policies cover direct losses only. Other policies cover some types of indirect losses. Homeowners policies cover increases in living expenses after a covered loss renders the home untenable.

Direct loss

A reduction in the value of property that results directly and often immediately from damage to that property.

Indirect loss

A loss that arises as a result of damage to property, other than the direct loss to the property.

Are the Amounts of Loss or Damages Covered?

Claims representatives should always check the policy to determine whether the amounts of loss are covered. For property damage claims, the amount of loss payable is usually limited to physical damage to, destruction of, or loss of use of tangible property. The amount is usually based on the cost to repair or replace the damaged property with that of like kind and quality. Claims for indirect loss, such as loss of business income, can be payable if indirect loss coverage is included or has been added to the policy.

For liability claims, damages for which the insured may be liable are of two types:

Compensatory damages, which include **special damages** (which pay for specific, out-of-pocket expenses, such as medical expenses, wage loss, funeral expenses, or repair bills) and **general damages** (which pay for losses, such as pain and suffering, and do not involve specific measurable expenses), reimburse, or compensate, claimants for their bodily injury or property damage.

Punitive damages punish a wrongdoer for a reckless, malicious, or deceitful act and deter similar conduct. See the exhibit "Damages."

Compensatory damages

A payment awarded by a court to reimburse a victim for actual harm.

Special damages

A form of compensatory damages that awards a sum of money for specific, identifiable expenses associated with the injured person's loss, such as medical expenses or lost wages.

General damages

A monetary award to compensate a victim for losses, such as pain and suffering, that does not involve specific, measurable expenses.

Punitive damages (exemplary damages)

A payment awarded by a court to punish a defendant for a reckless, malicious, or deceitful act to deter similar conduct; the award need not bear any relation to a party's actual damages.

Damages

```
                          Damages
                   ┌─────────┴─────────┐
              Compensatory           Punitive
           ┌──────┴──────┐
        Special       General
```

[DA03111]

Some policies do not define or list the types of damages payable under the policy. For example, the insuring agreement for the PAP liability coverage section begins, "We will pay damages for 'bodily injury' or 'property damage' for which any 'insured' becomes legally responsible because of an auto accident."[7]

Generally, the term "damages" refers only to compensatory damages, such as expenses for medical bills, lost wages, and pain and suffering. In some states, the insurer is not permitted to pay for punitive damages because such payment by an insurer would not punish the insured.

In a liability insurance policy, the insurer agrees to pay judgments and settlements up to the policy limit. In addition, some liability policies contain deductibles. They may also include coverage for certain expenses, such as defense costs and bail bonds, outside the limit of liability. Others may have a self-insured retention (SIR) in which the insured organization adjusts and pays its own losses up to the SIR level. Once that SIR is exceeded, the insurer makes payment. The claims representative must verify all the policy limits applicable to a loss before making a settlement to ensure that any payment made falls within the available limits of coverage.

In addition to ensuring that the type of loss and types of damage are covered, claims representatives must verify that the amount of damages is within the policy limits. A first party property policy will have limits of liability and may also have sublimits for certain types of property or types of losses. For example, the HO-3 contains a limit on the dwelling and contents as well as special limits for loss of money and theft of jewelry and silverware. First-party losses are also subject to deductibles, provisions that specify how the loss is to be valued (either actual cash value or replacement cost), and coinsurance clauses designed to ensure that the appropriate amount of insurance is maintained on the property.

Is the Location of the Loss Covered?

The location where the loss occurred must be within the policy's territorial limits and, for property policies, be shown on the policy as a covered location. To illustrate, the PAP defines policy territory as:[8]

1. The United States of America, its territories or possessions;

2. Puerto Rico; or

3. Canada.

   This policy also applies to loss to, or accidents involving, "your covered auto" while being transported between their ports.

Accidents occurring in Mexico would not be covered because they are outside the territory covered by the policy. Property policies cover buildings only at the locations listed in the declarations, but personal property can be covered at other locations.

Do Any Exclusions Apply?

Some losses may be excluded in the policy. For example, the HO-3 excludes losses caused by deterioration, such as a wooden garage door that rots. The PAP excludes damage caused by wear and tear, such as the wear on a tire. Exclusions to coverage can involve these elements:

- Persons
- Causes of loss
- Types of property
- Types of damage
- Other circumstances

When claim circumstances fall within a specific exclusion, coverage does not apply. An exclusion applies even if other coverage requirements are met. For example, suppose that an insured uses his car as a taxi and is involved in an accident, severely damaging the driver's side door. The insured subsequently submits a claim. That claim appears to be covered according to these criteria:

- Is the person involved covered? The driver is the named insured.
- Did the loss occur during the policy period? In this case, it did.
- Is the cause of loss covered? The policy covers physical damage to the insured's car.
- Is the damaged property covered? The vehicle is listed in the policy's declarations.
- Is the type of loss covered? The policy covers collisions.
- Are the amounts of loss or damages covered? The amount of the loss is within the policy limits but more than the deductible.
- Is the location of the loss covered? The loss occurred within the policy's territorial limits.

Then the claims representative would ask another question: "Do any exclusions apply?" On reviewing the exclusions, the claims representative would find that the PAP excludes loss that occurs while the car is used as a public or livery conveyance, and the claims representative would rightfully deny the claim.

Sometimes exclusions contain exceptions, meaning they clarify what is excluded. For example, the PAP excludes liability coverage for damage to property used by the insured. However, an exception in the exclusion states that the exclusion does not apply to property damage to a residence used by the insured. Claims representatives who carefully read the policy can avoid incorrectly denying coverage based on an exclusion when an exception applies. See the exhibit "Adjusting Tip."

Adjusting Tip

A claim representative must make sure that the exclusion upon which the denial is based has not been declared invalid by a court having jurisdiction over the claim or by a state statute.

[DA05560]

Does Other Insurance Apply?

Some policies are intended to apply only if no other insurance applies or only above the limits provided by other insurance. For example, the PAP states that coverage provided under that policy is excess over other collectible insurance for vehicles the insured does not own. In other cases, a policy may pay a portion of the loss based on the limit of insurance available from other policies. Having answered all the questions in the framework for coverage analysis, the claims representative can apply the policy to the facts of the claim and make a coverage determination.

APPLYING THE CLAIMS HANDLING PROCESS AND THE FRAMEWORK FOR COVERAGE ANALYSIS

To ensure good-faith handling of property and liability claims, insurers' claims departments adopt specific procedures and guidelines.

Claims representatives can use the claims handling process and apply the framework for coverage analysis as a guide for every claim they handle. Specific information about handling property, liability, and bodily injury claims will help dictate the procedures for each claims handling activity.

Case Facts

Susan and Thomas Reed live at 104 Fremont Street in Malvern, Texas. They have two children: Ann, age 16, who lives at home, and John, age 19, who lives at home when not attending Columbus College in New Mexico. Susan's mother, Marie, also lives with them. Susan is a schoolteacher, and Thomas is the owner of a small company called Universal Widgets.

Susan and Thomas own their home and three cars. The ABC Loan Company holds a mortgage on their home. They also have a car loan, from Union Trust Company, on their 2015 Lexus. They do not have lienholders for their other two cars (a 2012 Toyota Camry and a 2011 Honda Civic).

Susan and Thomas have an HO-3 policy covering their home. They have a Personal Auto Policy (PAP) covering all three cars.

On April 12, 20XX, Susan and Thomas received a phone call from John's roommate informing them that John had been in an auto accident while driving the Honda Civic. John suffered minor injuries after failing to obey a stop sign and then hitting another car. The driver of the other car, Karen Jones, was hospitalized.

Case Analysis Tools

To handle a claim such as the one provided in this case study, a claims representative would need to have an understanding of the coverages provided in the HO-3 policy form and in the PAP form. However, to resolve the case study, only a thorough understanding of the activities in the claims handling process and the framework for coverage analysis is required.

Activities in the Claims Handling Process

A thorough understanding of these activities in the claims handling process will lead to the conclusion described in the Correct Answer section and other possible conclusions to this case study:

- Acknowledging and assigning the claim
- Identifying the policy and setting reserves
- Contacting the insured or the insured's representative
- Investigating the claim
- Documenting the claim
- Determining the cause of loss, liability, and the loss amount
- Concluding the claim

Acknowledging and Assigning the Claim

After talking with John, Thomas called his insurance agent and reported the claim. The agent then reported the claim to the insurer. Claims Representative Jim Smith was assigned to handle all aspects of the claim.

After he received the claim assignment, Jim acknowledged receipt of the claim to the agent. Then he entered the claim information into the insurer's claims-processing system.

Identifying the Policy and Setting Reserves

Jim identified the Reeds' auto policy and performed an initial review. He established that the 2011 Honda Civic had liability coverage, collision coverage with a $1,000 deductible, and Personal Injury Protection coverage. Based on the limited information on the first notice of loss, Jim set up these parts of the claim with preliminary reserves:

- Bodily injury liability claim from Karen Jones—reserve $5,000
- Property damage claim from Karen Jones—reserve $2,500
- Collision coverage for the 2006 Honda—reserve $2,500
- PIP coverage for John's injuries—reserve $1,000

Contacting the Insured or the Insured's Representative

Jim contacted Susan and Thomas Reed. They gave him a brief description of the accident and asked Jim to contact John for all of the details about what happened. While talking with Susan and Thomas, Jim confirmed that they are the registered owners of the car, that the car is registered in Texas, and that John was using the car with their permission.

Jim called John and took a recorded statement that provided these facts:

- John is a full-time college student in New Mexico. He lives in a dormitory on campus. He has had the Honda at school since the beginning of the semester and parks it on a campus parking lot.

- The accident occurred at 11:30 AM on a Saturday morning. John was driving to a sandwich shop. He did not see a stop sign or the car on his right because of sun glare, so he entered the intersection without slowing down or stopping.

- John's car struck the car driven by Karen Jones on the driver's side door. John was wearing his seatbelt at the time of the accident. His air bag deployed on impact. He was taken to the emergency room, treated for minor cuts, and released.

- Karen Jones was also taken to the emergency room. John believed she had a concussion and a deep laceration on her forehead. John received a ticket for careless driving.

- The Honda was taken to Sam's Auto Body Shop in Columbus, New Mexico.

Investigating the Claim

After concluding his conversation with John, Jim requested a police report and reviewed the PAP to answer some questions he had regarding coverage for this claim. Jim had already confirmed that the Honda is listed on the Reeds' policy and that it has collision coverage. (Is the damaged property covered? Is the cause of loss covered?) He also confirmed that the accident date occurred within the policy period. (Did the loss occur during the policy period?)

Jim determined who is covered by the PAP. According to the liability coverage part, "insured" is defined in this manner:

1. You or any "family member" for the ownership, maintenance or use of any auto or "trailer".

According to the definition of insured, John is covered by the policy. (Is the person involved covered?) The insuring agreement states that the insurer will pay damages for bodily injury or property damage for which any insured becomes legally responsible because of an auto accident. The insuring agreement also states that the policy will pay defense costs in addition to the limit of liability. (Is the type of loss covered?)

Jim then checked the Part A exclusions. None of the exclusions appear to apply. (Do any exclusions apply?)

Next, Jim examined the policy period and territory provision of the PAP. The loss occurred during the policy period and within the policy territory of the U.S. (Is the location where the loss occurred covered?)

Based on the information obtained from Thomas Reed and John Reed, no other auto policies are applicable to this accident because all of the Reeds' cars are insured under this policy. (Does other insurance apply?)

The PAP provides out-of-state coverage, so the policy complies with New Mexico's financial responsibility laws. New Mexico does not have no-fault laws, so the liability portion of the Reeds' coverage will apply to Karen's bodily injury and property claims. (Do any other policies apply to the loss?) Based on the limited medical information available at this time concerning Karen, Jim believes that the liability limit on the Reeds' policy is sufficient to cover the bodily injury and property damage that Karen sustained. (Are the amounts of loss or damages covered?) However, Jim will have to review this portion of the claim frequently as more information about Karen and her injuries becomes available.

Jim confirmed that Karen was released from the hospital after she received treatment for her injuries and was kept for 24 hours of observation because of blood loss. He called her the next day to take her claim statement, which confirmed John's account of the accident. Karen's statement also revealed these details:

- Karen is 38 years old and single, and lives at 2227 North Casa Avenue, Apt. 215, Pueblo, New Mexico.

- Karen received sixty stitches for the wound in her forehead. While in the hospital, she received blood to replace blood she lost because of the laceration to her forehead. The emergency staff confirmed through an X-ray that she had suffered a minor concussion, and the physician prescribed a pain reliever for her headaches.

- Karen was placed under observation for one week to monitor any problems that might ensue because of the concussion.

- Karen's 2012 Buick was taken to Roy's Auto Damage, where an estimate for $3,800 was prepared to cover repairs to the driver's-side door and front fender. Karen agreed to mail the estimate to Jim.

- Based on the estimate, Jim adjusted the property damage reserve for Karen's auto to $3,800.

Documenting the Claim

Jim recorded all of the information he learned through the investigation in his file status notes for this claim. He included the police report with a diagram of the scene (that matched John's and Karen's accident descriptions), Karen's auto estimate, and the recorded statements of the two claimants with the claim file documents.

The claims diary system created an automatic entry for follow-up two weeks after the date of Jim's initial entry. Jim changed the diary date to two weeks from the date he completed this phase of the investigation. Documentation of changes in the claim information, reserves, and settlements will be ongoing.

Jim will also have to continue his investigation to determine who is liable for the accident.

Determining Cause of Loss, Liability, and Loss Amount

As part of his analysis of liability coverage, Jim answered some of the questions that needed to be asked when analyzing coverage for the damage to the Reeds' Honda:

- Did the loss occur during the policy period?
- Is the loss location covered by the policy?
- Do any other auto policies apply to this loss?

Based on the police report, the ticket issued to John, and John's own admission of fault, Jim determined that John was liable for the damages in the accident through tort liability. Because John is an insured under Susan and Thomas's policy, the policy will cover the damages up to the policy limits.

This investigation resolved the questions to which answers are required to ensure coverage under auto liability. (Did the claim arise out of the use of certain autos by certain individuals? Was the claim for bodily injury or property damage?) The investigation also addressed the PAP exclusion for intentional acts, as John did not intend the result of his actions or intend to commit the action that caused the injurious outcomes. After reviewing Part D—Coverage for Damage to Your Auto of the PAP, Jim confirmed that there is collision coverage on the Reeds' Honda. Based on the facts currently known, Jim reviewed the exclusions to Part D coverage and determined that none of the exclusions apply.

Property Damage Claims

Jim assigned an appraiser to assess the amount of damage to the Reeds' Honda and to Karen's Buick and to prepare estimates to repair the damages. Based on the description of the accident that John gave in his statement, Jim decided that the $2,500 reserve for the Honda is adequate. He will review the reserves after he receives the appraiser's estimates.

Jim changed the diary date to two weeks after the date he requested the estimate from the appraiser, so that he can follow up if he does not receive the reports. He also updated the file status notes with the cause of loss, liability, and coverage information.

Two days later, Jim received the appraiser's estimate for $3,700 in damages to the Reeds' Honda and an estimate for the damage to Karen's Buick that was $5 less than the estimate Karen submitted. He also received photos of the damage to both autos. Jim adjusted the reserve for this expected damage amount on the Reeds' auto to $2,700 (after application of the $1,000 deductible). The difference in the estimates for Karen's Buick was negligible, so he made no change to that reserve. Jim updated his file status notes and added the estimates and photos to the claim file.

John's Medical Claim

Jim reviewed the Personal Injury Protection (PIP) endorsement attached to the Reeds' auto policy. This endorsement provides unlimited medical expenses coverage to covered persons. Jim confirmed that the definition of insured applies to a family member. The insuring agreement states that PIP benefits will be paid to an insured who sustains bodily injury caused by an accident and resulting from the use of an auto. The medical expenses must be reasonable and necessary.

John had indicated that he suffered a laceration above his eye, which was treated at the emergency room. He also received treatment from a chiropractor for his sore neck and back. John will give his medical bills to Jim for review and reimbursement.

Jim also reviewed the exclusions in the endorsement and determined that none of them apply. Jim decided to raise the reserve on John's PIP claim to $2,500 to cover the emergency room bill and three months of chiropractic treatment.

Four months after the accident, Jim verified that John's treatment for his injuries had ended. John submitted medical bills and medical mileage expenses totaling $2,400. Jim examined the bills and mileage figures and determined that they were reasonable and necessary for John's injuries.

Karen's Medical Claim

Six weeks after the accident, Jim reviewed the medical receipts and medical mileage records he received from Karen for treatment of her injury. He determined that they were reasonable and necessary for the injuries she sustained. He reviewed an early photo of Karen's injured forehead and a recent photo showing that scarring was minimal.

Jim submitted a query in an injury database to which his employer subscribes. It showed that Karen had never sustained any injuries that were submitted to a workers compensation or liability insurer. This indicated that her injuries from this accident were new injuries.

Jim totaled the medical receipts and medical mileage claim at $4,200. Because she was hospitalized over a weekend and was able to report to work the following Monday, Karen incurred no loss of income. Jim added 10 percent to the total to compensate Karen for her "pain and suffering." Jim then confirmed that the total of $4,620 plus $3,800 for Karen's Buick, or $8,420, was within the Reeds' PAP liability policy limit.

Concluding the Claim

Before issuing any payments, Jim checked the federal and state databases to ensure that neither Karen nor any of the Reeds had any outstanding legal obligations that would require payment before they could receive any payment for their claims.

After Karen's auto was repaired, Jim issued a check payable to Roy's Auto Damage and to Karen Jones for $3,800. He then closed Karen's property damage reserve. After the Reeds' Honda was repaired, Jim issued a check payable to Sam's Auto Body and Thomas and Susan Reed for $2,700 and closed the Reeds' property damage reserve.

Jim arranged a settlement review with Karen, in which he offered her the calculated total of $4,620 for her medical expenses. Jim explained how he arrived at that amount and that he believed it was a reasonable settlement. He also showed Karen the total amount of the bodily injury and property damage claims paid by the Reeds' insurer for Karen's damages. (At this time, Jim noted that the scar on Karen's forehead was barely visible). Karen accepted Jim's settlement offer. He issued her a check for her medical expenses and obtained a full release from liability for the claim, which Karen signed. Later, Jim closed Karen's bodily injury claim reserve.

Jim contacted the Reeds and offered to pay $2,400 for John's PIP claim. Because John was at fault for the accident, no "pain and suffering" compensation was warranted. Jim noted that they had already paid $2,700 ($3,700 less the $1,000 deductible) for repairs to the Honda. The Reeds accepted Jim's settlement offer. He mailed them a check for $2,400, along with full releases for their property damage claim and for John's PIP claim. The Reeds signed the forms and returned them to Jim's office the following day. Jim closed John's PIP reserve.

Jim included the signed releases in the claim file and completed his file status notes to indicate the outcome of Karen's settlement meeting and the Reeds' settlements. Then he marked the claim file as closed on the insurer's claims information system. See the exhibit "Correct Answer*."

Correct Answer*

Claim Payments for Reed/Jones Accident, DOL: 04/12/20XX

- Bodily injury liability claim payment for Karen Jones—Final payment, $4,620
- Property damage claim for Karen Jones's 2008 Buick—Final payment, $3,800
- Collision coverage for the Reeds' 2006 Honda—Final payment, $2,700
- PIP coverage for John Reed's injuries—Final payment, $2,400

*This solution might not be the only viable solution. Other solutions could be exercised if justified by the analysis. In addition, specific circumstances and organizational needs or goals may enter into the evaluation, making an alternative action a better option.

SUMMARY

Two primary goals of the claims function are complying with the contractual promise and supporting the insurer's financial goals. The insurer fulfills its contractual promise to the insured through the claims handling process. Claims departments provide claims information that is used by marketing, underwriting, and actuarial departments to perform their functions.

Insurers and other insurance organizations have claims departments, which can be structured in various ways. Claims personnel may be staff claims representatives, independent adjusters, employees of TPAs, or producers. Public adjusters can also handle claims by representing the insured's interests to the insurer. Claims Department performance can be measured by a loss ratio and the use of internally identified best practices, claim audits, and customer-satisfaction data.

Insurers use a combination of compliance measures to meet legal and regulatory requirements and promote good-faith claims handling practices. These measures include (1) claims guidelines, policies, and procedures; (2) controls, such as reports, access security, authority levels, and tracking; (3) supervisor and manager reviews; and (4) claims audits.

Claims representatives must be able to apply the information contained in the policy to the activities in the claim handling process. This process creates consistency in claims handling and helps ensure that claims are handled in a manner that conforms with legal and ethical standards. These activities are performed on every claim, to some degree:

- Acknowledging and assigning the claim
- Identifying the policy
- Contacting the insured or the insured's representative
- Investigating and documenting the claim
- Determining the cause of loss, liability, and the loss amount
- Concluding the claim

Claims representatives use a framework for coverage analysis that involves every policy component, ensuring that all parts of the policy will be considered when making a coverage determination. Using the framework, the claims representative answers these questions:

- Is the person involved covered?
- Did the loss occur during the policy period?
- Is the cause of loss covered?
- Is the damaged property covered?
- Is the type of loss covered?
- Are the amounts of loss or damages covered?
- Is the location where the loss occurred covered?

- Do any exclusions apply?
- Does other insurance apply?

Claims representatives can use the framework for coverage analysis and the claims handling process as guides for every claim they handle. The language of the policy and the facts of the claim will provide the details.

ASSIGNMENT NOTES

1. Includes copyrighted material of Insurance Services Offices, Inc., with its permission. Copyright, ISO Properties, Inc., 2003.
2. Includes copyrighted material of Insurance Services Offices, Inc., with its permission. Copyright, ISO Properties, Inc., 2010.
3. Includes copyrighted material of Insurance Services Offices, Inc., with its permission. Copyright, ISO Properties, Inc., 2003.
4. Includes copyrighted material of Insurance Services Offices, Inc., with its permission. Copyright, ISO Properties, Inc., 2010.
5. Includes copyrighted material of Insurance Services Offices, Inc., with its permission. Copyright, ISO Properties, Inc., 2010.
6. Includes copyrighted material of Insurance Services Offices, Inc., with its permission. Copyright, ISO Properties, Inc., 2003.
7. Includes copyrighted material of Insurance Services Offices, Inc., with its permission. Copyright, ISO Properties, Inc., 2003.
8. Includes copyrighted material of Insurance Services Offices, Inc., with its permission. Copyright, ISO Properties, Inc., 2003.

Actuarial Operations

Educational Objectives

After learning the content of this assignment, you should be able to:

▷ Summarize the actuarial function in insurer operations and the actuarial services required by insurers.

▷ Describe the insurer goals of ratemaking and the ideal characteristics of rates.

▷ Describe the components of an insurance rate and common ratemaking terms.

▷ Explain how the following factors can affect ratemaking:
- Estimation of losses
- Delays in data collection and use
- Change in the cost of claims
- Insurer's projected expenses
- Target level of profit and contingencies

▷ Compare the following ratemaking methods:
- Pure premium
- Loss ratio
- Judgment

▷ Describe the steps in the ratemaking process.

▷ Evaluate how the following ratemaking factors vary by type of insurance:
- Experience period
- Trending
- Large loss limitations
- Credibility
- Increased limits factors

7

Educational Objectives, continued

▸ Analyze loss reserves in terms of purpose and types, importance of accuracy, and analysis techniques used by actuaries.

Actuarial Operations

7

THE ACTUARIAL FUNCTION

Actuaries are professionals who evaluate the financial consequences of future events. As such, they play a critical role in the fields of insurance and risk management.

The actuarial function is responsible for ensuring that the insurer operates effectively and conducts its operations on a financially sound basis. The two most prominent actuarial functions for an insurer involve ratemaking and estimation of unpaid liabilities and adequacy of loss reserves. Actuaries are also instrumental in developing an insurer's predictive models, and they perform other important functions for insurers, including analyzing reinsurance structure and participating in corporate planning and budgeting.

What Is an Actuary?

There are many definitions of what an actuary is. First, actuaries are professionals; they have a formal educational process, a set of standards for performance, and a code of conduct. Focusing on the financial effects of risk, actuaries are found throughout the business world, often employed by either insurance companies or firms supplying services to insurers. Actuaries often rely heavily on mathematical models and statistical techniques, but their examination process also covers insurance operations, accounting, insurance law, and financial analysis.

Actuarial Functions

One of the major functions of actuaries is to direct insurer ratemaking operations. Actuaries also develop factors that are applied to loss costs in order to reflect individual insurer experience and expenses. The ratemaking process involves estimation of trends that will affect claim costs during the future effective period of the rates. Thus, the actuary must consider economic and regulatory factors that will affect the potential cost of coverage.

Another major function of an actuary involves the estimation of an insurer's unpaid liabilities and adequacy of its loss reserves. Insurers are required by both accounting standards and law to set aside funds for the future payments on claims for which they are liable. Actuaries use various methods to estimate the amount of these liabilities. In the U.S., insurers are required to submit, with their statutory annual statement, a statement of opinion by a qualified actuary as to whether the carried reserves make a reasonable provision for this liability. The actuary providing this statement must have been approved by the insurer's board of directors and is named individually in the statement.

Actuaries are also instrumental in developing insurer's predictive models using **data mining** tools. Predictive modeling is increasingly being applied in areas such as ratemaking, underwriting, claims analytics, customer segmentation, and target marketing, which can lead to increased profits for an insurer.

Because of their quantitative background and familiarity in dealing with uncertain events, actuaries often perform other tasks, primarily related to assessment of insurer risks, including these:

- Analyzing reinsurance needs to determine the level and concentration of risk the insurer can retain versus the cost of reinsurance

- Estimating future cash flows so that assets will be available when claims are to be paid

- Assessing corporate risk by testing the adequacy of surplus under potential adverse conditions (catastrophe, sudden change in asset values, soft pricing, and inflation, for example)

- Providing financial and statistical information to regulators and applicable statistical agents (with accounting and finance areas)

- Participating in corporate planning and budgeting

Data mining

The process of extracting hidden patterns from data that is used in a wide range of applications for research and fraud detection.

Actuarial Services

Many large insurers employ a number of actuaries. Although small insurers may have a few actuaries on staff, most tend to rely on actuarial consultants. Some actuaries are concentrated in specialized departments, such as reserving. Insurers may also use actuaries within regional offices or in other functional areas, such as underwriting.

Insurers that employ staff actuaries may also retain actuarial consultants. Outside actuaries can supplement staff knowledge with specialized expertise, provide independent opinion when needed, and ease workload peaks. Regulatory authorities and reinsurers sometimes require insurers to provide a consulting actuary's opinion verifying the accuracy and reasonableness of the staff actuaries' work.

Insurers with limited data for ratemaking rely on rates or loss costs prepared by actuaries at advisory organizations, such as Insurance Services Office, Inc. (ISO), the American Association of Insurance Services (AAIS), or the National Council on Compensation Insurance (NCCI). The actuaries at these organizations collect premium and loss data from many insurers to use in calculating expected loss costs for various types of insurance. Advisory organizations also maintain contact with regulatory authorities to facilitate approval of rate filings. Advisory organizations also provide some services that are not actuarial, such as drafting insurance policies.

INSURER RATEMAKING GOALS

Even with years of statistics and insurance records as a resource, it is impossible for insurers to predict the future with complete certainty. Therefore, they must accept some risk when it comes to setting rates that they hope will cover the future, forecasting the fortuitous losses their policyholders will suffer, and estimating associated expenses.

Through the ratemaking process, insurers strive to be profitable while also meeting all insurance policy obligations. An ideal insurance rate has a number of different characteristics, including some that are contradictory.

Ratemaking Goals

From the insurer's perspective, the primary goal of **ratemaking** is to develop a rate structure that enables the insurer to compete effectively while earning a reasonable profit on its operations. To accomplish this, the rates must result in premiums that adequately cover all losses and expenses and that leave a reasonable amount for profits and contingencies.

This ratemaking goal complements the underwriting goal of developing and maintaining a profitable book of business. To be profitable, the insurer must have adequate rates, but to maintain its customer base, the insurer's rates must be competitive. These goals can easily conflict with each other. The rate chosen by an insurer is often a compromise between maximizing profit and maintaining (or expanding) market share.

To be approved, rates must comply with applicable regulations, which generally mandate rates that are adequate, not excessive, and not unfairly discriminatory.

> **Ratemaking**
> The process insurers use to calculate insurance rates, which are a premium component.

Ideal Characteristics of Rates

Ideally, rates should have five characteristics:

- Be stable
- Be responsive
- Provide for contingencies
- Promote risk control
- Reflect differences in risk exposure

Rates do not always have all these characteristics. Also, some characteristics conflict with others, and compromises are often necessary. For example, maintaining rate stability could conflict with being responsive, which suggests that rates should change promptly in response to external factors that affect losses.

Stable

Stable rates are highly desirable because it is expensive to change rates, involving a fair amount of time and expense to calculate rate indications, obtain needed approval, and then implement the new rates. Generally, rates are not changed more than once a year. Rates should also be stable from one rate adjustment to the next. Sudden, large rate changes can cause dissatisfaction among customers and sometimes lead to regulatory or legislative actions.

Responsive

Rates should include the best possible estimates of losses and expenses that will arise from the coverage. Because external conditions change over time, the most recent claims experience ought to predict future experience better than older experience. For this reason, most insurers and advisory organizations review their rates at least annually.

Provide for Contingencies

Future events cannot be predicted with absolute certainty. Because the insurer has a responsibility to pay all valid claims even if costs are higher than estimated, the rates charged for coverage should provide for contingencies, such as unexpected variations in losses and expenses. This provision also provides greater security that the insurer will be able to meet its obligations to potential claimants.

Promote Risk Control

Ratemaking systems help promote risk control by providing lower rates for policyholders who exercise sound risk control. For example, policyholders who install burglar alarm systems receive a reduction in their crime insurance rates. Lower fire insurance rates are charged to policyholders who install automatic sprinkler systems at their premises. However, policyholders who engage in activities that tend to result in more losses, such as using their own cars for business, generally pay higher rates.

Reflect Differences in Risk Exposure

Ideal rates reflect the amount of risk the insured is exposed to. For example, the owner of a wood-frame home would ideally pay more for fire insurance than someone who lives in a building made of concrete because the former faces a greater risk from fire. By differentiating the rates in this way, the insurer increases its chances of keeping the owner of the concrete home as a customer and encourages the owner of the wood-frame home to take protective measures, such as installing a sprinkler system, that could decrease his or her insurance rate.

Treating both insureds equally would probably cause the owner of the concrete home to look elsewhere for more reasonably priced coverage, affecting the insurer's income and ability to cover any losses the owner of the wood-frame building may suffer. Therefore, it is beneficial for insurers to use all data available to them to rate each exposure individually.

Apply Your Knowledge

Enhancing an insurer's ability to handle the economic impacts of unforeseen losses or expenses is an example of which one of these characteristics of an ideal rate?

a. Promote risk control

b. Reflect differences in risk exposure

c. Provide for contingencies

d. Be stable

Feedback: c. A rate's ability to provide for contingencies allows the insurer to handle the economic impacts of unforeseen losses or expenses.

RATE COMPONENTS AND RATEMAKING TERMS

Insurance premiums can sometimes seem like amorphous, arbitrary constructions. They are based on definitive rates that consider various factors, however, and having a thorough understanding of these factors will help insurance professionals explain the financial impacts of insurance to insureds.

Knowledge of the specific components and terms used in ratemaking provides a foundation to understanding the process. Understanding how investment income can affect an insurer's ratemaking can create further transparency in the process.

Rate Components

An insurance **rate** consists of three components:

- An amount needed to pay future claims and loss adjustment expenses (prospective loss costs)

- An amount needed to pay future expenses, such as acquisition expenses, overhead, and premium taxes (expense provision)

- An amount for profit and contingencies (profit and contingencies factor)

The first component of an insurance rate is related to the prospective loss costs developed by advisory organizations or by insurers with large pools of loss data. The second and third components are related to an expense multiplier. Once the insurance rate is calculated, it is multiplied by the appropriate number of exposure units to produce a **premium**.

Rate
The price per exposure unit for insurance coverage.

Premium
The price of the insurance coverage provided for a specified period.

Ratemaking Terms

These are common terms used in the ratemaking process:

- Exposure base (sometimes just exposure) is a variable that approximates the loss potential of a type of insurance. For property coverage, the exposure base is the value being insured; for product liability, the exposure is sales.

- Earned exposure unit is the exposure unit for which the insurer has provided a full period of coverage. The periods are typically measured in years.

- **Pure premium** is the amount included in the rate per exposure unit required to pay losses. This component is also sometimes called the loss cost.

- **Expense provision** is the amount added to the pure premium required to pay expenses. Such expenses include acquisition expenses; general expenses; premium taxes; and licenses and fees paid to government, regulatory, and advisory organizations. This component is sometimes referred to as underwriting expenses.

- **Loss adjustment expenses (LAE)** are the expenses associated with adjusting claims. These expenses are often split into either **allocated loss adjustment expenses (ALAE)** or **unallocated loss adjustment expenses (ULAE)**. Some ALAE, such as legal fees to defend a claim, may be included in the pure premium instead of the expense provision. An example of LAE included in the expense provision is the cost of an insurer's in-house claims adjusters.

- Insurers add a loading, or additional cost, to profit and contingencies. This loading protects the insurer against the possibility that actual losses and expenses will exceed the projected losses and expenses included in the insurance rate. If excessive losses or expenses are not incurred, the funds generated by the loading produce additional profit for the insurer.

Pure premium

The average amount of money an insurer must charge per exposure unit in order to be able to cover the total anticipated losses for that line of business.

Expense provision

The amount that is included in an insurance rate to cover the insurer's expenses and that might include loss adjustment expenses but that excludes investment expenses.

Loss expense (loss adjustment expense or LAE)

The expense that an insurer incurs to investigate, defend, and settle claims according to the terms specified in the insurance policy.

Allocated loss adjustment expense (ALAE)

The expense an insurer incurs to investigate, defend, and settle claims that are associated with a specific claim.

Unallocated loss adjustment expense (ULAE)

Loss adjustment expense that cannot be readily associated with a specific claim.

Apply Your Knowledge

Which one of the following terms represents expenses associated with adjusting claims?

a. Expense provision

b. Pure premium

c. Loss adjustment expenses

d. Earned exposure unit

Feedback: c. Loss adjustment expenses are expenses associated with adjusting claims.

Investment Income

A property-casualty insurer performs two distinct operations: insurance operations and investment operations.

The insurance operations write policies, collect premiums, and pay losses, resulting in an underwriting profit. The investment operations use these funds to buy or sell bonds, stocks, and other investments to earn an investment profit, which is called investment income.

Historically, property-casualty insurers did not directly consider their investment returns when calculating insurance rates. They may, however, have informally considered investment returns when determining allowances for profits and contingencies.

Today, insurers often consider investment results explicitly in rate calculations. Some states even require this practice. Sophisticated models are available that can be used to include investment returns in the insurance rate.

The investment return earned by an insurer depends largely on the types of insurance written, the loss reserves, and associated unearned premium reserves. Property losses are usually paid relatively quickly, while liability losses often are not paid until years after losses occur.

Consequently, an insurer's loss reserves for liability insurance are usually much greater than its loss reserves for an equivalent amount of property insurance. Because the assets that support the loss reserves are invested to produce income for the insurer, investment returns have a much larger effect on liability insurance rates than property insurance rates.

FACTORS THAT AFFECT RATEMAKING

It is never easy to predict the future, to which any weather forecaster can attest, but that is exactly what insurers are expected to do when setting rates for insurance coverage. Several factors can have varying degrees of effect on a coverage's rate, but a good understanding of those factors can help insurance professionals keep unexpected rate increases to a minimum for their clients.

These areas of ratemaking can be affected by the inherent uncertainty of trying to predict events and estimate future costs:

- Estimation of losses
- Delays in data collection and use
- Change in the cost of claims
- Insurer's projected expenses
- Target level of profit and contingencies

Estimation of Losses

Properly estimating the amount of losses for future claims is the key to developing adequate insurance rates. Past loss experience is generally used as a starting point to estimate future losses. Ratemaking is based on estimating losses from past coverage periods and adjusting those losses for future conditions. For example, adjustments for anticipated future inflation or for changes in benefits mandated by legislation could be made to past loss experience.

However, past loss experience may not be completely known because not all covered losses are paid immediately. At any point in time, many claims have been incurred but not yet paid (for example, the losses for an auto accident are not paid immediately after the accident is reported; there is lag time as the claim is processed). The difference between the estimated amount that is set aside to ultimately pay for claims and the actual loss amount paid to date is the loss reserves. Insurers face the challenge of estimating **ultimate losses** for past experience as accurately as possible because of the difficulty of estimating future payments.

Insurance rates are based partly on incurred losses. **Incurred losses** include both paid losses and outstanding loss reserves. Loss reserves are estimates of future payments for covered claims that have already occurred, whether the claims are reported or not. Insurers are legally required to set aside funds for these future payments; these are shown as liabilities on their balance sheets. Because loss reserves are estimates of future events, they are somewhat imprecise. Nonetheless, rates are based partly on such estimates. Therefore, if loss reserve estimates are too low, rates will probably be too low. If loss reserves are too high, rates will probably be too high as well.

To illustrate, assume that rates for auto liability insurance are calculated based on losses that occurred in the most recent three-year period. The insurer's past experience indicates that 25 percent of losses are paid in the year the accident occurs, 50 percent are paid in the second year, and 25 percent are paid in the third year. See the exhibit "Hypothetical Auto Liability Loss Experience at Year 3 End."

Ultimate loss

The final paid amount for all losses in an accident year.

Incurred losses

The losses that have occurred during a specific period, no matter when claims resulting from the losses are paid.

Hypothetical Auto Liability Loss Experience at Year 3 End

Year	(1) Paid Losses	(2) Loss Reserves	(3) Incurred Losses
1	$10,000,000	$0	$10,000,000
2	7,500,000	2,500,000	10,000,000
3	2,500,000	7,500,000	10,000,000
Total	$20,000,000	$10,000,000	$30,000,000

[DA03362]

The exhibit shows the losses for each year in the three-year period, with Year 1 being the earliest year and Year 3, the most recent year:

- The paid losses in Column (1) are the amounts paid from January 1 of Year 1 up to and including December 31 of Year 3. The insurer has already paid this money to claimants.

- The loss reserves shown in Column (2) are the insurer's best estimates, as of December 31 of Year 3, of the amounts it will pay in the future for losses that occurred during each one-year period. Because all losses that occurred in Year 1 have been paid, no loss reserve exists for Year 1.

- Column (3), which is incurred losses for a given period, is the sum of Columns (1) and (2).

If the insurer in this exhibit insured 100,000 cars each year during this three-year period, it provided 300,000 car-years of protection. A car-year represents the loss exposure of one car insured for one year. If the 300,000 car-years are divided into the $30 million of incurred losses, the insurer needs a pure premium—the amount needed to pay losses—of $100 per car per year ($30,000,000 ÷ 300,000 = $100) to pay its losses during this past three-year period. This example includes not only paid losses but also loss reserves.

If the pure premium indicated by this **experience period** were used to develop rates for a future year, any inadequacy in past loss reserves would also make future rates inadequate, assuming conditions remain the same. Using the preceding example, assume that the loss reserves were underestimated by 15 percent; that is, the company had only $8,500,000 in loss reserves at the end of Year 3 instead of $10,000,000. The total incurred losses for the years would then be $28,500,000, and the calculated pure premium would be only $95 per car per year ($28,500,000 ÷ 300,000). Rates based on underestimated losses could lead to underwriting losses and possibly even insolvency.

Experience period
The period for which all pertinent statistics are collected and analyzed in the ratemaking process.

In theory, an insurer could avoid this problem by waiting for all claims to be paid before using loss experience to calculate rates. When all claims incurred during a given period have been paid, there is no need for loss reserves. In practice, however, waiting would create problems. If the rate filing were delayed for several years to permit all claims to be settled, then factors such as inflation, changes in traffic conditions, and so forth would have a greater chance of changing the loss exposure. The effects of these factors might be greater than the effects of errors in estimating loss reserves.

Delays in Data Collection and Use

Responsiveness is a desirable ratemaking characteristic. Because conditions are constantly changing, any delay between when data is collected and when it is used tends to reduce rate accuracy. Unfortunately, delays between when losses are incurred and when they are reflected in rates charged to customers are unavoidable and can span several years. During this period, factors—economic and otherwise—can increase or decrease the rates the insurer should charge if the premium is to reflect the expected losses. The delay in reflecting loss experience in rates stems from several sources, including these:

- Delays by insureds in reporting losses to insurers
- Time required to analyze data and prepare a rate filing
- Delays in obtaining state approval of filed rates
- Time required to implement new rates
- Time period during which rates are in effect, usually a full year

When a rate is in effect for a full year, the last policy issued under that rate could be issued 365 days (one year) after the effective date of the rate filing, and the policy's coverage under that rate continues until policy expiration, yet another year later. See the exhibit "Policy Year Time Frame."

Policy Year Time Frame

1/1/X1	12/31/X1	12/31/X2
Beginning of Policy Year First Policies Issued	Last Policies Issued for This Policy Year	Policies Issued 12/31/X1 Expire

[DA03368]

A typical schedule for developing, approving, and implementing new rates for auto insurance might have a six-year cycle, assuming the insurer is basing its new rates on its loss experience for a prior three-year period, called the experience period. Data from the experience period is collected and analyzed in the ratemaking process. See the exhibit "Chronology of a Rate Filing."

Chronology of a Rate Filing

1/1,	Year 1	Start of experience period, first loss incurred
12/31,	Year 1	
12/31,	Year 2	
12/31,	Year 3	End of experience period
3/31,	Year 4	Start of data collection and analysis
7/1,	Year 4	Rates filed with regulators
9/1,	Year 4	Approval of rates received
1/1,	Year 5	New rates initially used
12/31,	Year 5	Rates no longer used
12/31,	Year 6	Last loss incurred under this rate filing

[DA03369]

If the first experience period begins on January 1 of Year 1, data will be collected for a three-year period beginning on that date and ending on December 31 of Year 3. For most insurers, the analysis phase of the ratemaking process begins three months after the end of the experience period.

The exhibit assumes that the new rates will become effective on January 1 of Year 5, one year after the end of the experience period. They will remain in effect until December 31 of Year 5, two years after the end of the experience period. However, the policies issued on December 31 of Year 5 will remain in force until December 31 of Year 6. Consequently, the last claim under these rates will be incurred three years after the end of the experience period and six years after the beginning of the experience period, when the first losses on which the rate calculation was based occurred.

Change in Cost of Claims

Both loss severity and loss frequency affect an insurer's loss experience during any given period. Economic inflation or deflation during the inevitable delay also affects the average cost of a loss (severity). Finally, legislative or regulatory changes, such as modification in rules governing claim settlement, can affect the number of losses (frequency). Rates calculated without regard to these factors could prove to be grossly inadequate or grossly excessive.

These factors are difficult to quantify, but they clearly affect losses. Some factors that affect the size and frequency of losses cannot be identified or measured directly, but their aggregate effect on losses can be determined with reasonable accuracy by trending. The effects of historical changes can be employed to adjust the experience used in the ratemaking analysis. In addition, the rates must include a provision for changes that may arise during the period rates will be in effect.

Insurer's Projected Expenses

Insurance rates are also based on the insurer's projected expenses. Like losses, expenses can change over time, and projected changes must be considered in the ratemaking process. Rather than past expenses, it is sometimes more relevant to use judgment or budgeted expenses, especially when conditions change dramatically. For example, if a new agent commission plan was introduced, past commission expense would not necessarily be a good estimate of the costs for new policies.

Ratemakers are also challenged to allocate general administrative expenses properly among different types of insurance. Changes in the allocation of these expenses may need to be reflected in the rates.

Target Level of Profit and Contingencies

The insurer must decide what provision for profit and contingencies should be included in the rate. Consideration is given to the overall desired rate of return, including likely returns from **investment income** versus underwriting profit, respectively. An insurer's target profit may also depend on other factors. For example, an insurer may initially accept a lower profit (and thus charge lower rates) for a new insurance product in order to build a customer base.

Investment income

Interest, dividends, and net capital gains received by an insurer from the insurer's financial assets, minus its investment expenses.

Apply Your Knowledge

Which one of the following is not considered a cause for the delay in reflecting loss experience in new rates?

a. Delays by insureds in reporting losses to insurers

b. Time required to predict future losses

c. Delays in obtaining state approval of filed rates

d. Time required to implement new rates

Feedback: b. The delay in having new rates reflect loss experience can be caused by insureds delaying the reporting of losses to insurers; delays in obtaining state approval of filed rates; and the time it takes to implement new rates. The time required to predict future losses does not factor into the use of loss experience.

RATEMAKING METHODS

Although there are a few methods for adjusting existing rates or developing new rates, each serves its own purpose and has strengths and weaknesses that an insurance professional should be familiar with.

Insurers commonly use three ratemaking methods:

*   Pure premium method
*   Loss ratio method
*   Judgment method

Each method calls for different data to be put to use. See the exhibit "Ratemaking Methods."

Pure premium method

A method for calculating insurance rates using estimates of future losses and expenses, including a profit and contingencies factor.

Pure Premium Ratemaking Method

The **pure premium method** uses loss per exposure based on past experience as the basis for the rate. This method relies on past experience but is independent of any current rates.

Ratemaking Methods

Method	Data Required	Uses
Pure premium method	• Incurred losses • Earned exposure units • Expense provision • Profit and contingencies factor	To develop rates from past experience (cannot be used without past experience)
Loss ratio method	Actual loss ratio, calculated from: • Incurred losses • Earned premiums Expected loss ratio, calculated as: 100%—Provision for expenses, profit, and contingencies	To modify existing rates (cannot be used without existing rates; cannot be used to determine rates for a new type of insurance)
Judgment method	Rates based on experience and judgment	To develop rates when data are limited (requires skilled judgment)

[DA03381]

The pure premium method has four steps, the first of which is to calculate the pure premium. This is done by dividing the dollar amount of incurred losses by the number of earned exposure units.

$$\text{Incurred losses} = \$4 \text{ million}$$

$$\text{Earned car-years} = 100{,}000$$

$$\text{Pure premium} = \frac{\text{Incurred losses}}{\text{Earned car-years}}$$

$$\text{Pure premium} = \frac{\$4{,}000{,}000}{100{,}000} = \$40$$

The second step is to estimate expenses per exposure unit based on the insurer's past expenses (except investment expenses and possibly loss adjustment expenses). Whatever loss adjustment expenses are included in the pure premium are excluded from the expenses. Investment expenses are not directly reflected in rate calculations. If expenses are $1.7 million, then expenses per exposure unit are as shown:

$$\frac{\$1{,}700{,}000}{100{,}000} = \$17$$

Determining the profit and contingencies factor comes next. This example uses a factor of 5 percent, but it can vary. A provision for net investment income is generally included within the profit provision.

$$\text{Rate per exposure unit} = \frac{\text{Pure premium} + \text{Expenses per exposure unit}}{1 - \text{Profit and contingencies factor}}$$

$$= \frac{\$40 + \$17}{1 - 0.05}$$

The final step is to add the pure premium and the expense provision and divide by one minus the profit and contingencies factor. As an example, if the pure premium is $40, the expenses per exposure unit are $17, and the profit and contingencies factor is 5 percent, the formula would be this:

$$\text{Rate per exposure unit} = \frac{\text{Pure premium} + \text{Expenses per exposure unit}}{1 - \text{Profit and contingencies factor}}$$

$$= \frac{\$40 + \$17}{1 - 0.05}$$

$$= \frac{\$57}{0.95}$$

$$= \$60$$

The rate per exposure unit of $60 is equal to the pure premium of $40 (the amount required to pay losses) plus an additional $17 (the amount required to pay expenses) and $3 (for profit and contingencies).

Some insurers separate their expenses into two components: fixed expenses and variable expenses. Fixed expenses are stated as dollar amounts per exposure unit. Variable expenses are stated as percentages of the rate.

For example, the insurer in the preceding example might decide that its cost for issuing a policy and collecting the premium is $2.50 per car year, regardless of premium size, rating class, or rating territory. Its other underwriting expenses, such as commissions and premium tax, vary by premium size. The variable expenses equal 12 percent of the final premium, so this would be the rate per exposure unit:

$$\text{Rate per exposure unit} = \frac{\text{Pure premium} + \text{Fixed expenses per exposure unit}}{1 - \text{Variable expense percentage} - \text{Profit and contingencies factor}}$$

$$= \frac{\$40 + \$2.50}{1 - 0.12 - 0.05}$$

$$= \frac{\$42.50}{0.83}$$

$$= \$51 \text{ (rounded)}$$

The new $51 rate per exposure unit is equal to the sum of pure premium of $40 (the amount required to pay losses or loss costs), fixed expenses of $2.50, variable expenses of $6 (rounded), and profit and contingencies of $2.50 (rounded).

Loss Ratio Ratemaking Method

The **loss ratio method**, in its simplest form, uses two loss ratios—the actual loss ratio and the expected loss ratio of the insurer during the selected experience period:

Loss ratio method
A method for determining insurance rates based on a comparison of actual and expected loss ratios.

1. Actual loss ratio $= \dfrac{\text{Incurred losses}}{\text{Earned premiums}}$

2. Expected loss ratio $=$ 100% $-$ Expense provision

Because this method modifies a current insurance rate, profit and contingencies are included in the expense provision. The expected loss ratio plus the provision for expenses, profit, and contingencies always adds up to 100 percent. The basic loss ratio ratemaking equation looks like this:

$$\text{Rate change} = \frac{\text{Actual loss ratio} - \text{Expected loss ratio}}{\text{Expected loss ratio}}$$

If the rate change percentage is negative, it indicates a rate reduction. If positive, it indicates a rate increase. For example, if the actual loss ratio equals 54 percent and the expected loss ratio equals 60 percent, then the rate change is a decrease of 10 percent.

$$\frac{\text{Actual loss ratio} - \text{Expected loss ratio}}{\text{Expected loss ratio}} = \frac{(0.54 - 0.60)}{0.60}$$

$$= \frac{-0.06}{0.60}$$

$$\text{Rate change} = -0.10 = -10\%$$

Here, the insurer's actual loss ratio was better than expected. Based only on this information, the insurer could likely lower its rates and still make the desired profit on business. Lower rates could also attract additional business, further producing profits.

The loss ratio ratemaking method cannot be used to calculate rates for a new type of insurance, because there is no actual loss ratio for the calculation and no existing rate to adjust. Either the pure premium method or the judgment method must be used for a new type of insurance.

Judgment Ratemaking Method

Judgment ratemaking method

A method for determining insurance rates that relies heavily on the experience and knowledge of an actuary or an underwriter who makes little or no use of loss experience data.

The **judgment ratemaking method** is the oldest ratemaking method. Although its application is no longer as widespread as it once was, it is still used for some types of insurance (such as ocean marine insurance, some inland marine classes, aviation insurance, and terrorism coverage). Although this method might use limited or no loss experience data, an experienced underwriter or actuary generally has a sense of what rates have produced desired results in the past.

Apply Your Knowledge

The two ratemaking methods best suited to establishing rates for a new type of insurance are the:

a.   Pure premium and loss ratio ratemaking methods.

b.   Pure premium and judgment ratemaking methods.

c.   Loss ratio and judgement ratemaking methods.

Feedback: b. The two ratemaking methods best suited to establishing rates for a new type of insurance are the pure premium and judgment ratemaking methods. The loss ratio ratemaking method cannot be used to calculate rates for a new type of insurance, because there is no actual loss ratio for the calculation and no existing rate to adjust.

RATEMAKING PROCESS OVERVIEW

Advisory organization

An independent organization that works with and on behalf of insurers that purchase or subscribe to its services.

Understanding what is involved in the ratemaking process can help insurance professionals contribute to each step in that process.

To create or revise insurance rates, either an insurer's staff or an **advisory organization** working on behalf of the insurer follows these steps:

1.   Collect data

2.   Adjust data

3.   Calculate overall indicated rate change

4.   Determine territorial and class relativities

5.   Prepare rate filings and submit to regulatory authorities as required

Loss cost multiplier

A factor that provides for differences in expected loss, individual company expenses, underwriting profit and contingencies; when multiplied with a loss cost, it produces a rate.

An insurer follows a similar process when reviewing loss costs. For companies that rely on loss cost filings made by advisory organizations, the ratemaking process involves calculating and filing an appropriate **loss cost multiplier**.

Collect Data

Before collecting ratemaking data, the insurer must determine the kinds of data needed. Generally, the data falls into these categories:

- Losses, both paid and incurred (including loss adjustment expenses to be included in the pure premium)
- Earned premium and/or exposure information
- Expenses, including factors for profit and contingencies

If rates are to vary by rating class and/or territory, data must be identified for each class and territory. For example, if an insurer is establishing a new class of business, it would first identify experience for this class separately.

Ideally, the incurred losses, earned premiums, and earned exposure units should be based on the same group of policies. This isn't always practical, though, so approximations are used. For example, it's sometimes most practical to compare premiums during one twelve-month period with losses for a slightly different twelve-month period, even if these two periods don't involve the same policies.

Depending on the circumstances, different aggregations of data may be used. For example, loss payments for a single claim, such as a liability or workers compensation claim, could be made over several successive calendar years, so the **calendar-year method** would be unsuitable because the delay in loss payment can be long, and the loss reserves can be large compared to earned premiums. For those types of insurance, either the **policy-year method** or **accident-year method** should be used.

For fire, inland marine, and auto physical damage insurance, losses are paid relatively quickly, and loss reserves tend to be small compared to earned premiums, so the calendar-year method may work with these policies. However, it's not as accurate as the other two methods.

Adjust Data

After data is collected, it must be adjusted because the raw exposure, premium, and loss data reflect conditions from present and past periods, while the new rates will be used in the future.

Actuaries adjust premium and loss data in these ways:

- Adjust premiums to current rate level
- Adjust historic experience for future development
- Apply trending to losses and premium

Calendar-year method
A method of collecting ratemaking data that estimates both earned premiums and incurred losses by formulas from accounting records.

Policy-year method
A method of collecting ratemaking data that analyzes all policies issued in a given twelve-month period and that links all losses, premiums, and exposure units to the policy to which they are related.

Accident-year method
A method of organizing ratemaking statistics that uses incurred losses for an accident year, which consist of all losses related to claims arising from accidents that occur during the year, and that estimates earned premiums by formulas from accounting records.

Adjust Premiums to Current Rate Level

If rates charged in the experience period were written at different rate levels, then premiums must be adjusted to the current level. The ideal way is to calculate the premium for each policy in the experience period at current rate level. For example, 20X1 personal auto premiums at 20X4's rate level would be calculated by pricing each auto insured in 20X1 at 20X4 rates. However, re-rating every exposure requires storing, retrieving, and using every rating factor for each policy of each exposure, which may make this method unfeasible. An alternative is to adjust historic premiums in total to current levels.

For example, assume that a book of business has $100 of losses each year. In Year 1, a premium of $200 is charged, but the insurer decreases rates by 20 percent in each of the next two years. So an insured that paid $1,000 premium in the first year would pay only $640 after the two rate decreases. Say the insurer had a 50 percent loss ratio the first year, 63 percent the second year, and 78 percent the third year. It would be inappropriate to project the coming year's loss ratio as the average of those ratios. The 50 percent loss ratio in Year 1 was based on premiums that would not be charged as of Year 3, so it should not be used directly for ratemaking. The premium that had been charged must be adjusted to what would be charged in Year 3, the most recent year. See the exhibit "Effect of On-Level Premium Adjustment."

Effect of On-Level Premium Adjustment

	(1)	(2)	(3) = (1)/(2)	(4)	(5)	(6) = (2)×(5)	(7) = (1)/(6)
Year	Developed Losses	Collected Premium	Collected Loss Ratio	Rate Level Index	On-Level Factor	On-Level Premium	On-Level Loss Ratio
1	$100	$200	50%	1.00	0.64	$128	78%
2	$100	$160	63%	0.80	0.80	$128	78%
3	$100	$128	78%	0.64	1.00	$128	78%

[DA06289]

On-level factor

A factor that is used to adjust historical premiums to the current rate level.

Column 4 in the table shows the rate level relative to Year 1. This rate level index reflects that rates decreased 20 percent from the prior year in both Year 2 and Year 3. The **on-level factor** in Column 5 adjusts rate levels for each year to the most recent period's rate levels. It equals the rate level index for the most recent period (Year 3) divided by the rate level index for each year. At the most recent year's rate level, each year's losses would have a 78 percent loss ratio.

Premiums may also have to be adjusted because of changes in the levels of coverage being purchased. For example, an automobile liability insurer finds it's now selling much more of its $100,000 per accident limits than the $25,000 limit it had in the past. The premiums (and perhaps losses) need to be adjusted for this change.

Adjust Historic Experience for Future Development

When policy-year or accident-year experience is used to predict future results, the experience might not be complete. There may still be open claims that require future payment, or a claim for which the insurer is liable could be reported late. The insurer must estimate the values of these future payments and add them to the payments to date to estimate the losses in each period.

For example, at the end of a year, payments for medical malpractice claims that occurred during that year may be only 10 percent of the final payment. Because of the complexity and long discovery period of these claims, even the incurred losses tend to increase over time. Conversely, for automobile physical damage, an insurer's net loss payments might decrease over time as it collects salvage and subrogation recoveries on claims it paid.

The future development of the losses can be estimated using several methods. The most common is applying **loss development factors** to the current experience. With any method, the goal is to estimate the final, total cost to pay all the claims within each year. These projections are used as the basis for estimating the losses that will be incurred in the proposed policy period.

Apply Trending to Losses and Premium

Another way to adjust losses for ratemaking is with trending—reviewing historic environmental changes and projecting changes into the future. Examples of such changes are inflation of claims costs, the increasing safety of newer cars, and changes in legal liability.

Trend data can come from various sources. For example, external indexes such as the Consumer Price Index or one of its components may be used in trending. The most frequently used source of trends is historical experience. This experience can be reviewed by an insurer using its own data or by a statistical agent, such as Insurance Services Office, Inc., or the National Council on Compensation Insurance, using the combined experience of numerous companies. A trend adjustment commonly involves using historical experience to project past trends into the future.

Loss trending is usually reviewed using separate severity and frequency components. These trends can be projected into the future using an **exponential trending** method, which assumes that data being projected will increase or decrease by a fixed percentage each year from the previous year. For example, claim frequency will increase 1.3 percent each year, or claim severity will increase 8.2 percent each year. Exponential trends have a compound effect over time. For example, price inflation would be expected to follow an exponential trend. See the exhibit "Claim Severity Trend Calculation."

Claim Severity Trend Calculation

(1)	(2)	(3)	(4)	(5)
		Developed	= (2)/(3)	
	Developed	Number of	Average Claim	Change From
Accident Year	Losses	Claims	Severity	Prior Year
20X1	$11,000,000	9,167	$1,200	
20X2	$10,287,750	7,913	$1,300	8.3%
20X3	$11,112,000	7,880	$1,410	8.5%
20X4	$10,659,000	6,995	$1,524	8.1%
20X5	$11,275,000	6,860	$1,644	7.9%
			Average	8.2%

The losses and claims are the estimated final values for each accident year, projected using development factors or other methods.

[DA06290]

Losses may need to be adjusted to current conditions if significant external changes have affected loss payouts in recent years. For example, workers compensation insurance benefits are established by statute; if legislation or a court decision changes the benefits, past losses must be adjusted to current benefit levels.

Premiums may also need to be adjusted to reflect changing conditions. For example, if home prices rise, more homeowners insurance premiums might be collected on a house just because of its increase in value.

Calculate Overall Indicated Rate Change

The purpose of adjustments, development, and trending is to bring prior experience to a level likely to match what will happen in the future policy period. Based on the adjusted experience, an indicated rate is calculated. In some cases, a new rate is calculated directly. But in most cases, the indicated rate shows a change from the current rate—a 2.7 percent increase, for example. Several methods, such as the **loss ratio method** and the pure premium method, can be used to produce an indicated rate. The method used depends on the experience data available.

Loss ratio method

A loss reserving method that establishes aggregate reserves for all claims for a type of insurance.

Apply Your Knowledge

Three Hills Insurance Company is establishing a new class of business. When collecting ratemaking data for the new class of business, the insurer's staff must first

a. Adjust premiums to current rate level.
b. Identify experience for this class separately.
c. Adjust historic experience.
d. Apply trending to losses and premium data.

Feedback: b. If an insurer is establishing a new class of business, it would first identify experience for this class separately.

Determine Territorial and Class Relativities

If rates vary by territory and/or class, they are reviewed after the calculation of the overall rate change. Further analysis is performed to determine territorial and/or class relativities. These relativities show which subsets of insureds in a state deserve different rates than the statewide average rate. For example, in a territory with many congested highways, auto insurance rates might be 8.6 percent higher than the statewide average rate. Similarly, a frame-constructed building has a different exposure to fire loss than a fire-resistive steel and concrete building, so different rates are warranted.

Territorial relativities can be determined by comparing the estimated loss ratio (or pure premium) for each geographic territory to the statewide average loss ratio (or pure premium). This comparison helps determine experience in each geographic territory. If a territory has limited experience, its loss ratios are likely to vary widely from other territories, and differences from the overall average rate must be supported by credible experience. So if a territory has limited experience, even very good (or very poor) experience will produce only minimal difference from the average rate because it's more likely that chance played a role in the experience.

Class relativities, which are determined similarly to territorial relativities, are used to develop rates for each rating class. Once class relativities have been determined, the insurer can prepare a rate table showing rates for each territory and each rating class.

Prepare and Submit Rate Filings

Rate filings must be prepared after data has been collected and adjusted and after territorial and class relativities have been determined. Rate filings are submitted to state regulatory authorities.

Forms and requirements vary by state but generally must include these items:

- Schedule of the proposed rates
- Statement about the percentage change in the statewide average rate
- Explanation of differences between the overall statewide change in rate and the percentage change of the rates for individual territories and/or rating classes
- Data to support the proposed rate changes, including territorial and class relativities
- Expense provision data
- Target profit provision included in the rates, if applicable, and supporting calculations
- Explanatory material to help state regulators understand and evaluate the filing

In some states, rates must be approved before they are used. In others, formal approval is not required, but many insurers prefer to obtain approval before use to avoid the possibility of having to withdraw the rates if regulators decide that the rates do not meet statutory requirements. Actuaries are best qualified to answer technical questions that regulators might raise. Still, some insurers delegate contact with regulators to the Legal Department or filing specialists and involve actuaries only as needed.

If an advisory organization files rates or loss costs on behalf of an insurer, it handles follow-up or negotiations. Generally, companies that use an advisory organization are assumed to adopt the filings made by the organization automatically. When loss costs are filed by an advisory organization, the insurer is responsible for filing its expense provisions, which yield its final rates.

RATEMAKING FACTOR VARIANCES BY TYPE OF BUSINESS

Ratemaking is a critical component of insurance, and the process is made up of many factors. Understanding how and why the use of these factors changes is essential to ensuring that the ratemaking process is completed correctly and efficiently.

The use of ratemaking factors such as experience period, trending, large loss limitations, credibility, and increased limits factors can vary widely, based on the type of insurance being evaluated. In addition, variations can result from the characteristics of loss exposures, regulatory requirements, and other factors.

Experience Period

An experience period of one to three years is common for auto insurance and other types of liability insurance. For fire insurance, a five-year period is used almost universally because many states require it. But the experience for each of the five years is usually not given equal weight. The most recent years are given greater weight.

The experience period used for other property causes of loss, such as wind, is even longer—frequently twenty years or more—to avoid the large rate swings that would otherwise result after a major hurricane, series of tornadoes, or other natural catastrophe strikes an area.

Typically, three factors are considered when determining the experience period: legal requirements, if any; variability of losses over time; and credibility of the resulting ratemaking data.

Trending

Trending practices also vary. For property insurance, loss claim frequency is low and generally stable, so trending may be restricted to claim severity. But since infrequent large claims can distort the average property insurance claim, the average claim is not used to measure claim severity. As a result, an external composite index, composed partly of a construction cost index and the consumer price index, is used for trending.

For liability insurance, separate trending of claim severity and claims frequency is common because many factors can affect them individually. For example, economic inflation or deflation over the course of payments can affect the average cost of a claim (severity). Meanwhile, legislative, regulatory, or other external changes, such as modification in rules governing claim settlement, can affect the number of losses (frequency).

In some lines, such as fire insurance, trending both losses and premiums is necessary. Losses are trended partly to reflect any effects of inflation on claims costs. For example, inflation can elevate property values. But people also tend to increase the amount of property insurance purchased to reflect the increased values. This increases insurer premium revenue. So insurers trend both losses and premiums and offset the growth in losses with the growth in premiums.

Premiums are also trended in other types of insurance for which the exposure units are affected by factors typically tied to inflation, like workers compensation (which uses payroll as its exposure base) and some general liability insurance (which uses sales). But a trending problem exists in workers compensation insurance, because the benefits can be changed by legislation or a court decision unexpectedly. So a law amendment factor is used to adjust rates and losses. Actuaries can estimate the effects of a statutory benefit change on the losses that insurers will incur.

For equipment breakdown insurance, trending is applied to the inspection and risk control services because they are a significant portion of the rate, often exceeding the pure premium.

Large Loss Limitations

Unusual rate fluctuations can result from occasional large losses, whether from individual losses or accumulated smaller losses from a single event, such as a hurricane. In liability insurance, these fluctuations are controlled by using only **basic limit** losses in calculating incurred losses. Losses capped at a predetermined amount, such as $100,000, are an example of basic limit losses.

Workers compensation insurance ratemaking follows a similar practice. Individual claims used for ratemaking must be lower than a specified amount. Another limitation applies to multiple claims arising from a single event. Both limitations vary over time and by state.

Loss limitations also apply in property insurance ratemaking. When a large single fire insurance loss occurs, only part of it is included in ratemaking calculations in the state in which it occurred. The balance is spread over the rates of all states. The amount included in a state rate depends on the fire insurance premium volume in that state.

Most losses from catastrophic events are excluded from ratemaking data and replaced by a flat catastrophe charge. This charge is determined by catastrophe data collected over a long period to smooth the fluctuations that would otherwise result. A **catastrophe model**, which incorporates past experience with scientific theory, is often used to calculate an appropriate charge for these potential losses.

In addition, commercial insurers may have to quote a charge related to terrorism loss exposures.

Credibility

Credibility is a measure of the predictive ability of data. In ratemaking, the credibility of past loss data is important when projecting future losses. To be fully credible, ratemaking data must contain sufficient volume to provide an accurate estimate of the expected losses for the line, state, territory, and/or class being reviewed. The volatility of the loss data determines how much volume is needed to be fully credible—the higher the volatility, the more data that is required to provide a reasonable projection of future losses. For example, a smaller amount of automobile liability experience is needed for full credibility than for fire insurance, because the larger number of claims per exposure and smaller average claim size in auto insurance leads to less volatile results.

Basic limit
The minimum amount of coverage for which a policy can be written; usually found in liability lines.

Catastrophe model
A type of computer program that estimates losses from future potential catastrophic events.

Credibility
The level of confidence an actuary has in projected losses; increases as the number of exposure units increases.

In auto insurance, advisory organizations and some larger insurers consider statewide loss data to be fully credible. But that data might be inappropriate for some small insurers that base rates solely on their own loss data.

When an advisory organization identifies territories and classes with loss data that is not credible, rates are calculated as a weighted average of the indicated rate for the territory or class and the statewide average rate for all classes and territories. The **credibility factor** indicates the amount of weight to give to the actual loss experience for the territory or class compared with an alternative source—in this case, the statewide average loss experience. A credibility factor is a number between 0 (no credibility) and 1 (full confidence).

For property insurance, because of the low claim frequency, advisory organizations might determine that even the statewide loss data is not credible. In that case, a three-part weighted average could be used, combining the state loss data for the rating class, regional (multistate) loss data for the rating class, and state loss data for a major group encompassing several rating classes. Again, credibility factors are used as weights.

The pure premiums for workers compensation insurance developed by the National Council on Compensation Insurance (NCCI) are composed of pure premium charges for medical and indemnity costs. Separate credibility standards exist for each of these categories.

Increased Limits Factors

Liability insurance coverage is provided at various limits. Actuaries have numerous ratemaking techniques for pricing coverage amounts in excess of the basic limit. Although developing separate rates for each limit of liability coverage offered is possible, that approach would require credible ratemaking experience at each limit, as well as significant, often duplicative, efforts.

So the most common way to establish rates for coverage greater than the basic limit is to develop **increased limits factors**. A base rate is first developed using losses capped at the basic limit. Increased limits factors can then be applied to the basic limit rate. For example, the additional charge to increase the general liability limit to $2 million for any one occurrence might be expressed as 70 percent of the basic coverage limit rate, producing an increased limits factor of 1.70.

Charges to increase liability limits frequently exceed 100 percent of the charge for basic limits. There are several reasons for this.

First, the additional coverage purchased by the customer can be much higher than the basic limit. For example, in personal auto liability, the basic limit might be $50,000 per accident, but the customer purchases $1 million in coverage to protect his or her assets. Second, higher limits can also require a portion of the coverage to be reinsured, with the additional expense of reinsurance included in the rate. Finally, because large losses occur less frequently than small losses and take longer to settle, the variability of losses in higher

Credibility factor
The factor applied in ratemaking to adjust for the predictive value of loss data and used to minimize the variations in the rates that result from purely chance variations in losses.

Increased limit factor
A factor applied to the rates for basic limits to arrive at an appropriate rate for higher limits.

Risk charge

An amount over and above the expected loss component of the premium to compensate the insurer for taking the risk that losses may be higher than expected.

coverage layers is greater than for the basic limit losses, and the credibility is lower. This greater variability requires a greater **risk charge**.

Apply Your Knowledge

Weiland Insurance Company is trying to set property insurance rates for an area that was struck by a hurricane in the past three years. Which one of the following would be used in the ratemaking data to smooth the loss fluctuations that resulted from the hurricane?

a. Catastrophe charge

b. Credibility factor

c. Increased limits factors

d. Risk charge

Feedback: a. Most losses from catastrophic events, such as hurricanes, are excluded from ratemaking data and replaced by a flat catastrophe charge in the rates. This charge is determined by catastrophe data collected over a long period to smooth the fluctuations that would otherwise result.

LOSS RESERVES AND ANALYSIS

Insurers must hold the appropriate amount of loss reserves to ensure that they can pay valid claims and avoid insolvency, so it's important to understand the different types of loss reserves and how to calculate them.

Adequate loss reserves provide assurance that an insured's claim will be paid. They are generally the largest liability on an insurer's balance sheet and a significant part of an insurer's financial condition. An accurate estimation of future claims liabilities provides the insurer with an understanding of the actual costs of business and ensures its ability to pay claims. Actuaries use various techniques to estimate the liability for future payments.

Purpose of Loss Reserves

Insurers are required by law to have reserves for losses they can reasonably assume they will incur. These reserves have to be able to cover both reported claims and claims that have occurred but have not yet been reported. Insurers may also have to make payments on current claims well into the future. An insurer must estimate these future payments in order to calculate its financial position, and creating reserves requires setting aside current income (premiums) to pay for losses in the future.

The liability an insurer carries on its books for future payments on incurred claims is commonly called a loss reserve. However, the liability is not just for payments of claimants' losses; the insurer is also responsible for future loss adjustment expenses (LAE). Those expenses include both allocated loss adjustment expenses (ALAE) and unallocated loss adjustment expenses (ULAE).

An insurer's senior management selects the amount of loss reserves the insurer must hold, and actuaries and other professionals provide estimates of unpaid claims to assist in the decision.

Types of Loss Reserves

There are two principal types of loss reserves: case reserves and bulk reserves.

Case reserves represent the estimated loss value of a claim. The Claims Department usually sets these reserves, but the Actuarial Department might assist with complex claims. Bulk reserves exist because insurers cannot identify specific claims with inadequate or excessive case reserves or predict which claims will be reopened.

Bulk (or aggregate) reserves are the provisions insurers make for additional reserves. They can be a substantial part of an insurer's liabilities. Bulk reserves can have these components:

- **Incurred but not reported (IBNR) reserves**
- Reserves for losses that have been reported but for which the established case reserves are inadequate (sometimes called incurred but not enough recorded [IBNER] reserves)
- Reserves for claims that have been settled and then reopened

Incurred but not reported (IBNR) reserves

A reserve established for losses that reasonably can be assumed to have been incurred but not yet reported.

Importance of Accurate Loss Reserves

Analyzing loss reserves determines whether the carried loss and LAE reserves can be expected to adequately cover the losses that have been incurred but not yet paid. The following parties may conduct this analysis for various reasons:

- The insurer's auditors, to determine whether the insurer's financial statements accurately indicate its financial condition and performance
- Management, as part of its analysis of costs of doing business
- Rating agencies (such as A. M. Best or Standard & Poor's), on behalf of investors or creditors
- Regulators (on behalf of policyholders), to ensure that claims will be paid

The National Association of Insurance Commissioners (NAIC) Annual Statement requires insurers to have their loss reserves certified by an **actuary** or another qualified professional.

Overestimating loss reserves (higher than ultimately paid) can lower an insurer's financial strength rating, reduce statutory limits on premiums that can be

Actuary

A person who uses mathematical methods to analyze insurance data for various purposes, such as to develop insurance rates or set claim reserves.

written, or lead to dissolution of an insurer. If loss reserves are underestimated and future payments will exceed reserves, the insurer can become insolvent.

Analysis of Loss Reserves

Actuaries analyze loss reserves using a variety of methods. In most cases, estimates are made of the losses to be paid on the exposures to date. The loss reserve is then estimated by subtracting payments to date. Separate projections of the reserve are sometimes required for known claims and for IBNR claims, and those results are added together. ALAE reserves may be estimated with or separately from the loss reserve estimate. ULAE reserves are usually analyzed separately.

Because reserve analysis is a projection of future events, any reserve estimate is inherently uncertain to some degree, but actuarially sound reserve estimates should be based on reasonable assumptions using accepted methodology. Even so, actuaries cannot guarantee that actual future payments will be at or near the estimate.

Among the most common methods used to estimate ultimate losses are the loss development method, expected loss ratio method, and Bornhuetter-Ferguson method.

Loss Development—A Closer Look

The loss development method assumes that future changes in losses will occur similarly as in the past. Because of the widespread use of the loss development method and underlying loss development triangles, it's worth taking a closer look at this method. It's also used to project ALAE, claims counts, and even premiums.

The loss development method involves compiling the experience into a loss development triangle, calculating the age-to-age development factors, selecting the development factors to be used, and applying factors to experience to make projections.

The loss development triangle is a table showing values for a group of claims at different points in time. The table is arranged so that it's easy to see the values and the changes of different groups at similar ages of development. The claims are usually grouped by accident year or policy year.

For an example of how a loss development triangle is created, assume that accident year 20X1 has three claims, with payments made as shown. See the exhibit "Payments Made on Accident Year 20X1 Claims."

The payments at the end of each year can be summarized. See the exhibit "Cumulative Paid Loss as of Calendar Year-End."

Payments Made on Accident Year 20X1 Claims

Claim	Payment Made	Payment Amount
A	3/14/X1	$425
A	7/21/X2	$200
A	2/12/X3	$192
B	1/04/X2	$75
B	9/04/X2	$25
C	11/29/X2	$75

Paid as of 12/31/X1 = $425

Paid as of 12/31/X2 = Paid @ 12/31/X1 + Paid during 20X2

$\qquad$ = 425 + (200 + 75 + 25 + 75)

$\qquad$ = $800

Paid as of 12/31/X3 = Paid @ 12/31/X2 + Paid during 20X3

$\qquad$ = 800 + 192

$\qquad$ = $992

[DA06342]

Cumulative Paid Loss as of Calendar Year-End

Accident Year	Year-End 20X1	Year-End 20X2	Year-End 20X3	Year-End 20X4
20X1	$425	$800	$992	$992

[DA06343]

By the end of 20X4, payments have also been made for later accident years, so a more complete table of payments can be assembled. See the exhibit "Cumulative Paid Loss as of Calendar Year-End, Multiple Years."

Cumulative Paid Loss as of Calendar Year-End, Multiple Years

Accident Year	Year-End 20X1	Year-End 20X2	Year-End 20X3	Year-End 20X4
20X1	$425	$800	$992	$992
20X2		450	750	870
20X3			500	850
20X4				600

[DA06344]

It's easier to compare the different years' experience at the same age—for example, comparing accident year 20X1 at the end of 20X1 with accident year 20X2 at the end of 20X2. Rearranging the experience so that the columns now show the age of the experience produces a loss development triangle. See the exhibit "Cumulative Paid Loss as of Year-End by Age."

Cumulative Paid Loss as of Year-End by Age

Accident Year	After 12 Mos.	After 24 Mos.	After 36 Mos.	After 48 Mos.
20X1	$425	$800	$992	$992
20X2	450	750	870	
20X3	500	850		
20X4	600			

[DA06345]

This loss development triangle can be built up year after year.

The second step, calculating the age-to-age factors, is based on information presented in the loss development triangle. The triangle provides an overview of how each accident year's losses develop over time. Comparison between years is easier when looking at the change from one evaluation period to the next. For example, at 24 months, the losses paid for accident year 20X1 were 800, compared with 425 at 12 months. The ratio of the two values is 1.88 (800/425); so, losses increased by 88 percent from 12 months to 24 months. This ratio is an age-to-age factor. Similar factors can be calculated for each accident year's development, producing a loss development triangle of age-to-age factors. See the exhibit "Hypothetical Development of Loss Payments."

If the age-to-age factors down the column are relatively consistent, a pattern of development may be revealed that can be used to estimate future development.

The third step is calculating the loss development factors to be used. Assume that the average factors shown are a reasonable estimate of development. In an actual analysis, the factors selected might vary from the mean. For example, if the accident-year multipliers indicated an increasing trend, the analyst might use selected values higher than the mean. The expected development from each age to the final value can be derived by multiplying the factors together. See the exhibit "Expected Development Factors to Ultimate."

Hypothetical Development of Loss Payments

Accident Year	Months of Development			
	12	24	36	48
20X1	$425	$800	$992	$992
20X2	450	750	870	
20X3	500	850		
20X4	600	992	992	

Accident Year	Age-to-Age Development Factors		
	12 to 24	24 to 36	36 to final
20X1	1.88	1.24	1.00
20X2	1.67	1.16	
20X3	1.70		
Average	1.75	1.20	1.00

[DA06346]

Expected Development Factors to Ultimate

Expected development from 36 months to 48 months (final) =1.00

Expected development from 24 months to final
= Expected development from 24 to 36 months × Expected development from 36 months to final
= 1.20 × 1.00 = 1.20

Expected development from 12 months to final
= Expected development from 12 to 24 months × Expected development from 24 months to final
= 1.75 x 1.20 = 2.10

[DA06347]

The results are cumulative loss development factors that project from an age of development to a projected final value, or age-to-ultimate factors.

In this example, the experience shows no further development. In some cases, development may appear to continue beyond the last age for which there is experience. For example, liability claims may take many years to settle. An indication of further development is that factors for the most mature periods are still significantly different from 1.00. In those cases, a tail factor would have to be estimated using other information to account for further development.

Finally, the factors can be used to project immature loss data to full maturity. The paid losses are multiplied by the respective factors to produce a projected ultimate loss. See the exhibit "Projected Ultimate Losses Using Development Factors."

Projected Ultimate Losses Using Development Factors

Accident Year	Paid Loss at 12/31/X4	Development Age at 12/31/X4	Factor to Ultimate	Projected Ultimate Losses
20X1	$992	48 mos.	1.00	$ 992
20X2	$870	36 mos.	1.00	$ 870
20X3	$850	24 mos.	1.20	$1,020
20X4	$600	12 mos.	2.10	$1,260

[DA06348]

An estimated loss reserve can be calculated by subtracting the current paid losses from the projected ultimate losses. But any changes in business practices or external conditions could affect the usefulness of this method. Examples of such changes are changes in mix of business, policy limits purchased, and how case reserves are set. Also, large one-time events such as catastrophes would disrupt the historical pattern. In that case, there may be adjustments that can be made to the data, such as excluding catastrophe losses, which can correct for one-time conditions. In the end, the power and usefulness of the development method more than offset these limitations in most circumstances.

Apply Your Knowledge

To establish an accurate loss reserve for an insurer, an actuary wants to develop an estimate of ultimate losses for multiple accident years. To do this, the actuary wants to use the loss development method. What does the loss development method assume?

a.   The historical pattern of losses will change significantly over time.

b.   A catastrophe will strike at some point and disrupt the historical pattern.

c.   Future changes in loss will occur similarly as in the past.

d.   Insurers will make payments on current claims well into the future.

Feedback: c. The loss development method assumes that future changes in loss will occur similarly as in the past.

SUMMARY

Actuaries are trained professionals who estimate the cost of risk for insurers. Major responsibilities for an insurer include ratemaking and estimation of unpaid liabilities and adequacy of loss reserves. Actuaries are also instrumental in developing predictive models and perform other important functions for insurers.

Accurate ratemaking allows an insurer to offer competitive pricing while earning a reasonable profit. Ideal rates have these characteristics: stability, responsiveness, and reflection of differences in risk exposure, as well as the potential to promote risk control. They should also provide for unanticipated contingencies, such as unexpectedly high losses.

An insurance rate must be able to pay losses and LAE; pay expenses, such as acquisition expenses, overhead, and premium taxes; and provide a profit while covering unexpected contingencies. Common terms used in the ratemaking process are exposure, earned exposure unit, pure premium, expense provision, loss adjustment expenses, profit and contingencies, and investment income.

Ratemaking is based on adjusting estimated losses from past coverage periods for future conditions. However, because not all covered losses are paid immediately, past loss experience may not be completely known at the end of any specified period. This can cause issues of its own since conditions are constantly changing and any delay between when data is collected and when it is used can reduce rate accuracy. Other factors that affect ratemaking include changes in the cost of claims, the insurer's projected expenses, and the target level of profit and contingencies.

Three ratemaking methods are commonly used by insurers to set rates. The pure premium method involves calculating a pure premium, the amount needed to pay losses, and then adding an expense provision and applying a profit and contingencies factor. The loss ratio method determines a new rate by modifying an old rate, using a comparison of actual and expected loss ratios. The judgment method is used when little or no loss experience data is available for ratemaking. It relies heavily on the knowledge and experience of an actuary or underwriter.

When creating or updating insurance rates, an insurer or its advisory organization collects data, adjusts data, calculates the overall rate change, determines territorial and class relativities, and prepares and submits rate filings to regulatory authorities.

Ratemaking factors such as experience period, trending, large loss limitations, credibility, and increased limits factors, can vary significantly by type of insurance. The variations can result from the characteristics of loss exposures, regulatory requirements, and other factors.

Accurately calculating loss reserves is critical to insurers' ability to pay future claims costs and remain solvent. Actuaries use various techniques, like the loss development method, to estimate the liability for these future payments.

Reinsurance Principles and Concepts

Educational Objectives

After learning the content of this assignment, you should be able to:

▷ Summarize the principal functions of reinsurance.

▷ Describe the three sources of reinsurance.

▷ Contrast treaty reinsurance with facultative reinsurance.

▷ Given a case, determine the amount of a loss that would be payable under a pro rata reinsurance contract.

▷ Given a case, determine the amount of a loss that would be payable under an excess of loss reinsurance contract.

▷ Explain how finite risk reinsurance and capital market based methods are used as alternatives to traditional reinsurance.

Reinsurance Principles and Concepts

8

REINSURANCE AND ITS FUNCTIONS

A single insurer that sells a $100 million commercial property policy and a $100 million commercial umbrella liability policy to the owners of a high-rise office building may appear to be jeopardizing its financial stability. However, this transaction is possible when the insurers use reinsurance as a tool to expand their capacity.

Reinsurance is one way insurers protect themselves from the financial consequences of insuring others. This section introduces basic reinsurance terms and concepts, including the principal functions of reinsurance.

Basic Terms and Concepts

Reinsurance, commonly referred to as "insurance for insurers," is the transfer from one insurer (the **primary insurer**) to another (the **reinsurer**) of some or all of the financial consequences of certain loss exposures covered by the primary insurer's policies. The loss exposures transferred, or ceded, by the primary insurer could be associated with a single subject of insurance (such as a building), a single policy, or a group of policies.

An insurer that transfers liability for loss exposures by ceding them to a reinsurer can be referred to as the reinsured, the ceding company, the cedent, the direct insurer, or the primary insurer. Although all these terms are acceptable, "primary insurer" will be used to denote the party that cedes loss exposures to a reinsurer.

Reinsurance is transacted through a **reinsurance agreement**, which specifies the terms under which the reinsurance is provided. For example, it may state that the reinsurer must pay a percentage of all the primary insurer's losses for loss exposures subject to the agreement, or must reimburse the primary insurer for losses that exceed a specified amount. Additionally, the reinsurance agreement identifies the policy, group of policies, or other categories of insurance that are included in the reinsurance agreement.

The reinsurer typically does not assume all of the primary insurer's insurance risk. The reinsurance agreement usually requires the primary insurer to retain part of its original liability. This **retention** can be expressed as a percentage of the original amount of insurance or as a dollar amount of loss. The reinsurance agreement does not alter the terms of the underlying (original) insurance policies or the primary insurer's obligations to honor them. See the exhibit "Risk."

Reinsurance
The transfer of insurance risk from one insurer to another through a contractual agreement under which one insurer (the reinsurer) agrees, in return for a reinsurance premium, to indemnify another insurer (the primary insurer) for some or all of the financial consequences of certain loss exposures covered by the primary's insurance policies.

Primary insurer
In reinsurance, the insurer that transfers or cedes all or part of the insurance risk it has assumed to another insurer in a contractual arrangement.

Reinsurer
The insurer that assumes some or all of the potential costs of insured loss exposures of the primary insurer in a reinsurance contractual agreement.

Reinsurance agreement
Contract between the primary insurer and reinsurer that stipulates the form of reinsurance and the type of accounts to be reinsured.

Retention
The amount retained by the primary insurer in the reinsurance transaction.

> ## Risk
>
> Although "risk" is often defined as uncertainty about the occurrence of a loss, risk has several other meanings that are useful in understanding reinsurance practices. In reinsurance, the term risk often refers to the subject of insurance, such as a building, a policy, a group of policies, or a class of business. Reinsurance practitioners use the term risk in this way and include it in common reinsurance clauses.

[DA05756]

Ceding commission

An amount paid by the reinsurer to the primary insurer to cover part or all of the primary insurer's policy acquisition expenses.

Retrocession

A reinsurance agreement whereby one reinsurer (the retrocedent) transfers all or part of the reinsurance risk it has assumed or will assume to another reinsurer (the retrocessionaire).

Retrocedent

The reinsurer that transfers or cedes all or part of the insurance risk it has assumed to another reinsurer.

Retrocessionaire

The reinsurer that assumes all or part of the reinsurance risk accepted by another reinsurer.

The primary insurer pays a reinsurance premium for the protection provided, just as any insured pays a premium for insurance coverage, but, because the primary insurer incurs the expenses of issuing the underlying policy, the reinsurer might pay a **ceding commission** to the primary insurer. These expenses consist primarily of commissions paid to producers, premium taxes, and underwriting expenses (such as policy processing and servicing costs, and risk control reports).

Reinsurers may transfer part of the liability they have accepted in reinsurance agreements to other reinsurers. Such an agreement is called a **retrocession**. Under a retrocession, one reinsurer, the **retrocedent**, transfers all or part of the reinsurance risk that it has assumed or will assume to another reinsurer, the **retrocessionaire**. Retrocession is very similar to reinsurance except for the parties involved in the agreement.

Reinsurance Functions

Reinsurance helps an insurer achieve several practical business goals, such as insuring large exposures, protecting policyholders' surplus from adverse loss experience, and financing the insurer's growth. The reinsurance that an insurer obtains depends mainly on the constraints or problems the insurer must address to reach its goals. Although several of its uses overlap, reinsurance is a valuable tool that can perform six principal functions for primary insurers:

- Increase large-line capacity
- Provide catastrophe protection
- Stabilize loss experience
- Provide surplus relief
- Facilitate withdrawal from a market segment
- Provide underwriting guidance

Depending on its goals, a primary insurer may use several different reinsurance agreements for these principal functions.

Increase Large-Line Capacity

The first function of reinsurance is to increase **large-line capacity**, which allows a primary insurer to assume more significant risks than its financial condition and regulations would otherwise permit. For example, an application for $100 million of property insurance on a single commercial warehouse could exceed the maximum amount of insurance that an underwriter is willing to accept on a single account. This maximum amount, or **line**, is subject to these influences:

- The maximum amount of insurance or limit of liability allowed by insurance regulations. Insurance regulations prohibit an insurer from retaining (after reinsurance, usually stated as net of reinsurance) more than 10 percent of its policyholders' surplus (net worth) on any one loss exposure.

- The size of a potential loss or losses that can safely be retained without impairing the insurer's earnings or policyholders' surplus.

- The specific characteristics of a particular loss exposure. For example, the line may vary depending on property attributes such as construction, occupancy, loss prevention features, and loss reduction features.

- The amount, types, and cost of available reinsurance.

Reinsurers provide primary insurers with large-line capacity by accepting liability for loss exposures that the primary insurer is unwilling or unable to retain. This function of reinsurance allows insurers with limited large-line capacity to participate more fully in the insurance marketplace. For example, a primary insurer may want to compete for homeowners policies in markets in which the value of the homes exceeds the amount the primary insurer can safely retain. Reinsurance allows the primary insurer to increase its market share while limiting the financial consequences of potential losses.

Provide Catastrophe Protection

Without reinsurance, catastrophes could greatly reduce insurer earnings or even threaten insurer solvency when a large number of its insured loss exposures are concentrated in an area that experiences a catastrophe. Potential catastrophic perils include fire, windstorm (hurricane, tornado, and other wind damage), and earthquakes. Additionally, significant property and liability losses can be caused by man-made catastrophes, such as industrial explosions, airplane crashes, or product recalls.

The second function of reinsurance is to protect against the financial consequences of a single catastrophic event that causes multiple losses in a concentrated area. For example, an insurer might purchase reinsurance that provides up to $50 million of coverage per hurricane when the total amount of loss from a single hurricane exceeds the amount the insurer can safely retain.

Large-line capacity
An insurer's ability to provide larger amounts of insurance for property loss exposures, or higher limits of liability for liability loss exposures, than it is otherwise willing to provide.

Line
The maximum amount of insurance or limit of liability that an insurer will accept on a single loss exposure.

Stabilize Loss Experience

An insurer, like most other businesses, must have a steady flow of profits to attract capital investment and support growth. However, demographic, economic, social, and natural forces cause an insurer's loss experience to fluctuate widely, which creates variability in its financial results. Volatile loss experience can affect the stock value of a publicly traded insurer; alter an insurer's financial rating by independent rating agencies; cause abrupt changes in the approaches taken in managing the underwriting, claim, and marketing departments; or undermine the confidence of the sales force (especially independent brokers and agents who can place their customers with other insurers). In extreme cases, volatile loss experience can lead to insolvency.

Reinsurance can smooth the resulting peaks and valleys in an insurer's loss experience curve. In addition to aiding financial planning and supporting growth, this function of reinsurance encourages capital investment because investors are more likely to invest in companies whose financial results are stable.

Reinsurance can be arranged to stabilize the loss experience of a line of insurance (for example, commercial auto), a class of business (for example, truckers), or a primary insurer's entire book of business. In addition, a primary insurer can stabilize loss experience by obtaining reinsurance to accomplish any, or all, of these purposes:

- Limit its liability for a single loss exposure
- Limit its liability for several loss exposures affected by a common event
- Limit its liability for loss exposures that aggregate claims over time

The exhibit illustrates how reinsurance can stabilize a primary insurer's loss experience. See the exhibit "Stabilization of Annual Loss Experience for a Primary Insurer With a $20 Million Retention."

Provide Surplus Relief

Insurers that are growing rapidly may have difficulty maintaining a desirable capacity ratio, because of how they must account for their expenses to acquire new policies. State insurance regulation mandates that, for accounting purposes, such expenses be recognized at the time a new policy is sold. However, premiums are recognized as revenue as they are earned over the policy's life. When an insurer immediately recognizes expenses while only gradually recognizing revenue, its policyholders' surplus will decrease as its capacity ratio increases.

Surplus relief

A replenishment of policyholders' surplus provided by the ceding commission paid to the primary insurer by the reinsurer.

Many insurers use reinsurance to provide **surplus relief**, which satisfies insurance regulatory constraints on excess growth. State insurance regulators monitor several financial ratios as part of their solvency surveillance efforts, but the relationship of written premiums to policyholders' surplus is generally a key financial ratio and one considered to be out of bounds if it exceeds 3 to 1 or 300 percent. Policyholders' surplus (also called "surplus to policyholders"

Stabilization of Annual Loss Experience for a Primary Insurer With a $20 Million Retention

(1) Time Period (Year)	(2) Actual Losses ($000)	(3) Amount Reinsured ($000)	(4) Stabilized Loss Level ($000)
1	15,000	—	15,000
2	35,000	15,000	20,000
3	13,000	—	13,000
4	25,000	5,000	20,000
5	40,000	20,000	20,000
6	37,000	17,000	20,000
7	16,500	—	16,500
8	9,250	—	9,250
9	18,000	—	18,000
10	10,750	—	10,750
Total	$219,500	$57,000	$162,500

The total actual losses are $219.5 million, or an average of $21.95 million each time period. If a reinsurance agreement were in place to cap losses to $20 million, the primary insurer's loss experience would be limited to the amounts shown in the stabilized loss level column. The broken line that fluctuates dramatically in the graph below represents actual losses, the dotted line represents stabilized losses, and the horizontal line represents average losses.

Graph of Hypothetical Loss Data

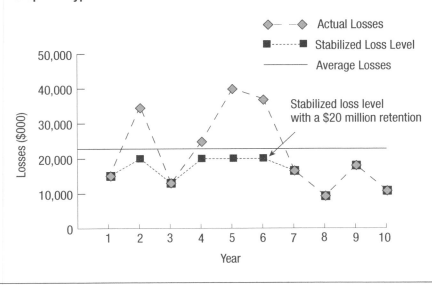

or simply "surplus") is an insurer's net worth as reported on the financial statement prescribed by state insurance regulators. It represents the financial resource the primary insurer can draw on to pay unexpected losses.

Some reinsurance agreements facilitate premium growth by allowing the primary insurer to deduct a ceding commission on loss exposures ceded to the reinsurer. The ceding commission is an amount paid by the reinsurer to the primary insurer to cover part or all of a primary insurer's policy acquisition expenses. The ceding commission immediately offsets the primary insurer's policy acquisition expenses for the reinsured policies and often includes a profit provision, or an additional commission, if the reinsurance ceded is profitable.

Because the ceding commission replenishes the primary insurer's policyholders' surplus, the surplus relief facilitates the primary insurer's premium growth and the increase in policyholders' surplus lowers its capacity ratio.

Facilitate Withdrawal From a Market Segment

Reinsurance can also facilitate withdrawal from a market segment, which may be a particular class of business, geographic area, or type of insurance. A primary insurer may want to withdraw from a market segment that is unprofitable, undesirable, or incompatible with its strategic plan. When withdrawing from a market segment, the primary insurer has these options:

- Stop writing new insurance policies and continue in-force insurance until all policies expire (often referred to as "run-off")
- Cancel all policies (if insurance regulations permit) and refund the unearned premiums to insureds
- Withdraw from the market segment by purchasing portfolio reinsurance

To withdraw from a market segment, an insurer can stop writing new business or, to the extent permitted by applicable cancellation laws, cancel all policies in effect and return the unearned premiums to its insureds. However, these approaches can be unwieldy and expensive and could create ill will among insureds, producers, and state insurance regulators. They also create uncertainty about the insurer's outstanding claims, which must be settled, and about new claims, which might continue to be filed even after the insurer ceases operations.

Portfolio reinsurance

Reinsurance that transfers to the reinsurer liability for an entire type of insurance, territory, or book of business after the primary insurer has issued the policies.

Another approach available to the primary insurer is to transfer the liability for all outstanding policies to a reinsurer by purchasing **portfolio reinsurance**. Portfolio reinsurance can facilitate withdrawal from a market segment and prevent the formation of ill will due to policy cancellation. It is an exception to the general rule that reinsurers do not accept all of the liability for specified loss exposures of an insurer.

In portfolio reinsurance, the reinsurer accepts all of the liability for certain loss exposures covered under the primary insurer's policies, but the primary insurer must continue to fulfill its obligations to its insureds. For example, the primary insurer may decide to use portfolio reinsurance to withdraw from the errors and omissions insurance market. In this situation, the reinsurer typically agrees to indemnify the primary insurer for all losses incurred as of, and following, the date of the portfolio reinsurance agreement. However, the primary insurer continues to pay claims to (or on behalf of) its insureds who are covered by the underlying insurance.

Sometimes a primary insurer wants to completely eliminate the liabilities it has assumed under the insurance policies it has issued. This can be accomplished through a **novation**. A novation is not considered portfolio reinsurance because the substitute insurer assumes the direct obligations to insureds covered by the underlying insurance. Usually, the approval of state insurance regulators or the insured is required to effect a novation.

Novation

The act of substituting a contract with another contract, an obligation with another obligation, or a party with another party or adding an obligation.

Provide Underwriting Guidance

Reinsurance may also provide underwriting guidance. Reinsurers work with a wide variety of insurers in the domestic and global markets under many different circumstances. Consequently, reinsurers accumulate a great deal of underwriting expertise. A reinsurer's understanding of insurance operations and the insurance industry can assist other insurers, particularly inexperienced primary insurers entering new markets and offering new products. For example, one medium-size insurer reinsured 95 percent of its umbrella liability coverage over a period of years and relied heavily on the reinsurer for technical assistance in underwriting and pricing its policies. Without such technical assistance, certain primary insurers would find it difficult to generate underwriting profits from coverages with which they have limited expertise.

Reinsurers that provide underwriting assistance to primary insurers must respect the confidentiality of their clients' proprietary information. Reinsurers often learn about the primary insurer's marketing and underwriting strategies but should not reveal insurer-specific information to other parties.

REINSURANCE SOURCES

Participants in the international reinsurance market can take many forms, including professional reinsurers that deal only in reinsurance, licensed insurers that also market reinsurance, and organized entities that allow small organizations to pool their resources so that they can participate in lines of reinsurance that would otherwise be out of reach.

Reinsurance not only strengthens the primary insurance market by providing insurers with a greater ability to take on risk, but also provides an extra stream of revenue for insurers that are able to take on excess risk from other insurers. As such, many kinds of participants are involved in the marketplace, each with their own strengths and shortcomings.

Professional Reinsurers

Professional reinsurers interact with other insurers directly or through intermediaries, as primary insurers do.

A reinsurer whose employees deal directly with primary insurers is called a direct writing reinsurer. However, most direct writing reinsurers in the United States also solicit reinsurance business through **reinsurance intermediaries**.

A reinsurance intermediary generally represents a primary insurer and works with that insurer to develop a reinsurance program that is then placed with one or more reinsurers. The reinsurance intermediary receives a brokerage commission—almost always from the reinsurers—for performing other necessary services in addition to placing the reinsurance, such as disbursing reinsurance premiums among participating reinsurers and collecting loss amounts owed to the insurer.

Although the variety of professional reinsurers leads to differences in how they are used and what they can offer, some broad generalizations may be made about professional reinsurers:

- Primary insurers dealing with direct writing reinsurers often use fewer reinsurers in their reinsurance program.
- Reinsurance intermediaries often use more than one reinsurer to develop a reinsurance program for a primary insurer.
- Reinsurance intermediaries can often help secure high coverage limits and catastrophe coverage.
- Reinsurance intermediaries usually have access to various reinsurance solutions from both domestic and international markets.
- Reinsurance intermediaries can usually obtain reinsurance under favorable terms and at a competitive price because they work regularly in this market with many primary insurers and can therefore determine prevailing market conditions.

Because the treaty reinsurer underwrites the primary insurer as well as the loss exposures being ceded, professional reinsurers evaluate the primary insurer before entering into a reinsurance agreement. To do so, the reinsurer analyzes the primary insurer's financial statements or reviews information developed by a financial rating service. Other information about the primary insurer may be obtained from state insurance department bulletins and the trade press.

Reinsurers also consider the primary insurer's experience, reputation, and management. The reinsurer relies on the quality of the management team, and a relationship of trust must underlie any reinsurance agreement. Whether it involves a one-time facultative agreement or an ongoing treaty agreement, the relationship between the primary insurer and the reinsurer is considered to be one of utmost good faith. This is because each party is obligated to and relies on the other for full disclosure of material facts about the subject of the agreement. It would be considered a breach of this duty of utmost good faith if the primary insurer withheld material facts relevant to the reinsurer's underwriting decision, intentionally underestimated prior losses, or failed to disclose hazardous conditions affecting loss exposures.

Just as the reinsurer should evaluate the primary insurer, the primary insurer should evaluate the reinsurer's claim-paying ability, its reputation, and management's competence before entering into the reinsurance agreement.

Reinsurance Departments of Primary Insurers

Unless prohibited from doing so by statute or charter, primary insurers may also provide treaty and facultative reinsurance through their reinsurance departments. A primary insurer may offer reinsurance to affiliated insurers, regardless of whether it offers reinsurance to unaffiliated insurers. To ensure that information from other insurers remains confidential, a primary insurer's reinsurance operations are usually separate from its primary insurance operations.

Many primary insurers are groups of commonly owned insurance companies. Intragroup reinsurance agreements are used to balance the financial results of all insurers in the group. The use of intragroup reinsurance agreements does not preclude using professional reinsurers. See the exhibit "How Blockchain Could Change Reinsurance."

How Blockchain Could Change Reinsurance

The development of blockchain applications for the insurance industry could simplify the reinsurance process by enabling quick, reliable validation of the information that reinsurance relationships are built on.

For example, instead of going through the usual, sometimes arduous, process of evaluating a reinsurer or primary insurer, potential parties to a reinsurance contract would be able to quickly consult the verifiable data held within a blockchain to confirm that the other organization is a viable partner for the contract.

Smart contracts could also facilitate this process by allowing primary insurers to place notification of the excess loss exposure they are seeking to place on the blockchain, and reinsurers could use algorithms to decide whether the terms offered are favorable. If they are, the contract could be accepted and verified on the blockchain. Additionally, if applicable, automatic triggers could be put in place to speed up payment of eligible losses or premiums.

[DA12800]

Reinsurance Pools, Syndicates, and Associations

The third source of reinsurance is **reinsurance pools, syndicates, and associations**. These entities provide member companies the opportunity to participate in a line of insurance with a limited amount of capital—and a

Reinsurance pools, syndicates, and associations

Groups of insurers that share the loss exposures of the group, usually through reinsurance.

proportionate share of the administrative costs—without having to employ the specialists needed for such a venture. Whether a pool is a reinsurance device is determined by the organizational structure, the type of contract issued, and the internal accounting procedures. The terms "pool," "syndicate," and "association" are often used interchangeably, although there are some fine differences.

Reinsurance pool
A reinsurance association that consists of several unrelated insurers or reinsurers that have joined to insure risks the individual members are unwilling to individually insure.

In a **reinsurance pool**, a policy for the full amount of insurance is issued by a member company and reinsured by the remainder of the pool members according to predetermined percentages. Some pools are formed by insurers whose reinsurance needs are not adequately met in the regular marketplace, while others are formed to provide specialized insurance requiring underwriting and claims expertise that the individual insurers do not have. Reinsurance intermediaries also form reinsurance pools to provide reinsurance to their clients. A reinsurance pool may accept loss exposures from nonmember companies or offer reinsurance only to its member companies. Some reinsurance pools restrict their operations to narrowly defined classes of business, while others reinsure most types of insurance.

Syndicate
A group of insurers or reinsurers involved in joint underwriting to insure major risks that are beyond the capacity of a single insurer or reinsurer; each syndicate member accepts predetermined shares of premiums, losses, expenses, and profits.

In a **syndicate**, each member shares the risk with other members by accepting a percentage of the risk. These members collectively constitute a single, separate entity under the syndicate name. For example, syndicates are a key component of Lloyd's (formerly Lloyd's of London), an association that provides the physical and procedural facilities for its members to write insurance. Each individual investor of Lloyd's, called a Name, belongs to one or more syndicates. The syndicate's underwriter, or group of underwriters, conducts the insurance operations and analyzes applications for insurance coverage. Depending on the nature and amount of insurance requested, a particular syndicate might accept only a portion of the total amount of insurance. The application is then taken to other syndicates for their evaluations.

Association
An organization of member companies that reinsure by fixed percentage the total amount of insurance appearing on policies issued by the organization.

An **association** consists of member companies that use both reinsurance and risk-sharing techniques. In many cases, the member companies issue their own policies; however, a reinsurance certificate is attached to each policy, under which each member company assumes a fixed percentage of the total amount of insurance. One member company is usually responsible for inspection and investigation, while a committee comprising underwriting executives from the member companies establishes the association's underwriting policy. Organizations of this type allow members to share risks that require special coverages or special underwriting techniques, and can increase the primary insurer's capacity to insure extra-hazardous risks.

REINSURANCE TRANSACTIONS

No single reinsurance agreement performs all the reinsurance functions. Each reinsurance agreement is tailored to the specific needs of the primary insurer and the reinsurer.

There are two types of reinsurance transactions: treaty and facultative.

Treaty reinsurance, also referred to as obligatory reinsurance, uses one agreement for an entire class or portfolio of loss exposures. The reinsurance agreement is typically called the treaty.

Facultative reinsurance uses a separate reinsurance agreement for each loss exposure being reinsured. It is also referred to as nonobligatory reinsurance.

Treaty Reinsurance

With treaty reinsurance, the reinsurer agrees in advance to reinsure all the loss exposures that fall under the treaty. Although some treaties allow the reinsurer limited discretion in reinsuring individual loss exposures, most treaties require that all loss exposures within the treaty's terms be reinsured.

Primary insurers usually use treaty reinsurance as the foundation of their reinsurance programs. Treaty reinsurance provides primary insurers with the certainty needed to formulate underwriting policy and develop underwriting guidelines. Primary insurers work with reinsurance intermediaries (or with reinsurers directly) to develop comprehensive reinsurance programs that address the primary insurers' varied needs. The reinsurance programs that satisfy those needs often include several reinsurance agreements and the participation of several reinsurers.

Treaty reinsurance agreements are tailored to fit the primary insurer's individual requirements. The price and terms of each reinsurance treaty are individually negotiated.

Treaty reinsurance agreements are usually designed to address a primary insurer's need to reinsure many loss exposures over a period of time. Although the reinsurance agreement's term may be for only one year, the relationship between the primary insurer and the reinsurer often spans many years. A primary insurer's management usually finds that a long-term relationship with a reinsurer enables the primary insurer to consistently fulfill its producers' requests to place insurance with them.

Most, but not all, treaty reinsurance agreements require the primary insurer to cede all eligible loss exposures to the reinsurer. Primary insurers usually make treaty reinsurance agreements so their underwriters do not have to exercise discretion in using reinsurance. If treaty reinsurance agreements permitted primary insurers to choose which loss exposures they ceded to the reinsurer, the reinsurer would be exposed to adverse selection.

Because treaty reinsurers are obligated to accept ceded loss exposures once the reinsurance agreement is in place, reinsurers usually want to know about the integrity and experience of the primary insurer's management and the degree to which the primary insurer's published underwriting guidelines represent its actual underwriting practices.

Facultative Reinsurance

With facultative reinsurance, the primary insurer negotiates a separate reinsurance agreement for each loss exposure it wants to reinsure. The primary insurer is not obligated to purchase reinsurance, and the reinsurer is not obligated to reinsure loss exposures submitted to it. A facultative reinsurance agreement is written for a specified time period and cannot be canceled by either party unless contractual obligations, such as payment of premiums, are not met.

Facultative certificate of reinsurance

An agreement that defines the terms of the facultative reinsurance coverage on a specific loss exposure.

The reinsurer issues a **facultative certificate of reinsurance** (or facultative certificate), which is attached to the primary insurer's copy of the policy being reinsured.

Facultative reinsurance serves four functions:

- Facultative reinsurance can provide large-line capacity for loss exposures that exceed the limits of treaty reinsurance agreements.

- Facultative reinsurance can reduce the primary insurer's exposure in a given geographic area. For example, a marine underwriter may be considering underwriting numerous shiploads of cargo that are stored in the same warehouse and that belong to different insureds. The underwriter could use facultative reinsurance for some of those loss exposures, thereby reducing the primary insurer's overall exposure to loss.

- Facultative reinsurance can insure a loss exposure with atypical hazard characteristics and thereby maintain the favorable loss experience of the primary insurer's treaty reinsurance and any associated profit-sharing arrangements. Maintaining favorable treaty loss experience is important because the reinsurer has underwritten and priced the treaty with certain expectations. A loss exposure that is inconsistent with the primary insurer's typical portfolio of insurance policies may cause excessive losses and lead to the treaty's termination or a price increase. The treaty reinsurer will usually allow the primary insurer to remove high-hazard loss exposures from the treaty through facultative reinsurance. These facultative placements of atypical loss exposures also benefit the treaty reinsurer. For example, an insured under a commercial property policy may request coverage for an expensive art collection that the primary insurer and its treaty reinsurer would not ordinarily want to cover. Facultative reinsurance of the collection would eliminate the underwriting concern by removing this loss exposure from the treaty. Often, the treaty reinsurer also provides this reinsurance through its Facultative Reinsurance Department. The facultative reinsurer knows that adverse selection occurs in facultative reinsurance. Consequently, the loss exposures submitted for reinsurance are likely to have an increased probability of loss. Therefore, facultative reinsurance is usually priced to reflect the likelihood of adverse selection.

- Facultative reinsurance can insure particular classes of loss exposures that are excluded under treaty reinsurance.

Primary insurers mainly purchase facultative reinsurance to reinsure loss exposures they do not typically insure or for exposures with high levels of underwriting risk. Consequently, primary insurers use facultative reinsurance for fewer of their loss exposures than they do treaty reinsurance. Primary insurers that are increasingly using facultative reinsurance may want to review the adequacy of their treaty reinsurance.

The expense of placing facultative reinsurance may be high for both the primary insurer and the reinsurer. In negotiating facultative reinsurance, the primary insurer must provide extensive information about each loss exposure. Consequently, administrative costs are relatively high because the primary insurer must devote a significant amount of time to complete each cession and to notify the reinsurer of any endorsement, loss notice, or policy cancellation. Likewise, the reinsurer must underwrite and price each facultative submission. See the exhibit "Hybrids of Treaty and Facultative Reinsurance."

Hybrids of Treaty and Facultative Reinsurance

Reinsurers sometimes use hybrid agreements that have elements of both treaty and facultative reinsurance. The hybrid agreements usually describe how individual facultative reinsurance placements will be handled. For example, the agreement may specify the basic underwriting parameters of the loss exposures that will be ceded to the reinsurer as well as premium and loss allocation formulas. Although hybrid agreements may be used infrequently, they demonstrate the flexibility of the reinsurance market to satisfy the mutual needs of primary insurers and reinsurers. The two hybrid agreements briefly described next illustrate common reinsurance agreement variations.

- In a *facultative treaty*, the primary insurer and the reinsurer agree on how subsequent individual facultative submissions will be handled. A facultative treaty could be used when a class of business has insufficient loss exposures to justify treaty reinsurance but has a sufficient number of loss exposures to determine the details of future individual placements.

- In a *facultative obligatory treaty*, although the primary insurer has the option of ceding loss exposures, the reinsurer is obligated to accept all loss exposures submitted to it. Facultative obligatory treaties are also called *semi-obligatory treaties*.

[DA05757]

TYPES OF PRO RATA REINSURANCE

Primary insurers have unique needs, so each reinsurance agreement between a primary insurer and reinsurer must be uniquely designed to meet those needs. As a result, several types of reinsurance have been developed. The more you know about these different types of reinsurance, the better you'll be able to navigate the reinsurance process.

Unlike primary insurance contracts, reinsurance agreements are not standardized, and a primary insurer's reinsurance program can combine several of the various types of reinsurance agreements to meet the insurer's specific needs. See the exhibit "Types of Reinsurance."

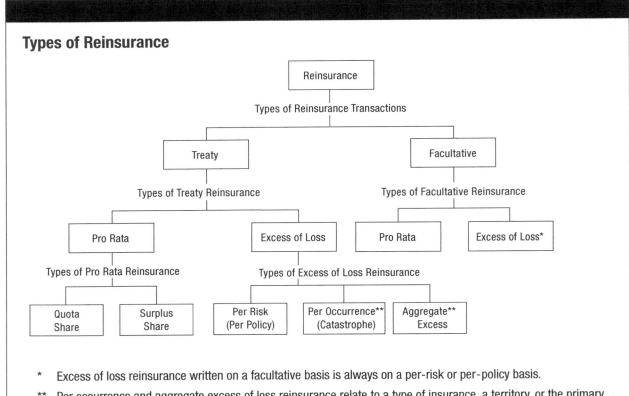

Types of Reinsurance

*   Excess of loss reinsurance written on a facultative basis is always on a per-risk or per-policy basis.

**   Per occurrence and aggregate excess of loss reinsurance relate to a type of insurance, a territory, or the primary insurer's entire portfolio of in-force loss exposures rather than to a specific policy or a specific loss exposure.

[DA05080]

Under the two primary types of reinsurance transactions—treaty reinsurance and facultative reinsurance—are two principal approaches that insurers and reinsurers use to share the amounts of insurance, policy premiums, and losses. Those principal approaches are pro rata reinsurance and excess of loss reinsurance. Here, you'll learn how **pro rata reinsurance** is defined, used, and calculated.

Pro rata reinsurance

A type of reinsurance in which the primary insurer and reinsurer proportionately share the amounts of insurance, policy premiums, and losses (including loss adjustment expenses).

Pro Rata Reinsurance

Under pro rata reinsurance, or proportional reinsurance, the amount of insurance, premium, and losses (including loss adjustment expenses) is divided between the primary insurer and the reinsurer in the same proportions as the loss exposure. For example, if the reinsurer covers 60 percent of the liability for each loss exposure that is insured by the primary insurer, then the reinsurer is entitled to 60 percent of the policy premiums and is responsible for 60 percent of each loss. Loss adjustment expenses related to a specific loss are also usually shared proportionately.

The reinsurer usually pays the primary insurer a ceding commission for the ceded loss exposures. A **flat commission** is commonly the type of ceding commission used. However, **profit-sharing commission** or **sliding scale commission** arrangements are also used often and provide an incentive to the primary insurer for ceding profitable business. The amount of ceding commission paid to the primary insurer is usually negotiated and is taken from the reinsurance premium remitted to the reinsurer.

Pro rata reinsurance is generally chosen by newly incorporated insurers or insurers with limited capital because it's effective at providing surplus relief. This results from the payment of ceding commissions, a practice that is uncommon under excess of loss treaties.

Two Classifications of Pro Rata Reinsurance

Pro rata reinsurance can be classified as either **quota share reinsurance** or **surplus share reinsurance**. The principal difference is how each structures the primary insurer's retention.

Quota Share Reinsurance

The distinguishing characteristic of quota share reinsurance is that the primary insurer and the reinsurer use a fixed percentage when sharing the amounts of insurance, policy premiums, and losses (including loss adjustment expenses). For example, an insurer may arrange a reinsurance treaty in which it retains 45 percent of policy premiums, coverage limits, and losses while reinsuring the remainder. This treaty would be called a "55 percent quota share treaty" because the reinsurer accepts 55 percent of the liability for each loss exposure subject to the treaty. Quota share reinsurance can be used with both property insurance and liability insurance but is more frequently used in property insurance. See the exhibit "Quota Share Reinsurance Example."

Under quota share treaties, even policies with low amounts of insurance that the primary insurer could safely retain are reinsured. In addition, a **variable quota share treaty** enables a primary insurer to retain a larger proportion of the small loss exposures it's capable of absorbing, while maintaining a safer and smaller retention on larger loss exposures.

Most reinsurance agreements specify a maximum dollar limit above which responsibility for additional coverage limits or losses reverts back to the primary insurer (or is taken by another reinsurer). With a quota share reinsurance agreement, that maximum dollar amount is stated in terms of the coverage limits of each policy subject to the treaty. For example, a primary

Flat commission
A ceding commission that is a fixed percentage of the ceded premiums.

Profit-sharing commission
A ceding commission that is contingent on the reinsurer realizing a predetermined percentage of excess profit on ceded loss exposures.

Sliding scale commission
A ceding commission based on a formula that adjusts the commission according to the profitability of the reinsurance agreement.

Quota share reinsurance
A type of pro rata reinsurance in which the primary insurer and the reinsurer share the amounts of insurance, policy premiums, and losses (including loss adjustment expenses) using a fixed percentage.

Surplus share reinsurance
A type of pro rata reinsurance in which the policies covered are those whose amount of insurance exceeds a stipulated dollar amount, or line.

Variable quota share treaty
A quota share reinsurance treaty in which the cession percentage retention varies based on specified predetermined criteria such as the amount of insurance needed.

Quota Share Reinsurance Example

Brookgreen Insurance Company has a quota share treaty with Cypress Reinsurer. The treaty has a $250,000 limit, a retention of 25 percent, and a cession of 75 percent. The following three policies are issued by Brookgreen Insurance Company and are subject to the quota share treaty with Cypress Reinsurer.

- Policy A insures Building A for $25,000 for a premium of $400, with one loss of $8,000.
- Policy B insures Building B for $100,000 for a premium of $1,000, with one loss of $10,000.
- Policy C insures Building C for $150,000 for a premium of $1,500, with one loss of $60,000.

Division of Insurance, Premiums, and Losses Under Quota Share Treaty

	Brookgreen Insurance Retention (25%)	Cypress Reinsurance Cession (75%)	Total
Policy A			
Amounts of insurance	$6,250	$18,750	$25,000
Premiums	100	300	400
Losses	2,000	6,000	8,000
Policy B			
Amounts of insurance	$25,000	$75,000	$100,000
Premiums	250	750	1,000
Losses	2,500	7,500	10,000
Policy C			
Amounts of insurance	$37,500	$112,500	$150,000
Premiums	375	1,125	1,500
Losses	15,000	45,000	60,000

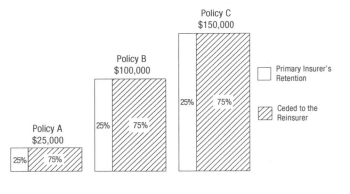

[DA05081]

insurer and a reinsurer may share amounts of insurance, policy premiums, and losses on a 45 percent and 55 percent basis, respectively, subject to a $1 million maximum coverage amount for each policy.

In addition to a maximum coverage amount limitation, some quota share reinsurance agreements include a per occurrence limit, stated as an aggregate dollar amount or as a loss ratio cap, which restricts the primary insurer's reinsurance recovery for losses originating from a single occurrence.

Surplus Share Reinsurance

A distinguishing characteristic of surplus share reinsurance is that when an underlying policy's total amount of insurance exceeds a stipulated dollar amount, or line, the reinsurer assumes the surplus share of the amount of insurance (the difference between the primary insurer's line and the total amount of insurance). Surplus share reinsurance is typically used only with property insurance.

Under surplus share reinsurance, the primary insurer and the reinsurer share the policy premiums and losses proportionately. The primary insurer's share is the proportion that the line bears to the total amount of insurance; the reinsurer's share is the proportion that the amount ceded bears to the total. For example, if the line is $50,000 and the amount ceded is $200,000, the primary insurer would receive 20 percent ($50,000 ÷ $250,000) of the policy premium and pay 20 percent of all losses, while the reinsurer would receive 80 percent ($200,000 ÷ $250,000) of the policy premium and pay 80 percent of all losses.

The **reinsurance limit** of a surplus share treaty is expressed in multiples of the primary insurer's line. For example, a primary insurer with a nine-line surplus share treaty has the capacity under the treaty to insure loss exposures with amounts of insurance that exceed its retention by a multiple of nine. So if the line is $300,000 for a nine-line surplus share treaty, the primary insurer has a total underwriting capacity of $3 million, calculated as the $300,000 line plus nine multiples of that $300,000 line. In addition to being expressed as a number of lines, the reinsurance limit of a surplus share treaty can be expressed as an amount of insurance the reinsurer is willing to provide, such as $2.7 million ($300,000 multiplied by nine lines). See the exhibit "Surplus Share Reinsurance Example."

Unlike the example in the exhibit, many surplus share treaties allow the primary insurer to increase its line from a minimum amount to a maximum amount, depending on the potential loss severity of the exposed limit. For example, Brookgreen's surplus share treaty may allow the company to increase its line on a quality loss exposure from $25,000 to $50,000. In this case, the nine-line surplus share treaty would give Brookgreen large-line capacity to insure loss exposures with amounts of insurance as large as $500,000, which is calculated as the $50,000 line, plus nine multiplied by the $50,000 line. The primary insurer's ability to vary its line also allows it to retain some loss exposures it would otherwise cede.

Reinsurance limit
The maximum amount that the reinsurer will pay for a claim and that is commonly stated in the reinsurance agreement.

Surplus Share Reinsurance Example

Brookgreen Insurance Company has a surplus share treaty with Cypress Reinsurer and retains a line of $25,000. The treaty contains nine lines and provides for a maximum cession of $225,000. Therefore, the retention and reinsurance provide Brookgreen with the ability to issue policies with amounts of insurance as high as $250,000. The following three policies are issued by Brookgreen Insurance Company and are subject to the surplus share treaty with Cypress Reinsurer.

- Policy A insures Building A for $25,000 for a premium of $400, with one loss of $8,000.
- Policy B insures Building B for $100,000 for a premium of $1,000, with one loss of $10,000.
- Policy C insures Building C for $150,000 for a premium of $1,500, with one loss of $60,000.

Division of Insurance, Premiums, and Losses Under Surplus Share Treaty

	Brookgreen Insurance Retention	Cypress Reinsurance Cession	Total
Policy A			
Amounts of insurance	$25,000 (100%)	$0 (0%)	$25,000
Premiums	400	0	400
Losses	8,000	0	8,000
Policy B			
Amounts of insurance	$25,000 (25%)	$75,000 (75%)	$100,000
Premiums	250	750	1,000
Losses	2,500	7,500	10,000
Policy C			
Amounts of insurance	$25,000 (16.67%)	$125,000 (83.33%)	$150,000
Premiums	250	1,250	1,500
Losses	10,000	50,000	60,000

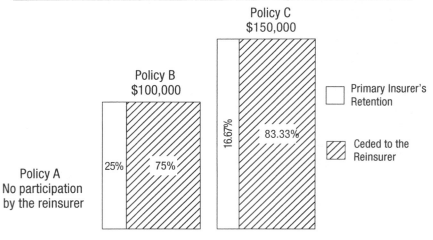

Apply Your Knowledge

Woodvail Insurance Company has arranged a reinsurance treaty with Markdall Insurance Company. Under the treaty, Woodvail will retain 40 percent of the policy premiums, coverage limits, and losses while reinsuring the rest with Markdall. What will the treaty be called?

a.   A 60/40 quota share treaty

b.   A 40/60 quota share treaty

c.   A 60 percent quota share treaty

d.   A 40 percent quota share treaty

Feedback: c. This treaty will be called a 60 percent quota share treaty because the reinsurer accepts 60 percent of the liability for each loss exposure subject to the treaty.

TYPES OF EXCESS OF LOSS REINSURANCE

Among the several types of reinsurance that have been developed to help insurers meet their goals and fulfill their promises is excess of loss reinsurance. Knowing how a loss would be paid under an excess of loss reinsurance program will put you in a better position to decide which reinsurance product would work best in a given situation.

Excess of loss reinsurance is one of the principal reinsurance agreements that insurers and reinsurers use to share the amounts of insurance, policy premiums, and losses. Here, you'll learn how excess of loss insurance is defined, used, and calculated.

Excess of Loss Reinsurance

Under an excess of loss reinsurance agreement, also called nonproportional reinsurance, the reinsurer responds to a loss only when it exceeds the primary insurer's retention, often referred to as the **attachment point**. The primary insurer fully retains losses below the attachment point. Sometimes, the reinsurer requires the primary insurer to retain a percentage of the losses that exceed the attachment point to provide the primary insurer with a financial incentive to efficiently manage losses that exceed the attachment point.

An excess of loss reinsurer's obligation to indemnify the primary insurer for losses depends on the amount of the loss and the layer of coverage the reinsurer provides. The reinsurer providing the first layer of excess of loss reinsurance shown in the following exhibit would indemnify the primary insurer for losses that exceed $250,000 (the attachment point) up to total incurred losses of $500,000. This reinsurer describes its position as "$250,000 in excess of (denoted as xs) $250,000." The reinsurer in the second layer of the excess

Excess of loss reinsurance (nonproportional reinsurance)
A type of reinsurance in which the primary insurer is indemnified for losses that exceed a specified dollar amount.

Attachment point
The dollar amount above which the reinsurer responds to losses.

of loss reinsurance program would indemnify the primary insurer for losses that exceed $500,000 up to total incurred losses of $1 million, or $500,000 xs $500,000. Losses that exceed the capacity of the primary insurer's excess of loss reinsurance (in this case, $25 million) remain the primary insurer's responsibility unless otherwise reinsured. See the exhibit "How Excess of Loss Reinsurance Is Layered."

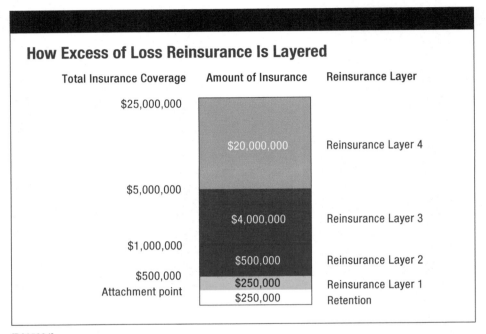

How Excess of Loss Reinsurance Is Layered

Total Insurance Coverage	Amount of Insurance	Reinsurance Layer
$25,000,000	$20,000,000	Reinsurance Layer 4
$5,000,000	$4,000,000	Reinsurance Layer 3
$1,000,000	$500,000	Reinsurance Layer 2
$500,000	$250,000	Reinsurance Layer 1
Attachment point	$250,000	Retention

[DA05084]

Excess of loss reinsurance premiums are calculated according to the likelihood that losses will exceed the attachment point. The premium is usually stated as a percentage (often called a rate) of the policy premium charged by the primary insurer (often called the **subject premium**, or underlying premium). Therefore, unlike with quota share and surplus share reinsurance, the excess of loss reinsurer receives a nonproportional share of the premium.

Reinsurers generally do not pay ceding commissions under excess of loss reinsurance agreements, but they may reward a primary insurer for favorable loss experience by paying a profit commission or reducing the rate used to calculate the reinsurance premium.

The primary insurer's attachment point is usually set at a level where expected claims would be retained. But if the primary insurer's volume of losses is expected to be significant, a lower attachment point may be set. This type of reinsurance agreement is sometimes referred to as a working cover. It enables the primary insurer to spread its losses over several years. Primary insurers selling a type of insurance with which they have little experience may select a working cover agreement until they better understand the frequency and severity of the losses for that type of insurance.

Subject premium

The premium the primary insurer charges on its underlying policies and to which a rate is applied to determine the reinsurance premium.

Five Types of Excess of Loss Reinsurance

These are the five types of excess of loss reinsurance and their specific uses:

- **Per risk excess of loss reinsurance** is often referred to as property per risk excess of loss and is generally used with property insurance. The attachment point and reinsurance limit apply separately to each loss to individual risks (loss exposures), with the primary insurer usually determining what constitutes one risk. The attachment point and reinsurance limit are stated in dollar amounts.

- **Catastrophe excess of loss reinsurance** protects the primary insurer from an accumulation of retained losses that arise from a single catastrophic event, such as a tornado, a hurricane, or an earthquake. As with per risk excess of loss reinsurance, the attachment point and reinsurance limit are stated in dollar amounts. The attachment point is subject to negotiation, but it's usually set high enough to be exceeded only if the aggregation of losses from a catastrophe would impair the primary insurer's policyholders' surplus. In addition, losses exceeding the attachment point are usually subject to a **co-participation provision**.

- **Per policy excess of loss reinsurance** is used primarily with liability insurance. It applies the attachment point and the reinsurance limit separately to the losses occurring under each insurance policy and is triggered when a loss exceeds the attachment point.

- **Per occurrence excess of loss reinsurance** is also typically used for liability insurance. It applies the attachment point and the reinsurance limit to the total losses arising from a single event, regardless of the number of policies or risks involved.

- **Aggregate excess of loss reinsurance** can be used for property or liability insurance and covers aggregated losses that exceed the attachment point and occur over a stated period, usually one year. The attachment point can be stated in a dollar amount of loss or as a loss ratio. When the attachment point is stated as a loss ratio, the treaty is called stop-loss reinsurance. Most aggregate excess of loss treaties also contain a co-participation provision of 5 percent to 10 percent to provide the primary insurer with an incentive to efficiently handle claims that exceed the attachment point.

Apply Your Knowledge

In the excess of loss reinsurance program for Bestmo Insurance Company (the primary insurer), Zates Insurance Company (the reinsurer) describes its position as being $250,000 xs $250,000. If a total amount of $600,000 in losses

Per risk excess of loss reinsurance
A type of excess of loss reinsurance that covers property insurance and that applies separately to each loss occurring to each risk.

Catastrophe excess of loss reinsurance
A type of excess of loss reinsurance that protects the primary insurer from an accumulation of retained losses that arise from a single catastrophic event.

Co-participation provision
A provision in a reinsurance agreement that requires the primary insurer to retain a specified percentage of the losses that exceed its attachment point.

Per policy excess of loss reinsurance
A type of excess of loss reinsurance that applies the attachment point and the reinsurance limit separately to each insurance policy issued by the primary insurer regardless of the number of losses occurring under each policy.

Per occurrence excess of loss reinsurance
A type of excess of loss reinsurance that applies the attachment point and reinsurance limit to the total losses arising from a single event affecting one or more of the primary insurer's policies.

Aggregate excess of loss reinsurance

A type of excess of loss reinsurance that covers aggregated losses that exceed the attachment point, stated as a dollar amount of loss or as a loss ratio, and that occur over a specified period, usually one year.

needs to be paid out under the program and Bestmo has no other reinsurance, how much of the $600,000 is Bestmo responsible for?

a. $100,000
b. $250,000
c. $350,000
d. $500,000

Feedback: c. Bestmo would be responsible for $350,000. Under the excess of loss agreement, Bestmo is responsible for any losses up to the attachment point ($250,000) and any total incurred losses above the reinsurance layer of $500,000 (which equals an additional $100,000).

ALTERNATIVES TO TRADITIONAL REINSURANCE

Alternatives to traditional reinsurance have emerged as the industry adapts to new economic and regulatory pressures. Knowing what's available can help primary insurers meet their changing reinsurance needs.

Some types of risk, particularly catastrophe risk, cannot always be suitably addressed through traditional reinsurance, so alternatives to traditional reinsurance have been developed. They include finite risk reinsurance and methods that use the capital market for risk financing.

Finite Risk Reinsurance

Finite risk reinsurance

A nontraditional type of reinsurance in which the reinsurer's liability is limited and anticipated investment income is expressly acknowledged as an underwriting component.

Under **finite risk reinsurance**, the reinsurer's liability is limited (or finite), and anticipated investment income is an underwriting component. It transfers a limited amount of risk to the reinsurer in order to improve the primary insurer's financial result. As a result, it's often called financial reinsurance.

Finite risk reinsurance can be arranged to protect a primary insurer against traditionally insurable loss exposures (such as building damage from an explosion) as well as traditionally uninsurable loss exposures (for example, loss from economic variables such as product demand and market competition). It also handles extremely large and unusual loss exposures, such as catastrophic losses resulting from an oil rig explosion or earthquake.

A finite risk reinsurance agreement typically has a multiyear term (for example, three to five years). This allows the reinsurer to spread the risk and losses over several years while imposing an aggregate limit for the agreement's entire term. With finite risk reinsurance, the primary insurer can rely on long-term protection and a predictable reinsurance cost over the coverage period, while the reinsurer can rely on a continual flow of premiums. Because of these benefits, both the primary insurer and the reinsurer tend to be flexible when negotiating the price and terms.

Finite risk reinsurance premiums can be a substantial percentage of the reinsurance limit (for example, 70 percent). This relationship between premium and reinsurance limit reduces the reinsurer's potential underwriting loss to a level that is much lower than that typically associated with traditional types of reinsurance.

Generally, finite risk reinsurance is designed to cover high-severity losses. The reinsurer commonly shares profits with the primary insurer when it has favorable loss experience or generates investment income. This profit-sharing income can compensate the primary insurer for the higher-than-usual premium of finite risk reinsurance. Also, the reinsurer will not assess any additional premium, even if losses exceed the premium.

Capital Market Alternatives

Capital markets have emerged as tools primary insurers can use to finance risk as an alternative to insurance. Instead of purchasing reinsurance to cover its potential liabilities, the primary insurer uses traded security instruments to finance insurance risk.

Some of the capital market instruments are rooted in the concepts of **securitization of risk** and **special purpose vehicles (SPVs)**, which allow primary insurers to exchange assets for cash. Others are based on **insurance derivatives** or **contingent capital arrangements**. A common theme in all of this: rather than working with a reinsurer, primary insurers obtain funding from capital markets (made up of investors and financial institutions) to help cover losses.

Although capital market alternatives can evolve rapidly, these are among the products and methods most often used:

- Catastrophe bond—A type of **insurance-linked security** that is specifically designed to transfer insurable catastrophe risk to investors. A bond is issued with a condition that if the issuer suffers a catastrophe loss greater than the specified amount, the obligation to pay interest and/or repay principal is deferred or forgiven by bondholders and used to pay losses. As long as catastrophe-related losses do not exceed the specified amount, investors earn a relatively high interest rate and receive a return of their principal. Catastrophe bonds are typically issued by the SPVs of insurers, large reinsurers, or large corporations for any type of catastrophic insurable risk, such as hurricanes, earthquakes, and other adverse weather and environmental risks.

- Catastrophe risk exchange—A means through which a primary insurer can exchange a portion of its insurance risk for another insurer's. The exchange can be, for example, an internet-based forum on which risks available for trade are advertised, negotiations are conducted, and trades

Capital market
A financial market in which long-term securities are traded.

Securitization of risk
The use of securities or financial instruments (for example, stocks, bonds, commodities, financial futures) to finance an insurer's exposure to catastrophic loss.

Special purpose vehicle (SPV)
A facility established for the purpose of purchasing income-producing assets from an organization, holding title to them, and then using those assets to collateralize securities that will be sold to investors.

Insurance derivative
Financial contract whose value is based on the level of insurable losses that occur during a specific time period.

Contingent capital arrangement
An agreement, entered into before any losses occur, that enables an organization to raise cash by selling stock or issuing debt at prearranged terms after a loss occurs that exceeds a certain threshold.

Insurance-linked security
A financial instrument whose value is primarily driven by insurance and/or reinsurance loss events.

are completed. The insurance risk traded may differ by geographic area, type of property, or cause of loss insured against. A primary insurer with a geographic concentration of loss exposures can use a catastrophe risk exchange to reduce its losses from a single loss occurrence. A primary insurer can also diversify the kinds of property insured to make it less susceptible to heavy losses from a single cause of loss.

Surplus note

A type of unsecured debt instrument, issued only by insurers, that has characteristics of both conventional equity and debt securities and is classified as policyholders' surplus rather than as a liability on the insurer's statutory balance sheet.

- Contingent surplus note—A **surplus note** that has been designed so a primary insurer, if it chooses, can immediately obtain funds by issuing notes at a previously agreed-upon rate of interest. A benefit of surplus notes is that they increase a primary insurer's assets without increasing its liabilities.

- Industry loss warranty (ILW)—An insurance-linked security that covers the primary insurer in the event that an industry-wide loss from a particular catastrophic event, such as an earthquake or a hurricane, exceeds a predetermined threshold. The distinguishing characteristic of this instrument is that its coverage is triggered by industry losses as a whole, rather than only a loss for the primary insurer.

Strike price

The price at which the stock or commodity underlying a call option (such as a warrant) or a put option can be purchased (called) or sold (put) during a specified period.

- Catastrophe option—An agreement that gives the primary insurer the right to a cash payment from investors if a specified index of catastrophe losses reaches a specified level (the **strike price**). The catastrophe loss index, such as that provided by Insurance Services Office, Inc., Property Claim Services, keeps track of catastrophe losses by geographic region, by cause of loss, and by time of occurrence.

- Line of credit—An arrangement under which a bank or another financial institution agrees to provide a loan to a primary insurer in the event that the primary insurer suffers a loss. The credit is prearranged so that the terms, such as the interest rate and principal repayment schedule, are known in advance of a loss. In exchange for this credit commitment, the primary insurer taking out the line of credit pays a commitment fee. A line of credit does not represent any risk transfer; it simply provides access to capital.

- Sidecar—A limited-existence SPV, often formed as an independent company, that provides a primary insurer more capacity to write property catastrophe business or other short-tail lines through a quota share agreement with private investors. Investors in the SPV assume a proportion of the risk and earn a corresponding portion of the profit on the primary insurer's book of business. The primary insurer charges a ceding commission and may receive an additional commission if the book of business is profitable.

The Rise of Parametric Insurance

Parametric insurance, a type of insurance-linked security, is becoming more common. It's a highly customizable form of coverage against losses caused by a specific event or movement in an index. Typically, the payment is a specific, agreed-upon figure, which is paid out if the parameters (parametric triggers) set around the event or index are reached.

Examples of parametric triggers could be earthquake magnitude, hurricane wind speed, level of precipitation, length of a drought, or a specific economic variable (like loss of income).

Because the triggering event is tied to a specific measure, determining when a payout is required is relatively easy. Combine that with the fact that the payout was determined from the outset of the agreement, and parametric insurance eliminates the need for a lengthy adjustment and claims process. For insureds, this means that they will receive funds rapidly once a qualifying event occurs.

[DA12801]

Apply Your Knowledge

Hamels Insurance Company has entered into an agreement with a financial institution under which the institution agrees to provide a loan to Hamels if Hamels suffers a loss. The terms have been prearranged, so the interest rate and repayment schedule are set before any loss occurs. What type of reinsurance product does Hamels Insurance have?

a.   Finite risk reinsurance

b.   A contingent surplus note

c.   An industry loss warranty

d.   A line of credit

Feedback: d. A line of credit is an arrangement in which a bank or another financial institution agrees to provide a loan to a primary insurer in the event the primary insurer suffers a loss. The credit is prearranged so that the terms, such as the interest rate and principal repayment schedule, are known in advance of a loss.

SUMMARY

Reinsurance is the transfer of insurance risk from one insurer to another through a contractual agreement under which the reinsurer agrees to indemnify the primary insurer for some or all the financial consequences of the loss exposures covered by the reinsurance contract. Reinsurance performs these principal functions for primary insurers: increase large-line capacity, provide catastrophe protection, stabilize loss experience, provide surplus relief, facilitate withdrawal from a market segment, and provide underwriting guidance.

Reinsurance is available from professional reinsurers; reinsurance departments of primary insurers; and reinsurance pools, syndicates, and associations. Each source has its own strengths and shortcomings, but all provide a means for insurers to expand their abilities to take on loss exposures.

The two types of reinsurance transactions are treaty reinsurance and facultative reinsurance. Treaty reinsurance agreements provide coverage for an entire class or portfolio of loss exposures and involve an ongoing relationship between the primary insurer and the reinsurer.

A primary insurer's reinsurance program can combine several types of reinsurance agreements to meet its specific needs. One of the principal approaches that insurers and reinsurers use to share the amounts of insurance, policy premiums, and losses is pro rata reinsurance. The two types of pro rata reinsurance are quota share and surplus share reinsurance.

Excess of loss reinsurance is one of the principal approaches that insurers and reinsurers use to share the amounts of insurance, policy premiums, and losses. The five types of excess of loss reinsurance are per risk excess of loss reinsurance, catastrophe excess of loss reinsurance, per policy excess of loss reinsurance, per occurrence excess of loss reinsurance, and aggregate excess of loss reinsurance.

Alternatives to traditional reinsurance have been developed in response to the economic and regulatory pressures the industry is under. Finite risk reinsurance is one example, and it can help protect a primary insurer against large and unusual loss exposures. Primary insurers can also use capital markets to finance risks, particularly those related to catastrophes.

Direct Your Learning ▶▶

9

Business Needs and IT Alignment

Educational Objectives

After learning the content of this assignment, you should be able to:

▷ Explain why information technology is important in insurer operations.

▷ Explain how data quality practices enable insurers to meet operational-, managerial-, and strategic-level information needs.

▷ Explain how insurers use these technology systems to optimize decision making, customer service, and daily transactions:

- Transaction processing systems

- Decision support systems

- Expert systems

- Customer-focused collection and safety systems

▷ Evaluate the security risks in information systems and appropriate responses to those risks.

▷ Explain why an insurer's information technology strategy should align with its overall business strategy.

Business Needs and IT Alignment

IMPORTANCE OF INFORMATION TECHNOLOGY TO AN INSURER

As the insurance industry's collection and use of data continue to evolve, so does the power structure that manages those tasks. Chief information officers (CIOs), who manage an insurer's information technology (IT), and chief data officers (CDOs), who oversee the organization's data collection, work together to provide a clear path and directive that enables an insurer to better meet the needs of its customers.

Insurers are always looking for ways to improve their operational efficiency and growth, as well as to understand and exceed customers' expectations. Insurers are more likely to meet these challenges if business and IT professionals collaborate to leverage IT capabilities in an effort to meet these goals:

- Gain a competitive advantage
- Optimize operations and resources
- Provide information to support strategy and decision making
- Facilitate governance, risk, and compliance initiatives

Gain a Competitive Advantage

Information is essential to effective underwriting, and IT capabilities improve the speed with which information can be stored, processed, and retrieved. This enables insurers to collect and validate data using outside sources—such as motor vehicle registration and licensing records or an individual's claims history—to create a data resource that can become the basis for enhanced business decisions.

In the modern insurance environment, insurer differentiation—and therefore competitive advantage—may hinge on intelligence, customer relationships, and speed. Business and IT professionals should collaboratively use predictive analytics to develop intelligence using **database** information, such as customer behaviors and preferences, the markets the insurer serves or might consider entering, and the risks and opportunities it might encounter. For example, analytics that incorporate medical information, claims history, and fraud incidence might suggest that an insurer should withdraw from writing auto liability insurance in a particular region.

Database

A collection of information stored in discrete units for ease of retrieval, manipulation, combination, or other computer processing.

Internet of Things (IoT)
A network of objects that transmit data to computers.

Data from the **Internet of Things (IoT)**, such as telematics that create a picture of an insured's driving habits or information collected from a home heating system that monitors temperature or water pressure, can help an insurer provide an insured with the most protection necessary at the lowest price possible. In other words, IT intelligence gives insurers better insight for underwriting, product development, and pricing.

IT supports tools such as smartphone applications that offer policy self-service, auto maintenance reminders, and route planning. The intelligence could suggest solutions that improve collaboration and communication with insurers' stakeholders, such as a web portal for producers that aggregates customer information to suggest **endorsements**, new policy features, and other products, all customized for each insured. It could also assist the insurer with governance by, for example, embedding building code requirements into a database to help claims representatives accurately estimate reconstruction costs.

Endorsement
A document that amends an insurance policy.

Business intelligence (BI)
The skills, technologies, applications, and practices used to improve decision-making insights and reinforce information integrity.

The blending of business and IT can combine **business intelligence (BI)** with web-enabled capabilities, social media, and innovation to craft marketing programs, explore distribution channels, and develop new products and services that entice customers and boost **retention** and loyalty by engaging producers and policyholders.

Personnel from both the business and the IT sides of an insurer must work together to manage the quality of its data. Successful insurers identify data that has the greatest impact on their business strategy and focus on defining and validating that data. An insurer's data might reveal purchasing trends or demographics that suggest a profitable emerging or **niche market**. For example, analytics might reveal locations with aging populations that have strong financial resources and an interest in fitness. This information may lead the insurer to develop a commercial policy offering customizations to fitness and spa facilities that cater to customers over age fifty-five.

Retention
The percentage of policies in force that are renewed at the policy anniversary.

Niche market
A small segment of a total market.

Underwriters increasingly use analytical engines with predictive modeling to experiment with pricing changes and predict their effect on key performance indicators. It also enables underwriters to integrate cost and demand to find the optimum premium that is likely to gain regulatory approval, be low enough to attract customers, and be high enough to meet or exceed the organization's profit and growth objectives.

For example, an underwriter might cull an insurer's data and find that parents of young drivers are likely to shop for low-cost auto insurance. To encourage customer retention and reduce the risk of claims from young drivers' errors, an underwriter might use a predictive model to determine a premium discount that encourages young drivers to take a safe-driver course every two years. The insurer might also negotiate a discount with a national course provider.

Underwriting, claims, and accounting personnel and their IT partners must examine the needs of insurance consumers who use web-enhanced tools and mobile applications to get instant insurance quotes from multiple insurers and price changes on their current policies, as well as to submit new applications, change requests, and cancellation requests. These capabilities can be enhanced through IT's collaboration with outside entities such as motor vehicle departments, credit rating agencies, and insurance subscriber services that share information from their own databases. This partnering reduces customer entries and provides accurate quotations through a channel that speeds delivery of insurance products.

Because all these processes rely on accurate, secure, and often personal data, efficiently capturing data from and about consumers is crucial to innovation. This data is often captured by smart products, which can sense their environment, process data, and communicate with other smart products and smart operations through the IoT, generating data to which advanced analytics can be applied. The security and integrity of this data then becomes paramount, as does accessibility.

Blockchain technology—which offers a virtual distributed ledger that maintains a dynamically updated list of records (blocks) and confirms the data within them through a consensus process—is a possible solution for this need. By allowing cooperating entities to share data quickly, it expands the information available for predictive modeling and analysis beyond what would be available to an organization acting on its own.

Increase Operational Efficiency

IT capabilities can increase the operational efficiency of nearly every functional area of an insurer's business. When considering whether to develop or purchase new technology, the costs of efficiency enhancements should be weighed against the savings and benefits that the new IT would produce to determine the return on investment (ROI).

In addition to the cost of purchasing and installing the equipment, as well as any development costs, insurers should consider these costs when calculating ROI:

- Staff's time for training and any associated fees or materials costs
- Time lost until staff become proficient using the new technology
- Maintenance of the technology
- Required services associated with the technology
- Any costs associated with building or structural modifications and equipment needed to house and protect the new IT equipment

The savings/benefit calculations should consider any salary and benefit costs eliminated through staff reductions; the savings from eliminated expenses incurred for the use, support, and maintenance of the old technology; the realized value of employees' reduced time once the learning curve has been eliminated; the value of customers' satisfaction with the improved technology; and new business volume that results from the IT upgrade.

Insurers that align all their objectives with their vision, mission, and goals might decide to use a transformational approach to evaluating IT system and process upgrades rather than a cost/benefit approach. In a transformational approach, insurers focus on the future state of the organization based on its vision and strategic goals. If IT initiatives align with the organization's goals, then they are worthy of pursuit. For example, if a corporate goal is to improve operational efficiency by reducing costs and risk, an appropriate improvement may be a technology improvement allows the insurer to monitor its operations online in real time to identify backlogs and workflow bottlenecks.

Improvements in mobile technology and declining costs have made adoption of portable IT enhancements imperative for operational efficiency. The benefit is evident for field claims representatives, who access and verify policy information and transmit claims information while adjusting property losses at loss sites. IT features enable them to settle losses or make partial payments immediately so that displaced families can return to their homes as soon as possible. The customer service and satisfaction benefits of this technology are exponential compared with the costs of the technology.

Insurers can also increase operational efficiencies using enhanced IT models. For example, insurers might use cloud technology to eliminate the costs of purchasing and owning expensive computer equipment and to enjoy the processing speeds of newer equipment. However, they must also consider the potential trade-offs, which include losing control over data and the risk that the cloud vendor might not properly protect the data.

Apply Your Knowledge

Andy is the new manager of the Claims Division of a regional insurance company. At a recent claims association conference, he learned about a user-friendly, image-enabled workflow system with built-in analytics and networking capability that integrates with Insurance Services Office, Inc.'s (ISO's) database services to improve fraud detection, theft recovery, and exposure analysis. Andy is not certain that the system is compatible with his company's current network operating system or database, but he is so impressed by it and the value he believes it would deliver to his employer that he thinks the organization should purchase it and let the IT Division work out any compatibility issues later. What flaw in Andy's thinking could undermine adoption of this new system?

Feedback: Andy's expectations are shortsighted. Before considering any new technology purchase, business professionals should collaborate with their IT professionals to determine user needs and current system capabilities. Together, they should explore system options, their costs and benefits, and the feasibility of adopting new technology. In Andy's scenario, even if the new system were compatible with his company's existing network, the insurer would still be likely to incur costs to integrate the new system with the existing one. If conversions were required to adapt data for the new system, reduced retrieval speeds would create operating inefficiencies. In either case, the time to complete the integration might outdate the proposed claims system, as technology continually evolves.

Support Strategy and Decision Making

Managerial decision making requires analyzing complex business information from multiple sources that often change. Unfortunately, human decision makers have limitations. The volume of information to be analyzed increases the time people need to make informed decisions, but the pace of change makes timely business decisions essential. Further complicating these decisions is the fact that while a manager with considerable education and experience could potentially make superior decisions, personal biases and values may negatively influence those decisions, rendering them less effective.

IT decision-support capabilities can help people overcome these limitations. Decision-support systems analyze large databases of BI to supply managers with suggested fact-based outcomes for the business problem the manager inputs. Each database is logically organized for efficient processing, and the results can include graphics and other tools that support a decision. The number of outputs is limited to a few that are best supported by the data. The manager must still exercise good judgment to select the best solution, but the software improves the speed and quality of decisions and may help the manager recognize flaws in his or her thinking. Another benefit is that the manager can add to or change details of the problem and then rerun the application to produce better-defined or more specific solutions. In addition to the speed with which decision-support applications produce results, they incorporate business rules with knowledge that has developed over time, and they easily transfer the knowledge to new managers, resulting in more consistent, rational decision making, whether by one individual or many.

Because decision-support systems include business rules and vast databases of BI, they have become essential tools for developing business strategy. Predictive analytics tools are often paired with decision-support functionality. When managers input data that they deem strategic to the organization, these systems can project the outcomes of various strategies. Managers can examine the suggested results in conjunction with the organization's vision, mission, and objectives to produce optimum strategies that will help set the insurer apart from its competition.

At various points during the year, managers may reassess their strategies by rerunning the analytical decision-support systems—using new and developing data that have periodically been added to the database—to ensure that the strategy remains effective to meet the insurer's goals or to tweak its strategies based on new BI.

Facilitate Governance, Risk, and Compliance Initiatives

An insurer's governance, risk, and compliance programs create rules, processes, and controls that support the insurer's operating policies and strategic goals. They create transparency that offers the insurer's management and stakeholders a macro view of all of the organization's daily activities and helps them identify potential credit, market, or operational risk exposures so that they can react quickly and appropriately.

Modern IT support and decision-making tools enable insurers to proactively analyze various scenarios and conduct tests for corporate exposures to risk. The results of these tests and analyses help insurers anticipate and identify risk and react to it promptly and effectively. IT controls help insurers better understand financial market risks and changes in laws and regulations; threats and vulnerabilities to IT systems; and threats caused by environmental issues, political unrest, and terrorism.

Governance, risk, and financial reporting features that are embedded in an insurer's IT-enabled end-to-end processes and controls on an enterprise-wide basis are, in effect, integrated into that insurer's daily processing. This integration can reduce the insurer's administrative burden and provide ongoing compliance and risk monitoring. This holistic view of enterprise risk allows the insurer to respond promptly to changes in its environment and markets, enabling it to use strategic risk and return to sustain a competitive advantage.

The National Association of Insurance Commissioners (NAIC) monitors insurers' corporate governance practices through annual and quarterly reports that insurers develop and transmit. The NAIC guides insurers on corporate governance, requiring them to have adequate top-level controls, checks, established structures, and communications.

IT capabilities can assist with auditing by preventing unauthorized entries, such as a reserve that exceeds the authority level of the claims representative who set it. Control features might also select files for auditing based on established criteria and provide the list of files to a manager or an internal auditor. Control functions can even audit the IT systems to provide real-time alerts to IT staff concerning system problems and errors; unauthorized attempts to access secured data or systems; and failures of other systems, such as malfunctions of the cooling and humidity controls that protect computer equipment.

Accurate data reporting is crucial to government oversight, the industry, and stakeholders. State insurance regulators require the use of statutory accounting principles (SAP) for insurers' financial statements, which help regulators monitor insurer solvency. SAP accounting uses a conservative approach to the valuation of assets and liabilities (the insurer's obligations) and the recording of income to ensure that the insurer has adequate capital to meet solvency requirements. Accurate solvency data protects policyholders and public interests, ensuring that insurers have the capital to meet their claims obligations and remain solvent, even if disaster strikes or the economy slumps. IT tools and capabilities simplify categorizing data according to SAP requirements and developing standardized SAP reports that are required by state insurance regulators. Standardized data formats and electronic report submissions improve regulators' ability to maintain oversight of all insurers.

Accurate data is equally important for insurers' generally accepted accounting principles (GAAP) financial reporting. GAAP reporting provides investors, members, or other stakeholders with financial information in a uniform format, enabling them to analyze and compare an insurer's profitability and earnings with those of other insurers and types of business organizations. Credit rating agencies, such as Moody's, analyze insurers' GAAP financial reports to assign ratings that help investors, creditors, and additional stakeholders make sound financial decisions. IT tools and capabilities also categorize information for GAAP reporting. Credit rating agencies require standardized data formats for GAAP reporting. They run IT analytics to apply rules and algorithms consistently and, in so doing, to develop and assign a financial strength rating for each insurer. IT ensures the reliability of the ratings so that agency customers can use them to make sound business decisions.

THE IMPORTANCE OF DATA QUALITY IN MEETING INSURER INFORMATION NEEDS

Almost every crucial insurance decision is based on data. So insurance professionals who have a well-rounded understanding of how quality data is collected, stored, and used are in a better position to help insurers best meet their goals and serve customers.

Collecting and managing quality data are critical insurer functions. Such data is needed to set pricing, control risk, evaluate new markets, manage finances, and support compliance efforts. To support insurers' goals, data managers must ensure that data quality standards are met and that the data is protected, used, and enhanced in the best ways possible. To facilitate this, the data needs of insurers are split into three levels: operational, managerial, and strategic.

Usage and Characteristics of Quality Data

In insurance, data serves many purposes, and in many cases, the same data serves multiple purposes. For example, policyholder zip codes are stored as part of insureds' addresses, and insurers also use zip codes to evaluate loss exposures in a region for policy pricing or for decisions to expand or withdraw from writing coverages in that region.

Quality data is data that is appropriate, reasonable, and comprehensive enough to accomplish its given use. Certain traits determine whether data is appropriate, such as its timeliness or historic value, the source from which it was collected or derived, its independence from or dependence on other appropriate data, and the suitability of the data to produce a reliable result or assessment. Reasonable data is data that's been validated using outside sources or audited for consistency and accuracy. Comprehensive data contains the full range of information needed to produce a reliable result or analysis.

For example, data for evaluating auto rates by insureds' ages must include age groupings that have been used consistently within the organization and in nationwide claims databases. The data must also include claims data that help determine rates for various coverages, such as claims for which losses were paid; their settlement amounts; the territory; the types of claims paid (property damage or bodily injury); and causes of loss. A quality control audit should be performed on the selected data to ensure accuracy, validity (quality as a permitted value in a dataset), and consistency.

Quality data is free of any factors or limitations that could adversely affect an outcome. If any such factors exist and reasonable alternatives are available, alternatives should be used. For example, when selecting data for a study to determine the number of auto accidents that are likely to occur while the driver is using autonomous or semi-autonomous driving aids, claims that occurred before the year 2015 would be limited because of the growing frequency in the use of those driving aids after that year. Viable alternative data to reflect current trends would be claims from the two most recent years.

Users must also consider the validity of the data sample. In the auto example, claims that occurred more than two years prior would produce an invalid sample because so many more people used the driving aids in the years since.

The Casualty Actuarial Society (CAS) and the Insurance Data Management Association (IDMA) are two examples of business associations that have been formed to develop data-quality standards and best practices for gathering, organizing, analyzing, and distributing information to support insurers' decisions. The IDMA Value Proposition states that poor data quality can be costly, so the best approach is to proactively address quality at the moment data is created—by engineering the processes to create quality data.

Data warehousing

The use of a database or a collection of databases developed for an organization or an enterprise for analysis and support of management decisions.

Data managers achieve data governance (creating rules and processes to protect and enhance data) by creating data definitions and metadata (information describing the data); developing data standards; ensuring compliance with standards; and monitoring and assisting with data analysis, **data warehousing**, predictive modeling, business intelligence, and risk management. Data managers also advocate for standardized data across the industry.

To effectively manage data quality, a data manager must understand the insurer's data needs, which are divided into operational, managerial, and strategic levels.

Operational-Level Information Needs

Insurers' operational-level data needs are triggered by necessary activities such as setting rates, underwriting, producing policies, collecting premiums, reserving and paying claims, defending insureds and claims decisions, supporting producers, developing sales information, financing, auditing, and controlling losses.

The subsequent in-depth examination of some of these operational functions depicts the types and extent of data required.

Customer Information

Both producers and insurers benefit from learning as much as possible about their customers and prospects. This drives product development, sales, and customer service. In addition to personal identifying information, insurers need customers' current and past insurance information—including detailed exposure information and specifics about customers' risk retention and risk management efforts—to underwrite and rate coverages.

Underwriting Information

Underwriters are charged with selecting profitable **exposures** and developing rates that produce a profit. So underwriters need specific, detailed data on the coverage requested and claims history. Selection and rating data must be accurate, complete, and granular enough to support decisions. Underwriters need data on the insurer's rating formulas; reinsurance criteria; loss costs; and, for workers compensation cases, **National Council on Compensation Insurance (NCCI)** classification codes. Poor data quality results in improper pricing.

Underwriters also need data from outside organizations, such as credit ratings; loss experience data; driver records; authorized medical records; wildfire, flood plain, and National Weather Service data; vehicle valuation data; stolen equipment data; and more. This data is structured data because it can be standardized. Underwriters also need access to unstructured data, such as claims representatives' notes; images of correspondence; photos; and audio and video files.

Exposure

Any condition that presents a possibility of gain or loss, whether or not an actual loss occurs.

National Council on Compensation Insurance (NCCI)

An advisory association that manages a database of workers compensation insurance information, analyzes industry trends, prepares workers compensation rate recommendations, assists in pricing legislation, and provides data products.

Apply Your Knowledge

Underwriters for Maldeen Insurance Company have been asked to determine whether certain commercial property insurance exposures will be profitable. To do so, they will look at detailed data on the coverages requested and claims history. To support the underwriters' decisions, this selection and rating data must be accurate and have which one of the following traits?

a. It must come from the same source.

b. It must come from outside organizations.

c. It must be structured data.

d. It must be complete and granular.

Feedback: d. Selection and rating data must be accurate, complete, and granular enough to support decisions.

Claims Information

Claims representatives require extensive information. When a claim is reported, they must gather data from numerous sources. They get policy information from the insurer's database and the loss notice to verify that coverage existed at the time of loss, identify **policy limits**, and determine whether **aggregate limits** or reinsurance applies. Claims representatives should also resolve entry or processing errors to ensure data quality.

When conducting an investigation, claims representatives develop the claim information using additional loss details, claimant information, investigation details, claim reserves, loss payments, **salvage** and reinsurance recoveries, notes, digital images, correspondence, and audio and video files. This data is recorded in the insurer's database along with data from outside sources such as fire and police departments, motor vehicle departments, medical providers, claims history and fraud databases, property damage estimators, valuation services and salvage buyers, stolen property registries, social media, independent adjusters, lawyers and courts, and others. The insurer's claim file must provide documentation to support its decisions and avoid or defend against **bad faith**.

Claims managers also need information from the insurer's defense and corporate legal counsel and from state insurance departments. Ideally, all of an insurer's data is stored and accessed in a central database.

Accounting and Financial Information

Accounting staff need all billing and collection information stored in the insurer's database, and they need access to premium and claims information. In addition, accounting and financial staff need digital information from banks and other financial institutions.

Finance extracts most federal, state, and local tax reporting information from the insurer's database(s), but it also needs information and systems for tracking depreciation on business property, processing and filing state statistical and rating information, and completing and filing tax returns and reporting payments to employees and vendors. Additionally, financial staff need data from analytic engines and predictive modeling for investment planning and fulfillment of reporting and legal requirements.

Managerial-Level Information Needs

Managers need accurate information to control and monitor the performance of the enterprise. This information should indicate the insurer's progress toward meeting objectives and suggest changes to improve performance and achieve profitability.

Policy limits

The maximum that can be paid on the claim, regardless of the actual value of the property damaged.

Aggregate limit

The maximum amount an insurer will pay for all covered losses during the covered policy period.

Salvage

The process by which an insurer takes possession of damaged property for which it has paid a total loss and recovers a portion of the loss payment by selling the damaged property.

Bad faith

An insurer's denial of coverage without cause, which can result in extracontractual damages, punitive damages, or both.

Financial Reporting and Premium Determination

For financial reporting, accountants need complete, accurate, and detailed current and historical data for tracking the insurer's assets and liabilities. Financial reports are required by state insurance departments to evaluate insurers' solvency and are submitted to rating bureaus to assist with investor decision making. Managers also use financial reports to analyze the insurer's profitability, determine where problems might be occurring, and prepare budgets based on expected premiums, losses, and expenses. The data aids the organization's planning process and ensures that department goals are aligned with strategic goals.

Actuaries need premium and loss information for ratemaking to determine the insurer's standard premiums. Financial reports enable underwriters to monitor premium and loss data and to discover new loss exposures that may merit a premium change.

Product Development and Pricing, Producer Relations, and Reinsurance

Underwriters and actuaries often monitor sales trends and profit margins to identify markets in which the insurer can grow its business. Insurers can use predictive modeling to simulate market conditions and change policy terms and coverages to estimate future loss patterns and develop pricing structures for new products. Quality historical data must form the foundation of these new product prices to ensure profitability.

Insurers analyze their policy and financial data to determine the volume and profitability of business provided by each producer. They also analyze premium and loss information to determine the type and level of reinsurance protection the insurer should seek. Insurers analyze data on exposures by geographic concentration, industry, and coverage limits to suggest the appropriate mix of reinsurance protection. They use financial data to monitor their books of business for new patterns in risk assumption and to review their reinsurance programs regularly for continued adequacy.

Strategic-Level Information Needs

Insurers examine their vision, mission, and goals and align their strategies to achieve them. An insurer needs data and output from analytics and predictive modeling to determine what products to produce, what processes to adapt, which customers to serve, and the optimum size and composition of the organization.

Executive managers need extensive, high-quality data resources and analytics to determine the insurer's strategic path. Executive information systems combine the insurer's financial data with data from external databases containing news feeds, market research, population trends, trade activity, and economic activity to create powerful decision-support systems.

Strategic use of quality data enables insurers to improve their customers' experiences and determine which technologies to use. Conversely, an insurer's use of faulty data for customer-facing tools could alienate customers and become a liability.

TYPES OF BUSINESS INFORMATION SYSTEMS

Insurers rely heavily on technology to compete against other insurers and enhance the customer experience. As a result, the more you know about the tools and systems insurers use, the better equipped you'll be to aid in insurance transactions and organizational decision making.

A business information system (BIS) consists of the technological tools insurers use to remain competitive and serve customers. A BIS can include one or more databases, decision-support tools, information management controls, and applications needed for an insurer to conduct thorough and accurate business analysis.

A BIS consists of four systems that help insurers make sound business decisions and deliver information and products to customers: transaction processing system (TPS), decision support system (DSS), expert system (ES), and customer-focused collection and safety system.

Transaction Processing Systems

TPS is the generic name for a collection of software, databases, procedures, and devices that can perform a high volume of routine and repetitive business transactions and analyses. A TPS can include database management systems, multipurpose databases, data mining and **big data** systems, **telematics** devices, cloud storage, and **blockchain** technology.

Insurers can use a TPS for efficient collection, modification, and retrieval of transaction data. TPS data is useful for policy and claims processing, managing purchasing and inventory, accounting within ledger systems, managing financial investments, and more.

Database Management Systems

A database management system (DBMS) stores and organizes data flowing from a TPS in a database. It also provides a user interface for retrieving information using a TPS.

A DBMS manages information from each TPS and stores it in a central repository database or in individual databases that function together as a central repository. A DBMS collects data from the beginning of a policy life cycle and makes that data available for reuse in other systems or by other departments. This prevents duplicate entries, errors, and confusion, which can be created

Big data

Sets of data that are too large to be gathered and analyzed by traditional methods.

Telematics

The use of technological devices in vehicles with wireless communication and GPS tracking that transmit data to businesses or government agencies; some return information for the driver.

Blockchain

A distributed digital ledger that facilitates secure transactions without the need for a third party.

when the same or similar information is entered through multiple systems at different touchpoints.

Consider this example of how a TPS and DBMS work together for efficient data collection, access, and modification: After receiving an insurance application, a producer enters the customer's name, address, contact information, vehicle identification numbers (VINs), policy limits, **deductibles**, and so forth into the agency's TPS, which stores the data in the insurer's DBMS, where it will be available for use by multiple departments. The insurer's underwriting TPS retrieves the information from the DBMS for underwriting review and policy issuance. The information does not need to be reentered, so potential data entry errors are avoided. Any updates for the policy, including final premium information, are entered in the underwriting TPS and updated in the DBMS. All this data can then be fed to the insurer's accounting TPS, which uses it to generate billing information and financial reports and handle electronic payments.

When the insured reports a claim, a customer service representative can key the policy number into the claims TPS, and the policy and premium information stored in the DBMS is automatically fed into the claims TPS for reuse. No one in the Claims Department must retype the information to process claim payments because it was already captured in the underwriting TPS, passed to the DBMS, and made available for the claims TPS and other systems. Again, the DBMS ensures that crucial information is accurate and consistent among each TPS.

Multipurpose Databases

Multipurpose databases, or data warehouses, can be used for structured and unstructured data. Structured data is made up of standardized fields, whereas unstructured data can include open text fields and objects such as emails, audio and video files, webpages, customer intelligence retrieved through social media (such as "likes" and group affiliations), and data transmitted from vehicles and smartphones.

With unstructured data, an insurance manager can develop actionable information by selecting and sorting the data by territory code, policy limits, loss amount, or policy term. Using unstructured data, however, can involve searching the data using tags (labels) or terms such as "fraud" or "arson." Searching for the tag "SIU" (**special investigative unit**), for example, could enable the manager to identify suspicious claims that may be related.

Data Mining and Big Data

Database and data warehouse features enable data mining, the analysis of large quantities of data to find patterns, trends, and correlations. Data mining offers users new perspectives on information, leading to better decisions, new products, new customer groups, and recognition of emerging exposures, all of which can create a marketing advantage. Data mining has also been used to

Deductible

A portion of a covered loss that is not paid by the insurer.

Special investigation unit (SIU)

A division set up to investigate suspicious claims, premium fraud, or application fraud.

identify fraud activity, predict customer buying patterns, and increase operating productivity. For example, data mining can generate a report of a city's suspicious rear-end collision claims, including those involving injured pedestrians, in which the injured are treated by the same physicians and specialists and the treatments extended beyond six months. Another example of a data mining report is one of claims in which all damaged autos were repaired by one of three auto repair facilities for less than $2,000. Any patterns revealed in either of these reports could suggest that fraud rings are causing the claims.

Large database systems are also used to store and process big data. This term refers to any data that is too vast and/or complex for traditional data processing or analysis techniques. Big data systems take large quantities of information and apply statistical modeling and **artificial intelligence** (AI) to it to produce forecasts of future events, losses, and risks. Big data can influence functions, such as underwriting, ratemaking, claims processing, and marketing.

Artificial Intelligence (AI)
Computer processing or output that simulates human reasoning or knowledge.

Telematics

The variety, volume, and velocity (speed with which data is transmitted) of data involved in telematics exemplify big data. A telematics device installed in an auto or a mobile device senses behaviors—such as hard braking, fast turns, quick acceleration, and speed—and other information—such as miles driven, location, and the time of day driven (variety and volume)—in real time (high velocity), then transmits this large amount of data wirelessly to an insurer, enabling the insurer to offer usage-based rating for auto insurance.

A drawback of big data, like the kind continuously generated through telematics, is that managing the versions and locations of the various files can be time consuming. One solution is a sophisticated enterprise-wide index with a user-friendly interface that can tag data and store its location and metadata (information about the data and their attributes), and then locate particular data.

Cloud Storage

Cloud storage is another data model that allows insurers to efficiently store, modify, and retrieve data. In this model, data is stored on remote servers that can be accessed using the internet ("the cloud"). An advantage of cloud storage is that insurers and their employees can remotely access valuable data from just about anywhere the internet is available. Insurers can choose what kind of data can be stored in the cloud, what kind of data can be pulled from the cloud, and who can access and alter the data.

A disadvantage of cloud storage is that it can be more difficult to secure sensitive data that is stored in the cloud than data that is stored in an insurer's traditional database. However, like with many big data systems, a variety of tools can be used to protect data from hackers and thieves.

Blockchain

Blockchain technology is a giant leap forward in digital record keeping. It is a decentralized data-storage technology and real-time ledger that contains a history of transactions that cannot be hacked. Blockchain is a shared database that does not require an official record keeper or third party to act as an intermediary. An advantage of blockchain for both insurers and insureds is that it enables the data and financial transactions of authorized participants to be approved and recorded (in digital "blocks") immediately. It creates an instant, permanent transaction record that can be viewed, in read-only format, by authorized entities, like an insurer.

Due to their security, blockchains can eliminate the need to verify the accuracy of insureds' data. As a result, rather than spending time trying to double-check past data—like policy terms and limits—claims and audit teams can now spend more time on forward-looking functions, like predictive analysis or forecasting. This could lower expense ratios and improve ratemaking.

In addition, blockchains can store and execute smart contracts—digital contracts that follow a computer protocol and are executed automatically when conditions of the contract are met. For example, if a homeowner's flood insurance policy is stored on a blockchain, his insurer could automatically issue him a claim payment when a weather service informs the insurer that the area in which his home is located has been flooded.

Decision Support Systems

A DSS is an organized collection of hardware, software, databases, and procedures used by a BIS to support strategic decision making. It typically examines and manipulates a vast amount of information collected by a TPS.

A DSS provides an interface that allows users to enter details about a problem and obtain suggested solutions. The database used in a DSS contains information, rules, and modeling and analytical tools relevant to those problems. By entering details on new markets they are considering, insurers can use a DSS to more accurately predict return on investment (ROI) from strategic changes they might make, as well as the time it will take to realize that ROI. A DSS can also help insurers identify declining markets they may want to abandon.

A DSS can perform analyses based on these factors (and the questions insurers might ask related to them):

- Changes to one or more situational details (what-if factor)—For example, an insurer might ask, "What if we reduce the insured's deductible by $50 for one year of accident-free driving?"
- Repeated changes to a single detail (sensitivity factor)—For example, an insurer might ask, "How would the insured react if his premium is increased by 10 percent each year?"

- Changes to several details aimed at achieving a target result (goal-seeking factor)—For example, an insurer might ask, "At what premium and deductible will insureds be willing to purchase a vanishing deductible?"
- Experimentation to find the best combination of details subject to certain constraints (optimization factor)—For example, an insurer might ask, "How much can we increase the premium and deductible before a ten-year policyholder will research policy prices with other insurers?"

A DSS can predict the ROI from offering alternatives for auto identification cards, such as transmitting insurance details to an electronic device installed in an auto so that, in the event of an accident, the information can be accessed by police. A DSS can identify consumers' needs for a type of insurance coverage or policy feature and determine potential ROI for providing them.

Expert Systems

An ES stores knowledge and makes inferences. It is designed to emulate human decision making using AI. An ES contains case-based or hierarchical facts about a specific subject along with rules that explain to the system how it can use expert reasoning. Using AI, an ES can analyze vast amounts of complex information faster than a human and either recommend solutions or actually make decisions.

For example, life insurers have developed AI systems that allow individuals to obtain insurance quotes using photos of themselves. The AI technology behind the process uses complex health data to analyze a photo and determine the subject's age, gender, and body mass index. Insurers can then use that information to help them assess risk.

The benefits of using an ES to supplement or support human decision making include speed and consistency, its preservation and use of the knowledge of multiple experts, and the fact that it does not suffer human limitations (distraction, stress, or fatigue). An ES is also objective and not prone to bias. Insurers can use an ES to underwrite complex accounts, handle complex claims, offer potential medical diagnoses, and detect fraud.

Customer-Focused Collection and Safety Systems

Insurers are increasingly using information produced by systems that interact with customers. They enable insurers to collaborate with customers to provide individualized pricing or discounts.

Telematics is one example. Telematics, used in what is called pay-as-you-drive or pay-how-you-drive (usage-based) insurance, enables insurers to rate drivers based on their driving habits rather than assumptions based on segmentation (such as age, gender, marital status, and auto model). Some regulators prohibit insurers from using personal characteristics as the basis of price because doing so can penalize good, law-abiding drivers. Telematics provides a solution: individualized pricing. Because safe drivers are attracted to telematics' benefits, insurers can gain a competitive advantage by attracting the most profitable customers.

Cutting-edge safety and security features are being installed in motor carriers, personal autos, homes, and commercial buildings. These technologies may use Internet of Things (IoT) devices, or smart devices, such as cameras, sensors, global positioning systems, and other devices to transmit data to insurers and/or security vendors and local authorities. Information transmitted and/or collected by these devices can be used by insurers to investigate losses, determine causes of loss, and serve as evidence that can potentially bring justice to those who have committed fraud.

IoT and smart devices can even help prevent losses. For example, if a property in a floodplain has a sump pump to prevent water damage, a smart moisture sensor in the home could detect if moisture in the home rose above a set level, indicating that the sump pump failed. The sensor, which is connected to the internet, could then send a signal to the insurer and/or the homeowner, who could call a repair company to replace the pump before a major loss occurs.

Insurers can offer attractive policy pricing to more-profitable prospects that use safety and security devices like these so they are less likely to suffer a loss.

Apply Your Knowledge

Erin, a claims representative for Alvva Auto Insurance, is researching information on an insured's auto claim. She is looking for emails, audio and video files, or data transmitted from the insured's car related to the claim. This data would be characterized as

a.   Structured data.

b.   Unstructured data.

c.   Metadata.

d.   Mined data.

Feedback: b. Unstructured data can include open text fields and objects such as emails, audio and video files, webpages, customer intelligence retrieved through social media, and data transmitted from vehicles and smartphones.

SECURITY AND CONTROL IN INFORMATION SYSTEMS

Technology has been a boon to the economy in general, but its increased use and our increased dependency on it also creates new forms of risk. These risks must be identified and addressed to minimize potential damages.

Threats to data security can come from any area: internal sources, external sources, or a combination of both. For insurers, security risks can center on the destruction of data or programs, espionage, invasion of privacy, social networks, employee fraud, human error, cloud computing, and mobile devices. While security teams can minimize data security risks and subsequent losses by remaining vigilant, all employees should be aware of these concerns, trained in best practices, and held accountable for data safety as directed by the security team.

Sources of Security and Control Risks

Weaknesses in data security allow for risk sources that can be internal, external, or collusive (a combination of the first two). Employees who could exploit such weaknesses pose an internal risk for organizations. This risk can be mitigated by segregating duties—for example, by not permitting any one person to have both custody of and access to the records concerning an asset. This separation restricts the ability of employees to steal an asset and then conceal the theft by, for example, altering computer records.

Two major sources of external risk are customers and vendors that process transactions: both have indirect access to an organization's assets and records. Former employees also constitute a risk to computerized data, as they may have intimate knowledge of data systems and their control weaknesses. Unknown criminals that pose an external risk include hackers, who may be more motivated by the challenge than the theft; competitors attempting to gain an advantage; or members of organized crime, who may want to exploit weaknesses in data security to defraud an organization of its assets.

Collusive sources of risk exist when two or more individuals conspire to defraud an organization and to conceal the theft by altering records. Internal collusion occurs when employees cooperate to bypass an organization's controls, steal an asset, and conceal the theft. External collusion exists when an employee acts with a nonemployee to defraud the organization.

Security Risks and Responses

Specific organizational risks may arise from internal, external, and collusive sources.

Destruction of Data or Programs

Data and files vital to an organization's operation may be difficult to reconstruct if destroyed. Intentional data or program destruction could arise from disgruntled employees or former employees gaining unauthorized access to various systems to destroy or modify files as a form of revenge, or from hackers, proving they can bypass the security features of the system to introduce a virus or malware. For general network security, it is important to invest in quality antivirus and spyware software on a regular basis.

Sometimes the destruction of data or programs happens accidentally. This risk can be minimized by hiring capable, trained, and responsible employees; continually retraining and updating the skills of those employees; providing manuals and resources for safeguarding data; and maintaining high standards of data protection and adhering to them. Following prescribed backup policies ensures that data can be retrieved in the event of a fire, flood, or other physical damage to storage hardware. See the exhibit "Best Practices for Backup."

Best Practices for Backup

To ensure data integrity and restoration, an organization can adopt best practices for backup, including these:

- Determine what data on which computers will be backed up
- Select the appropriate program(s) for backing up the data
- Determine an offsite location for backup archives
- Set up a regular backup schedule
- Periodically monitor the backups for occurrence and accuracy
- Periodically pursue data restoration in a test environment

To ensure data integrity during the backup process, an organization can adopt best practices for employees, including these:

- Save data often and always at the end of the workday
- Report any scheduled backups that are missed
- Do not alter or change the scheduled backup times
- Store data in designated locations (such as certain drives or certain folders) to maximize backup efforts
- If overnight backup is scheduled, leave computers in the correct mode

If data backup will be on the cloud, organizations should ensure that the above best practices align with those of the cloud provider.

[DA10517]

Espionage

Executives who are concerned about the actions and plans of competing companies can acquire useful information about competitors, such as financial, production, or employee records, by gaining access to proprietary data. Information could be stolen by using a Universal Serial Bus (USB) flash drive or a keystroke logger to monitor a company's emails, passwords, and newly inputted data. See the exhibit "USB Flash Drives and Security Failures."

USB Flash Drives and Security Failures

The United States Department of Homeland Security conducted a security check by leaving Universal Serial Bus (USB) flash drives in the parking lots of federal buildings and private contractors. The majority of those that were found were plugged into company computers, particularly the flash drives that had official logos on them. While this was only a test, it did confirm that hackers can leave tempting USB flash drives in the paths of individuals and wreak potentially devastating results. A flash drive can introduce an executable program to collect information or spread a virus. In addition, it can be programmed to accomplish its activities weeks later, convincing the user in the short term that it is safe and can continue to be used. A damaging flash drive may appear on screen to be blank, luring the user into a false sense of security.

[DA10518]

Companies operating internationally may be victims of espionage from competitors in a foreign country, where certain spying techniques might be legal.

To thwart such efforts, companies should secure wireless connections by encrypting all information between wireless devices and their router. Because the router may be set up with a default setting that is commonly available to anyone on the internet, companies should secure a wireless access key and change router settings often.

Invasion of Privacy

Computerized data files can contain a large amount of personal information regarding clients, partners, and employees. Disclosure of this information is an invasion of privacy, with implications of possible criminal or civil liability at the local, state, and federal levels. Employees should be able to assume that their information, such as age, address, wages, and pension records, will be kept private, while customers expect confidentiality concerning current balances, credit ratings, and payment histories.

Threats to privacy can come from hackers or employees, but general network security procedures can protect private data that should remain confidential. Internally, routine training regarding company standards and the applicable laws addressing privacy issues can be good reminders for employees to keep personal file information secure.

Because insurers gather personal information from applicants, insureds, and claimants, they must be aware of the relevant legal and regulatory requirements around invasion of privacy. These include the Health Insurance Portability and Accountability Act (HIPAA) and, for insurers that do business in Europe, the General Data Protection Regulation (GDPR), which standardizes controls for the protection of personally identifiable information across all member nations of the European Union. Insurers can limit their loss exposures by reducing the amount of acquired and stored personal information and only requesting, receiving, and storing the personal information necessary for a claim or insurance application.

Social Networks

While social networking sites can encourage communication and connections, ideally creating an atmosphere of sharing and trust, they can also present another loss exposure for employers. An organization's internal secrets might be obtained indirectly by analyzing employees' public postings on social networking sites. Employees visiting these sites during business hours or detailing company plans or projects can leave their employers vulnerable to information leaks, no matter how unintentionally. Posted company information can become public information within minutes over the internet.

Organizations may find an explicit social media policy helpful in educating their employees of the potential threats, providing detailed standards and guidelines, and proactively minimizing exposures before any damage occurs.

Employee Fraud

Fraud is the risk that most often affects the accuracy of accounting records by misstating assets and expenses in financial statements. Major fraud endangers the ability of an organization to continue its operations.

Although many controls protect against fraud by lower-level employees, managers may be in a position to override these controls. Additionally, when employees collude internally or externally, controls may fail to prevent or detect fraud.

Human Error

Human error, including unintentional errors from users, programmers, and service providers, can cause information loss. It, rather than technical failure, is generally considered the most frequent cause of security lapses.

Human error takes multiple forms. For example, if someone casually reveals a personal password and that same password is used for all of his or her business applications, a company's security could be jeopardized. Or if an employee is uneducated about **phishing** expeditions, that may put his or her business data at risk. These types of risk associated with human error can be minimized by hiring technicians with the appropriate amount and type of experience and

Phishing

A fraudulent email scheme by which an unauthorized party acquires a victim's personal or confidential information.

by emphasizing security training and certifications for information technology (IT) employees.

Cloud Computing

Cloud computing, or the cloud, allows a company to access and run many programs and applications without buying or maintaining them for each employee and without needing to install the best and fastest computer hardware.

Through the cloud, employees can sign in from any location and store data on remote computers. The cloud also provides data backup with digital storage devices and keeps a copy of all company information to ensure retrieval in case of a breakdown. The risk is allowing others to have this access—there is uncertainty in placing a company's ideas and secrets in someone else's control.

Other risks to consider are a cloud provider's security standards and procedures, which can vary by provider. To date, little conclusive research exists on the cost of losses from cloud computing. Insurance for covering these losses, offered as part of a service agreement, is an option to consider when choosing a provider.

If a company's files are stored on the cloud, that company becomes dependent on the servicing company or network to provide its data. If the service is disrupted, for example, by damage to a fiber-optic cable, the network will be down. Although backup data would be available, and thus no actual information lost, a company may merely be inconvenienced, but at worst, it could experience devastating results, depending on when the disruption occurred and for how long.

Security and Control Measures

Internal security controls consist of the methods, policies, and procedures used by an organization to ensure the safeguarding of assets, the accuracy and reliability of financial records, the promotion of administrative efficiency, and compliance with management and regulatory standards. Examples of external controls include a well-maintained network with firewalls and access control lists.

An organization's security team should understand senior management's goals for the company and integrate a security plan that helps meet those goals. In this way, the security team should be supported by senior management and enlist the help of the entire organization. A security team that has familiarized itself with all aspects of an organization's departments can more easily identify and respond to emerging risks.

An education and training program is especially important for organizations such as insurers, which value their stakeholders' trust by safeguarding personal information. Employees must understand the reasons that safety measures are created, the structure and hierarchy of the security system, and the need for periodic audits to measure and improve compliance. An insurer should impress upon employees that they are partners with senior management and the security team in accomplishing the goal of attracting new customers, retaining existing insureds, and continuing an insurer's reputation for privacy and confidentiality.

A technology-usage statement is a policy that identifies levels, responsibilities, and roles for all internal employees and external partners. It should be in writing, identifying any practices deemed essential, such as access to the internet, password requirements, and use of mobile devices. The statement, along with corrective actions for noncompliance, should be explained in detail; signed by employees; and then revisited, revised, reinforced, and re-signed as needed.

A process should be in place for detection and correction of any possible breaches, restoration of the system if necessary, and analysis and revision of the process for any future incidents.

To the extent possible, a company should be forward-thinking and aware of emerging technology, new risks, and possible solutions, such as the use of blockchain technology. Blockchain provides a cloud-like storage system for information, but disperses the information across a network of servers. For a limited-access blockchain to be compromised, a hacker would have to simultaneously alter the records stored on more than half of the participating servers, all of which would have their own security measures.

Apply Your Knowledge

Cassandra works in the IT Department of a large insurer. Her manager has asked her to send a communication to all employees explaining how their use of social media on computers linked to the organization's network could present a danger to the organization's data security. Describe the threats and risks Cassandra might touch on in this communication.

Feedback: In her communication, Cassandra can explain that an organization's internal secrets might be obtained indirectly by analyzing employees' public postings on social networking sites. Employees visiting these sites during business hours or detailing company plans or projects can leave their employers vulnerable to information leaks, no matter how unintentionally.

ALIGNING INSURER AND IT STRATEGY

Practically every insurer, whether large or small, must address the challenges of aligning information technology (IT) strategies with business strategies. Despite the difficulty of the task, aligning current and new technologies with business objectives can result in more efficient and expanded operations in all departments.

Key subjects concerning the alignment of business and IT strategy include these:

- Importance of IT and business strategy alignment
- Benefits and challenges
- Plan for alignment
- Metrics of successful alignment

Importance of IT and Business Strategy Alignment

How IT is aligned with core insurer operations and the integral relationships between IT and senior leadership are essential to the success of an insurer. Insurers are continually evolving operationally in response to market and regulatory influences as well as new trends in technology. Technology can create a competitive advantage as an insurer's dependencies on information and data increase.

As insurers become more transaction-focused, the value of IT investments increases. IT is no longer a stand-alone cost center. For an insurer to grow to its full potential, IT initiatives must be aligned closely with an insurer's key strategic goals and objectives. See the exhibit "Example of an IT Initiative That Is Not Aligned With an Insurer's Business Goals."

Example of an IT Initiative That Is Not Aligned With an Insurer's Business Goals

An insurer's chief information officer (CIO) visited the vendor booths at an underwriting conference, where he found a workers compensation policy processing system he believed could replace the outdated system the insurer was currently using. The new, off-the-shelf application would be easy for the IT staff to master and was designed to interface easily with several external databases and state workers compensation rating bureaus. The CIO conferred briefly with the vice president of workers compensation underwriting, and she concurred.

Only after purchasing this software package and migrating policy processing off the old system did they realize that the new system did not capture and store key data elements necessary for both internal reports and external regulatory reports.

What went wrong? Although the CIO did consult with the underwriting vice president, the new system still did not align with business needs. In this instance, they failed to consult with personnel in the business units who use the system: underwriters, data quality managers, business analysts, and compliance staff.

[DA10559]

Benefits and Challenges

Alignment of IT goals with business goals creates both benefits and challenges. Part of the responsibilities of each of an insurer's department managers is to identify what benefits can be expected from an IT initiative and what challenges may prevent its successful implementation.

Benefits

These are among the numerous potential benefits to all of an insurer's departments of increasing alignment between IT and business objectives:

- Sustainable improvements in service level realized for internal and external customers
- Cost reduced
- Compliance with a state's insurance department regulations attained
- Private or privileged information protected
- Best practices standardized
- Productivity increased
- Communications enhanced
- Production workflows expedited
- Competitive advantage obtained via faster implementation of new technology

These benefits can result from an IT initiative's helping an insurer reach a business goal, such as operational excellence, that promotes efficient operations. An example of a sustainable improvement in service level for internal and external customers is the use of cost-of-repair estimating software that can generate more consistently accurate estimates. An example of cost reduction is a program that allows employees to report their monthly expenses more quickly than the previous method, which should result in more available time for employees to perform productive tasks.

Properly aligned and successfully implemented IT projects can create a chain reaction of benefits. Elevated performance can lead to improved customer satisfaction, which, in turn, may lead to fewer complaints to the insurer and state department of insurance, a lower loss ratio and lower loss adjustment expenses, and higher revenue and market share.

Challenges

Every insurer has its own set of unique challenges, which can hinder the complete alignment of IT and business strategies. Challenges that can affect IT and the business functions it serves include these:

- Controlling expenses—This is often the primary concern. The benefit delivered by the investment in the IT project must exceed its expense. To determine whether the investment will earn an acceptable return, assess the insurer's ability to implement the IT project successfully.

- Changing IT or business metrics—Frequently, in IT, when a trend that management may want to act on is detected, a change occurs that causes current metrics to become obsolete. Be ready to make adjustments mid-cycle. For example, changes in traffic regulations—such as increasing the legal speed limit on a state highway—will change the predicted frequency and severity of insured bodily injuries and property damage.

- Clearly understanding customers' needs—This is essential for both internal and external customers. Understanding their needs will help IT guide customers through the learning curve and encourage acceptance of IT initiatives. When IT is aligned to serve the business, the business can best align with customer needs.

- Management financial support—Substantial infrastructure changes can be a significant investment for an insurer. Senior management may not always see the enterprise-wide picture and may have varying opinions about how to spend budget dollars. Showing a positive correlation between successfully implementing IT initiatives and achieving business goals can help obtain IT funding.

- Lack of prioritization—IT project to-do lists do not get shorter. Projects must be prioritized to ensure that adequate resources will be available for successful implementation. Projects without a high enough priority and sufficient resources may cause the insurer to incur unnecessary costs and consumption of time.

- Lack of trust—Because an insurer's IT professionals may not believe their jobs are secure, they may pursue training to obtain skills that would be desirable to another employer rather than the IT skills the current employer needs. Assurances of job security can help prevent this inefficiency.

Legacy system

Typically an outdated computer system that continues to meet users' needs and is still in use even though newer technology is available that can meet those needs more efficiently.

- Overly complex IT infrastructure—A **legacy system** that is retrofitted onto the business structure can become difficult to modify and can have trouble supporting overlying business functions. In such a case, comparative analysis should be performed to determine the costs and benefits of retaining the old infrastructure as opposed to updating to a new one.

- IT as a separate unit—IT personnel too often see themselves as a separate unit apart from the rest of the organization, rather than as people who can help a customer perform a business function. It should be emphasized to IT personnel that, for an IT initiative to be considered a success, it must have a business driver; there is a business need for an IT solution rather than an interesting state-of-the-art technology seeking an application.

- Lack of understanding of insurer and its needs—Some IT personnel need to better understand the insurance business and the insurer's operations to be able to more effectively align business needs with an IT solution. The corporate culture needs to be one in which IT personnel are considered part of the business. Training, education, and job rotation and shadowing can help resolve this concern.

- Lack of understanding of IT and its capabilities—Businesspeople need to understand the technology and what it is, and is not, capable of. The same solutions that have been suggested for improving understanding of an insurer can be applied here.

Plan for Alignment

To substantially increase the chances of success, IT management must be involved in the insurer's strategic planning. Insurers that make a significant investment in the planning process in the beginning will likely save time and money as the alignment continues. These savings are probable for a variety of reasons, which include the insurer's being able to more quickly and accurately anticipate challenges to the implementation of an alignment plan. This advance knowledge regarding which challenges will be problematic allows management to allocate resources more economically and to have them available when needed. Initially, the planning process should focus on determining the insurer's business needs.

Once the insurer's strategic goals have been established, a plan should be drafted in which the business objectives are mapped with measurable IT services. Preferably, business and IT management do this jointly. By charting a path that aligns business and IT objectives, they can be prioritized and placed in the order of execution that optimizes allocation of IT resources and the business value of each IT initiative. The charted path should be a map that also shows the key touch points and interdependencies between business processes and technological opportunities.

Key resources, both internal and external, should be identified. These resources should be aligned so that the entire staff can function efficiently. The vision and strategy created through the planning process should be shared with the entire staff, as well, so they can see the direction in which the insurer intends to go.

Metrics of Successful Alignment

Some insurers measure the value of a project by selecting an internal baseline with a goal of improving it by a certain percentage. Other insurers may supplement that measurement by using industry benchmarks to compare their performance with competitors'. However, when performing this analysis, management should not lose sight of the key issue of whether an IT project is enabling the associated business goal to be met and business benefits to be realized. An IT initiative may be implemented successfully, but if it does not support or improve a process that results in a business benefit or attainment of a goal, it has failed. Tracking and measuring value from a project's design throughout its implementation should help avoid such a situation and support the realization of benefits.

An important way to track and measure the success of an IT project is to evaluate the efficiency and effectiveness of the business process it is intended to improve and to show tangible results. Although it is recommended that metrics be developed that are tailored to a specific insurer's objectives, some standard metrics can work well for any organization:

- Percentage of uptime—Consider how downtime affects the functionality and value of the system. What costs are incurred, including missed opportunities, because of the downtime of the system?

- Functionality—What is the purpose of the project, and which business process is it supporting or improving? Determine whether the project is meeting that purpose.

- Problem resolution—Are the concerns of internal and external (if applicable) customers being addressed efficiently? Is there one central office or point of contact to which customers can go for the project? How long does it usually take for a customer's problem to be resolved?

SUMMARY

IT capabilities that deliver the right data to the insurer or customer at the right time, in the right place, and in the right form can provide an insurer with a competitive advantage. IT capabilities can increase the operational efficiency of nearly every functional area of an insurer's business, as well as support the insurer's strategy, decision making, and governance and compliance initiatives.

Quality data is needed in just about every part of an insurer's business. For this reason, data managers ensure that quality data standards are met. But to effectively manage data quality, a manager must understand the insurer's information needs, which are split into three levels: operational, managerial, and strategic.

A BIS uses multiple tools to conduct accurate business analysis. It can help insurers maintain and develop competitive advantages, enter new markets, and improve the customer experience. To optimize decision making, a BIS uses transaction processing systems, decision support systems, expert systems, and customer-focused collection and safety systems.

An organization's data security can be threatened internally, externally, and collusively. Risks to a company include the destruction of data or programs, espionage, invasion of privacy, social networks, employee fraud, human error, cloud computing, and mobile devices. An organization's security team plans and executes control measures in response to these specific risks in accordance with the organization's overall needs and goals.

Key subjects concerning the alignment of business and IT strategy include these:

- Importance of IT and business strategy alignment
- Benefits and challenges
- Plan for alignment
- Metrics of successful alignment

Insurer Strategic Management

Educational Objectives

After learning the content of this assignment, you should be able to:

▷ Summarize the stages in the strategic management process.

▷ Explain how the Five Forces and SWOT methods can be used to analyze the environment in which an insurer operates.

▷ Explain how strategies are developed at the corporate, business, functional, and operational levels.

▷ Given information about an insurer's business strategies, conduct a SWOT analysis of its strategy.

Insurer Strategic Management

STRATEGIC MANAGEMENT PROCESS

The strategic management process is critical to any organization's success. However, effective strategic management is especially important for insurers because they must distinguish themselves in a highly regulated business where products may not widely vary.

Organizations can be successful in the long term if they have effective strategies that efficiently deploy resources. Therefore, the heart of any successful business strategy is the alignment between the internal resources of the organization and external factors. This alignment allows an organization to create a sustainable competitive advantage.

The **strategic management process** involves three interdependent stages:

- Strategy formulation—creating a plan
- Strategy implementation—putting the plan into action
- Strategy evaluation—monitoring the results to determine whether the plan works as envisioned

Strategy Formulation

Strategy formulation depends on an organization's mission or value statements. Throughout the strategic management process, these statements should serve as a focal point for the organization's management and board of directors.

Mission and Vision Statements

A **mission statement** is a broad expression of an entity's purpose or goals, while reflecting the entity's character and spirit. The mission statement specifies the products or services the organization provides, its stakeholders, and what is important to the organization. Mission statements frequently refer to customers, shareholders, employees, and other corporate stakeholders. For insurers, mission statements frequently mention financial strength, customer service, and integrity.

Mission statements may also include, or be accompanied by, vision or value statements that provide additional information about company values or principles important to the organization. Values such as integrity, honesty,

Strategic management process
The process an organization uses to formulate and implement its business strategies.

Mission statement
A broad expression of an entity's goals.

customer focus, flexibility, and compassion are often included in these statements.

Strategy Formulation Steps

Considering the organization's mission and vision statements, board members and senior-level executives develop strategies through a three-step process. Although business theorists differ over the labeling and numbering of the steps (and some divide individual steps into more than one), strategy formulation has these basic components:

- Analysis of external and internal environments
- Development of long-term strategies and organizational goals
- Determination of strategy at different organizational levels

The first step of strategy formulation involves an internal analysis of the organization and an analysis of external factors including competitors, current and prospective customers' needs, the current and anticipated economy, and government regulations. Typically, a **SWOT analysis** may enable executives to determine how receptive the market would be to its products and services and its competitive position within the market. Opportunities can be categorized as those that "can" or those that "should" be pursued. With this approach, the framework for a strategic plan begins to emerge.

The second step in the process involves development of long-term strategies and organizational goals to support the mission statement within the framework developed during the analysis step. An organization's goals should reflect an understanding of its identity, customers, and purpose. Companies establish these goals to set the priorities or direction for the organization, to establish a measurement of success, and to align its people and actions.

Normally, the chief executive officer (CEO) and executive officers will develop these strategies and goals, often with input from the board and operational-level managers. Depending on the organization, executives and others in management will then develop short-term financial objectives that are aligned with long-term strategies and goals.

The third step in strategy formulation is to determine strategies at different levels of the organization. This involves agreement on more specific action and delegation of responsibilities to achieve long-term strategies and goals. These strategies are based on an organization's core competencies, the competitive nature of the business, the potential customer base, and other factors. This step in the strategic management process involves formulating the "who," "what," and "when" responsibilities.

Strategy Implementation

The second stage of the strategic management process is strategy implementation, also called strategy execution. Strategy implementation is the process of

SWOT analysis
A method of evaluating the internal and external environments by assessing an organization's internal strengths and weaknesses and its external opportunities and threats.

making strategies work. In relation to the strategy formulation stage, this stage is more difficult to complete and requires more time.

The first consideration and a crucial component of strategy implementation is designing the structure of the organization. The most appropriate organizational structure for a company will be determined by its strategic goals. In a single-business company, a **functional structure** might be most suitable, with departments defined by the operation they perform. Examples of such departments would be claims, underwriting, and marketing and sales, among others. A diversified company is more likely to use a **multidivisional structure** to organize its operations and to segregate each division into separate profit centers.

Other possible structures organize company operations by region or by type of product or customer. A large insurer, for example, might have separate underwriting departments for commercial, marine, and personal lines insurance. This way, the expertise and resources required for specific customers is concentrated within the related department. Such an approach supports a differentiation strategy, in which the company seeks to provide unique products for specific market segments.

Structure can also determine the reporting relationships or the company's level of vertical differentiation, which is the extent to which an organization is stratified from its lowest to highest levels. Some companies are tall organizations, with many levels between functional-level positions and executive-level positions. Conversely, a flat organization has fewer levels from the top of the organization to the bottom. When following a **cost leadership** strategy, a flat organization helps to eliminate costs related to maintaining multiple reporting relationships within the company.

Companies should also decide what degree of centralization is needed to operate efficiently and to meet organizational goals. The degree of centralization determines whether authority is maintained at top levels of the organization or is delegated throughout headquarters, into regions, or even to the local level. For example, some insurers retain underwriting authority at the headquarters level, while others extend authority to local offices or to managing general agents. Their claim departments make similar decisions about whether claim-settling authority resides with home office claim staff or is extended to regional claim managers or local company adjusters.

Ultimately, the entire organization is responsible for successful strategy implementation. However, the plans for implementation begin with a filtering-down process, where organizational goals are communicated by top management. See the exhibit "Strategy Implementation Steps."

Strategy Evaluation

Strategy evaluation, also called strategic control, provides a method for measuring a strategy's success. Control mechanisms allow management at each

Functional structure
An organizational structure in which departments are defined by the operation they perform.

Multidivisional structure
An organizational structure in which divisions are organized into separate profit centers.

Cost leadership
A business-level strategy through which a company seeks cost efficiencies in all operational areas.

Strategy Implementation Steps

Mid-level managers are typically responsible for strategy implementation and may follow these five steps:

- Create a documented roadmap of the specific processes, tasks, and responsibilities necessary to disseminate the corporate strategies throughout the organization.

- Communicate information regarding the strategies clearly, frequently, and completely throughout the organization.

- Assign specific responsibilities, tasks, authority, and accountability throughout the organization.

- Allocate adequate resources for successful implementation. Resources include finances, staff, training, time, equipment, data, and technology.

- Manage variances between the goals and the mid-year results; make necessary adjustments to achieve the goals.

[DA06247]

level to gauge the progress of the integration of established strategies into the organization's activities and toward achieving the goals that have been set. The control process has four steps:

1. Establish standards
2. Create and apply measurements
3. Compare actual results to standards
4. Evaluate and implement corrective actions if goals are not met

Following these steps provides a structured approach to strategy implementation. See the exhibit "Example of Steps in the Control Process Applied to an Underwriting Department."

Example of Steps in the Control Process Applied to an Underwriting Department

1. Establish standards—A combined ratio of under 100 was established as the standard. Combined ratios are usually readily available, which makes the ratio an appropriate and easily-applied standard.

2. Create and apply measurements—Measurement would consist of compiling all premium, expense, and loss data required to develop a combined-ratio figure for this individual office, as well as determining a format for reporting the data.

3. Compare actual results to standards—An inherent part of this process is for managers to communicate the importance of meeting this standard to all employees and to motivate them to do so. These premium, expense, and loss reports would then be used in comparing actual results to the established standard of a combined ratio under 100. If the standard has not been met, managers will need to determine the reason and then implement changes.

4. Evaluate and implement corrective actions if goals are not met—Depending on the results of this comparison, corrective actions might involve training initiatives for employees, strengthening communications with producers, examining marketing activities, or taking other corrective actions. If the goal has been met, management should reward and recognize all employees involved to provide motivation to achieve future strategic goals.

[DA06248]

These are categories of organizational controls that may be used to monitor goals:

- Financial controls—In the insurance industry, loss ratios, expense ratios, and combined ratios are financial controls typically used to evaluate over-all corporate performance. They also measure the performance of business units, regional offices, and individual books of business. Other financial controls include stock price, return on investment formulas, cost/benefits analysis, or budget measurements.

- Operational or process controls—These include processes to monitor work flow, production processes, and customer service. In an insurance claims department, such controls could include the average cost of settle-ment, average case load per adjuster, or file turnover rates for individual adjusters.

- Human or behavior controls—This category includes rules, policies, and procedures that provide operating guidelines for employees within an organization, including measurement of individual performance.

As a result of evaluation, strategic plans may be reformed, and/or the manner in which they are implemented may need to be adjusted. The evaluation may indicate that results are off target in ways that cannot be addressed through moderate adjustments. Or it may reveal that the plan's concepts were not completely connected in the implementation stage, which requires an adjustment to the implementation approach.

THE FIVE FORCES AND SWOT METHODS OF ANALYZING THE ENVIRONMENT

An insurer's success depends on its ability to analyze changing environmental factors and influences and to formulate sound business strategies based on its analysis.

Insurers rely on the strategic management process to achieve long-term goals. Strategy formulation is a crucial component of the strategic management process and involves the interrelated steps of analysis of external and internal environments, development of long-term strategies and organizational goals, and determination of strategy at different organizational levels.

In the first step of the process, managers consider factors in both the general environment and the task environment. The general environment affects all businesses, regardless of the specific industry in which they operate, and includes demographic, sociocultural, legal, technological, economic, and global factors. The task environment, which includes an organization's customers, competitors, and suppliers, describes the environmental factors specific to the industry in which the organization operates. The task environment for an insurance company might include customers, competitors, suppliers, reinsurance providers, and regulators.

Many methods can be used to analyze the environment in which an organization operates. Two commonly used methods are the Five Forces Model and SWOT analysis.

The Five Forces Model

Five Forces Model

A method of evaluating the external environment in which a company operates. Involves assessing five forces that drive competition: threat of new entrants, threat of substitute products or services, bargaining power of buyers, bargaining power of suppliers, and rivalry among existing firms.

The widely used **Five Forces Model**, developed by Harvard Business School professor Michael E. Porter, deals with the external task, or competitive, environment and is often used to analyze customers, competitors, and suppliers. Porter describes five forces that drive competition:[1]

- Threat of new entrants
- Threat of substitute products or services
- Bargaining power of buyers
- Bargaining power of suppliers
- Rivalry among existing firms

By analyzing these forces and their effect on the organization, managers can better understand their company's position in the industry. This increased understanding allows management to construct strategies that build a competitive advantage.

Threat of New Entrants

The threat of new entrants in a market is one force that drives competition, although the strength of this force depends on how difficult it is for outsiders to enter the market. Barriers to entry include economies of scale, which contribute to lower overall costs by decreasing the unit cost of products as volume increases. Many insurers writing homeowners or personal auto policies have achieved economies of scale through technology. The standardized nature of personal insurance policies allows some insurers to use automated processes to issue large numbers of policies with relatively low overhead costs. These insurers have lower expenses than insurers relying on more labor-intensive processes, allowing them to charge lower premiums and thus raise barriers to entry for this market segment.

Insurers can also raise barriers to entry by offering unique products or services through the establishment of leadership in certain distribution methods (for example, having a long-term relationship with producers or creating an online direct application system known for its ease of use) or by having established advertising or group marketing programs. The ability for one insurer to access distribution channels in a marketing system can create barriers to entry for others and pose a competitive disadvantage for potential new entrants. For insurance products, the insurance distribution system and channel can be important components of the overall marketing plan.

State statute and regulatory policy can act as a barrier to entry if they deter potential entrants from considering the highly regulated insurance industry. Regulatory requirements within a given jurisdiction can also discourage insurers from entering certain states. For example, the state of Massachusetts once discouraged new entrants to the personal auto insurance market with state-made rates and restrictions on distribution.

Threat of Substitute Products or Services

A second force that drives competition is the threat of substitute products or services. This threat arises when products that are capable of performing the same function as those from another industry become widely available. This threat makes it difficult for any one seller to substantially increase prices and tends to hold down profits for all participants in the original industry.

The threat of substitute products or services to the insurance industry has been limited thus far, but remains an important force for insurers to consider. One example of such a threat is alternative risk transfer mechanisms including self-insured retention, formation of captive insurance companies, catastrophe bonds, and finite risk transfer.

Bargaining Power of Buyers

The third force that drives competition is the bargaining power of buyers. When buyers have significant power, they can increase competition within an industry and demand lower prices. This force affects the insurance industry, principally in the personal insurance market, in which customers have exerted great pressure on insurers to lower prices and increase availability. The bargaining power of buyers is the reason that many government-sponsored or -mandated residual market plans were created. Auto assigned risk plans and property insurance plans (particularly those serving coastal markets) were created where the market would not support the prices needed for insurers to voluntarily offer coverage. Further, the bargaining power of buyers led to the explosive growth in a number of coastal property insurance plans and wind pools as property owners would not, or could not, pay rates sought by the private market.

When formulating strategy, companies should consider customer buying power. In some cases, insurers might decide not to enter markets where they feel pressure from buyer groups would inhibit their ability to be profitable.

Bargaining Power of Suppliers

A fourth force driving competition is the bargaining power of suppliers. In some industries, suppliers can exert power over companies by increasing prices, restricting supply, or varying product quality. For example, in the energy industry, oil-producing countries can exert tremendous power over the supply and price of petroleum products.

In the insurance industry, reinsurers are a supplier to primary insurers. Without access to reinsurance, many insurers would lack sufficient capacity to write certain types and amounts of insurance. Reinsurers are in a position to control the price and amount of capacity they provide depending on the market conditions. For example, in periods when large losses occur, such as multiple devastating hurricanes in a single year, reinsurance capacity may shrink. Insurers may also underestimate anticipated loss amounts from such unanticipated events. Such uncertainty in the marketplace generally results in tighter capacity, rising rates, and more restrictive terms.

Another example of the bargaining power of suppliers is the power exerted by auto manufacturers to mandate use of original equipment manufacturer (OEM) parts for auto physical damage repairs. Where suppliers have successfully limited the acceptance or use of less expensive non-OEM (aftermarket) parts, physical damage loss costs may increase for insurers.

Rivalry Among Existing Firms

Rivalry among existing companies is the fifth force that drives competition. Rivalry is reflected in pricing wars, aggressive advertising campaigns, and increased emphasis on customer service. Competitors are constantly striving to be at the top of their industry and to outperform other companies. This type of rivalry exists among personal lines auto insurers.

A high level of competition can be expected in industries having many companies, little product differentiation, or high exit costs. All of these characteristics are present in the insurance industry, making the market strongly competitive. While some insurers can use economies of scale to gain a competitive edge, the individual market share of insurers at the top of the market is still relatively small compared to that of other industries. No single insurer has enough market share to dominate the overall property-casualty market. For example, the leading property-casualty insurer's market share is only approximately 10 percent.

SWOT Analysis

SWOT analysis, or situational analysis, is another method used to analyze the competitive environment. SWOT (Strengths, Weaknesses, Opportunities, and Threats) analysis allows organizations to consider both the general environment and the task environment. This method was devised by Albert S. Humphrey, a business scholar and management consultant who specialized in business planning and change.

Strengths and Weaknesses

Identifying internal strengths and weaknesses involves consideration of financial, physical, human, and organizational assets. Managers use SWOT analysis to determine the current state of their companies. These are some of the assets that management considers:

- Managerial expertise
- Available product lines
- Skill levels and competencies of staff
- Current strategies
- Customer loyalty
- Growth levels
- Organizational structure
- Distribution channels

It would be a strength if an organization has an executive training program that is considered an industry standard. If a company is having financial difficulty or is experiencing unfocused growth, it would be a weakness. In an insurance operation, an insurer that had been cutting prices to gain market share might identify loss of premium volume as a substantial weakness when an unanticipated rise in losses is projected as part of the SWOT analysis. Unfavorable loss results cause financial constraints.

Opportunities and Threats

Managers determine potential opportunities or threats by analyzing the external environment, including both general and task environment factors.

Trend analysis

An analysis that identifies patterns in past data and then projects these patterns into the future.

One way to achieve this is through **trend analysis**, which identifies patterns related to specific factors in the past and then projects those patterns into the future to determine potential threats or opportunities. Insurers might determine opportunities and threats through trend analysis. Opportunities might be presented by new markets, possible acquisition targets, or a reduction in competition, while threats might include new competitors, an increase in competition levels, economic downturns, or changes in customer preferences.

For example, projection of various demographic trends might reveal new marketing opportunities or a shrinking market for an existing core product. See the exhibit "SWOT Analysis Table."

SWOT Analysis Table

	Strengths	Weaknesses
Internal	List assets, competencies, or attributes that enhance competitiveness	List lacking assets, competencies, or attributes that diminish competitiveness
	Prioritize based on the quality of the strength and the relative importance of the strength	Prioritize based on the seriousness of the weakness and the relative importance of the weakness
	Opportunities	**Threats**
External	List conditions that could be exploited to create a competitive advantage	List conditions that diminish competitive advantage
	Prioritize based on the potential of exploiting the opportunities	Prioritize based on the seriousness and probability of occurrence
	Note strengths that can be paired with opportunities as areas of competitive advantage	Note weaknesses that can be paired with threats as risks to be avoided

[DA03626]

The approach used by organizations varies based on each company's needs. A company should not only identify strengths, weaknesses, opportunities, and threats, but should also thoroughly analyze how they affect its strategic plan.

Once the SWOT analysis has been completed, managers can develop strategies that position the company to gain a competitive advantage by leveraging organizational strengths and offsetting or reducing weaknesses. The company should also find ways to capitalize on identified opportunities and to neutralize existing threats.

DETERMINING STRATEGY AT DIFFERENT ORGANIZATIONAL LEVELS

Strategic plans encompass a variety of organizational activities. Because organizations vary widely, every organization requires its own approach. Strategies can be categorized based on the levels at which they are carried out within an organization, how they relate to the development stage of the organization, and how they align with the organization's overall business approach.

Different kinds of strategies are carried out at various levels within an organization. Strategies at all levels should be aligned to support the organization's overall mission and vision. On any given day, insurance professionals may participate in implementing multiple strategies simultaneously. See the exhibit "Types of Organizational Strategies."

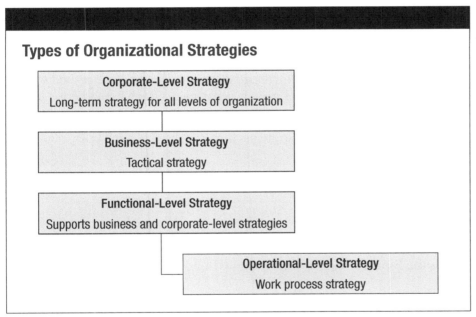

Types of Organizational Strategies

Corporate-Level Strategy
Long-term strategy for all levels of organization

Business-Level Strategy
Tactical strategy

Functional-Level Strategy
Supports business and corporate-level strategies

Operational-Level Strategy
Work process strategy

[DA06291]

These are the most prevalent types of organizational strategies:

- Corporate-level strategy represents the highest strategy level for a diversified organization. It determines the types and potential profitability of businesses or activities the organization will undertake.

- Business-level strategy may be implemented by a single operation or, in the case of a diversified corporation, a strategic business unit (SBU). Managers develop strategies at this level to support the corporate-level strategy, to be competitive, and to respond to changes in the external environment.

- Functional-level strategy is carried out by individual departments performing specific organizational functions, such as marketing or underwriting.
- Operational-level strategy relates to a department's narrowly defined day-to-day business activities. Operational strategies include workflows and production processes.

Corporate-Level Strategy

At the corporate level, the chief executive officer (CEO) and the executive team determine the businesses in which the company will be involved, allocate organizational resources properly, and coordinate strategies at all company levels to maximize profits. Corporate-level strategies are relatively long term, established for a five-year period and beyond.

Competitive advantage is reinforced when each department or unit in an organization creates value for the customer. In insurance operations, the marketing, underwriting, claim, customer service, and other departments must align to build value and to support corporate-level strategy in a continuous chain. This alignment can also provide additional advantages in the form of reduced operating expenses or increased differentiation of products and services through the interaction of various departments, such as marketing and underwriting.

Three generic corporate-level strategies are available for companies in a growth mode:

- Single business
- Vertical integration
- Diversification

There are different corporate-level strategies for companies in a decline mode, such as the bankruptcy, divestiture, turnaround, and harvest strategies.

Concentration on a Single Business

Based on a business environmental assessment, a company might determine that the best corporate-level strategy for it to pursue is concentration on a single business. By concentrating its efforts and resources on one industry, product, or market, a company can build distinctive competencies and gain a competitive advantage. Many property-casualty insurers pursue a single-business strategy, even though they write many types of insurance.

Concentrating on a single business, however, has some potential disadvantages. Most are related to missing opportunities to build a competitive advantage through either vertical integration or diversification into related areas.

Vertical Integration

A **vertical integration strategy** can be either backward or forward. If an organization produces inputs for processing (such as an insurer printing policy forms in-house instead of purchasing them from a printing supplier), it is backward integration. When an organization sells its product directly to the customer rather than through a wholesaler, it is called forward integration. Direct writer insurers are an example of forward integration being put to use.

Companies choose vertical integration to decrease expenses or increase efficiency. However, vertical integration could have an opposite effect due to a lack of expertise or the cost of resources in different stages of the production process.

Vertical integration strategy

A corporate-level strategy through which a company either produces its own inputs or disposes of its own outputs.

Diversification

Diversification for the property-casualty insurance industry can be advantageous. Because the industry is affected by the weather cycles, diversifying into lines of insurance or financial products that are unaffected by the weather can help smooth the demand for both financial and human resources. Because the insurance underwriting cycle does not coincide with the general business cycle, some insurers may benefit from diversification into non-insurance businesses to offset lower insurer profits during troughs in the insurance profit cycle. In pursuit of diversification, companies can pursue either related or unrelated diversification strategies.

Related diversification allows companies to gain economies of scope by sharing resources, such as the same distribution system or research and development facilities. For example, a property-casualty insurer may also provide life or health insurance and thus utilize its existing technology and agency system to grow its business while spreading risk. Another benefit of related diversification is the ability to leverage fixed expenses with additional revenues from diversified operations, resulting in a lower unit cost for each product or service offered. For example, insurers may enter into third-party administration of claims as some of their customers choose alternative risk financing approaches instead of traditional insurance. This allows the insurers to obtain additional revenue from their existing technology platforms, claim expertise, and other internal resources.

Related diversification strategy

A corporate-level strategy through which a company expands its operations into areas that are similar to its existing operations.

Unrelated diversification strategy (also referred to as conglomerate diversification strategy) involves acquiring companies that have no relationship to the existing business operations and is riskier than related diversification. The negative aspects of unrelated diversification include additional costs of coordinating the divergent businesses, a loss of synergy among business units, and diminishing returns from any economies of scale or scope. Companies that have succeeded with an unrelated diversification strategy excel at making the right types of acquisitions. These companies have also developed strong structure and control mechanisms to offset some of the difficulties stemming from managing an extensive and varied group of profit centers.

Unrelated diversification strategy

A corporate-level strategy through which a company expands its operations into areas that have no relation to its existing operations.

Decline Mode Strategies

All of the strategies discussed to this point involve companies operating in growing markets. However, some companies might not be growing, might be encountering substantial marketplace obstacles, or might have numerous internal weaknesses and external threats. The problems that these companies encounter could include decreasing profits, loss of market share, or changing economic conditions. When a company is operating in a market in which demand for its products or services is decreasing, it is in a decline mode and its strategic options are different than those of companies in a growth mode.

Corporate-level strategies for such companies are defensive. In the worst-case scenario, the company might determine that the only option is bankruptcy or liquidation. In bankruptcy, companies seek court protection from creditors to reorganize and improve their financial standing. If a company cannot recover from bankruptcy, it is liquidated and any remaining proceeds are used to satisfy outstanding obligations.

Business-Level Strategy

Business-level strategies are developed at the business or division level by managers who are responsible for supporting the stated corporate-level strategy. These managers must find ways for their business units to be competitive and to respond to changes in the external environment. Business-level management also budgets for needed resources and coordinates the functional-level strategy within the division. The time frame for business-level strategies, sometimes referred to as tactical strategies, is three to five years in most organizations. There are three business-level strategies:

- Cost leadership
- Differentiation
- Focus

Cost Leadership

Cost leadership enables a company to charge a lower price for its products or services. It involves eliminating costs in every aspect of the operation, from product development and design to distribution and delivery. However, cost leadership involves more than just charging the lowest price in the industry. Even when prices for similar products are comparable, the cost leader can earn higher overall profits than its competitors because of its lower costs. Cost leaders can also better withstand prolonged price wars.

One requirement of a cost leadership strategy is that most products or services must be fairly standardized. Introducing varied types of products increases expenses and erodes any cost leadership advantages, so cost leaders do not tend to be first movers within an industry.

For insurers, price cutting might be limited by regulatory constraints. Insurers must closely examine the three components of an insurance rate (allowances for loss payments, expenses, and profit) to determine where costs can be reduced. When evaluating how to decrease costs, insurers can consider reducing acquisition expenses by lowering producers' commissions, using a direct writer system for some or all of their marketing, or exploring alternative distribution channels.

Loss expenses can be reduced by streamlining claim adjusting processes, managing litigation expenses, or implementing cost containment practices, such as negotiation of repair or medical reimbursement rates with vendors. Underwriting expenses can be reduced by using expert computer systems or standardizing underwriting guidelines. Technology can automate processes, improve interaction among departments, and speed policy processing times. All of these efforts combine to execute the cost leadership strategy.

Differentiation

A successful **differentiation strategy** requires products and services that customers perceive as distinctive and that are difficult for rivals to imitate. Companies using this strategy must accurately determine the needs and preferences of their customers, or revenue and market share will be lost. Market share will also be lost if competitors can match or improve upon the product's unique features.

Insurers employing this strategy may choose to differentiate products or services to gain market share and to establish a competitive advantage. Insurers that offer special programs for commercial or homeowners insurance are examples. When an insurer writes only homeowners or personal auto insurance and targets multiple markets (such as teachers, retired persons, and military personnel), it is following a differentiation strategy. If an insurer offers a wide range of specialized coverages, but offers them only to municipalities, it is following a focus strategy.

Focus

A focus strategy involves concentrating on a group of customers, a geographic area, or a narrow line of products or services while using a low-cost approach or a differentiation strategy. The two types of this strategy are **focused cost leadership strategy** and **focused differentiation strategy**.

Many insurers follow one of the focus strategies. Niche marketing programs, which offer tailored coverages to specific groups of customers, are examples of focused differentiation. Alternatively, an example of a focused cost leadership approach is when an insurer that sells to a specific group of customers, such as retail hardware stores, and offers discounted commercial packages or automobile policies using standard forms. The use of standard forms is an important factor because any significant level of specialization increases costs and erodes profits.

Differentiation strategy

A business-level strategy through which a company develops products or services that are distinct and for which customers will pay a higher price than that of the competition.

Focused cost leadership strategy

A business-level strategy through which a company focuses on one group of customers and offers a low-price product or service.

Focused differentiation strategy

A business-level strategy through which a company focuses on one group of customers and offers unique or customized products that permit it to charge a higher price than that of the competition.

Functional-Level Strategy

Functional-level strategies are the plans for managing a particular functional area, such as finance, marketing, underwriting, actuarial, risk control, premium audit, and claims. These strategies establish how functional departments support the organization's business-level and corporate-level strategies. The time frame for these strategies is short term, usually one year.

Companies build value and competitive advantage through efficiency, quality, customer responsiveness, and innovation. Some combination of these factors must be incorporated into its activities at the functional level for a company to pursue either a cost leadership or differentiation strategy at the business level. For example, without efficiency and innovation, cost leadership cannot be attained. Similarly, quality and customer responsiveness must be included in the development, production, and marketing functions for a company to execute a differentiation strategy effectively.

In insurance operations, functional-level strategies specify how the underwriting, claim, actuarial, and other departments advance business-level strategies. For an insurer to be successful at garnering market share using a cost leadership strategy, it must become a highly efficient organization. For example, human resources, in cooperation with the underwriting, claim, customer service, and marketing departments, should find ways to improve productivity. The information technology department should provide innovative solutions to lower overall production costs and improve the speed of organizational communications, both internally and externally. Likewise, an insurer that is pursuing a differentiation strategy will consider innovation and quality at all functional levels to be critical to providing a distinctive product that meets the customer's needs.

Operational-Level Strategy

Operational-level strategies involve daily business processes and workflows, and are implemented at the department level to support the strategies of the functional, business, and corporate levels. For example, a claim office with a high volume of claims and a functional-level strategy to improve efficiency might decide to obtain more information through the claim reporting process in order to assign the claim properly and eliminate redundant communication with insureds. A premium auditing department, striving to achieve a functional-level budget strategy, might use pre-audit screening as an operational-level strategy to make the most effective use of resources to achieve its budget goals.

STRATEGIC MANAGEMENT CASE STUDY

A SWOT (strengths, weaknesses, opportunities, and threats) analysis can improve an insurer's planning process and the resulting outcome, particularly if those participating in the process represent a variety of perspectives and ask and find answers to difficult questions. It also may be used to evaluate whether an insurer's business strategies will contribute to its success.

A SWOT analysis can be used to examine an insurer's internal and external environment, and is frequently used in the strategic management planning process. The analysis is a step in action planning—not an end in itself. Results of SWOT analyses can change over time; therefore, the first step in the process of evaluation of business strategies should be to complete a current analysis. The current analysis can then be used to examine the insurer's business strategies, placing emphasis on any issues that have prompted the current evaluation. Strategies can then be evaluated to determine whether they are appropriate in guiding the insurer to meet its goals and objectives.

Case Facts

To evaluate an insurer's strategies, the reviewer or team of reviewers needs information about the insurer's strategic goals, as well as its internal and external environment. In addition, an understanding of the purpose of the evaluation will help narrow the review's focus.

Given background information on an insurer, the overall question to be answered is, "Will this insurer's current business strategies allow it to achieve its goals, or is a change required?"

Greenly Insurance Company—Internal and External Environment

Greenly Insurance Company (Greenly) is a sixty-year-old regional mutual insurance company authorized and operating in eight states. The company is headquartered in Pennsylvania, but maintains at least one satellite claims office in each state in which it writes.

Greenly writes only personal lines risks, with automobile insurance being the core of its business. Auto customers may be offered coverage in Greenly's "preferred" automobile insurance company, or in its "nonstandard" (high risk) company. The company offers generous discounts for drivers between the ages of thirty-five and sixty, based on the favorable loss ratios of this group. Greenly does not offer a rating discount based on longevity, although long-term households also show consistently favorable loss ratios.

The company's operations are consistent with core values it established sixty years ago: to protect policyholder assets, to gain customer loyalty, be a good corporate citizen, and to comply with all legal requirements. Throughout its existence, the company has enjoyed a consistently superior financial rating. A conservative investment strategy, favorable underwriting results, and conservative policy growth have allowed Greenly to maintain ample policyholder surplus even in years of high catastrophe losses and lackluster returns on investments. Greenly does not compete based on price, but rather on financial strength and core values.

Greenly uses independent agents to sell its products, and a monthly poli-cyholder magazine accounts for the majority of its advertising. Greenly's customer-focused philosophy stresses personalized service to gain customer trust and loyalty. Therefore, Greenly's website does not provide quotes, direct purchase options, claim reporting, or premium payment options.

Over the past decade, the automobile insurance market has changed dramati-cally. Policyholders demand customer service, yet also want lower premiums. The line between "preferred" and "nonstandard" companies has blurred as the use of credit-based insurance scoring and other tools effective in predicting risk of loss have resulted in more refined pricing and increased use of rating tiers. More sophisticated coverage and rating options mean that insurers are able to rate and compete for segments of business that they may not have in the past.

Some automobile insurers invest millions of dollars annually in high-profile advertising. Celebrity spokespersons, mascots, special effects, and humor have led to name recognition for certain companies and remind consumers that they can easily switch companies. Generally, younger consumers tend to seek information from insurers' websites when shopping for automobile insurance, and those shoppers are more likely to seek an automobile insurance quote directly from a website or mobile application than older consumers.

Greenly Insurance Company—Goals

An organization's goals provide the overall context for what the organization seeks to achieve. Greenly's goals have remained fairly constant for many years, and it establishes metrics based on these goals annually:

- Maintain financial strength to protect insureds
- Build long-term customer loyalty and maintain high customer satisfaction by meeting customer needs
- Contribute to charitable community efforts through time and financial support
- Comply with legal requirements

Greenly Insurance Company—Business Strategies

Based on its goals of financial strength, customer loyalty and satisfaction, and charitable giving, Greenly has developed business strategies to direct its actions. See the exhibit "Greenly Insurance Company—Business Strategies."

Issues That Prompted the Evaluation

Greenly has failed to meet its automobile insurance written premium and policy growth goals for the past two years. Greenly's new business has declined steadily over the past few years, and **retention ratios** of existing business have decreased at an even greater pace. After accounting for the impact of the

Retention ratio

The percentage of insurance policies renewed.

Greenly Insurance Company—Business Strategies

1. Financial Strength: We will protect our policyholders' security by maintaining financial strength. To accomplish this, we will:

   - Increase policyholders surplus and maintain our superior financial rating
   - Achieve a combined ratio of 98% or less (automobile and homeowners)
   - Increase written premium by 5%
   - Gain a net increase of automobile policies in force by 2%

2. Customer Focus: We will commit to providing the outstanding customer service that our customers deserve and demand, and will strive to build long-term relationships with our policyholders. To accomplish this, we will:

   - Offer quality products, while meeting or exceeding established product delivery goals
   - Increase average household longevity by providing consistently superior service
   - Achieve 98% customer satisfaction as expressed on post-claim settlement and annual policyholder renewal surveys

3. Technology and Data Management: We will provide the best service possible to our agents and policyholders by adopting current and efficient technologies intended to enhance our business. To accomplish this, we will:

   - Safeguard all customer data
   - Expand use of data-driven products in the claims settlement process

4. Corporate Leadership: We will show leadership in the communities in which we operate through organizational effort and through the dedication of our employees. To accomplish this, we will:

   - Dedicate our time and financial support to community activities
   - Encourage employee participation in community charitable efforts
   - Achieve a 50% positive response on recognition of our community efforts as measured by annual policyholder renewal surveys

[DA06385]

economic downturn, it has become clear that the negative trends likely stem from its current business practices.

A survey of Greenly's agents has revealed that Greenly insureds who were insured under their parent's policies seem increasingly less likely to stay with Greenly when they establish their own households. Further, many cited customer dissatisfaction with claims service as a primary reason for obtaining coverage elsewhere, despite the fact that post-claim surveys continue to show acceptable results. See the exhibit "SWOT Analysis Table."

SWOT Analysis Table

	Strengths	Weaknesses
Internal	List assets, competencies, or attributes that enhance competitiveness	List lacking assets, competencies, or attributes that diminish competitiveness
	Prioritize based on the quality of the strength and the relative importance of the strength	Prioritize based on the seriousness of the weakness and the relative importance of the weakness
	Opportunities	**Threats**
External	List conditions that could be exploited to create a competitive advantage	List conditions that diminish competitive advantage
	Prioritize based on the potential of exploiting the opportunities	Prioritize based on the seriousness and probability of occurrence
	Note strengths that can be paired with opportunities as areas of competitive advantage	Note weaknesses that can be paired with threats as risks to be avoided

[DA03626]

Case Analysis Tools and Information

To evaluate business strategies for Greenly Insurance Company, the reviewer or review team will need these:

- A current SWOT analysis
- The company's business strategies
- An explanation of the reason for the evaluation
- The company's goals and objectives that relate to the reason for the evaluation

Case Analysis Steps

Evaluating an organization's strategies involves a series of decision-making steps. Following these steps minimizes the effort required by focusing on the issues, strategies, and desired outcome:

1. Conduct a current SWOT analysis of the organization's internal and external environments
2. Determine the business strategies relevant to the business issue that generated the need for evaluation
3. Evaluate the relevant business strategies using the SWOT analysis

Conduct a Current SWOT Analysis

The SWOT analysis is a methodical assessment of an organization and its business environment that usually is completed by those involved in planning and decision-making for the organization. While determination of strengths and weaknesses may be based on subjective criteria, the overall process allows for an objective view of the environments in which the organization operates. See the exhibit "SWOT Analysis Process."

SWOT Analysis Process

One method of conducting a SWOT analysis is through a group activity that involves an organization's managers and is organized by a facilitator.

Brainstorming

- If the group is large, the facilitator may divide the managers into smaller groups to encourage participation.
- Through brainstorming, factors are listed under each of the SWOT headings.
- This activity will produce many factors randomly organized under each SWOT heading.

Refining

- To make the list easier to examine, similar items are clustered together.
- Items of high importance are noted under each of the SWOT headings.

Prioritizing

- Strengths are ordered by quality and relative importance.
- Weaknesses are ordered by the degree to which they affect performance and by their relative importance.
- Opportunities are ordered by degree and probability of success.
- Threats are ordered by degree and probability of occurrence.
- Strengths that require little or no operational changes and can be paired with opportunities are designated for potential action to maximize competitive advantages that entail low risk.
- Weaknesses that can be paired with threats are designated in the prioritized list for potential action to minimize consequences that entail high risk.

[DA03650]

The SWOT analysis of Greenly reveals that the company faces a high-risk threat because it has not kept pace with the needs of existing customers or the buying preferences of prospective customers. Customer satisfaction surveys may be unreliable because they are outdated and fail to ask the right questions, or fail to reach a broad enough audience. Further, the company's normal avenue of direct communication with policyholders, the monthly magazine, may have little impact on customer relations or loyalty.

A review of the survey questions asked and their target audience may reveal whether such surveys need to be revised. For example, Greenly could be relying only on input from current satisfied customers rather than from former customers who may have left due to dissatisfaction, which would skew responses toward positive results. See the exhibit "SWOT Case Table— Greenly Insurance."

Determine Business Strategies to Be Evaluated

The organization's business strategies are its long-term approach to attaining its goals and objectives. Because an organization's strategies can be extensive, it is helpful to narrow the focus of the examination by understanding the business issue that has prompted the evaluation. The strategies relevant to the issue can then be targeted for evaluation.

Which business strategies have contributed to the failure of Greenly to meet its customer satisfaction and loyalty goals and policy growth target?

Assuming that customers are leaving because they are either dissatisfied with the company's products, services, or prices, the company may need to reevaluate its customer-focused strategy:

> 2. Customer Focus: We will commit to providing the outstanding customer service that our customers deserve and demand, and will strive to build long-term relationships with our policyholders. To accomplish this, we will:
>
> · Offer quality products, while meeting or exceeding established product delivery goals
>
> · Increase average household longevity by providing consistently superior service
>
> · Achieve 98% customer satisfaction as expressed on post-claim settlement and annual policyholder renewal surveys

This goal seeks to meet the needs of customers but fails to address identification of changes in the marketplace. The company's business strategies also lack commitment to respond to the changing needs or buying habits of insurance consumers.

Evaluate Relevant Business Strategies

After an organization's internal and external environments and its business strategies have been examined, the next step is to determine whether a change in course is required to achieve its goals.

Will the current business strategies for Greenly continue to be the most effective approach toward attaining its goals, or should its business strategies be changed?

Greenly's current customer-focused strategy will not lead to successful achievement of the company's growth goals. Greenly has committed to

SWOT Case Table—Greenly Insurance

	Strengths	Weaknesses
Internal	Strengths are apparent in the organization's financial stability: • Superior financial rating and policyholders' surplus • Branding based on customer satisfaction allows the company to focus on financial stability • Commitment to charitable efforts and community involvement • Established method of monthly communication with policyholders • Representation by independent agents fosters goal of customer loyalty (for example, trust and service) • Experienced employees	Weaknesses have emerged in the types of services that the organization has not developed and the needs it is not meeting: • Customer surveys are inadequate in measuring customer feedback • Technology in use has not kept pace with consumer demands/lack of development of website options for quotes and applications • Claim handling complaints increasing (distant locations may have resulted in inadequate oversight, training, or focus on company values) • Inadequate advertising/lack of branding • Reliance on products with few unique options/lack of new products (for example, "green" insurance options)
	Opportunities	**Threats**
External	Opportunities provide potential actions that the organization can take to meet the needs of its current and potential policyholders. • Generation Y insurance consumers less sensitive to price—ability to target younger prospective policyholders based on factors other than price • Ability to enhance branding through focus on charitable and community involvement efforts • Ability to pilot discounts or incentives based on customer longevity • Claims staff can be retrained and customer evaluation materials can be revised to improve reliability of results • Ability to expand into additional states • Ability to pilot direct writing option, and Internet-based partnership options with independent agents	Threats have surfaced as some are better positioned to meet the needs of the company's customers. • Current business is vulnerable to price leaders' advertising efforts, particularly of national writers • Agency force may lean toward better-recognized brands or companies that advertise lower prices • Increasing percentage of consumers looking for direct purchase options and interactive website capability • Dissatisfaction with claims processes may damage the company reputation, particularly if dissatisfied customers tell others or if complaints are filed with state departments of insurance • Competitors offer more pricing options, reducing likelihood of declinations and nonrenewals and enhancing customer stability

[DA06389]

customer satisfaction but has not devised an effective method of determining customer needs and opinions. Although the company is committed to soliciting feedback through renewal and post-claim surveys, those surveys may not be worded appropriately to invite the type of feedback needed for the company to truly evaluate its operations. For example, if the surveys only request feedback on current issues, the company will not have the benefit of hearing how customers believe the company has changed, improved, or even declined over time—or the benefit of hearing suggestions for the future. Perhaps even more important, Greenly has no established method of seeking input from former customers to determine why they left.

If the company revises its customer surveys and establishes additional methods of reaching out to current and former customer and agents, it may determine that additional changes are needed as well. For example, the company may wish to revise its business strategies to include opportunities identified to attract and retain policyholders and to help meet the company's goals. Such changes may include these:

- Redesign its website to add online quote capability or other interactive options

- Expand into a new state as a direct writer

- Implement a pilot program to test new products or coverage options

- Redesign the company magazine to emphasize new developments and to better target second-generation policyholders

- Refocus community involvement efforts on issues more likely to appeal to second generation policyholders and effectively promote those efforts

- Retrain claims staff to improve customer satisfaction

SWOT Case Correct Answer

The Greenly Insurance Company has failed to meet its automobile insurance written premium and policy growth goals for the past two years because customer satisfaction goals are not being met and lapse ratios are increasing. A SWOT analysis indicates that Greenly has not adequately identified or kept pace with the changing needs of customers.

Using that information to evaluate its business strategies, Greenly must revise its customer-focused strategy to meet its goals. As a well-capitalized company, Greenly is in a good position to implement changes, including updating technology and implementing pilot marketing programs designed to attract and retain business.

[DA06390]

SUMMARY

The strategic management process is employed by organizations to align external factors and internal resources to create a sustainable competitive advantage. The strategic management process includes strategy formulation, strategy implementation, and strategy evaluation.

The Five Forces Model can be used to thoroughly assess an organization's external environment by identifying factors related to customers, competitors, and suppliers. A SWOT analysis can then be used to determine internal strengths and weaknesses related to the company's financial, physical, human, and organizational assets. An examination of the external environment is then conducted to determine opportunities and threats.

Strategy is planned and implemented at the organization's corporate, business, functional, and operational levels. Corporate-level strategies are developed by the executive team. Business-level strategies are employed by divisional managers within the organization. Functional areas of insurers include marketing, underwriting, claim, risk control, premium audit, actuarial, and finance. Operational-level strategies are implemented at the department level to support the strategies of the functional, business, and corporate levels; these strategies focus on daily business operations.

A SWOT analysis is a structured examination of an organization's internal and external environment as a prelude to action planning. When used to evaluate an organization's business strategies, the SWOT analysis focuses on the event that prompted the evaluation. The results of the business strategies relevant to the cause of the event are examined to determine whether those strategies will continue to be effective in achieving the organization's goals.

ASSIGNMENT NOTE

1. Michael E. Porter, Competitive Strategy: Techniques for Analyzing Industries and Competitors (New York: The Free Press, 1980), p. 4.

Index

Page numbers in boldface refer to pages where the word or phrase is defined.